BRIDGE
TO THE SUN

BRIDGE
TO THE SUN

The Secret Role of the
Japanese Americans Who Fought
in the Pacific in World War II

Bruce Henderson

Alfred A. Knopf
New York | 2022

THIS IS A BORZOI BOOK
PUBLISHED BY ALFRED A. KNOPF

www.aaknopf.com

Knopf, Borzoi Books, and the colophon are
registered trademarks of Penguin Random House LLC.

Library of Congress Cataloging-in-Publication Data
Names: Henderson, Bruce B., [date] author.
Title: Bridge to the sun: the secret role of the Japanese Americans who fought
in the Pacific in World War II / Bruce Henderson.
Description: First edition. | New York: Alfred A. Knopf, [2022] |
Identifiers: LCCN 2021053217 (print) | LCCN 2021053218 (ebook) |
ISBN 9780525655817 (hardcover) | ISBN 9780525655824 (ebook)
Subjects: LCSH: World War, 1939–1945—Participation, Japanese American. |
Japanese American soldiers—History—20th century. | Japanese American soldiers—
Biography. | World War, 1939–1945—Japanese Americans. |
World War, 1939–1945—Campaigns—Pacific Area.
Classification: LCC D769.8.A6 H46 2022 (print) | LCC D769.8.A6 (ebook) |
DDC 940.53089/956073—dc23/eng/20220107
LC record available at https://lccn.loc.gov/2021053217
LC ebook record available at https://lccn.loc.gov/2021053218

Jacket photograph: U.S. Army Signal Corps
Jacket design by Jenny Carrow

Manufactured in the United States of America
First Edition

For them all

CONTENTS

INTRODUCTION

Bridge to the Sun tells the little-known story of the U.S. Army's Japanese American soldiers who fought in the Pacific theater during World War II, and their decisive role in the defeat of Japan. Thousands of Nisei—first-generation American citizens born in the United States whose parents were immigrants from Japan—served as interpreters, translators, and interrogators throughout the Pacific, participating in all the major battles. Guadalcanal. New Guinea. Solomons. Iwo Jima. Burma. Leyte. Okinawa. Tantamount to a secret weapon in the war against Japan, they were intent on proving their loyalty even as their families were being held in internment camps. They fought two wars simultaneously: one, against their ancestral homeland; the other, against racial prejudice at home.

After America's declaration of war against Japan following the surprise attack on Pearl Harbor, the Japanese immigrants (Issei) living in the U.S. were branded as "enemy aliens." Their Nisei offspring were seen by many Americans not as fellow countrymen but as the face of the hated enemy. It was unsafe for them to walk down the streets of some U.S. communities. As a result of this nation's failure to correctly gauge their loyalty and patriotism, coupled with the widespread xenophobia regarding anyone and anything Japanese, President Franklin D. Roosevelt signed Executive Order 9066 in February 1942 that authorized the removal of some 110,000 men, women, and children of Japanese ancestry from four western states to hastily built camps run by the War Relocation Authority. An estimated two-thirds of them were U.S. citizens. Stripped of their constitutional rights, they were rounded up and forced into internment camps.

In a few short months, the War Department, desperate to find sufficient numbers of Japanese speakers to serve in the Military Intelligence Service (MIS) in the Pacific, concluded that training the Nisei for this vital role might be the answer. But there was a key question to be addressed: Would Japanese Americans be willing to fight against their ancestral homeland? The Army sent recruiters to relocation camps to find out. In one camp after another, the irony was inescapable to the internees. They were being kept behind barbed-wire fences because the U.S. government questioned their loyalty, and now the Army needed them to volunteer in the war against Japan, the very country they were suspected of being sympathetic toward? Even the most patriotic Nisei harbored strong feelings that their rights as U.S. citizens had been violated. And yet, from their bleak, barracks-like quarters inside guarded compounds in desolate locations, waves of young Japanese Americans answered their nation's call. Implored one tearful mother to her departing nineteen-year-old son as he left to join the Army: "Make us proud."

In 1942, the first Nisei recruited by the U.S. Army for the newly opened Military Intelligence Service Language School (MISLS) arrived at Camp Savage, Minnesota. Initial plans called for a new class to graduate every year, but the pressure to have Japanese-speaking MIS teams in the field resulted in a compressed timetable, with graduation in half that time. The War Department ordered the school to supply enough Japanese-language teams to support every division fighting in the Pacific. As a result, each succeeding class was larger than the one before it, with the curriculum ever more focused and specialized. By spring 1946, the MISLS had produced nearly six thousand graduates.

The war planners in Japan believed their language so complex that few Westerners would fully understand it. As a result, many Japanese military communications were sent in the open without being coded. Trained Nisei linguists in the field were able to rapidly translate these messages and other captured documents and provide U.S. commanders with timely intelligence about enemy defenses and plans, the condition and morale of its troops, and technical specifications of their weapons, all of which were put to use in winning battles and saving American lives.

The story of the Japanese American soldiers who served in the Pacific theater is one of action, pride, courage, and sacrifice. That U.S. combat units fighting throughout the Pacific had the ability to understand the enemy's language and read their communications was among the best kept secrets of the war. In the decades that followed, a veil of secrecy stayed in place over matters pertaining to military intelligence. Even when the World War II records started to be declassified decades later, much of this story remained untouched in dusty storage bins at national archives. The buried and scattered records of their service were often incomplete or not easily found. The fact that their small intelligence teams were attached to larger units made finding detailed accounts of their wartime activities all the more challenging. Astonishingly, no roster of the Japanese American soldiers who served in the Pacific was ever compiled by the Army. (See Appendix for the first list of more than three thousand Nisei veterans of the Pacific war.)[*]

For decades, there were no reunions of the MIS Nisei; they had gone through the war without having much contact with others like themselves except for the few men on their own team. After the war, they were disinclined to join veterans' organizations, as their race and ancestry made them unwelcome in the usual circles of military fraternal groups. Some local posts of the Veterans of Foreign Wars prohibited Japanese Americans from joining. Many Nisei veterans, satisfied with having done their duty and proven their loyalty to America, did not speak openly of their wartime experiences for years, even to their families.

Bridge to the Sun tells this dramatic, poignant, and inspirational story at a pivotal time in this country's history. Japanese Americans, with

---

[*] Before the war ended, approximately thirty-one thousand Nisei served in uniform, the majority of them sent to Europe. While more than three thousand Japanese American soldiers served in the Pacific with little public notice due to wartime secrecy around intelligence activities, the exploits of the all-Nisei infantry units—the 100th Infantry Battalion and the 442nd Regimental Combat Team—fighting the Germans in North Africa and Europe received widespread recognition during and after the war.

ancestral ties to a nation with which we were at war and distrusted for that reason, became huge assets to the U.S. military because they knew the enemy better than anyone and were highly motivated to defeat them. In an America that too often prejudges people based on race and ethnicity, their timeless message of courage and patriotism should not be forgotten.

Bruce Henderson
Menlo Park, California

PROLOGUE

Tokyo Bay: September 2, 1945

The sky was dull gray with low-hanging clouds over the battleship on which the war that began with the attack on Pearl Harbor more than a thousand days before was to now end with Japan's formal surrender.

The USS *Missouri*'s trio of sixteen-inch guns mounted in forward turret No. 2 had hurled one-ton, armor-piercing projectiles in bombardments of Iwo Jima and Okinawa months earlier, and more recently at the Japanese homeland. But now the sixty-six-foot-long barrels were pointed straight up to provide headroom on the verandah deck, where some of the highest-ranked military leaders of the victorious Allied nations were standing in designated spots. The teak deck shone with the colors of red-striped Russians, beribboned British, olive-drab Chinese, and khaki-clad American admirals and generals. In the center of the narrow space was a long, collapsible table borrowed at the last minute from the crew's mess and covered with a coffee-stained green cloth from the officers' wardroom—stand-ins for a showy mahogany table (a gift from the British Navy for the momentous occasion) that proved too small to spread out the surrender documents for signing. A straight-back chair had been placed at either side of the table. In the superstructure rising high above, every level and catwalk was filled with hundreds of cheering white-capped sailors gawking at the scene below as the ship's band played a rousing rendition of the Navy march song, "Anchors Aweigh."

Standing thirty feet away on a subdeck with a group of U.S. news

correspondents was twenty-seven-year-old Thomas Sakamoto, a tall
Japanese American with thick black hair and large, penetrating eyes
whose intelligence and dedication to duty had been rewarded with two
promotions in the past four months. Born in San Jose, California, he
now wore a single gold bar collar device as one of the newest second
lieutenants in the Pacific. On a chain around his neck was the same
"Press" tag worn by the newsmen he had escorted from Manila two
days before as their official interpreter.

At precisely 9:04 a.m., the gaiety aboard the battleship ceased when
a small launch came along the starboard side carrying a delegation of
Japan's government officials and military officers. One by one they
climbed a steep ladder to the *Missouri*'s gangway. First to the top was
Foreign Minister Mamoru Shigemitsu, who had trouble on the ladder
because of his wooden leg—the result of a Korean terrorist attack a
decade earlier. No American reached out to help as he pulled on the
ship's ropes to bring himself up the last rungs. Like his two aides from
the Foreign Office behind him, Shigemitsu was dressed in formal
attire: a frock coat, striped trousers, and a silk top hat. Leaning heavily on a cane, he awaited the rest of his party, which included three
representatives each from Japan's War and Navy Departments. He
then hobbled slowly with them to where they were directed to stand
mid-deck near the signing table. Shigemitsu was known in diplomatic
circles for his efforts to stave off armed conflict with America; a year
before Pearl Harbor, he spent two weeks in Washington trying to
arrange a face-to-face meeting between Prime Minister Fumimaro
Konoe and President Franklin D. Roosevelt, a summit that never took
place. Shigemitsu had been appointed foreign minister a year before.
By signing the surrender on behalf of Japan's government this day,
Shigemitsu would be formally ending a war he had never wanted.

Next to Shigemitsu stood Japan's other signee to the surrender: a
grim-faced General Yoshijiro Umezu of the Imperial General Staff, his
uniform replete with dress gloves and knee-high boots, and his chest
covered in campaign ribbons and draped with loops of gold braid.
His dress uniform usually included his steel-bladed samurai sword,
but this morning he was not wearing his prized *shin-guntō*. Umezu,
who had commanded armies in China and Manchuria, had opposed
surrender to the last moment. Even after the atomic bombs were

dropped on Hiroshima and Nagasaki, killing more than a hundred thousand of his countrymen, he had lobbied to fight on and force the U.S. and their allies to sustain such heavy losses in an invasion of the homeland that Japan would be able to negotiate for peace under better terms. Considering himself a soldier born to command an army, he

Surrender ceremony aboard the USS *Missouri* in Tokyo Bay,
September 2, 1945

had threatened to commit hara-kiri in protest if ordered to sign the surrender. It took the emperor's personal persuasion before Umezu reluctantly accepted his appointment as the signee to the instrument of surrender on behalf of Japan's armed forces.

In the hush that followed the delegation's arrival, Tom Sakamoto could hear only his own breath. The Japanese party waited, not knowing what to expect, as there had been no rehearsal or other instructions given them. Nothing spelled defeat more than having to board their enemy's massive battleship anchored in the bay of their own capital city, and they were left to stand as the vanquished before a thousand hate-filled stares. A Chinese general swiped his hand under his chin in a cut-the-throat gesture. It reminded Sakamoto of the thumbs-down sign that sealed the fate of defeated gladiators in the Roman Colosseum. The Japanese, their downcast eyes having gone dull, stood like statues in the harsh silence. Had they looked at a nearby bulkhead, they would have seen the gray surface painted with row after row of miniature rising suns representing the number of Japanese planes and ships shot down or sunk by the *Missouri*.

When General Douglas MacArthur at last stepped out from a sea cabin, he strode stiffly to a cluster of microphones. The only sign of emotion Sakamoto detected from the man who had orchestrated the defeat of Japan in a strategic island-hopping campaign through the Southwest Pacific was the slight trembling of his hands as he held his prepared remarks.

"We are gathered here, representatives of the major warring powers, to conclude a solemn agreement whereby peace may be restored," he said in the sonorous voice familiar to many. "It is my earnest hope, and indeed the hope of all mankind, that from this solemn occasion a better world shall emerge out of the blood and carnage of the past—a world founded upon faith and understanding, a world dedicated to the dignity of man and the fulfilment of his most cherished wish for freedom, tolerance, and justice." Promising to discharge his duties as supreme commander for the Allied powers in the peaceful occupation of Japan with "justice and tolerance," MacArthur said, "I now invite the representatives of the emperor of Japan and the Japanese government and the Japanese Imperial General Headquarters to sign the Instrument of Surrender at the places indicated."

Sakamoto realized that no attempt was made to translate MacArthur's message for the Japanese delegation, and he wondered just how many of the vanquished understood the words of the victor.

Shigemitsu was the first to sit at the table. He signed his name in three distinct Japanese ideographs inside a pair of forty-by-twenty-inch bound books; one held the surrender document in English that would be taken to Washington, and the other had a Japanese translation he would take to Tokyo later that day. Next came Umezu, the swordless old warrior who had pushed for his country to fight on.[*]

As MacArthur approached the table, he motioned forward two of his generals, Jonathan Wainwright, who was captured when Corregidor fell, and Arthur Percival, the British commander who surrendered Singapore; both had been prisoners of the Japanese since 1942 until being freed two weeks earlier. Hurriedly flown in the day before to attend the surrender ceremonies, they were still shockingly emaciated. With pressed uniforms hung on bony apparitions but heads held high, Wainwright and Percival stood at attention behind MacArthur, who took from his pocket five silver-tipped fountain pens. He began his signature, then stopped and handed the pen to Wainwright, who saluted and stepped back. Percival received the next pen. Of the three remaining pens MacArthur used to complete his signature, one was for him, one would be kept aboard the *Missouri* for posterity, and one sent to President Harry S. Truman. Then a succession of representatives of the nine Allied nations at war with Japan strode one by one to the signing table to add their signatures.

Studying the American generals and admirals lined up on the deck, Sakamoto could almost read their expressions. Most of them were in their fifties and sixties, and they looked as if they knew this was not

---

[*] Japan's two signees to the surrender instrument took divergent postwar paths. Umezu was convicted of multiple war crimes, most committed by his forces in China, and sentenced to life in prison, where he died in 1949 at the age of sixty-seven. Despite his well-known opposition to the war and over the objection of U.S. officials, including Joseph Grew, a former U.S. ambassador to Japan, Shigemitsu was convicted of "waging aggressive war" against the Allies. After serving five years in Sugamo Prison in Tokyo, he was elected to the Lower House of the Diet of Japan, and in 1955 became the deputy prime minister of Japan.

only the end of the war but the climax of their long military careers. They were dressed informally in khaki uniforms with open collars and no ties. "We fought them in our khaki uniforms," MacArthur had decreed, "and we'll accept their surrender in our khaki uniforms." In the front row was Fleet Admiral Chester Nimitz, whose ships and planes had defeated the Japanese fleet at Midway six months after the surprise attack on Pearl Harbor in the first decisive victory for the U.S. in the Pacific. Directly across from Sakamoto stood Admiral William "Bull" Halsey, who was MacArthur's favorite admiral because he wasn't afraid to risk losing ships while aggressively taking the fight to the enemy. And there was General Joseph "Vinegar Joe" Stilwell, who the *Time* correspondent Theodore H. White, standing nearby, thought "bristled like a guard dog" at the enemy officials as they came aboard. Stilwell had been traveling with the British army when the Japanese chased them out of Burma in 1942, but he returned eighteen months later with two well-equipped, U.S.-trained Chinese infantry divisions and a band of tough American jungle fighters called Merrill's Marauders to kick the Japanese out of northern Burma and open the crucial Allied supply route into China.

Sakamoto felt honored to be a witness to history—something he appreciated even more when he learned that he was one of only three Japanese Americans in attendance. But he was discomfited by all the double-takes he received from sailors who he knew must be wondering who the hell he was and what *he* was doing here with all the brass.

After twenty-five months spent in the Southwest Pacific, Sakamoto was greatly relieved that the harrowing savagery of the war with Japan was over. Like millions of GIs, he was eager to return home. But that morning aboard the *Missouri*, he experienced a range of other emotions.

A decade earlier, he had spent four years at a boarding high school in Kumamoto, Japan, where his immigrant parents in California sent him to learn about their homeland. His schoolboy memories of Japan were mixed in with the scenes of devastation he had seen the past few days in a country he knew well but now barely recognized. He thought about the families he had known and the school friends he had made in Kumamoto, just across Shimabara Bay from Nagasaki. How many had survived the war? And what kind of life and future would they have in a wrecked nation rife with homelessness and poverty? He knew he was likely one of the few Americans aboard the *Missouri* that day who had even an ounce of empathy for the people of Japan. His feelings weren't solely because this was his parents' homeland, but because he had lived among the people of Japan and knew them to be a peaceful and humble people, not the cartoonishly evil, bucktoothed, myopic, war-mongering "Japs" portrayed by much of the U.S. press. The average Japanese conscript—many had been farmers before the war—fought well and hard and sacrificed much, believing in their cause as much as the American GIs believed in their own. But Sakamoto did blame the most fervent of the Japanese, and the country's military and government leaders, for the war that had cost so many lives on both sides.

Sakamoto did not have divided loyalties. He was an American by birth and upbringing, and Japanese by ancestry. He was proud of his lineage, but during his years in Japan he had been a student of the culture, not a convert. He didn't have dual citizenship like many Japanese Americans, whose parents only had to register a child's birth in America with a Japanese consulate for them to receive dual citizenship. Military training was mandatory in high schools in Japan, and Sakamoto, a good student, had excelled in his military studies. Knowing he was an American, some students ribbed him that one day they could face each other on a battlefield, not realizing the truth of their foretelling. With his graduation only days away, he had been summoned to the office of the school's military commandant, a major in the Imperial Japanese Army who went around campus in his dress uniform complete with a long sword rattling at his side. He required any of his young charges who came before him to stand rigidly at attention. Once Sakamoto was in the proper stance with head up, stomach in, and chin out, the major announced that he had been selected to become a probationary officer in the army.

Sakamoto understood that it was a supreme compliment. By then—the spring of 1938—Japan had been at war in China for nearly a year, and its army had already captured Shanghai and the Chinese capital of Nanking. Martial arts songs about the nobility and purity of dying for the emperor were played nonstop on the radio, and were sung by children of all ages in assemblies in the nation's schools. Every morning at his high school, students gathered in the chapel and prayed for their country's warriors. He had been dispatched with other students to bid farewell to trainloads of soldiers going to war in China from stations packed with family, friends, and neighbors waving flags and cheering, *"Banzai!"* On the trains, officers held their swords high in salutes, and young soldiers recited aloud Psalm 23 as they prepared to walk through the valley of the shadow of death and fear no evil because they believed that dying for the emperor was the greatest honor, as did their families, who were ready for their sons to earn such an honor even though it meant losing them. In the Japanese army, young men went off prepared to sacrifice their lives, having been taught that anything short of victory was a disgrace to their family. It was the opposite in the U.S. Army, Tom later learned; soldiers went off to do their duty with every intention of returning home. But those days in Japan, the atmosphere of militarism and patriotism was all-encompassing and impossible to escape. The best students with a demonstrated acumen for the military who were given the opportunity to become officers after graduation were expected to jump at the chance, and most did. All of this made what Sakamoto knew he had to say to the major not easy to vocalize, but he steeled himself and did so anyway, explaining that he was not a Japanese citizen but an American, and he would not be accepting the military appointment but going home. Before dismissing the young man, the major angrily berated him for being a traitor to the emperor.

Then eighteen, Sakamoto returned that summer of 1938 to America, where he borrowed $800 from the Farm Bureau to lease forty-three acres in California's Santa Clara Valley, carpeted with orchards and several million apricot, plum, citrus, and other fruit trees. He rented a farmhouse, bought a used tractor and an old truck, and grew fruit and produce for the wholesale market until he was drafted in early 1941.

The journey that brought Tom Sakamoto to the *Missouri* that morning began a month before the attack on Pearl Harbor, when he reported with fifty-seven other Japanese American soldiers to the Army's new Japanese-language school at the Presidio in San Francisco. Nearly all of them had spent at least a few years attending school in Japan, and as a result were fluent in the language. A small cadre of Army intelligence officers who had been stationed in Japan in the

1920s and 1930s had sounded the alarm in Washington as tensions worsened between the two countries that there would be enormous language difficulties in the event of war with Japan. They argued that very few Americans of European ancestry had a real mastery of the incredibly complex Japanese language, and a school was needed to start training interpreters, translators, and interrogators.

When Sakamoto arrived at the new school in November 1941, he entered an old, empty hangar at Crissy Field on the edge of the San Francisco Bay. The cavernous space with cement floors had been used to park mail delivery planes in the 1920s; it had no seats, no tables, and no sleeping quarters. Before classes could start, the student-soldiers brought in abandoned orange crates and boxes for chairs and desks, built wooden partitions to separate classrooms from offices and sleeping quarters, and constructed three-tiered bunks. Typewriters and other supplies were borrowed from wherever they were found. Bookstores and libraries were searched for old Japanese-language books, and using a decade-old Japanese army manual as a reference, a handful of newly hired civilian teachers assembled course materials. When classes began, the students faced a challenging curriculum of not only advanced Japanese reading, writing, translation, and interpretation, but also the social, political, economic, and cultural background of modern-day Japan. They pored over documents and maps, and studied Japanese military structure, organization, and technical terms. Fifteen of the students dropped out when they failed to meet the academic rigors and were returned to their units. By the time the first class graduated in May 1942, the U.S. and Japan were at war, and American field commanders in the Pacific were clamoring for Japanese-language teams to read captured enemy documents and interrogate prisoners of war. Thirty-five of the first graduates were dispersed throughout a vast theater of operations, ranging from Alaska in the north to Guadalcanal and Papua New Guinea in the Southwest Pacific. The remaining ten—all top-ranked graduates, including Sakamoto—were retained to join the teaching staff at the new Military Intelligence Service Language School being set up at Camp Savage, Minnesota. With the push on for more Japanese-language teams, the next two classes graduated nearly six hundred students. Sakamoto taught at Camp Savage for a year before his request for overseas duty was granted in July

1943, and he was sent to the Pacific in charge of his own ten-man Military Intelligence Service team.

The surrender ceremony aboard the *Missouri* took no more than thirty minutes from the time the Japanese delegation came aboard until they were curtly given the signal to leave shortly after MacArthur proclaimed, "These proceedings are closed."

As if on command, the skies parted and the sun broke through the clouds. Rays of light found the slate-gray hulls of the nearest ships, and a distant drone soon turned into a deafening roar. Several hundred U.S. bombers and smaller fleet carrier planes rumbled over the armada of Allied ships anchored in the bay in a final salute to victory.

For Tom Sakamoto and many others, it had been long in coming.

PART ONE

One

THE TYPE OF SOLDIER WE WANT

Kazuo Komoto was born in the heart of California's Central Valley. He was the first of six boys. His father, Yoshikazu, had immigrated on his own from Japan at the age of seventeen in 1907. Landing in Seattle, he worked as a railroad and field laborer for ten years before returning to Japan and marrying Hisano Waki from their hometown of Okayama, a city on the western shore of Japan's main island of Honshu, bounded on the south by the Island Sea and known for its traditional gardens and a samurai-era castle. Together, the newlywed couple migrated to America in early 1918, settling in Sanger, California. Kazuo was born nine months later.

Infant Kazuo in arms of
his mother, Hisano, 1919

It was a hardscrabble life on cracked, sunbaked land made fertile thanks to the miracle of irrigation. Hisano, who had a comfortable upbringing in Japan, cried herself to sleep the first night in her new home. The wind howled through the slats of the shack in the middle of a treeless field, and stars were visible through holes in the roof. This was not the life she had envisioned. As the years passed and her babies came, she grew concerned about what she saw as America's discriminatory society weighted against Japanese immigrants and their children, fearing that it would be difficult for her sons to get ahead in life. She had seen many young Nisei men unable to find decent jobs, having to work as farm laborers or in produce stands. In her mind, acquiring an education was paramount. To complement the local public school, she enrolled seven-year-old Kazuo and his school-age brothers in a Japanese school two miles away. She walked them there every Saturday, signaling to her young sons the importance she placed on their education.

By the time Kazuo was ten years old, his father was making a decent living growing grapes and strawberries on twenty acres, much of which he delivered himself to the 7th Street farmers' market in Los Angeles over the winding road through the Tehachapi Mountains known as the Grapevine. Like other immigrants from Japan, Kazuo's parents were not allowed to hold U.S. citizenship. And since they were ineligible for citizenship, under California's restrictive Alien Land Laws of 1913 and 1920, they could not own land or hold long-term leases, which meant Kazuo's father could farm only rented land. A quiet man who worked long hours, he didn't have much time or energy for the children, and they were largely reared by their strong-willed mother. It was she who, in 1928, decided to take her oldest son to Japan so he could learn more about his ancestral culture and receive a traditional Japanese education.

Kazuo gave his mother no argument when she left him in the care of his paternal grandparents in Okayama and returned to California. His grandfather, a Shinto priest, made an immediate impact on young Kazuo, although the boy was influenced more by his elder's conduct than his words. The old man lived, to the end, a disciplined life, yet was always kind to others. Kazuo tried his best to follow his grandfather's example.

It didn't take Kazuo long to learn firsthand that Japan had its own immigrant discrimination. Anyone of Japanese ancestry coming from America (and elsewhere) was considered lower class by native-born Japanese. Being the only American in school targeted him for teasing and bullying. He looked like them, but the other kids did not accept

High school student
Kazuo in Japan, 1937

him as one of their own. In America, he was Japanese; in Japan, he was American. But the personable boy dismissed the insults and began to make friends.

After two years in elementary school, Kazuo entered intermediate school. He read voraciously, anything he could find, which helped him with basic Japanese grammar as well as memorizing some two thousand commonly used ideographs known as kanji—characters adopted from Chinese that are used in the Japanese writing system—which the students were expected to know by the sixth grade.

Thanks to his extracurricular reading, his vocabulary expanded greatly. After graduating from sixth grade, he took the admission test for preparatory high school. Of the more than one thousand students in the region taking the exam, 250 passed. Kazuo was one of them. Already thinking about what he would study after high school at university, he seemed on track to get the education his mother wanted for him. By then, both grandparents had passed away, and Kazuo was living with his mother's sister.

During his decade in Japan (1928–38), Kazuo witnessed the country moving steadily toward militarism. Japan's national policy to spread influence politically and militarily led to the 1931 invasion of Manchuria, which was colonized and used as a base from which to attack China in 1937. In this rising tide of imperialism, the legions of the soldiers going off to "protect Japan" were revered as saviors. *But protect and save Japan from what?* Kazuo often wondered. It seemed that Japan was always the aggressor. But this was not an opinion he could freely express. On occasion, in fact, he had to stand compliantly with other students cheering trains filled with soldiers yelling the slogan first used centuries ago to express respect for the emperor but which was now a battle cry.

"Banzai! Banzai! Banzai!"

Playing with friends one day in a park, Kazuo watched a platoon of Japanese army reservists drilling, then breaking for lunch. When three of the soldiers returned a few minutes late, their sergeant beat them, one by one, first with his fists, then kicked them after they fell to the ground. The soldiers took the beatings without a whimper, as the other soldiers and their officer watched. Although only twelve at the time, Kazuo wanted to yell at the sergeant to stop. *Why are you beating your own soldiers?*

As he grew older, Kazuo worried that if he stayed in Japan he would be drafted and sent off to some faraway war. His high school years passed quickly; he was a good student, popular with his peers, and a star on the track team, setting school records in the hundred yard dash. After his graduation in June 1938, he wrote his mother saying he wanted to come back to the U.S. for college. Although he had enjoyed his time in Japan, he had strong feelings that he did not belong, and did not see himself spending the rest of his life here. He disliked how the people were conditioned to think and act the way the government wanted them to. Here, it was about conforming, and being docile. When a teacher made a statement, that was it, right or wrong, with no discussion. The students didn't dare ask questions that might embarrass the teacher. As early as first grade, children were taught in *shushin* (ethics) courses about virtues such as fidelity, diligence, and frugality, and also to obey the emperor and be willing to die for him. Life itself was but a feather, they were told, compared to their obligation to the emperor. But through all the indoctrination, Kazuo never forgot he was an American, and he never accepted all the fuss about what he later derided as "emperor love."

But there was more to Kazuo's desire to leave Japan. He had brothers he had not seen in ten years; the youngest ones he hardly knew. He missed his intelligent and supportive mother, and even his father, although he was at times harsh. Kazuo was crestfallen when his mother wrote to him to stay in Japan for college. But his mind was made up. When it was apparent she wasn't going to send the money for his return, he borrowed enough from his sympathetic aunt for a steamship ticket to California. He didn't tell anyone at home he was coming, but waited to telephone them when his ship docked in San Francisco. Within a few days of arriving back in Sanger, he told his parents of his plan to enroll in college and become an American diplomat—maybe even one day the U.S. ambassador to Japan, a lofty notion first put in his head years before by his dear grandmother in Okayama.

His father had other ideas. *Enough school! As the eldest son, you must work on the farm and work for the family.*

Kazuo now understood why his mother had wanted him to stay in Japan for college; she must have known of his father's plans to put him to work. She protested now, but to no avail. Kazuo felt guilty about being away so long and not helping the family. He was nineteen, and he had never earned a penny, while his brothers had been working on the farm and had part-time jobs in town. Kazuo agreed to put his dream on hold.

He worked hard on the farm, and enjoyed making new friends. His chiseled good looks, quiet sense of humor, and winning smile made him popular with the girls, Japanese as well as Caucasian. But he soon discovered that when he went on a Friday night date in town he could not expect to receive table service anywhere other than the Chop Suey House.

Two years after returning home, he received his draft notice from the Selective Service, and was inducted into the peacetime U.S. Army in March 1941. He was sent to Camp Roberts near San Luis Obispo for ninety days of basic training. One sweltering June day, after finishing a grueling run in the back hills with a full pack, he was ordered to clean up, change his uniform, and report to an administrative office on the double.

Waiting for him was a tall, square-jawed Army officer named Kai Rasmussen, who was touring camps to interview Nisei soldiers as possible candidates for the new Japanese-language school starting up that fall at the San Francisco Presidio. Rasmussen had immigrated to America from Denmark at the age of twenty in 1922, unable to speak a word of English on his arrival. He enlisted in the U.S. Army, and two years later won admission to West Point, graduating in the class of 1929. From 1936 to 1940, he served as a military attaché at the U.S. embassy in Tokyo, during which time he learned Japanese, which he spoke with a heavy Scandinavian accent. For six months, he had embedded as an observer with the Imperial Japanese Army in China. Few U.S. military officers knew Japan and its military as well as he did. Now, with tensions rising between the two countries, he had been among a handful of career officers the War Department had charged with organizing the school to train Japanese-speaking soldiers for military intelligence work. That summer, Rasmussen and two other Japanese-speaking officers were visiting camps to interview more than a thousand Nisei soldiers on active duty. Rasmussen had presumed that many young men raised by Japanese immigrants would be fluent in their parents' language, but he discovered that was not the case. His unofficial survey found that less than 10 percent of Nisei soldiers could read, write, and speak Japanese. The rest had been so thoroughly Americanized in U.S. schools and society that they knew little or no Japanese. Those findings were a shock to Rasmussen as well as the War Department. The statistics would have been even more discouraging were it not for the Kibei—literally, "returned to America"—the name given to those Japanese Americans who came back to the U.S. after receiving some schooling in Japan. Rasmussen estimated that one in ten Nisei had gone to school in Japan. While their years in Japan and retention of the language varied, many of them had returned home to the United States speaking Japanese as well as or better than English. They were a unique generation that was both Japanese and American in language, attitude, and cultural heritage. And Rasmussen recognized early on just how valuable they would be to the U.S. Army in the event of war with Japan.

Kazuo was astonished when the blond, fair-skinned officer launched into passable Japanese. In turn, Rasmussen was impressed with Kazuo's ten years of education in Japan. He handed Kazuo a Japanese military field manual and asked him to translate some passages, which Kazuo did with the ease of reading the Sunday comics. In truth, after spending the majority of his school years in Japan, Kazuo was now more fluent in Japanese than English. They talked about his time in Japan—some of the same years Rasmussen had been there—and of places they had both been and the natural beauty of the Land of the Rising Sun. They shared stories and memories of the country they both loved. However, in the course of their conversation, it became clear to Rasmussen that Kazuo had fully assimilated back into life in America, and his loyalty to the United States, the country of his birth, was clear and unambiguous.

After explaining the Army's plans for the new language school, Rasmussen said, "Private Komoto, you are the type of soldier we want. I'd like you to volunteer for the school. You'll be trained in intelligence work. Should war break out with Japan, we'll have a special job for you."

The word *volunteer* popped out at Kazuo.

"You want volunteers, sir?"

"Yes, the school is voluntary."

Kazuo didn't want to volunteer for anything. Truthfully, he was fed up with others telling him what he should be doing with his life.

"Sir, I was drafted for one year of military service. When I get out I want to go to college. I'm sorry, but I'm not interested in volunteering."

A disappointed Rasmussen said he understood.

Six months later, Pearl Harbor was attacked. When Kazuo, still at Camp Roberts, heard the terrible news that morning, he thought, *It finally happened.* He was not shocked by Japan's aggression like many Americans because of the direction in which he had seen the militarists taking the country, but he hated the thought of fighting his parents' homeland, where he had left behind many relatives and friends. But he knew he had no choice. First and always, his loyalty was to the country of his birth. The United States of America.

The next day, Kazuo's platoon boarded a Greyhound bus to Barstow, a railroad town in the California desert. For the next three weeks they protected the switching yards from sabotage. Then, on December 28, his unit was sent to Downey, near Los Angeles, to guard an aircraft manufacturing plant. Kazuo and another Nisei soldier happened to be on duty at the front gate one day when a local newspaper reporter and photographer arrived to tour the plant. A few pictures were taken, and the next day a photo of the two men ran on the front page below the alarming headline:

JAP SOLDIERS GUARDING AIRCRAFT PLANT!

Later that day, the company commander called Kazuo and the other soldier into his office. "Boys, I gotta take you off the front gate," he said. "You'll guard the back gate from now on."

Kazuo heard reports of Nisei soldiers being kicked out of the Army, and how those who had spent time in Japan were being particularly targeted. He recalled the officer recruiting for the Japanese-language school saying how valuable those same individuals would be in event of war with Japan. That they were now being culled from the ranks seemed nonsensical.*

Not long after, Kazuo and other Nisei soldiers mysteriously pulled from their units boarded a train to El Paso, Texas, where they were placed in segregated barracks at Fort Bliss, with no regular duties. Rumors circulated about what the Army had in store for them. When he received new travel orders a few weeks later, Kazuo's first thought was that he was being booted out of the Army. When he was bused to the train station with thirty other Nisei from Fort Bliss, he was convinced of it.

They arrived in the middle of the night in St. Paul/Minneapolis, where they loaded into a convoy truck. Let out in the dark after a bumpy ride, they were herded into dimly lit, log cabin barracks filled with cots and not much else. It wasn't until morning that they found out that the gloomy cabins had most recently been a state home for indigent elderly men.

Soon, there were two hundred Nisei soldiers in camp. They were to comprise the first class of the Military Intelligence Service Language School at Camp Savage, the expanded successor to the Fourth Army's language school at the Presidio that had graduated fewer than fifty students (including Tom Sakamoto) in May 1942. Hundreds of Japanese-language interpreters, translators, and interrogators were urgently needed now for the war in the Pacific.

So much, he thought, *for not volunteering.*

But it was war now, and Kazuo Komoto was ready to do his part.

---

* A confidential War Department communiqué, dated January 23, 1942, sent to all commanding generals in the U.S. Army, ordered that soldiers of Japanese descent "not be assigned to positions in units or installations where they might gain valuable information or be able to execute damage to important installations."

TWO

"HARM THEM . . . HARM ME"

Nobuo Furuiye was born in the spring of 1918 in a Colorado farmhouse near the base of the eastern slope of the Rocky Mountains twenty miles north of Denver. It was here, about two miles outside the hamlet of Lafayette, where Nobuo's nomadic father, Daijiro, had at long last put down roots a decade earlier to become a farmer.

Daijiro had left Japan in 1900, at the age of seventeen, to work for his own father, a sugarcane plantation foreman in Hawaii. Three years later his father returned to Japan, where his wife had stayed behind with their other children when he went to Hawaii for work. But Daijiro decided against going back to Japan, and thereby avoided being drafted into the army, as many young Japanese men were for the Russo-Japanese War (1904–05), which, eerily similar to the attack on Pearl Harbor thirty-seven years later, began with Japan's surprise attack on the Russian fleet at Port Arthur three hours before the Russian government received Japan's declaration of war. By the time that conflict ended, it had taken the lives of some 150,000 Japanese and Russian soldiers.

Daijiro worked his way to America in 1903 as a deckhand on a freighter bound for San Francisco. He picked hops in the Central Valley during the summer harvest, and after long days in the fields went to night school to learn English. He signed on with the Western Pacific Railroad and laid untold miles of tracks in California. After a

stint working in coal mines in Wyoming, he drifted to Colorado, where
he found a job at a Pueblo steel mill. When a Chinese immigrant was
badly beaten by workers who were angry that he had taken a job away
from a white man, Daijiro decided to hit the road again. He ended up
in Denver, where the only work he could find was as a dishwasher in
a restaurant. However, it was there that his fortunes began to change,
when he met a man from a small Japanese community north of Denver who convinced him there was a future in farming. Daijiro found a
Caucasian landowner willing to rent him acreage near Lafayette. With
a borrowed horse and plow, he set out to succeed in farming, which
he eventually did. But as he neared thirty, he knew what was missing
in his life, and he wrote to his father in Japan asking for help in finding
a suitable wife willing to join him in America.

Daijiro's father knew a young woman and her parents, who lived
in Kamotogun, a neighboring village in Kumamoto Prefecture.* Her
name was Tamaye Tsukamoto. She was nineteen years old, and could
read and write. Deeming her worthy of becoming his son's wife, Daijiro's father approached her family and made the arrangements. Like
many Japanese immigrant couples of the era, the spouses-to-be had
never met, but only exchanged photographs. In those days, "picture
brides" were married by proxy before departing, and traveled under
their new married name. When Tamaye's ship, the *Sado Maru*, arrived in
Seattle on August 29, 1912, an eager Daijiro was there to meet her. But
during a medical examination in U.S. Customs, Tamaye was discovered to have conjunctivitis, an eye infection that had to be cleared up
before she entered the country. After being quarantined for a month,
Tamaye was allowed entry on October 7. Daijiro was again waiting
to greet her. They walked downtown to the Buddhist church where
he had arranged for a traditional wedding ceremony. After stopping
at a nearby Japanese tailor shop that made Western clothing for new
arrivals, Daijiro took his bride home to the farm. Nine months and
three weeks later, Tamaye gave birth to Albert, their firstborn.

There were several Japanese families in the Lafayette area, and

---

* Since 1888, Japan has been divided into forty-seven regional prefectures. Similar to the functions of counties and states in the United States, they serve as a
first level of governmental jurisdiction.

Nobuo, the third of six children born to Daijiro and Tamaye, grew up playing with those children as well as his own siblings. He didn't have much chance to make Caucasian friends until he started at the two-story, redbrick schoolhouse that went from first through fourth grades downstairs and fifth through eighth upstairs, with one teacher per floor. Coming from a Japanese-speaking household, he didn't know enough English when he started school to tell his teacher when he had to go to the bathroom. The teacher was sympathetic, and allowed him to slip out of class without asking for permission whenever nature called.

Nobuo had daily chores to perform before and after school. He was up before dawn to milk their old Guernsey cow, which provided the family's milk, cheese, and butter, and to feed the plow horses a mixture of grass hay and alfalfa for their upcoming day of labor. Come afternoon, another milking, then mucking out the stalls, which, for a time, he thought was the worst job on the farm. But Nobuo came to enjoy caring for livestock so much that he joined the local 4-H club. His specialty was steer raising, and one year his steer won third place at the county fair. Summer was not vacation time for Nobuo, as he worked every day in his father's fields, weeding and irrigating, and harvesting tomatoes, lettuce, cabbage, and cucumbers to be crated and then trucked into Denver, where they were sold to produce houses. Most Japanese farmboys had similar responsibilities; they, like Nobuo, became hardworking and serious before their time. Nobuo did, however, envy the way some white friends spent their summers, swimming and fishing.

The nearest high school was in Denver. When Nobuo graduated from eighth grade, his father arranged for him to board at a Buddhist temple in the Mile High City. About a dozen other Nisei boys were staying at the temple. Every day after school, they were required to come back to the temple for two hours of Japanese classes, which were taught by visiting teachers from Japan who were enrolled at the University of Denver or the Colorado School of Mines. Over the course of three years, Nobuo learned much about the language, customs, and history of his parents' homeland. His two older siblings had gone to school in Japan for several years, not an uncommon practice among families with Japanese-immigrant parents who could afford it.

But he had never been to Japan, and his curiosity was piqued. Nobuo's chance came as he was finishing at Manuel High School in Denver. When his father asked if he wanted to go to Japan, Nobuo said yes. The only catch was that his father wanted him to enroll in high school there in order to learn more about the country of his ancestors. While he wasn't excited about spending more time in high school, Nobuo thought it would be worth it for the experience of seeing Japan. Graduating in Denver a semester early, he arrived in Japan in the spring of 1936 to stay with his father's cousin, a schoolteacher in the city of Kumamoto, about sixty miles from Nagasaki. Because of his studies at the temple, Nobuo did well enough in a placement exam to enter the third year at a private boarding school, Kyushu Gakuin, one of the top high schools in Japan.

Nobuo was surprised that English was taught to all the students at Kyushu Gakuin. In fact, they had to take three courses: conversational English; translating Japanese to English; and translating English to Japanese. Nobuo had his own work to do improving his skills in advanced Japanese writing, grammar, and literature. Whether one was American or Japanese, becoming fluent in both languages was difficult and challenging. He soon won friends by offering to tutor them in English in exchange for them helping him in math and science courses, which included biology, chemistry, physics, horticulture, botany, algebra, geometry, and trigonometry. There were no electives as in U.S. high schools, only academic subjects necessary for graduation.

For Nobuo, the hardest aspect of living in Japan, and his biggest culture shock, were the rules, regulations, and restrictions on daily life. Many of the freedoms that young people took for granted in America were nonexistent in Japan. It partly had to do with Japanese culture, which required children to obey their elders without protest. There were also traditional walls of separation between the genders that didn't exist in American society. For instance, all the high schools were single-sex. The increased militarism in 1930s Japan also impacted personal liberties. Male students in high school wore dark-colored military-style uniforms with collar devices that identified each student by his class and group. While on the streets, they had to wear caps and salute upperclassmen and any military men they passed. Young Japanese males were taught about Bushido, the code of the samurai, in mandatory classes led by Japanese military officers assigned full-time to schools. Many of these officers preached that until a young male became a military man, he was not a man at all.

Of all his courses, Nobuo most dreaded the military classes, two hours every Tuesday and Thursday. They were taught at Kyushu Gakuin by an artillery major who Nobuo decided was looking for another war to fight before he got too old. Every semester he made the students take a thirty-six-hour forced march, carrying a full military pack while lugging a heavy, bolt-action rifle. It was always an agonizing ordeal for the boys.

Kumamoto had five military bases, and was home to the 6th Infantry Division of the Imperial Japanese Army. This division, Nobuo learned, was revered throughout the country for capturing Port Arthur in 1905 during the Russo-Japanese War. The division paid a price for its glory, as nearly half of its men were killed in the battle before the port finally fell.*

Also in the city was a unit of the Kenpeitai, the secret police arm of the Japanese army composed of fanatical nationalists. With duties similar to the Nazi SS, these military police sometimes wore civilian clothes to blend in and other times a uniform and white armband with the kanji characters representing *ken* (law) and *hei* (soldier). They carried swords, bayonets, and pistols, and watched everywhere for enemies or suspicious persons, both military and civilian. Nobuo and the other dozen or so Nisei in his school were warned by their teachers that the Kenpeitai kept close watch on Americans in Japan—adults and teenagers—and knew who they were by the way they "walked, talked and acted." The teachers told the students to be careful about what they said or did publicly or they could be taken in by the Kenpeitai for interrogation. Nobuo and the other Americans kept a low profile and didn't dare step out of line.

During Nobuo's second year in Japan, the country went to war with

---

* In December 1937, the 6th Division took part in the Battle of Nanking and the Nanking Massacre, which involved widespread rape and looting and resulted in the slaughter of tens of thousands of Chinese civilians. Subsequently sent to fight in the South Pacific, the division was annihilated by Allied forces on Bougainville Island in 1945.

China, following the Marco Polo Bridge Incident on July 7, 1937, a two-day battle between Chinese and Japanese army units in Peking. He and the other students heard the news at school, and talked about it after class. Most of the boys didn't consider it a major concern that would affect them. In fact, Nobuo had observed that many of his classmates resented the army types as much as he did, and a few really hated their guts, especially the Kenpeitai, who strode down the streets like bantam roosters. The boys he knew had no desire to go forth and die for Japan or the emperor in a foreign war.

When he graduated from Kyushu Gakuin in early 1938, Nobuo was twenty years old. He was surprised to learn for the first time that he had dual citizenship as a result of his American birth having been registered with the Japanese consulate. With the war in China going full tilt, Nobuo did not want to stay in Japan and chance being drafted into the army. (Some of his Nisei classmates at Kyushu Gakuin, he would later learn, stayed too long in Japan and were drafted into the Imperial Japanese Army.) So he said farewell to his father's cousin, who had been so hospitable during the previous two years, and on March 9, 1938, boarded the *Taiyo Maru*, an ocean liner heading to California, on a third-class ticket paid for by his father.*

During the voyage, Nobuo met a pretty Nisei woman who was three years older. California-born Toshie Suminaga was returning with her mother to their home in Redondo Beach after visiting relatives in Japan. He and Toshie saw each other daily aboard ship, sitting together

---

* The *Taiyo Maru* was to play a role in the prelude to Japan's attack on Pearl Harbor. On October 22, 1941, it departed Yokohama with several hundred foreign passengers, and three Imperial Japanese Navy officers disguised as crew members. One was an aviator gathering intelligence on U.S. airpower and aircraft carriers in Hawaii, and the others were submariners. After the ship docked, the three officers reconnoitered the entrance to Pearl Harbor and the activities of the U.S. fleet and aircraft. They met with the local Japanese consul aboard ship, and learned that the U.S. fleet's pattern of leaving harbor early in the week and returning for the weekend had been followed without variation for months. The *Taiyo Maru* left Hawaii on November 5 and arrived back in Japan in time for the officers to provide intelligence to some of the personnel, including the crews of midget submarines, which would take part in the Pearl Harbor attack on Sunday, December 7, 1941.

for meals and trading stories about their experiences in Japan and growing up in America with fathers who were farmers. She had an innocence and quiet strength that Nobuo found appealing. As the ship slipped under the Golden Gate Bridge on March 24 and Nobuo prepared to leave the ship—Toshie and her mother stayed aboard to disembark in Los Angeles two days later—he asked Toshie for her address and promised to write to her.

Nobuo took the train to Denver, where he was met by his parents. It was good to be home, and he was happy to once again be helping his father on the farm. Come winter, he took the train to California, where he visited a Nisei classmate from Kyushu Gakuin, who lived in San Jose. They contracted with orchard owners to trim their fruit trees, and Nobuo did that until it was time to return and help his father with spring planting. But before he left California, he paid a visit to Redondo Beach to see Toshie, with whom he had been corresponding. Again in her company, he felt the same connection he had on their voyage across the Pacific. Given their age difference, Toshie was cooler toward the idea of becoming serious with the tall, stocky Nobuo, although he looked older and more sure of himself than his years suggested. She told Nobuo she had broken off an earlier engagement to a man in Japan that had been arranged by their families. Facing the reality of marrying someone she didn't know, she reneged, and it would have meant living in Japan when she couldn't even read or write the language. "I am American," she told Nobuo. "I didn't want to live in Japan." Nobuo didn't take anything she said as a rejection of him or their blossoming friendship. But as he headed back to Colorado, he knew he had a long way to go to win the heart of the woman he loved.

Nobuo worked on the family farm during the spring and summer of 1939, then over the winter lull he got a job at a Japanese import store in Denver called Nippon Mercantile, which had the largest selection of Japanese foods in the city. The position came with a room upstairs in the back of the store where he could stay. The owner, a widow named Mrs. Uyehara, who knew his parents, appreciated Nobuo's intelligence and the fact that, unlike many young Nisei, he could read and write Japanese. She soon had him on an assistant managerial track. She also agreed that Nobuo could leave in the spring and summer to help his father on the farm. For the next year and a half, that was Nobuo's routine: working in Denver until spring, then leaving to work on the farm, and returning to the store for the fall and winter.

When Congress enacted a draft in 1940, Nobuo had to register, but due to his farmwork he was granted an agricultural exemption. He read in the newspapers about the tensions between Japan and the United States, but like many Americans he considered that the realm of international relations and believed it would have little to do with his daily life. Yes, he well knew that the militarists were in power in Japan, but he had also seen for himself that it was a nation of limited resources and manufacturing capabilities. In reality, Japan was a poor nation, lacking a modern transportation system and many other conveniences that were taken for granted in America. And, of course, they were already fighting one war in China; he couldn't imagine Japan wanting to fight America at the same time. It would be such a reckless act. The day soon came, of course, when he realized how mistaken he was, and how his life and the lives of so many others in both countries would be forever changed.

On that fateful day—December 7, 1941—Nobuo was at the farm for Sunday lunch. As was often the case, his parents had invited his employer, Mrs. Uyehara, to join the family, and Nobuo rode with her from Denver. They were all seated around the table, eating and chatting, when a little past noon the music on the radio stopped mid-song for the startling news bulletin about Japan's surprise attack on Pearl Harbor.

The room was stunned to silence.

His father spoke first. "What a *stupid* thing to do!"

Mrs. Uyehara had a stricken expression. "We'd better hurry back, Nobuo! There might be vandalism at the store."

Nobuo and Mrs. Uyehara jumped in her car and rushed the twenty-five miles back to Denver in record time. When they reached the store, they were relieved to see it was quiet in front, with no sign of any anti-Japanese protests. The store was located downtown on Larimer Street, and there were several other Japanese businesses in the neighborhood, but Mrs. Uyehara's was by far the biggest and best known. As a precaution, she had Nobuo get a ladder, take down the sign above the entrance, and scratch out NIPPON. When he put the sign back up, it read MERCANTILE.

Like countless Americans, Nobuo decided to enlist within days of Pearl Harbor. When he told his parents, they supported his decision, even though they knew it meant he would be fighting against their ancestral homeland. "This is your county," his father said, not at all sadly. "It's been good to you. Serve it."

Daijiro and Tamaye had always wanted their children to know their homeland, but in that moment Nobuo realized that their truest loyalties lay not with their own country of origin, but with America, the land that had taken them in and where their children had been born and they had built lives for them all. While his parents would worry about the safety of relatives in Japan, with whom they would not be able to correspond for years, that country was to receive no sympathy or support in the Furuiye household in its war with the United States.

Nobuo drove to his draft board in Boulder, twelve miles away, and told them he no longer wanted an agricultural exemption.

"I'm volunteering for the draft," Nobuo said.

The official found his name in their records, then looked at a long list of draftees. "Tell you what, son," he said. "We've had so many volunteers this month, we'll call you up next month."

"Okay, thank you."

That gave him another month as a civilian. Nobuo now faced having to tell Toshie, who, after his many letters and phone calls and another visit to California, had at last agreed to marry him even after turning down his first proposal. But now, more than three years after they met crossing the Pacific, their wedding plans would have to be postponed indefinitely. He decided a letter was better than a phone call. It was a sad and difficult missive for him to write because he didn't want to lose her. But he tried his best to explain his desire to do his part in the war, and only hoped she would understand and wait for him.

In early January it was announced that all Japanese residents must turn in their firearms and cameras to local authorities. Everyone knew that Daijiro was good friends with the county sheriff, who for years had come out to the farm to buy his produce, so a lot of guns and cameras were dropped off at the house for Daijiro to turn in. It was quite a collection, and Nobuo helped his father, who was turning in his own shotgun and camera, load the contraband into the back of their old pickup. They drove into town together.

The sheriff took one look at the stockpile and complained, "I don't need all this stuff!" But he really had no choice but to take it. He had a deputy unlock a cell in the back of the jail and Nobuo and Daijiro stacked everything inside, then the cell door was shut and locked.

"I've known you folks thirty years," the sheriff said. "I know you aren't going to do anything." He shook his head. "But orders are orders."

The official at the local draft board made good on his promise, and Nobuo received instructions to report for active duty on January 16, 1942. He started telling friends he would soon be leaving, and a few of them lived in Longmont, ten miles up the road. Somehow word got to the editor of the Longmont newspaper, who contacted Nobuo and confirmed the date he was leaving. Since he was the first local boy to leave for the war, the editor added, "Let's see if we can have a send-off for you."

Sure enough, a few days before he left, there was a big farewell party for Nobuo at the Elks Lodge in Longmont. Friends, neighbors, and some residents he didn't even know showed up to say goodbye and wish him good luck. He left feeling how lucky he was to be living where Pearl Harbor and the war with Japan had not gotten in the way of the long-standing goodwill between local Caucasian and Japanese residents. Many of their white neighbors gave the local Japanese much credit for arriving in the country penniless and working hard to establish themselves.

On January 16, Nobuo reported to Fort Logan, a military post in southwest Denver. There he was processed into the U.S. Army, given a haircut, issued uniforms, and assigned to a barrack. More men poured in daily, and four days after his arrival, Nobuo was in a group of inductees herded onto a troop train and sent south to Camp Roberts, in California, the largest Army basic training installation in the nation, to undergo an intensive seventeen-week training cycle to mold them into fighting men. After all his hard labor on the farm, Nobuo was quick to adjust to the physical demands of the training even as some of the city boys struggled.

Four weeks later came FDR's Executive Order 9066, and thereafter the stipulation that all persons of Japanese ancestry—U.S. citizens and noncitizens alike—were to be removed from the western states. Nobuo was shocked to learn that the order applied to Japanese American soldiers, too. He couldn't understand how anyone would think they posed a threat to the nation they were in uniform to defend. There were about fifty Nisei recruits at Camp Roberts, and they were all pulled out of their training units and loaded into a special car on a train with armed MPs guarding them. Destination: across the country to Camp Robinson, Arkansas.

The situation was so ludicrous Nobuo didn't know whether to laugh or to cry. The choice was made for him several days into the mind-numbing trip when the train diverted onto a side track in west Texas to enter Fort Bliss, where they were to pick up supplies. The MPs went through the car ordering all window shades drawn because the Nisei soldiers were not permitted to see the military reservation for "security reasons." That announcement underscored the idiocy of the scene, and Nobuo and the others started laughing, and kept laughing, releasing their pent-up frustration and stress. Nobuo laughed until his sides ached.

When they arrived at Camp Robinson, located ten miles north of Little Rock, they were trucked to their new units. Nobuo and three of the Nisei who came with him on the train from California ended up in the same platoon. For the next eight weeks of basic infantry training, one day blended into the next—marching, hiking, running, shooting, studying. Nobuo took it all in stride, thinking, *This is nothing*. He didn't say a word to anyone, of course, but he knew that the rigorous military training he had received in high school in Japan had been tougher.

After graduation, all the Caucasian soldiers were shipped out as replacements to infantry units, while the Nisei soldiers were again pulled from the ranks, this time to stay behind at Camp Robinson. Their feelings of being treated like second-class soldiers were amplified by their assignments; one by one, they were sent off to motor pools, garbage collection, clerical duties, kitchen police, and other assignments that Nobuo saw had one thing in common: they would not be bearing arms.

Nobuo was assigned to the Quartermaster Corps, responsible for providing supplies and material support to the base. Once there, he fell into a cushy job as chauffeur for the commandant. Given the use of a staff car, he picked up the colonel in the morning, drove him to breakfast, then to the office, and waited until he was ready to go to lunch. That went on all day and into the evening until, after dinner, he dropped the colonel back at his quarters. Because of these duties, Nobuo was exempt from cleaning barracks, standing guard duty, or doing any of the other onerous jobs that lowly enlisted men got stuck with. On top of that, the colonel was a nice man and treated him well, as did the rest of the men in the Quartermaster Corps, who did not seem to even notice his race.

All of this went into Nobuo's decision not to volunteer for the Military Intelligence Service when two recruiters came to Camp Robinson in the fall of 1942 to interview Nisei soldiers. The recruiters, a white officer and a Nisei sergeant, knew about the years Nobuo had gone to high school in Japan and about his fluency in the language. Nobuo heard them out, and answered their questions about his background. *But why start over with something new when he had such a plush job?* If he volunteered, he was told, he would be sent to a language school in Minnesota.

That sealed it for Nobuo, as he had a very good reason to stay in Arkansas. He and Toshie had been writing all along, but he hadn't heard anything for a while until her recent letter revealing that she and her parents had been rounded up in Los Angeles and taken to the Jerome Relocation Center—in Arkansas! He wrote back and let her know he was in Arkansas, too. Looking at a map, he saw they were only about a hundred miles apart. He had no idea how or if he could visit her at Jerome, but he hoped to get permission to do so; it was another reason to continue working for his colonel.

Nobuo also received a letter from his parents, confirming that there was no relocation of Japanese living in Colorado because it was so far inland. His family was safe at home, and his father continued to farm.

In fact, thousands of Japanese rounded up in California were being sent to Colorado, whose governor, Ralph Carr, was the only western governor to publicly welcome Japanese to his state even though he abhorred the idea of anyone being interned in camps without "proof of misconduct." Carr's position stood in stark contrast to those of his peers. "The Japs live like rats, breed like rats, and act like rats," Chase

Clark, the Republican governor of Idaho, said. "I don't want them." Kansas Republican Governor Payne Ratner declared, "Japs are not wanted and not welcome in Kansas," and promised to call up the Kansas National Guard to enforce his will. Republican Governor Nels Smith of Wyoming threatened that any Japanese that came to his state would be found "hanging from every pine tree."

Construction began on the Granada Relocation Center in the southeast part of Colorado, and would eventually receive eight thousand men, women, and children starting in May 1942. Governor Carr's welcome mat for the displaced Japanese was not popular with all Coloradans, however. In March, when he heard that mobs might take the law into their own hands, and that vigilante groups were forming and threatening to hang all arriving Japanese from telephone poles, he addressed an angry crowd of five hundred people gathered in a junior high school gym in La Junta, seventy miles west of the new internment camp. His voice booming, he lectured the locals, many of them farmers, that a U.S. citizen of Japanese descent had the same rights as any other American citizen. "If you harm them," he went on, "you must first harm me. I was brought up in small towns where I knew the shame and dishonor of race hatred. I grew up to despise it . . . In Colorado, they will have full protection."*

Shortly before Thanksgiving 1942, Nobuo received orders to report to the Military Intelligence Service Language School at Camp Savage, Minnesota, for a six-month class that began in December. He was caught off guard since he had declined to volunteer for the school, but the Army had surprised him before and doubtless would again.

Mostly, he was disappointed at having to leave Toshie behind.

But if he was needed as a translator and interpreter in the war in the Pacific rather than as a driver for a supply colonel on a quiet base in the middle of Arkansas, then that's what Nobuo Furuiye was ready to do.

---

* Ralph Carr, a Republican, lost his bid for U.S. Senate that year to Democrat Edwin "Big Ed" Johnson, who criticized Carr's welcoming of Japanese Americans. The defeat came in a year when other Republican candidates were swept into statewide offices. He never again held elective office. In 1999, *The Denver Post* named Ralph Carr Colorado's "Person of the Century" for taking a moral stand that cost him a bright political future.

Three

"WHERE IS PEARL HARBOR?"

At the dawning of the twentieth century, there were exactly ten Hira-bayashi households in the township of Hotaka located in Nagano Prefecture, a mountainous region known as the "Roof of Japan." With snowy peaks rising to ten thousand feet, Nagano would host that nation's second winter Olympics a hundred years later. Ironically, *Hirabayashi* translates literally to "level ground."

Those ten households had branched out from a single Hirabayashi family that settled in Hotaka in the seventeenth century, so all who came after were related in some way. More than distant cousins, the Hirabayashis were a close-knit clan. Few were surprised when four Hirabayashi cousins decided to immigrate together to America. The young men were intrigued by the success story of a local man said to have made a fortune in the United States in five years. In prepara-tion for their planned migration, they signed up for English lessons at a private academy whose principal was a Christian evangelist and disciple of a secular movement similar to the Quakers. Their tenets were to live a Christian life of faith and morals, study the scriptures, and look after the welfare of fellow members. Devotees met in small fellowship gatherings hosted in their homes. The cousins, all from Buddhist families, became converts.

In 1907, the four cousins booked steerage on a steamship bound for Seattle. When they cleared U.S. Immigration, entry records noted that three of them each carried $50 in cash (equivalent to about $1,300 today), the minimum amount required to enter the country without a financial sponsor, and one had $70. They found railroad jobs, then worked at a sawmill, hotels, restaurants, and stores before going into farming, which they had learned back home in Hotaka, Japan's largest wasabi-producing region (the spicy paste, made from ground rhizome, a Japanese horseradish, had long been used in cuisine there). In time, the men arranged to have picture brides sent from home. Their American-born children became U.S. citizens at birth, as guaranteed by the citizenship clause of the Fourteenth Amendment to the U.S. Constitution.

Twelve years after arriving in America, two Hirabayashi cousins joined with two other immigrants from Nagano to buy a run-down forty-acre farm in the White River Valley near the rural hamlet of Thomas, twenty miles south of Seattle, Washington. They formed a cooperative farming venture they named White River Gardens. Together they worked the ground, planted and harvested, and owned in common all machinery, tools, barns, horses, and equipment. For them, cooperation was not a theory but a daily practice. The property had once been a dairy, and the land, swampy and strewn with tree stumps, was not tillable. The priorities that first year were to build a small but sturdy house for each couple, and make drainage ditches to carry the land's excess water into holding ponds that could be drawn on for irrigation. They next began to clear the land, which turned into a multiyear project. Each spring they were able to plant more acreage in crops, primarily lettuce and cauliflower, but also celery, berries, peas, and tomatoes, which they sold at farmers' markets.

Toshiharu was one of the four Hirabayashi cousins to immigrate to America. He had believed he had no choice but to depart Japan since he was a younger son; according to custom, his oldest brother would inherit the family estate. A high school graduate, Toshiharu was considered the most knowledgeable of the cousins. Soft-spoken and religious, he enjoyed reading, especially the Bible, which he quoted when reprimanding his children for their misdeeds rather than spanking them. His wife, Midori, from a well-to-do Nagano family, was also a high school graduate, which was unusual at the time because daughters in Japan weren't generally sent to school for that long. She was on her school tennis team and did well in competition, she claimed, because she was ambidextrous. Hitting with either hand gave her a

Grant Hirabayashi family, 1922

powerful forehand from both sides. She later observed that being able
to use her hands equally well aided her at home with eight children. In
1919, the same year they moved to White River Gardens, their second
child, Grant, was born. Toshiharu insisted that the children be named
after Christian heroes. Grant was named for Ulysses Grant Murphy, a
Methodist minister and former missionary to Japan, who himself was
named for the Civil War general and former U.S. president. Their oldest, Martin, named for the church reformer Martin Luther, was then
three. Their other six babies came at intervals of one to two years.
As his family grew, Toshiharu kept adding on to an extension at the
back of their house.

One of Grant's earliest memories was being jolted awake by early-
morning dynamite blasts. One by one, the stumps and roots had to
be blown up because plows would hit them and break a blade or
overturn. A fonder memory: family suppers following Sunday fellowship gatherings. The meal did not start until his father led everyone
in prayer, which always ended by giving thanks to God. The Sabbath
was for rest and reflection, with no sports allowed or work, except
during harvest. Everyone was encouraged to contemplate his or her
beliefs and behavior. Moral values such as honesty, helping others,
and being responsible for the good name of the family were drilled

into the children, all of whom were required to help on the family farm. For the youngest, it started with collecting eggs each morning in the henhouse, while the older children worked in the fields hoeing, planting, and harvesting.

The families at White River Gardens lived near each other in their simple bungalows surrounded by well-tended roses, dahlias, carnations, and asters. There was soon a multitude of children, most of whom chose playmates close to their own age. For Grant, that included Gordon, the son of another Hirabayashi cousin, Shungo, who, unlike Grant's father, was the eldest son in his family. However, his family's dire finances had convinced him to leave Japan and make his own way.

As the families worked hard to build for their futures, White River Gardens drew the attention of the prosecuting attorney for King County, where the property was located. The county filed suit accusing them of fraud for having placed the title in the name of one of the minor children to skirt the anti-alien land law passed in Washington State in 1921. The law read: "The ownership of lands by aliens, other than those who in good faith have declared their intention to become citizens of the United States, is prohibited in this state." The catch was that immigrants from Japan—known as Issei—had long been prevented by federal law from obtaining U.S. citizenship. The partners were made aware of the state law before purchasing the property, but with the benefit of legal advice they believed they had complied by not placing it in their own names. However, with a strong anti-immigrant sentiment prevailing locally and elsewhere on the West Coast—particularly among powerful agricultural interests that considered Japanese farmers an economic threat—going concerns such as White River Gardens had come under increased scrutiny. The suit alleged that the minor child, an American citizen by birth, had been used as a subterfuge, and petitioned to have White River Gardens confiscated. The families hired an attorney to represent them, but it was a losing fight. In February 1924, a trial judge ruled in favor of King County. The property was confiscated and leased to a Caucasian businessman in a sweetheart deal for $10 an acre per year. With nowhere to go, the families stayed on, paying rent to the new owner and working the land they had bought with their hard-earned savings and labored to make into a productive farm. Prejudice trampled fairness, and along with it their dreams. The families would never again own their own land.*

The sons and daughters of White River Gardens walked to Thomas Middle Grade School a mile away. Other children came in from all directions, as it was the only public school in the area. Fully half of the students were born in America to parents who had emigrated from Japan. Each morning the children stood in their classrooms before a U.S. flag, right hand over their heart, and recited the Pledge of Allegiance.

After school, Grant liked to fish a nearby creek with two friends from school, Kenji Nomura and Tom Horiuchi. None of the boys had store-bought tackle. They cut sturdy tree branches for poles and made hooks out of nails, which they filed down and bent into a loop. On the end they stuck freshly dug-up earthworms, and tied the hooks to the pole with string used to train pea vines. One sunny afternoon, the fish weren't biting and the boys were perched lazily on the bank when Grant's friends started talking about Japan, which they both had visited the previous summer with their families.

"They drive on the wrong side of the road!" Tom exclaimed.

"You walk barefoot whenever you go inside," said Kenji.

The more he heard, the more curious Grant became about Japan. He had listened to his parents talk about the beauty of their country and knew they had many relatives living there, but he had never thought of it as a place to visit. In fact, he had been unenthusiastic about attending a Japanese-language school in Thomas his parents made him go to every Saturday. He considered it a tedious duty to

* The case of *White River Gardens v. State of Washington* was appealed to the U.S. Supreme Court. On April 23, 1928, the Court upheld the lower court decision, ruling that "withholding from aliens the privilege of land ownership" was not a violation of the equal protection clause of the Fourteenth Amendment. In 1962, the Washington state legislature determined that the immigrant owners of White River Gardens had in fact been unjustly treated nearly forty years earlier. They were awarded redress in the amount of $12,000 for the property—now rich farmland—that the four Japanese partners had paid $15,000 for in 1919, unimproved.

learn the ideographs necessary to read and write Japanese, and could not imagine why he needed to do it. For him, the best part about the Japanese school was its baseball team, for which he pitched and played shortstop. His cousin Gordon, a good fielder and hitter, was on the same team. Now, as Grant thought about visiting his parents' homeland, he was glad they had insisted he study Japanese for the past several years.

A few days later, Grant's father gave him a haircut, always the best time for them to have a one-on-one conversation out of earshot of others.

"I'd really like to go there, Dad," Grant said. "Can I this summer?"

When his father didn't answer, Grant kept talking about Japan.

"Son, there's eight of you kids in our family," his father finally replied. "We can't afford to send each of you to Japan for a vacation."

Grant understood what his father was saying, as frugality was a way of life in the Hirabayashi household. But still he waxed on for weeks about visiting Japan. One day in exasperation, he exclaimed, "Dad, if you're not going to send me, I'm going to swim across the Pacific Ocean."

His father had to smile at his son's boyish determination.

Toshiharu and Midori agreed that they should not dampen their son's sudden interest in their ancestral homeland, but should find a way to support it. They knew Japan's schools to be excellent, and thought the academic discipline would be good for their second son, who seemed to prefer sports to books. They made Grant an offer. If he agreed to go to school in Japan for at least two years and get good grades, the expense could be justified. In short, he was not going there for a vacation, but to learn. It could be arranged for him to live with his father's oldest brother and his wife. An elated Grant, ready for his own adventure across the Pacific as his parents had been nearly half a lifetime earlier, eagerly agreed.

Summer could not come fast enough. When it was time to depart, Grant was surprised when his father introduced him dockside in Seattle to the captain of a gleaming ocean liner flying the Japanese flag. The captain was Kokohu Mizuno, and the two men had been boyhood classmates at the Christian academy in Hotaka. Known as a "cultivated man and sincere Christian," Mizuno was a member of

The *Heian Maru*

a peace movement in Japan. The ship he commanded was the *Heian Maru*. It had made its maiden voyage a year earlier, and was a fast, modern, midsized ship capable of taking 330 passengers across the Pacific in comfort. The three-week voyage was especially luxurious for Grant, even though he was traveling on the least expensive ticket. The captain not only turned over his sea cabin to the boy, but also assigned his steward to wait on him and make his bed every morning. When the ship reached Yokohama, the captain handed Grant a white flag on which had been printed his name, Hirabayashi, in large Japanese ideographs: 平林. He told the boy to wave it on the crowded dock so his aunt and uncle would find him.

When Grant arrived in Japan in the summer of 1932, he was just shy of thirteen. After two days of sightseeing in Yokohama, he and his aunt Kinoe and uncle Taneju boarded a passenger train for the eight-hour journey to their home in Hotaka, two hundred miles to the northwest. Soon after arriving in his father's hometown, Grant realized how different his life would be there. He went from being one of eight children competing for attention to receiving the benefits of an only child, as his aunt and uncle had lost their only children, two young sons, to childhood illnesses. Grant-san became their surrogate son and was doted on by everyone.

In other ways, he faced some difficulties adjusting. At school, all the boys had buzz cuts that left them as bald as monks, while Grant's thick black hair shot straight past his ears. Everyone wore sandals that they unobtrusively slipped out of before entering class. His first day at school, Grant, wearing his new school uniform—a black tunic with a mandarin collar and five gold buttons down the front—strolled into the classroom in his oxfords, which caused much snickering. It seemed that only teachers wore shoes in class. Understanding that he was fresh off the boat from America, the teacher was sympathetic, and allowed him some leeway for his Western ways. Before long, however, he had a shorn head to go along with a new pair of sandals, and looked like all the other boys.

More problematic was the language. Grant was perplexed by all the different dialects spoken in the country. It wasn't like in America, where people spoke English with regional accents. In Japan, more than a dozen local dialects not only involved pitch accents, use of inflections, and varied vocabularies, but also varied in the use of vowels and consonants. It was possible for a dialect from one region to be incomprehensible to people from other parts of Japan. In Japanese school in America, Grant had learned what was known as standard Japanese, which was also taught in Japan's schools and served as the nation's official language. Grant could speak standard Japanese reasonably well, and though there were hundreds of ideographs he had not yet learned, the same was true for many of the students in his class, so he was not too far behind. Standard Japanese, or the "common language," as it was called in Japan, was spoken predominantly in Tokyo and other parts of eastern Japan. Grant knew a smattering of words and terms from the Nagano dialect his parents spoke with one another at home, but had trouble understanding people from other areas who spoke their own dialects. As he came to learn more Japanese history, Grant better understood the reasons for all the different dialects: the natural barriers created by the mountainous terrain; the existence of secluded *Shōgun* estates or territories, and the isolation of the island nation. It had not yet been a hundred years since Commodore Matthew Perry had sailed his ships into Tokyo Bay and forced the opening of feudal Japan to the outside world.

After Grant completed two years of intermediate school, he took the national test for admission to high school, and flunked. Even though he was due to return home, failing the national exam—given annually—angered and humiliated him, and he asked to stay for another year to try again. The second time he passed, finishing in the top thirtieth percentile. At least he wouldn't be leaving Japan an academic failure. He wrote his parents to tell them the good news, and then asked, "Can I come home now?" They had given him the opportunity to live in Japan, and in turn he had kept his promise to study hard and excel in school. But now fifteen, he was ready to come home and go to high school with his old friends. The letter he received back from his father congratulated him for his achievements, but, to Grant's dismay, his father said that since he had passed the national entrance exam and had been accepted to high school, he should stay and continue to get a good education in Japan. When he graduated from high school, he would be sent a steamship ticket home.

The edict issued by his father was difficult for Grant to hear. He had made friends in Japan, and his aunt and uncle had not stopped treating him royally. But he still had pangs of homesickness. He missed his brothers and sisters, his mother and father, and his friends in Thomas. In every way, he was ready to come home. But he had always accepted what his father said, and despite his disappointment Grant did not question his father's decision now. He would continue to strive to do his best in Japan.

Since there was no high school in Hotaka, Grant commuted ten miles every day by train to Matsumoto, with more than 100,000 residents one of the largest cities in Nagano Prefecture. The city, surrounded by mountains capped with snow in the winter, was known for its beautiful views in all directions. Matsumoto was his mother's hometown, and a benefit of going to school there was that he had the opportunity to spend time with her family. But not only was he starting over in a new city and a new school with many new classmates, the schoolwork was also more challenging than ever: algebra, physics, chemistry, history, Chinese classics—all in Japanese, of course—and English, where he had an advantage over the other students as well as the teachers, since his pronunciation was better than theirs. He never openly corrected the teachers, but occasionally they asked for his assistance with a word or phrase. A required class called Moral Education (*Dotoku*) focused on good behavior and upstanding values. And in their mandatory military training, the boys were taught marching drills,

Grant Hirabayashi in Japan, 1939

tested on military manuals, and in their last two years were issued their own rifle and gas mask, which they learned how to use in field exercises. One reading assignment—an article in a youth magazine, *Shonen Kurae*, circa 1937—gave the numbers of warships and aircraft various countries possessed, showing how the tonnage and numbers did not favor Japan. In any future war with America, the article speculated, Japan would likely launch a surprise attack against the U.S. military in the Philippines and Hawaii. That scenario left Grant uneasy, but he thought it unlikely. Japan already had thousands of troops deployed in China; why attack mighty America?

After his first year of high school, he again asked to come home. His father's response: "You have to finish." And so he did. During the next three years, he continued to do well in his studies, and was named captain of the track team and president of the Alpine Club, whose members made regular ascents of nearby peaks. At the end of his final year, he was one of two boys in his graduating class recommended for an appointment to the prestigious Imperial Japanese Army Academy.

The offer to attend Japan's elite officer training school astonished Grant, because he wasn't interested in the military, nor did he think he had shown much aptitude for it. Yet he had been singled out for an academy appointment? He wondered if it could have anything to do with his father's cousin from Hotaka, Morito Hirabayashi, now a lieutenant general in command of the 17th Infantry Division in occupied China. Morito had visited White River Gardens in the mid-1920s. Grant was only seven or eight years old at the time, but he well remembered their cousin from Japan being treated as an honored guest. A portrait was taken of the adult cousins—in suits and ties—including

Grant's father, Toshiharu, and Gordon's father, Shungo, with the oval-faced officer seated in the middle. At the time, Morito Hirabayashi was passing through America on his way to Berlin, where he was a military attaché at the Japanese embassy.*

Grant knew Japan's military academy was on a par with West Point or Annapolis. The other graduate accepted his appointment. But Grant, who did not have dual citizenship because his birth was never recorded with the Japanese consul, had no interest in being in the Japanese army. He was more ready than ever to return home. Anyone living in Japan in those days heard ad nauseam the Japanese patriotic march, "Nihon Aikoku Koshinkyoku," from the radio, movies, newsreels, and every lantern parade through the streets celebrating victories in the China war. *"Miyo! Tokai no sora akete . . ."* (Look! Dawn breaks over the eastern sea . . .)

Grant said his goodbyes to friends and family and, with his diploma in one hand and boat ticket in the other, left Japan after eight years. He was twenty-one years old. When he arrived back in America on April 28, 1940, many things were different than he remembered. His mother and father had aged, and his younger siblings were no longer little. His friends had graduated from high school and were off working or in college. Of course, since leaving as a preteen, he had changed, too. He was now a well-traveled young man. Studious looking, he had probing eyes behind wire-rimmed glasses, and alert ears that refused to lie flat. Perpetually arched eyebrows suggested a questioning manner with a healthy dose of skepticism. Quietly confident without being arrogant, he had a trim frame that made him seem taller than his actual height (five foot three). Clearly meant for other endeavors, he was uninterested in becoming a farmer or working in groceries or produce

---

* Morito Hirabayashi was commanding general of the 17th Infantry Division in northern China when Japanese forces launched an offensive against China's National Revolutionary Army in November 1940. The five-day battle was a major defeat for the Japanese, who suffered more than five thousand dead and seven thousand wounded. Recalled to Tokyo in 1942, he was attached to the Army General Staff until retiring in 1943. He became mayor of Matsumoto, Japan, before being recalled to active duty in 1945 for the last few months of the war. He died in 1969 at the age of eighty-one.

markets. He wanted to get ahead, and to him that meant college. But for that he needed a U.S. high school diploma.

Grant went to see a counselor at Kent High School, two miles up the road from Thomas. He learned there was a precedent for Nisei who had gone to school in Japan and returned to receive course credits. In Grant's case, after his courses from Japan were accepted, he had to take four classes to graduate: U.S. history, English, and two electives, typing and accounting. He had been surprised how his English had declined from not using it on a daily basis. But by the time he finished the required coursework in June 1941, his native language had come back to him, making him truly bilingual.

After his return, Grant started helping his father by delivering vegetables to farmers' markets and grocery stores in and around Seattle. It was the one job on the farm that he really enjoyed, because he got to drive his father's truck. His father always had a Ford, while Gordon's father preferred Chevys. Gordon did some vegetable deliveries, too, and when it came to their trucks the cousins were as competitive as they had once been on the baseball diamond.

"I see you're driving another tin-can Ford," teased Gordon.

"Yeah, and I see you've got another Chev-it-or-leave-it."

They even held challenge races. Driving a few miles outside of town to Star Lake, they established a starting line at the bottom of a steep hill. The idea was to gun the engine, slam the transmission into high gear, and floor it all the way, getting as high up the hill as they could until the engine cut out and the truck stopped. A mark was made at that spot, and the other guy tried to better it in his truck. Some days Ford won, other days Chevy. What was miraculous for both boys was that they never blew a transmission or clutch, and their fathers never found out.

Gordon, always an excellent student, had entered the University of Washington in Seattle a year earlier. The cousins could have ended up in college together, but Grant mistakenly let the deadline pass for applying for fall 1941 admission. That opened the door for Uncle Sam to make a decision for him: Grant's number came up in the draft that fall. He was ordered to report to Fort Lewis, south of Tacoma, on December 4, 1941. His father drove him to the station at Kent, and promised to bring his mother to the base for a visit on Sunday. Grant knew it was not easy for his father to see a son leave for the Army. Two of his father's brothers had fought in the Russo-Japanese War in Manchuria (1904–05), and his father had heard from them enough to know he wanted no part of the military. In fact, one reason his father had left Japan nearly forty years earlier was so he would not be drafted. As a tenet of his religion, Toshiharu had become a conscientious objector.

Grant had mixed feelings of his own about being drafted. War was raging in Europe, but so far the United States had stayed out of it. Serving a hitch in the peacetime Army could be a good thing. In truth, he was tired of school; it seemed like he had been going all his life. If he could learn a trade that he could ply in civilian life, his time in the Army would be worthwhile. That's why at Fort Lewis, when given a choice of branches, which was common at the time, he selected the Army Air Corps, hoping to be trained as an airplane mechanic, as he knew he could never become a pilot due to his eyesight. Although he corrected to 20/20, without his glasses he was nearly blind in his right eye (20/200).

Grant was kept busy his first days in the Army with physical exams, inoculations and indoctrinations, and a battery of written tests. Sunday was a free day, and in the morning he walked to the base chapel. As he was heading back after the Protestant service, a booming voice that echoed across the base through a PA system announced Japan's attack on Pearl Harbor. "This is not a drill! Repeat, this is not a drill!"

Grant's first thought: *Where is Pearl Harbor?*

Hawaii! Of course. Just like the old magazine article he'd read that said if Japan went to war with America it would make a surprise attack in Hawaii and the Philippines. So it had happened: Japan had started a war with America! How stupid of the leaders of Japan, and how sad for the people of Japan. Already in uniform, if for only a few days, Grant had no qualms about fighting for America anywhere, anytime. But Japan was not an enemy of his choosing. He thought of all his friends and relatives. He could see their faces: his classmates, his cousins, his kindhearted aunt and uncle. What would become of them? He rushed back to the barracks. By the time he got there, orders were already being issued. All leaves and day passes were canceled. No visitors permitted on the base . . .

His parents! He must tell them not to come. Grant raced to the bank of pay phones for the soldiers to use, but none had a dial tone; they had all been cut off for security reasons. The camp was in lockdown.

Grant headed to the main gate to see whether his parents would show up as planned. They were his major concern at the moment. In a war between the U.S. and Japan, they, as citizens of an enemy nation, would be labeled "enemy aliens." What would that mean? He knew they could be vulnerable to some kind of government action in wartime. What kind of treatment would they and the other first-generation Japanese immigrants receive? He was less worried about his siblings; like him, they were all U.S. citizens. What could possibly be done to them?

At the closed gate, there was a large gathering of civilians outside the fence hoping to see their sons, husbands, and fathers. Scanning the faces in the crowd until he was ready to give up, thinking his parents must have heard the news and decided not to make the trip, he finally spotted them in the press of humanity. Grant was in a crowd on his side of the fence, too, and with soldiers struggling to get close enough to speak to loved ones, he couldn't reach the fence. Neither could his parents. At least they were able to see each other and wave. As it turned out, those gestures and glimpses would have to last a long time.

The next day, President Franklin D. Roosevelt went before Congress to ask for a declaration of war with Japan. Grant was among the soldiers who crowded around the radios listening with rapt attention to the short speech delivered in FDR's familiar and calm cadence.

Yesterday, December 7th, 1941, a date which will live in infamy, the United States of America was suddenly and deliberately attacked by naval and air forces of the Empire of Japan . . . The attack yesterday on the Hawaiian Island has caused severe damage to American naval and military forces. I regret to tell you that very many American lives have been lost . . . No matter how long it may take us to overcome this premeditated invasion, the American people, in their righteous might, will win through to absolute victory . . . With confidence in our armed forces, with the unbounding determination of our people, we will gain the inevitable triumph. So help us God. I ask that the

Congress declare that since the unprovoked and dastardly attack by Japan on Sunday, December 7th, 1941, a state of war has existed between the United States and the Japanese Empire.

Thunderous applause from Congress followed the last two sentences. In less than an hour, the Senate passed the declaration of war 82–0, and the House of Representatives likewise on a vote of 388–1.*

Twenty-four hours later, Grant was on a train to Missouri, headed to the Jefferson Barracks south of St. Louis. He was heartened to learn that the post was a training site for the Army Air Corps. But his optimism that he would soon start learning how to be an airplane mechanic was misplaced. When he arrived, he was taken directly to a barracks where he joined a group of twenty-five Nisei soldiers. At Fort Lewis, he had seen no more than a few Japanese Americans on the entire base. Now he was in a barracks with *only* Nisei soldiers?

"What is this?" Grant asked suspiciously.

"This is 'protective custody,'" someone said sarcastically.

They had all been yanked out of their units on the West Coast after Pearl Harbor. Some had been in the Army a lot longer than Grant, but no one had any idea what was going to happen next. They had no regular duties and were in limbo on the 1,500-acre base. They marched to the exercise field in the morning and the mess hall three times a day, but otherwise were confined to quarters. They were allowed no recreational activities; even the base bowling alley and movie theater were off-limits. Any time they left the barracks they had an armed escort. Did *protective custody* mean they were being *protected*? If so, from

---

* Representative Jeannette Rankin, a Montana Republican, cast the lone vote against war with Japan, which elicited a round of hisses from her colleagues. A pacifist and the first woman elected to Congress (in 1916), Rankin had been instrumental in initiating the legislation that eventually became the Nineteenth Amendment to the Constitution (1920), granting voting rights to women. About her antiwar vote, she explained, "As a woman, I can't go to war, and I refuse to send anyone else." Realizing her vote was political suicide, she did not run for reelection in 1942. In January 1968, Rankin led a women's peace march in Washington, D.C., to protest the Vietnam War. With five thousand participants, it was the largest march by women since the Woman Suffrage Procession of 1913.

whom? Civilians? Other soldiers? Or were they in *custody* because the Army did not trust them?

Scuttlebutt had it that a Nisei at a recruiting center had been assaulted by a Caucasian, and as a result Japanese Americans were being separated. There were reports of Nisei soldiers at different camps being summarily discharged. Were they about to be kicked out of the Army, too? After forty long days, they had their answer. They were released from custody, and assigned to regular jobs on the post.

Grant became a flight clerk for a squadron. He did so well that his commanding officer saw to it that he was promoted to corporal after a few months. For the first time since joining the Army he felt like a full-fledged soldier doing his part. The affront of being held in protective custody had lessened; he had even reached the conclusion that the Army had done so for their own good. Then one day in May, Grant and the other Nisei were told to be in front of their barracks early the next morning with all their belongings packed into their duffel bags.

Here we go again, Grant thought. *Now what?*

A truck took them to the train station, where each of them was handed a brown envelope containing new orders and train tickets to their destinations. They had been relieved of their duties with the Air Corps and reassigned to the regular Army. Grant was ordered to Fort Leavenworth, Kansas, where he went to work as a hospital clerk.

In the summer of 1942, Grant received a letter from the commandant of the Military Intelligence Service Language School in Minnesota, who explained that the top-secret school was seeking soldiers competent in Japanese. The letter asked Grant to submit a résumé detailing his Japanese-language skills. Intrigued, Grant responded. He assumed that the school was training translators, and given his grasp of Japanese he knew he would be an ideal candidate. But when he didn't hear back for a few months, he forgot about it.

Then, that fall, Grant Hirabayashi was ordered to report to Camp Savage.

Four

EXECUTIVE ORDER 9066

Hiroshi Matsumoto was his family's first U.S. citizen. He was born in Laguna, California, a farming community ten miles southeast of Los Angeles, in 1913. The first Matsumoto to farm here was his paternal grandfather, Wakamatsu, who had been one of the early contract laborers sent from Japan to Hawaii in the late nineteenth century to work in the pineapple and sugarcane fields. Migrating to the West Coast in 1906, he started small, planting vegetables on paddle-flat rented land that had grown only hay. He dug irrigation ditches and each year expanded his acres under till. Eventually, he summoned his teenage son, Wakaji, from Japan to help. When Wakaji was ready to take a wife, he exchanged photos with a woman in Japan, Tee Kimura, who joined him in 1911. Two years later, she gave birth to Hiroshi, their first of eight children.

Bright and hardworking, Tee had a head for business that her husband did not. As Wakaji detested farming, he was relegated to delivering their produce by horse-drawn wagon to Los Angeles, while Tee's father-in-law, Wakamatsu, began to turn over to her more responsibilities, such as bookkeeping and payroll, all of which she did in addition to taking care of the children and cooking for her family and their farmhands starting at 4 a.m.

In 1917, Wakamatsu decided to retire to Japan, where he and his wife could live comfortably on what he had made farming in America. He left the U.S. a recognized pioneer among Japanese farmers, having hired many Japanese immigrants who themselves became successful farmers.

With his taskmaster father gone and his capable wife running the hundred-acre truck farm, Wakaji was free to follow his own dream. He had already bought a mail-order camera and had taken a correspondence course, and he now enrolled in a photography class in San Diego.

For young Hiroshi, the departure of his grandfather left a void in his life. His *jii-chan* used to take him fishing and always seemed to have time for his firstborn grandson. When Hiroshi was eight years old, his father asked him if he would like to visit his grandfather. A cousin of his father's was going to Japan for the summer and could accompany Hiroshi and his younger brother Takeshi, then seven, on the voyage. Hiroshi was ecstatic, and counted the days to their departure. They left on a coal-fired steamship from the port of San Pedro in June 1921. Hiroshi and Takeshi had never seen the ocean, and they spent much of the three-week journey on deck, catching glimpses of flying fish, porpoises, and breaching whales.

After arriving in Yokohama, they boarded a train—another first for the boys. Having grown up on a farm, Hiroshi was astonished

Hiroshi, right, and his brother Takeshi, on ship to Japan, 1921

Hiroshi, left, and his
brother Takeshi in Japan

at how people lived so close together here, which was the case not only in the cities the train passed through but even in the small coastal village of Jigozen, ten miles west of Hiroshima, where his grandparents lived in a newly built house his grandfather had purchased upon his return to Japan. He had also bought a small fishing boat, and one of the first things he and Hiroshi did together was go fishing in the Seto Inland Sea, a body of calm waters stretching more than two hundred miles that separates three of Japan's main home islands: Honshu, Shikoku, and Kyushu. One day they brought home a large catch and his grandfather transferred the fish from buckets to an underwater bamboo cage.

Why keep the fish alive? Hiroshi asked.

When everyone has fish, the market price is low, his grandfather said. *When it storms and there are no fish to catch, we sell for a higher price.*

Hiroshi knew his grandfather wasn't saving the fish because he needed the money, as fishing was only his hobby. In addition to being a lesson in supply and demand, the takeaway for the boy was to avoid doing what everyone else did. Later, he learned that his grandfather had used the same strategy farming in California; he delayed planting by weeks, ensuring a late harvest so he could get higher prices after everyone else's produce was gone. That, and hard work, had been the formula for his success.

One morning they boated out to a small island in Hiroshima Bay that his grandfather told him was one of the most beautiful and spiritual places in all of Japan. Since ancient times, Miyajima (Shrine Island) had been revered as a place where "the people and gods live together." The hills were filled with cherry blossoms as far as Hiroshi could see.

They visited the sacred Floating Torii Gate shrine and temples and pagodas, the likes of which Hiroshi had seen only in picture books.

His grandfather tutored Hiroshi in Japanese history and geography that summer. The first thing the boy learned was to memorize the names of the nearly fifty *ken*, or prefectures, ranging from Hokkaido, the northernmost of Japan's islands, to the southernmost one, Okinawa.

At summer's end, Hiroshi expected his father's cousin to come to his grandparents' house to collect him and his brother for their trip home. But when he showed up, something quite different happened.

I came to say sayonara, said the cousin.

Hiroshi was confused. *What do you mean? Aren't we going with you?*

No, you are staying with Grandmother and Grandfather.

It came out that his grandparents had known what was coming, and had agreed to take in the boys and enroll them in the public school a block away. But they had said nothing to Hiroshi and Takeshi, believing it was not their place to do so. Hiroshi soon realized that this had been his parents' plan all along. The trip to visit their grandfather had been a trick to get them here. Hiroshi knew of families who sent their children, especially their oldest sons, to Japan for school. But his parents had not talked to him about it, and as much as he loved his grandfather he would have objected to leaving his family and friends. Feeling sad and abandoned, Hiroshi cried himself to sleep for several nights.

When Hiroshi entered middle school that fall, he had little time to be homesick. Soon settling into school life, he made friends and got a job delivering newspapers after school. Due to the language barrier—he could speak Japanese but had limited knowledge of the written language—he had to study hard to catch up. Because he spoke Japanese with an American accent he was pegged as an *imin no ko* (kid of an immigrant) by his classmates. Hiroshi developed a short fuse and got into frequent fistfights. One day while playing baseball, a player on the other team called him a "dumb immigrant." Hiroshi hit the boy over the head with a bat. The boy lay in a hospital unconscious for two days before waking up. Relieved that the boy hadn't died or been paralyzed, Hiroshi vowed to control his anger in the future. His grandfather suggested that he count to ten whenever he was upset, a practice Hiroshi adopted. He learned even more self-discipline in judo, a Japanese martial art that avoids the application of pressure against any joints in throwing an opponent.

Hiroshi's life in America appeared to be behind him, especially when his parents gave up the farm after a bad drought and moved the family to Japan in 1927. They settled in Hiroshima, where Hiroshi, now fourteen, was already commuting daily by train to attend high school. He was happy to move back in with his family. His father, Wakaji, by then a skilled photographer, opened a portrait studio in downtown Hiroshima.

In 1930, Hiroshi's path in life changed yet again. He had fallen for his pretty cousin, Fumiko. For them both it was a first love, and an innocent one at that. But their youthful infatuation caused upheaval in the family; not only were they cousins, but Fumiko's parents had long ago arranged a future marriage for her. Hiroshi's mother liked the young girl but encouraged her son to consider finishing high school in California, where he could stay with his uncle Yoshio, his father's younger brother.

For the second time in his life, Hiroshi was to be sent across the ocean. But this time the final decision had been his. He understood that it wasn't right to interfere with Fumiko's planned marriage, and besides, he was not ready to make that kind of commitment to her or anyone. At seventeen, he looked forward to a new adventure, although he knew that going to high school in America would be a challenge, as he would have to work on improving his English, which had deteriorated over the years in Japan.

Before Hiroshi departed, his mother expressed her sadness at his leaving. She said she was pleased he had had the opportunity to learn about Japan and to get to know his relatives. But she told him it was a good time in his life for him to return to the United States. She reminded him that Japan was her and his father's homeland, not his. Her parting words of advice: *You are American, Hiroshi. Don't forget that.* She bought him a one-way steamship ticket, and went with him on the train to the port of Kobe, where they said their goodbyes and he boarded the ship.

When he arrived in San Pedro that summer, Uncle Yoshio, who used to work on the family farm, didn't recognize him. His nephew went off a boy and returned a young man. Now a solidly built five foot two and 140 pounds, he carried himself like an athlete, well balanced and at the ready. But with an open face and a warm smile to go with it, he was still the gregarious youth Yoshio remembered, always quick to make friends.

Uncle Yoshio took Hiroshi home to Long Beach, where he enrolled in the local high school and got a part-time job at a vegetable stand. A teacher who found his name a tongue-twister Americanized Hiroshi to Roy. The name caught on, and thereafter only his family called him by his Japanese name.

After graduating in 1933, Roy moved to Los Angeles to find full-time work to support himself and help his brother Tsutomu, three years his junior, who had followed him to America after graduating from high school in Japan. Tsutomu enrolled in Los Angeles City College, and soon became known as Tom. Roy found a steady job, a difficult task in the middle of the Depression. Then one day at the barber shop he had the good fortune to meet a man who owned a small chain of Japanese grocery stores. They chatted in Japanese. As the man was leaving he asked if Roy spoke English. Roy answered in English. The man asked if Roy had a driver's license, which he did. "I might have a job for you," the man said.

Roy was hired and worked for Hinode Grocery for seven years delivering orders in a company pickup truck to customers all over Los Angeles, most of them Japanese immigrants who ordered rice in one-hundred-pound sacks, shoyu sauce by the keg, canned goods like *kamaboku* (fish cakes) in cases, and boxes of cucumbers and other fresh vegetables. Many of their customers

Roy Matsumoto, grocery deliveryman, in Los Angeles, March 1942

preferred to converse in their local dialects from the old country. Over the years, Roy learned the Northern Kyushu dialect, which was spoken in the major cities of Fukuoka, Kumamoto, Saga, Nagasaki, and Oita, and a southern dialect that took in Miyazaki and Kagoshima. Over time, he became fluent in several other regional dialects to which he otherwise would not have been exposed, a unique linguistic education that would one day serve him well in some unexpected ways.

After Roy's brother Tom graduated from junior college in 1940, he found a job as a bookkeeper. Later that year, Congress initiated the first peacetime military draft in U.S. history, requiring 20 million men between the ages of twenty-one and thirty-six to register with their local draft boards for the possibility of serving a one-year term of service.* Registration numbers were pulled out of a giant fishbowl that had been used for the same purpose in World War I. Tom received his draft notice in 1941 and was inducted in late October of that year. Roy, who was relieved that his draft number did not come up, saw Tom off at the train station. He had been ordered to Camp Roberts in central California for basic training.

Six weeks later, Roy was driving his 1935 Ford coupe to Long Beach to visit his aunt and uncle one Sunday morning and listening to the radio. The music stopped for a news bulletin that would change his life forever.

"We interrupt this broadcast to bring you this important bulletin from the United Press. Flash. Washington. The White House announces Japanese attack on Pearl Harbor."

Then the music returned.

Roy had clearly heard "Japanese attack" but didn't immediately place Pearl Harbor. Was the news flash a joke of some kind? Three years earlier a radio show had caused widespread panic with alarming reports of an "alien invasion" that turned out to be a dramatic Halloween episode on *The Mercury Theatre on the Air* narrated by the actor

* In August 1941, the duration of military service for draftees was extended another eighteen months. After the U.S. entered the war in December 1941, Congress expanded the age range to eighteen to thirty-seven, and changed the term of service to the "duration of war, plus six months." By war's end, some 10 million men had been drafted into military service.

Orson Welles. Was this "Japanese attack" a similar hoax? He switched to another station, but they were also broadcasting a bulletin about the Japanese attack on Pearl Harbor. Then he remembered: Pearl Harbor was in Hawaii. His ship had stopped in Honolulu years ago and entered the narrow lagoon harbor.

Japan had attacked the United States! As that undeniable fact seared his consciousness, it came with a rapid-fire mix of thoughts. Roy had seen for himself the differences between the two countries: America was much bigger and more advanced than Japan, which lacked its own natural resources. How did the leaders of Japan expect to win a war against a nation as big and strong as America? But he also knew the degree of indoctrination the Japanese people had been subjected to these past years because he had a shortwave radio set up at home that picked up Tokyo stations. He enjoyed listening to the music and local news, which made him feel closer to his family in Japan, but ignored all the nationalistic posturing and militaristic propaganda. Japan's airwaves these days were filled with brazen anti-American and anti-British statements, and wild claims about the invincibility of the Japanese military. Although these were not the topics of the letters he exchanged with his parents in Japan—his father wrote most of them, and always in his neat and precise Japanese cursive—Roy wondered just how many people there believed the propaganda they heard from their leaders. Did they think a war with America was necessary and winnable? How wrong, he thought. How foolish. How terrible. So many people will die.

For most of his years (1921–30) in Japan, it had been a peaceful nation with a benevolent emperor and a democratic government. That had begun to change around the time he left, as the country's military leaders became more influential under a new, young emperor, Hirohito, who was enthroned in 1928 at the age of twenty-seven. In 1931, the year after Roy left, Japanese troops moved in to occupy Manchuria, and the following year Japan quit the League of Nations after receiving international condemnation. Then came the invasion of China, led by a newly promoted army general, Hideki Tojo, and two military pacts with Hitler's Germany. Roy hated from afar the gang of militarists ruling Japan and was disgusted with the warpath they had chosen for the picturesque and peaceful country he knew, home to

so many he loved. And now, the surprise attack on Pearl Harbor, and
the sinking of U.S. warships and the killing of Americans. Surely the
United States would have no choice but to wage all-out war against
Japan.

Roy thought of his family in Japan, and what a world war would
mean for them. He had three brothers in Japan: twenty-seven-year-
old Takeshi, twenty-four-year-old Noboru, and twenty-year-old Isao.
They likely would be drafted into the Japanese military. And with Tom
now in the U.S. Army, would his brothers end up fighting against one
another in the Pacific? And what of his parents, grandparents, and
other relatives in Japan? At least they weren't in or near one of the
major cities, ports, or military installations likely to be targeted by U.S.
bombers. It gave him a sense of security that they were living on the
coast five hundred miles away from Tokyo.

He couldn't imagine that Hiroshima would be bombed.

———·———

On February 19, 1942, ten weeks after Pearl Harbor and without
ceremony at the White House, President Roosevelt signed Executive Order 9066, which authorized the War Department to designate
military areas and exclude any and all persons as "protection against
espionage and against sabotage." The order did not mention the Japanese by name. Two days later, Attorney General Francis Biddle gave
a formal opinion on the legality of the order, which he said was "very
broad" and allowed the Army to act anywhere in the country. However, he explained that it was not intended that U.S. citizens other than
those of Japanese descent would be affected. The order was meant
to solve "a Japanese problem," Biddle stated, and the only action that
was anticipated was on the West Coast.

The anti-Japanese hysteria that swept the nation after Pearl Harbor
was especially intense on the West Coast, whipped up, in part, by the
drumbeat of popular columnists. In late January 1942, three weeks
before Roosevelt's executive order, Henry McLemore of the Hearst
newspapers wrote, "I am for the immediate removal of every Japanese
on the West Coast to a point deep in the interior. I don't mean a nice
part of the interior either. Herd 'em up, pack 'em off and give 'em
the inside room in the badlands . . . Personally, I hate the Japanese.

And that goes for all of them." Walter Lippmann of the *New York Herald Tribune* weighed in with his opinion that the West Coast was in "imminent danger of a combined attack from within and from without." Westbrook Pegler of Scripps-Howard wrote that an attack on the West Coast and sabotage by Japanese was "inevitable." The *Los Angeles Times* took up the cry that Japanese Americans were as much the enemy as Japanese aliens: "A viper is nonetheless a viper wherever the egg is hatched—so a Japanese American, born of Japanese parents, grows up to be a Japanese, not an American." In such widespread fear and outrage, even moderate publications like the *The Christian Science Monitor* called for "drastic measures" that included roundups and internment of all Japanese.

Wild rumors spread that Japanese saboteurs were prepared to strike oil refineries and shipyards, that fishermen had their Imperial Japanese Navy uniforms wrapped in oilskins in their bait boxes, that houseboys were intelligence agents, and that agricultural workers were militiamen awaiting the signal to rise up and kill Americans. In truth, none of this was entirely surprising given the long history of prejudice directed toward Chinese and Japanese immigrants. A century of anti-Orientalism, punctuated by outbursts of physical and civil violence, as well as restrictive laws such as the Immigrant Act of 1924, which banned the immigration of Asians, had preceded Pearl Harbor. And, of course, there was all the disturbing early war news: week after week came word of successive Japanese victories in the Pacific. Suddenly, they seemed to many like a kind of superman race that threatened America's existence.

Four nights after Executive Order 9066 was signed, the Japanese submarine I-17 surfaced a few hundred yards off Santa Barbara, California, and fired two dozen rounds from its deck gun at aviation fuel storage tanks on a bluff behind the beach, badly missing the tanks but damaging a pier and a pumphouse. The event triggered anew a West Coast invasion scare, and led the next night to what would later be known as the "Battle of Los Angeles," a suspected Japanese air attack that proved to be a false alarm touched off by a weather balloon, but not before Army coastal units fired 1,400 artillery rounds into the air, which, when they fell from the sky, damaged buildings and vehicles and killed five civilians.

It took less than two weeks for the Army to act on the unilateral authority given it under Executive Order 9066. On March 1, the Army commander on the West Coast, Lieutenant General John DeWitt, declared much of California, Oregon, and Washington, as well as southern Arizona, as Military Area #1, and decreed that no Japanese would be allowed to reside in those regions, including not only Japanese nationals—now "enemy aliens"—but also those who were American citizens. "A Jap's a Jap," DeWitt explained to U.S. Representative Edouard Izac of California. "It makes no difference whether he is an American citizen or not . . . I don't want any of them. They are a dangerous element. The West Coast is too vital and too vulnerable to take any chances."

Eighty-five percent of all ethnic Japanese in the continental U.S. lived in Military Area #1. As plans were being laid for the mass internment of some 110,000 people of Japanese descent—79,000 of them U.S. citizens—the government encouraged for a short time a "voluntary exodus" from the designated areas, allowing Japanese residents to leave the West Coast of their own volition. (Fewer than 10,000 were able to do so.) After that, those who remained were to be rounded up and put in internment camps; even hospitals would be scoured for patients and orphans removed from foster homes if they were Japanese.*

For several weeks after Pearl Harbor, Roy Matsumoto continued delivering groceries around Los Angeles, ignoring "Hey, Jap!" invectives, and worse. He knew all about the racial bias that had long existed against Asians, but since the attack on Pearl Harbor those feelings had been greatly inflamed against everyone and everything Japanese. By February, his employer had closed several of his Japanese groceries, which people were afraid to be seen entering or leaving. When customers couldn't pay their bills because they lost their jobs or had

---

* "S.F. Clear of All But 6 Sick Japs," declared the *San Francisco Chronicle* on May 21, 1942. "For the first time in 81 years, not a single Japanese is walking the streets of San Francisco. The last group, 274 of them, were moved yesterday . . . Only a scant half dozen are left, all seriously ill in San Francisco hospitals. Last night Japanese town was empty. Its stores were vacant . . . The Japanese were gone from San Francisco."

their bank accounts frozen, Roy's boss was forced to close his remaining stores. In the process, his employer lost so much money that Roy declined his last paycheck.

Roy considered packing up his car and fleeing the state. He wasn't sure where he would go or what he would do once he got there, but at least he would be out of California by the time the roundups began. Then he discovered that his own account had been frozen at a Japanese bank. He lost his life savings of a few hundred dollars, and with it the wherewithal to leave. He decided that hitting the road wasn't such a good idea, anyway, after hearing stories about ethnic-Japanese drivers unable to buy gasoline or get a flat tire repaired and being left stranded. Crazy things were happening to anyone Japanese. That had been made clear to him when two FBI agents arrived at his door. A neighbor had reported Roy's rooftop antenna to police, and the agents wanted to make sure his radio could not transmit signals to enemy ships or submarines off the coast. When he proved it was only a receiver, they let him keep it.

Roy felt he had no choice but to stay and be rounded up. He left his radio, tools, and car with friends for safekeeping, telling them he hoped to one day return for them. He packed some clothes and a few personal items in a suitcase, per government instructions to bring only what he could carry. Everything else he sold for pennies on the dollar or left behind. It seemed grossly unfair, inasmuch as there were no roundups of Germans or Italians. And why not? he wondered. America was at war with those countries, too.

The roundup of Japanese in Los Angeles began at the end of March 1942. At the same time, the Army issued new orders applying to anyone of Japanese ancestry on the West Coast, setting an 8 p.m. to 6 a.m. curfew and banning ownership of firearms, radios, and cameras. "Let me warn the affected aliens and Japanese Americans," General DeWitt stated, "that anything but strict compliance will bring immediate punishment."

Troop trucks rolled into Roy's neighborhood in early April, disgorging armed soldiers who had printed lists of names and addresses and went door-to-door ordering Japanese families outside to the curb, where they waited with what few belongings they could carry. Roy was taken away on a bus crowded with men, women, and children. Most sat silent, dazed by the terror of the government's forced roundup. A few women wept quietly.

They were driven to the Santa Anita Park in Arcadia, thirteen miles northwest of downtown Los Angeles, and unloaded near a long row of horse stables. One of the world's premier Thoroughbred race-courses, where two years earlier thirty thousand spectators had filled the grandstands to cheer Seabiscuit in his last start, Santa Anita had been turned into one of fifteen assembly centers, all located in the western states. The centers, most of them at fairgrounds or racetracks due to their expansive spaces, were to provide temporary housing for the uprooted Japanese until permanent internment camps were built farther inland.

Each family was assigned to their own stall, but being bachelors, Roy and several other men shared a two-hundred-square-foot stall that reeked of its former equine occupants in spite of the newly white-washed walls. Each man got an Army cot, a straw tick, and a blanket.

Santa Anita was encircled by a chain-link fence topped with rolls of barbed wire. Its perimeter was overlooked by watchtowers manned by soldiers with rifles fixed with long, pointed bayonets. On the roof

Armed guards and machine gun in watchtower
atop grandstand at the Santa Anita Assembly Center, 1942

of each tower was a machine gun on a tripod, next to a box of belted ammunition. In addition to utilizing more than a thousand horse stalls as living quarters, rows of tar-papered barracks had been built. A curfew was strictly enforced, and the empty streets were swept by searchlights all night long. The internees were warned not to go near the fences or risk being shot, and word spread that several men who strayed too close to the fences at other camps had been shot and killed.

There were six warehouse-sized mess halls, each with bench seating for 850 people; at mealtimes, the wait in line to eat could be up to an hour long. Once inside the loud, cavernous building, everyone picked up a tin tray, a cup, and flatware. As they moved down cafeteria lines, they held out their trays for them to be filled by mess servers. The camp's daily food budget was 39 cents per person, which made for bland, institutional fare.

Sanitary and washing facilities were inadequate and overcrowded. Toilets were communal, separated by gender but lacking walls and stalls. People stood in lines to bathe in horse showers, with flimsy partitions between the men and the women. There were 150 shower-heads for the 18,700 internees in Santa Anita, the most crowded of all the assembly centers.*

Government administrators established a schedule of wages ranging from $8 to $16 a month for workers employed in tasks necessary to run the assembly centers. To stay busy and to do their part, one out of three persons at Santa Anita volunteered to work, some in their chosen professions, such as doctors, teachers, cooks, electricians, and typists. Others toiled as laborers digging up the oval track's grass infield and turning it into a giant vegetable garden to supplement meals. More than two thousand workers were assigned to the mess halls, and Roy was one of them. Given his experience in the grocery business, he was made a foreman in the vegetable department. Although they had a commercial potato-peeling machine, much of the

---

* Living with his family in one converted horse stall was a young Japanese American boy named Hosato George Takei, the future actor best known for his role as Hikaru Sulu, helmsman of the USS *Enterprise* in the television series *Star Trek*. When he first saw the family's assigned stall, Takei, then five years old, exclaimed joyfully, "We get to sleep where the horsies slept!"

work, such as cleaning turnips and chopping cabbage, was done by hand, with Roy overseeing the operation.

Harrowing stories were told by eyewitnesses to anti-Japanese demonstrations turned violent; people were badly beaten and businesses and properties damaged by Caucasian thugs. While no one liked being there, some thought it safer than staying in their hometowns. Without revealing much of his own story, Roy listened to those of others. So many had it worse than he did, especially families with young children and elderly relatives to worry about. They had lost everything: their homes, businesses, farms, life savings, investments, cars, trucks, tractors, crops, animals, farm equipment. There were so many sad stories, such as neighbors rushing in to take equipment without paying for it or pocketing the proceeds of the last harvest. Years of hard work in the land of opportunity had been lost, not because of any treasonous acts they had committed individually or collectively, but because they were the same race as a hated foreign enemy. The rallying cry "Remember Pearl Harbor!" became synonymous with "I hate Japs!" For anyone of Japanese ancestry, the day of infamy was also a day of pain and accusation; every one of them had been tarred by the actions of Japan's military on December 7, 1941.

Some internees were righteously embittered, especially those born in America. Thrown into a concentration camp without due process in violation of their constitutional rights, they asked aloud how they could ever trust the U.S. government again. Then there were those of the older generation, the Issei, who understood what Japan, the country of their birth, had done and that they were in the camps as a form of retribution. They seemed most forlorn knowing that they would not have the years left to start over. And yet, coming from the oldest ones, Roy heard one oft-repeated phrase said in barely audible murmurs: *"Shikata ga nai"*—It cannot be helped. It was meant, as it always had been in Japanese culture, to be a stoic acceptance in the face of unimaginable adversity.

In the midst of the stifling-hot summer of 1942, the emptying-out of Santa Anita's overcrowded stables and barracks began in late August with the transfer of a thousand men, women, and children by train and bus to a new internment camp on a Native American reservation in Arizona. They left as they had arrived, with a few changes of clothes and scant personal items.

Over the next two weeks, 4,500 more departed for the Heart Mountain Relocation Center in Wyoming. More followed, divvied up among a half-dozen other recently opened camps, all run by civilian administrators from the War Relocation Authority, a federal government agency established to handle the forced relocation and internment of Japanese Americans, with a company of U.S. Army Military Police (about a hundred soldiers and several officers) assigned to each camp. During the site-selection process, the Army had insisted that the permanent camps be built on federally owned lands a "safe distance" from military bases and other strategic locations. As a result, the sand-and-cactus locales chosen were some of the most desolate spots in America.*

After more than six months at Santa Anita, Roy was among the last to leave, just two weeks before the assembly center closed. On October 12, 1942, his group boarded a long line of passenger cars in a special train headed 1,800 miles east to Arkansas. The southern state that had counted fewer than ten Japanese residents in the 1940 census was about to receive an influx of some seventeen thousand dispossessed Japanese—men, women, and children, the majority of whom were U.S. citizens—at two newly built relocation centers named Jerome and Rohwer, located thirty miles apart and connected by rail and by Arkansas Highway 1.

For the first hours of the trip, soldiers went through the cars making everyone keep their window shades drawn—for what reason, they never explained. Roy suspected that it was not so they couldn't look

---

* The first director of the War Relocation Authority, Milton S. Eisenhower, the younger brother of Dwight Eisenhower, was opposed to the mass internment of Japanese, and had tried to limit it to adult men. When that idea failed, he pushed to resettle but not incarcerate Japanese in labor-starved farming communities outside the military exclusion zone, but this was opposed by the governors of the farm states. "When the war is over and we consider calmly this unprecedented migration of 120,000 people," Milton Eisenhower wrote in April 1942, "we as Americans are going to regret the unavoidable injustices that we may have done." In June, a disillusioned Eisenhower resigned his WRA post after only ninety days.

out at the scenery but so people couldn't look in and see all the Japanese faces. Indeed, once they left the populated areas, the soldiers were less strict about the window shades. By then, they were in the middle of the Mojave Desert, and there was nothing to see but cactus and periodic dust billows dancing across the horizon. The scenery remained unchanged for days as they crossed into Texas. Roy marveled at how much of America's landscape was empty, a sight he had never seen in Japan. The ride in hard, upright wooden seats inside compartments heavy with heat, humidity, and the smell of sweat seemed never-ending. The only break in the monotony was when box lunches were passed out, and once or twice a day when the train came to a screeching halt in the middle of nowhere, and the doors were flung open for those who wanted to step outside for some fresh air and to stretch their legs. Roy always did so, standing mutely with others under the glares of the armed guards watching over them.

After four long days, they arrived at their destination.

"Jerome!" the MPs yelled as they went through the cars. "Jerome!"

When Roy climbed down from the train, he saw they had halted next to a barbed-wire fence. Behind it stretched a sprawling camp comprised of long rows of familiar tar-papered barracks, and tall towers with spotlights and guns pointed into the compound. Their purpose was obvious: not to keep people out, but to keep people from leaving.

A sign at the entrance read:

> **JEROME RELOCATION CENTER**
> **Built for WAR RELOCATION AUTHORITY**
> **By Corps of Engineers, U.S. Army**

The five-hundred acre site, 120 miles from Little Rock, was in the marshy delta of the Mississippi River's floodplain; America's largest river was 12 miles away. The swamp was laced with cutoff meanders and bayous. Like water pouring off a soaked sponge, flash floods raced across the saturated ground whenever it rained, leaving stagnating pools of muddy water and swarming mosquitoes. The swamps surrounding the camp were inhabited by four species of the most deadly snakes in America, including water moccasins and copperheads.

Roy and the others who disembarked were among the first Japanese to arrive at Jerome, which had opened only a week earlier. Eventually, Jerome—the last of the ten WRA centers to start up—would confine more than eight thousand men, women, and children, nearly three thousand of them from Los Angeles and the rest from central California.

When his name was called, Roy stepped forward. An MP who towered over him attached to Roy's coat lapel a card that read "5-5-F," which stood for Block 5, Barrack 5, Unit F. Bag in hand, Roy climbed into the back of an open truck with others assigned to Block 5. They rode through the gate into a sprawling complex of about forty residential blocks, each containing a dozen rectangular barracks. In the center of every block was a building with showers, toilets, and a mess hall.

They got off the truck in the middle of Block 5. Roy found his barrack, then Unit F at the back end of the structure. He went up three wooden steps and opened the unlocked door. A blast of heat hit him in the face; it was hot and humid outside, but inside was like a furnace. He stepped into the room that was to be his new home: a sixteen-by-twenty-foot unfurnished space with no plumbing or running water and a potbellied woodstove in the center. Nevertheless,

Jerome Relocation Center internees arrived by train,
and were loaded into flatbed trucks for the ride into the camp.

Rows of barracks at Jerome

his first thought was a positive one: *Much better than a horse stall.* They were distributing Army cots at the mess hall, and he went down to get his. He was told he would be sharing the space with other single men who hadn't yet arrived. In fact, Barrack 5 was designated for men only, a mix of Issei who spoke little English and younger Nisei, some of whom didn't speak Japanese. Since Roy could speak both, he was soon acting as interpreter.

Since being rounded up off the streets of Los Angeles a half year ago, Roy had mostly managed to conceal his anger and resentment— a by-product, perhaps, of learning to control his temper after the near-tragic baseball bat incident in Japan. But it was not easy for him to keep quiet, as he felt strongly that the "assembly center" and the "relocation camp" were, in fact, government prison camps. As far as he could determine, nothing about Santa Anita or Jerome was making America safer or more secure. Forcefully interning Japanese simply because of their race was a clear case of prejudice trumping fairness.

Following Pearl Harbor, the option of serving in the U.S. military had been rapidly closed to Japanese Americans not already in uniform. First, the War Department stopped all new enlistments of Japanese, whether or not they were U.S. citizens. Next, the Selective

Farming at Jerome was difficult. The completion in late 1942 of an irrigation canal resulted in some agriculture success.

Service stopped drafting Japanese. Those who had previously been classified as "fit for military service" (1-A) were reclassified to "unfit . . . alien exempt" (4-C). When Roy received notice of his reclassification from 1-A to 4-C, it made his blood boil. Now he was *unfit* to defend his country? How dare they! It confirmed what he most feared: the relocation and internment without due process was the government saying he and the other Japanese Americans were not entitled to be treated as U.S. citizens. In effect, their birthright had been stripped from them, and he wondered if and when and how they would ever get it back.

To help pass the interminably long days, Roy volunteered to work in his barrack's mess hall. He had a lot of time to ruminate about what he might have done differently. Should he have borrowed the money to get to Colorado or Chicago and find a job and live free? Should he have escaped from Santa Anita or tried to sneak off the train as it headed eastward? Should he now be looking for an opportunity to escape? These and other wild notions passed through his head, but he always came back to the same unanswered questions: Where would he go? And what would he do? Even if he did escape, he could ultimately be caught, and then perhaps even tried as a spy or enemy agent given his years spent in Japan.

Now he was sorry that he hadn't been drafted along with his brother. At the time, it had seemed like an unlucky break for Tom, given that he had just found a good job as a bookkeeper after graduat-

ing from junior college. And Roy had been relieved that his number
didn't come up in the draft. But in retrospect, Tom had gotten into
the service at the right time. He was in uniform, serving his country,
and not subjected to the humiliations of internment. The brothers
had exchanged letters for the past year; Tom addressed his "Hello,
Niisan," an affectionate Japanese suffix meaning "older brother." Roy
knew Tom was a sergeant working as a clerk in headquarters at Camp
Savage in Minnesota. While Roy didn't know much about what was
going on there, Tom had mentioned in his letters that Camp Savage
was the Army's Japanese-language school.

Roy had been at Jerome about three weeks when he read a notice
on a bulletin board saying the Army needed men fluent in Japanese,
and that recruiters would soon be arriving to conduct interviews. With
the blanket ban against drafting and enlisting Japanese in effect, there
were grumblings around camp—particularly among the young and
rebellious but also some older Issei—about the Army recruiting for
a *supai gakkō* (spy school), and the hypocrisy of doing so inside an
internment camp where Japanese were being held because they were
not trusted. Now suddenly they were needed by America in the war
against Japan? Roy understood the frustrations being expressed—
some of the younger Nisei were particularly vociferous—because he
felt the same aggravations. But he was clear that if the U.S. Army
would have him, he would go.

He had his reasons. His first objective was to get out of the camp
and regain his freedom. He also yearned to prove that he was a patriotic American, not "unfit" for military service, as the draft board had
labeled him, or "a damn Jap," as he had repeatedly been called to his
face since Pearl Harbor. The possibility that he might join Tom at the
language school in Minnesota was appealing, too. Besides, he knew
Japanese as well as any native of Japan, and doing translations—verbal
and written—would be easy work for him. It would likely be an office
job like Tom had at Camp Savage. That sounded good to Roy.

When the Army recruiters arrived at Jerome in early November
1942, Roy went for an interview, some of which was conducted in
English by a white officer and some in Japanese by a Nisei sergeant.
Roy was surprised how much the Army already knew about his years
and education in Japan, but then recalled providing some of those

details when he registered at Santa Anita. The recruiters explained that the Army needed Japanese speakers to become interpreters, translators, and interrogators. Qualified candidates would be accepted for training at the language school in Minnesota, said the recruiters, who explained that they were particularly eager to sign up Kibei like Roy who had gone to school in Japan and already spoke and read the language fluently.

Roy was sent to the camp clinic for a physical examination. In all, the Army selected eleven volunteers in Jerome. They would be enlisting for the duration of the war, subject to a background investigation by the FBI. They gathered in a room before the recruiters. With right hands raised, they recited the Oath of Enlistment, first used in 1775 to swear in citizen soldiers in the Continental Army during the War of Independence:

> I do solemnly swear that I will support and defend the Constitution of the United States against all enemies, foreign and domestic; that I will bear true faith and allegiance to the same; and that I will obey the orders of the President of the United

Swearing in Army volunteers at internment camp

States and the orders of the officers appointed over me. . . . So help me God.

They boarded a train the next morning well before sunrise. Roy felt as if they were sneaking out in the dark—and they were. As yet unsure of the level of patriotism among interned Japanese, the Army was playing it safe by not making a public spectacle of taking young men out of a camp.

Roy Matsumoto was not conflicted. As his mother had advised him years earlier, he had not forgotten he was an American. He was ready to take the leap from feeling wronged to serving his country in time of war.

Five

ROPE IN THE OPEN SEA

Born in Waipahu, Hawaii, a sugar plantation town on Oahu, Takejiro Higa was two years old in 1925 when his mother, Ushi, took him, his five-year-old brother, Takemitsu, and their seven-year-old sister, Yuriko, to Okinawa for an extended visit to meet their grandparents. Their father, Takeo, who had immigrated to Hawaii from Okinawa ten years earlier, stayed behind to run his small grocery in Waipahu. When Takeo later came to Okinawa to take his family back to Hawaii, Ushi was sick with pleurisy, an inflammation of the lungs that causes sharp pain with breathing, and couldn't travel. As Takeo had to return to his store, it was decided that he would take the two older children with him, and the youngest, Takejiro, would stay with his mother and grandparents. Takejiro's parents never saw one another again. His father ended up losing his store during the Depression, and died not long after of a stroke at the age of forty-six. Then Takejiro's mother passed away when he was twelve. In between those losses, his grandparents died. Takejiro was taken in by his mother's sister and her husband, who had three children of their own. Their oldest, Hiroshi, was seven years older than Takejiro, but he was so kind to the younger boy and took such an interest in his well-being that Takejiro was soon calling him Hiroshi-*niisan*.

Okinawa translates to "rope in the open sea," which aptly describes this 620-mile stretch of more than 150 islands, most of them small and uninhabited, situated dead center in the East China Sea, 400 miles south of Japan and an equal distance east of China. Together, they were

Takejiro Higa with his mother, Ushi

known as the Ryukyu Islands. The oldest evidence of human existence
on the islands dates from the Stone Age. For a time in the late Middle
Ages, Okinawa was the center of a thriving import-export trade with
China, Japan, and Korea. But several hundred years of domestic and
political independence ended in 1879 when Japan, following a series
of military excursions, formally annexed the archipelago and established the Okinawa Prefecture. An assimilation program was under-
taken, and children were taught only Japanese in school and received
demerits for speaking Okinawan. Japanese also became the official
language for civic administration and the media. Due to the similarities of the languages, most Okinawans were bilingual, willing to use
Japanese when necessary but otherwise preferring their native tongue.

Takejiro's aunt and uncle had a small farm in the remote village of
Shimabuku in the center of Okinawa's main island (called Okinawa
Island), which is approximately seventy miles long and averages seven
miles wide. The village, the birthplace of Takejiro's parents, was the
family's ancestral home going back centuries. It was reached by a single
winding road through groves of banyan and twisted pines. Residents
lived on subsistence farms with terraced fields that were fertile and
neat, or in spotless little houses lining quiet roads. On the rooftops
or flanking the gates of nearly every domicile was a pair of carved
shisa (lion-dogs), one with its mouth open to ward off evil spirits and
the other with its mouth closed to keep in good spirits. The guardian

statuaries seemed to be performing their duties, as the village had no jail, no brothel, no theft, no divorce, and no drunkenness. Town elders, however, gave more credit to an American missionary who had visited Shimabuku a decade before on his way to Japan, and stayed long enough to make two influential converts: the town's mayor and its schoolmaster. The missionary taught them a few hymns and left a Japanese-language Bible, which he encouraged them to live by. The town adopted the Ten Commandments as its legal code and the Sermon on the Mount as a guide to social conduct for its residents.

A single school in the village of Kishaba served several neighboring villages, and Takejiro's walk twice a day was a little more than a mile if he went over a rugged hill instead of around it. So he climbed the hill every day. Trees and grass grew thickly along the trail strewn with craggy boulders on which habu snakes often basked in the sun. Aggressive and venomous, they grew up to eight feet long and fed mainly on rodents and other small mammals. Takejiro learned to carry a long stick to keep the snakes at bay. When he reached the top of the hill, he often paused to take in the unforgettable view: the Pacific Ocean to the east and the China Sea to the west. He grew up convinced that Okinawa was in the center of the world's greatest oceans.

Each morning at school, the students lined up in the classroom to sing the national anthem of Japan ("Kimigayo"), an unabashed ode to the emperor. Its lyrics, they were told by their Japanese teacher, were the oldest among the world's national anthems.

> *Kimigayo wa*
> *Chiyo ni yachiyo ni*
> *Sazare-ishi no*
> *Iwao to narite*
> *Koke no musu made*
>
> (May you reign
> For a thousand, nay,
> Eight thousand generations
> Until the pebbles
> Grow into boulders
> Lush with moss)

For his formative middle school years, Takejiro's teacher was Shun-sho Nakamura, who was a strict disciplinarian in the classroom but also an excellent teacher. He became like a father figure to the young boy, and under his tutelage Takejiro learned to read, write, and speak Japanese, while growing up fluent in the Okinawan dialect spoken by his family and everyone else he knew. Mr. Nakamura was also the athletic coach, and Takejiro was a star player on the sixth-grade basketball team that went to the district championship in the capital of Naha, which none of the boys had ever seen because it was an hours-long trip by horse-drawn cart over bumpy dirt roads. Even though they were soundly defeated by a much taller "city team," it was an unforgettable experience.

Since his uncle could not afford to send him to high school, Takejiro did not take the admission test. When a list went up on the principal's bulletin board in the spring of 1937 naming the students advancing to high school in the fall, Takejiro, who every year ranked first or second in his class, read the names with a heavy heart. It was hurtful to see lesser students moving on when he didn't have that opportunity. When his eighth-grade school year ended, so did Takejiro's education in Okinawa.

At the age of fourteen, he went to work for his uncle as a farmhand. Potatoes were their main crop, planted at staggered times throughout the year so that some were always ready to be dug up for a meal. The leaves of the plants were chopped up and fed to the goat that provided their milk and cheese. Every year they raised a pig, which was slaughtered when it reached about four hundred pounds. The meat—a year's supply for the family—was salted as a means of preservation and used sparingly, usually a few pieces in a steaming pot of miso soup. The slabs of fat were boiled down into oil that was stored in jars and used for cooking. They couldn't afford to buy fish from ocean fishermen at the coast, but caught their own in a nearby pond or stream—usually small carp (*funa*), which were boned and sliced up for soup.

For most Okinawans, life was hard. There were years when typhoons and floods ravaged their crops and other years when they struggled with drought. Like most of the neighbors, Takejiro's uncle grew sugarcane, which was his only cash crop. Between June and December, when the cane reached eight to twelve feet tall, they used sharp knives to cut off the shoots close to the ground, making sure not to damage the roots, since they were good for two or three crops before the land had to be replanted. Shimabuku had its own cooperative sugar mill where all the farmers brought their cane shoots, which were boiled down into a thick black syrup that was poured into large barrels. It hardened into black sugar, a rich, caramel-flavored sugar produced in Okinawa since the seventeenth century. Because his uncle had one of the village's few full-sized horses (a retired cavalry mount), Takejiro was tasked with delivering the village's hundred-pound barrels of black sugar—ten to twelve at a time—in a horse-drawn cart to the port of Naha, twelve miles away. The barrels were stored in a wharf warehouse until they were loaded onto a cargo ship for export to Japan.

In early 1939, as Takejiro's sixteenth birthday approached, he heard disturbing news. A recruitment drive by Japanese officials sought able-bodied Okinawan boys sixteen to nineteen years old for the Manchurian Youth Corps, a quasi-military organization. Trained in centers much like army camps, they were issued uniforms and rifles, and taught how to shoot before being sent to Manchuria to work in large-scale farming operations producing food for Japan. They were also a group from which the Japanese army drafted replacement troops. Some boys and young men stepped forward to volunteer, attracted by the idea of a new frontier, and perhaps the hope of acquiring farmland of their own in Manchuria. For many second and third sons of poor farming families, their options were limited in Okinawa. There were not, however, enough volunteers, and the recruiters began giving each village a draft quota to fill.

Radios were nearly nonexistent on the island, and Takejiro could count on his fingers the number of people with a newspaper subscription. Most people knew nothing about events outside their village other than the propaganda dispensed by the Japanese government. Still, Takejiro knew he did not want to go to Manchuria to farm, nor did he want to fight for Japan.

Okinawa was the only home he knew and he had strong emotional ties to it, but if he had to leave to avoid being drafted he wanted to join his sister and brother in Hawaii. Takejiro and Yuriko had rarely written any letters to each other in the years they had been apart, but he wrote to his sister now, asking her to bring him to Hawaii. The mail to Hawaii went by slow boat, and it took a couple of months to exchange letters. Yuriko was surprised to receive the letter from her youngest brother, but she sent money for his passage. That summer of 1939, fourteen years after he left his birthplace in the arms of his mother, Takejiro returned to Oahu.

Although genetically connected by ancestry, Okinawans regarded themselves as different from "mainlander" Japanese. And, in fact, Takejiro did not look Japanese to the casual observer. He had large brown eyes set below bushy eyebrows and rich copper skin tones. His torso, long and muscular, looked meant for someone taller. Because he was only sixteen, he still had some growing to do to reach his adult height of five foot six.

His sister, now twenty-one years old, took the youngest brother she hadn't seen since he was a little boy into her arms at the dock when he came off the ship, and from that day forward did not want to let him go. She was married to Yeyi Yomisato, a second-generation immigrant to Hawaii from Okinawa. Takejiro's brother Takemitsu, who now went by his American name, Warren, lived with them too, and attended the University of Hawaii. It was a modest house near downtown Honolulu, and his brother-in-law's salary was not large, but they had food and shelter. Happy to be with his siblings, Takejiro was also excited to have his own room and his first bed instead of sleeping on a mat on the ground. His sister bought him his first pair of shoes; in Okinawa, he had gone barefoot year round.

Takejiro's biggest problem in Hawaii was the language. His sister enrolled him in a private school that specialized in teaching English to new arrivals from Japan. But he was slow to learn, and his attempts in English were ridiculed even by the small children in the neighborhood. His uncle had told him before he left that if Hawaii didn't work out he was welcome to return to Okinawa. Discouraged and ready to call it quits after a year, he told his sister he regretted coming to Hawaii.

"I want to go back to Shimabuku," he said.

"Stick it out for one more year," she urged. "I'm sure you can learn."

So Takejiro stayed, continuing his studies at an English-speaking parochial school, and studying the daily newspaper to learn new

words. When it came to pronunciation, he was not shy about asking people, even young children,
for corrections when they had
difficulty understanding him. In
the process, he endured much
teasing about his poor English.

But after another year, he
could converse in passable English, albeit with a heavy accent.
He was admitted to Honolulu's
Farrington High School, after
Warren, a recent graduate, spoke
of his situation to the principal.
Although five years older than his
classmates, Takejiro entered as a
freshman. By then he was committed to staying in Hawaii. The
food was varied and plentiful, and

High school student
Takejiro Higa in Hawaii

he didn't have to work in the fields for it. It still amazed him that he
could walk down the street and buy a loaf of fresh-baked bread. He
was able to continue the education that he had been denied in Okinawa, and soon, he had his first paying job.

Shortly before 8 a.m. on the morning of December 7, 1941, Takejiro was hurrying to his part-time dishwasher job at the YMCA cafeteria in downtown Honolulu, not far from Pearl Harbor. He was a
block away when he heard aircraft flying low overhead. Oahu residents
were accustomed to the sound of military aircraft coming and going.
A few minutes later, he and his coworkers heard distant explosions.
They agreed that it must be some kind of Sunday-morning drill.

A short time later, a young Caucasian woman rushed in.

"Coffee! Coffee!"

Handed a cup of freshly brewed Kona coffee from the Big Island,
she shook so badly that half of it spilled as she tried to bring it to her
lips.

"It's war! I just dropped my husband at Pearl Harbor."

The lady raced out of the cafeteria.

Some of the young employees laughed at her as she departed.

"Maybe the wahine a little cuckoo," Takejiro agreed.

A thunderous boom sounded in the distance, rattling the windows. Now that *was* unusual.

Takejiro rushed to the roof with the others, and they all watched, shocked and horrified, as planes circled like a swarm of angry hornets over the ships in the harbor. Pillars of coal-black smoke wafted across the skyline. When an aircraft streaked past low overhead, he saw the distinctive *hinomaru* (circle of sun) on its wings and fuselage. He recognized it as the same crimson-red disc at the center of the national flag of Japan, representative of the country known as the Land of the Rising Sun. He had learned about its symbolism in his Japanese history courses on Okinawa—how the emperor was believed to be the direct descendant of the sun goddess Amaterasu, and that the *hinomaru* reflected the importance of the sun to all Japanese. He had seen the same insignia on planes that flew over Okinawa. And now, unbelievably, they were here, bombing Pearl Harbor! Starting a war with America!

Several spent artillery shells fired from U.S. antiaircraft guns landed with metallic thuds on the corrugated roof of the adjacent building. The near misses caused Takejiro and the others to flee their observation perch and head back downstairs, in time to hear a local radio announcer's panicked report: "Take cover, get off the streets! We are being attacked by Jap planes! This is the real McCoy!"

Crowding around the radio, everyone was in a state of disbelief, and no one said anything for a long while. After a short lull, there was a new round of explosions. A second wave of bombers? When would it end?

That night, with martial law having been declared by the Army as everyone feared an imminent land invasion by Japanese troops, a blackout curfew was instituted. All the streetlights were off, and no one was allowed outside after dark unless they had a pass or were serving as a block warden. Takejiro volunteered, and was issued a gas mask and flashlight with a blue cover over it. As he walked his rounds in the dark along Vineyard Avenue between the Miyagi Store and the Taiyo Bakery, he thought about what would have happened if he had stayed in Okinawa. With Japan and the United States at war, he would likely have ended up in the Japanese army fighting Americans. His sister's advice to remain in Hawaii might well have saved his life.

Over the next three days, FBI agents on Oahu rounded up nearly 500 civilians, including dozens of U.S. citizens, many for no reason other than that they were Japanese. This group consisted of Buddhist and Shinto priests, teachers, businessmen, and journalists. They were first held at the Honolulu Immigration Station, after which they took the short boat ride under armed guard to Sand Island, a tiny coral island inside the harbor that had facilities deemed suitable for confinement of civilians. Before the roundups were over, nearly 2,000 individuals of Japanese heritage were incarcerated in Hawaii. The rest of the some 160,000 Japanese residents of Hawaii, comprising more than a third of the population, were spared mass internment, unlike the Japanese on the West Coast. The reason, according to Secretary of War Henry L. Stimson, was because those in Hawaii were so "interwoven into the economic fabric of the islands that if we attempted to evacuate all Japanese aliens and citizens all business . . . would practically stop." But the thousands of Japanese, most of them U.S. citizens, who worked at Oahu's military bases lost their jobs because their race and ancestry stamped them as security risks.

Rumors and incendiary newspaper articles proliferated. A United Press report three weeks after the attack on Pearl Harbor claimed that "big arrows pointing to military objectives were cut in the sugar cane on plantations in the islands a few hours before the Japanese struck," as if arrows were necessary to find the U.S. fleet's anchorage in the sprawling harbor or other major military bases. Articles published in New York, Washington, D.C., Oregon, and elsewhere reported that Japanese fliers shot down over Oahu wore rings of Honolulu high schools and carried local street car tokens. Receiving less coverage was the type of sober reporting done by Robert J. Casey of the *Chicago Daily News*, who arrived in Honolulu a week after the attack. He interviewed the Navy surgeon who had examined eight corpses recovered from downed Japanese planes. "I've heard those stories," said the doctor. "But I never saw any rings. I never saw any street car tokens. None of the pilots had much of anything in his pockets. None wore any jewelry. Only one had a watch."

Over the next few weeks, the sight of the burned hulks of the war-

ships down in the harbor, many of them still smoking and leaking oil
into the water, and damaged ships being towed away one by one to be
repaired on the West Coast, was not something Takejiro ever forgot.

On January 5, 1942, the War Department declared that all Japanese
American civilians—in spite of their U.S. citizenship—were "aliens
ineligible to serve" in the armed forces. However, by year's end the
government was under increasing pressure to reconsider its hard-line
policy. More manpower was needed to replace growing casualties in
the two-front war, and influential individuals and groups (including
Japanese American organizations) were on record opposing the edict.

On February 1, 1943, nearly fourteen months after Pearl Harbor,
President Roosevelt issued a statement that signaled a retreat from
the military's Nisei ban. "No loyal citizen of the United States should
be denied the democratic right to exercise the responsibilities of his
citizenship, regardless of his ancestry. The principle on which this
country was founded and by which it has always been governed is that
Americanism is a matter of the mind and heart. Americanism is not,
and never was, a matter of race or ancestry."

Within weeks, the War Department began to again accept new
Nisei recruits for military service. In Hawaii, they answered the call in
large numbers: a total of some ten thousand young Japanese Americans volunteered.

"What are you going to do?" Warren asked Takejiro.

Takejiro had left Okinawa because he didn't want to be drafted
into one army, and he wasn't sure he wanted to sign up for another
one. Besides, he still had little confidence in his English. What if he
couldn't understand important orders from his superiors, or they him?
He told his brother he wanted to get his high school diploma, then
figure things out.

"Bullshit!" Warren said. "Everybody's volunteering. All the Nisei."

So both Higa brothers volunteered for the all-Nisei unit being
formed on the mainland in March 1943. Rumor had it that they would
be sent to Europe to fight the Germans. Warren was accepted, but
Takejiro, who had just finished his second year of high school, didn't
score well enough on the Army's English proficiency exam. Warren
left for training in the States, and Takejiro stayed behind.

Three months later, Takejiro received a letter from the War Department asking if he was still interested in serving his country. They wanted to know if he would be willing to volunteer for a special intelligence unit of Japanese-speaking soldiers to serve in the Pacific. The letter took Takejiro by surprise. Obviously his ability to speak Japanese was now more important to the Army than his lack of English skills. But fighting the Germans was one thing. What if he found himself in the Pacific facing someone he knew? A classmate from Okinawa or one of his cousins drafted into the Japanese army? And he could even end up fighting *on* Okinawa, in a war that pitted his two homelands against one another. He was torn between those dreaded prospects and the desire to do his part as Warren and so many others were doing. And if he refused, he could be branded as a Japanese sympathizer and hauled off to Sand Island. He had never before so agonized over a decision. Although his sister was against her youngest brother volunteering for anything dangerous, he could not bring himself to refuse to serve his country. After trying to join up earlier and being turned down, how could he say no now? Yes, he wrote back, he was willing to volunteer for the special unit.

A few weeks later, a War Department letter arrived directing him to the Dillingham Transportation Building on Bishop Street in Honolulu on a certain day at a specific time. When he arrived, he was shown into a room where he was seated across a table from an Army intelligence officer and an FBI agent who had a file in front of him. They asked him questions about his life and schooling, and as they did Takejiro was surprised at how much they already knew about his years in Okinawa and even his family situation. In fact, he was a bit shaken by how much information they had collected on him.

He was then handed a short article in Japanese.

"Can you read this?" the Army officer asked.

"Sure."

"What does it say?"

Takejiro read it, stumbling only on pronouncing a few words in English. Then he put the article down and looked across the table at his inquisitors. He had an idea the officer knew he had read it accurately.

"Okay," said the officer. "We'll let you know. Thank you."

Inducted into the Army not long after, he was among the first group of more than two hundred Nisei from Hawaii to enter the Military Intelligence Service (MIS). They arrived at Camp Savage in July 1943, part of the school's biggest wartime class of more than seven hundred students. He was placed in one of the higher sections because of his superior Japanese-language skills. He was the only one in his class who had not graduated from high school, and some had gone to college. While many of the volunteers from Hawaii had to study to improve their Japanese, Takejiro, once again, was working hard to improve his English, as well as learning *heigo*, the military terminology of Japan's army.

Warren, who was at Camp Shelby in Mississippi training with the 442nd Regimental Combat Team, received letters from Takejiro describing Camp Savage, and mentioning how they got fresh milk and eggs every morning for breakfast. Compared to Mississippi, where the men of the all-Nisei 442nd were learning to live, eat, and fight in the mud like true infantrymen (which would serve them well when they were sent to Europe), the Army school in Minnesota sounded like sleepaway camp. When an MIS recruiter came to Camp Shelby in the fall of 1943 seeking Nisei recruits for the Japanese-language school, Warren volunteered.

Takejiro was midway through the six-month course when Warren arrived at Camp Savage, but after graduation Takejiro still had

Warren (left) and Takejiro Higa

to go to Camp Blanding in Florida for twelve weeks of basic training. Meanwhile, their sister, Yuriko, protective of her younger brothers, hoped they could be together. But after the loss of the five Sullivan brothers when their Navy cruiser, the *Juneau*, was torpedoed and sank near the Solomon Islands in 1942, brothers serving together in the same unit required special approval from the War Department. So Yuriko wrote to Washington, explaining how her brothers would watch out for each other and Warren could assist

Takejiro with his English. Her unusual request was apparently viewed favorably, because after they completed their training the brothers were assigned to the same ten-man MIS team.

Their newly formed team took the train to Seattle, then a ship to Hawaii. Ordered to report to the 96th Infantry Division, which had been activated eight months earlier in Oregon and had not yet seen combat, they found the division camped in a sprawling tent city at Schofield Barracks. The Nisei arrived in time to take part in the division's jungle training in the rugged Ka'a'awa Valley on Oahu's north shore. It was a particularly hot and humid August, and drenching rains and endless practice crossings of swollen tropical streams kept everyone soaked and miserable much of the time. They learned how to survive on exotic fruits and coconut water, how to safeguard their equipment in such soggy conditions, and how to patrol through thick, trackless jungle.

The division next boarded large, flat-keeled LSTs (Landing Ship, Tank) for Maui, where they invaded Kihei Beach in a mock amphibious assault that involved landing thousands of troops and tons of supplies onto a "hostile" beach in the proper order of tactical importance. Several small craft were sunk or damaged in the exercise, and there was considerable confusion ashore, but the rehearsal was to work out just such kinks before making a combat landing.

At last, the exhausted GIs were given passes to enjoy the beaches of Waikiki and the bars on Hotel Street, but not for long. On September 11, 1944, the division loaded onto troopships for the war in the Pacific.

The 96th Division was now on a circuitous course that would take Takejiro toward what he had long feared, as they would soon bear the brunt of what historians have called the "cruelest battle of the Pacific."

The Battle of Okinawa.

PART TWO

Six

—·—

CAMP SAVAGE

S un Tzu, the ancient Chinese general and philosopher revered as one of history's greatest military strategists, advised in his treatise, *The Art of War*, that the way to victory is through the procurement of information on the enemy. Such information has been referred to as "military intelligence" since the American Revolution, when George Washington pressed his subordinates to spare neither expense nor effort in learning the enemy's strength, disposition, and movements.

The U.S. Army established military intelligence as a specialty during the Civil War, and in every war since it has played an expanded role.

There are two major categories of military intelligence. *Strategic intelligence* is the big-picture product of planning for large-scale campaigns, such as the D-day invasion of Nazi-occupied Europe. *Tactical intelligence* concerns the enemy's strength and location, and is used to make timely decisions on the battlefield. The gathering of intelligence usually requires fluency in the enemy's language, both written and verbal.

Japan's military leaders long believed their language so complex that they were confident few Westerners would fully understand it. The Japanese had incorporated much of the Chinese language into their own more than a thousand years ago, and there was a Japanese interpretation in addition to a Chinese reading for most of the written ideographs. A rough equivalent would be incorporating the Russian language into English and then adding a complex system of picture writing. Also, much of the Japanese written language is divided into the formal and informal, each with different structures.

In June 1941, Major Carlisle C. Dusenbury, a former Japanese-language student assigned to Army headquarters in Washington, was the first to propose a new school to train Japanese-speaking soldiers as interpreters, interrogators, and translators in the event of war with Japan. Given the difficulty of the language and realizing how few Caucasians had the necessary fluency, he advocated recruiting Nisei already in the Army for such roles. It was a controversial proposition—even before the attack on Pearl Harbor—as there was widespread skepticism as to whether Japanese American soldiers could be trusted in a war against their ancestral homeland. It was even suggested that they should not be used in a war with Japan. "It's one thing for them to kill Germans," a skeptical Navy officer told Dusenbury, "but will they shoot their own kind?"

Plans for a Japanese-language school were nearly derailed after a group of Army intelligence officers returned from a summer 1941 trip to England, where they had observed the methods taught at the British army's interrogation school. The British had been fighting Erwin Rommel's Afrika Korps for more than a year, and had adopted a harsh, dominant method of interrogating captured Germans that was effective in deflating Nazi conceit and arrogance. Theorizing that the same method could work with Japanese, these officers pushed for a centralized training center near Washington, D.C., to teach the British method for interrogating both German and Japanese soldiers.

But knowing the psychology of the Japanese, a handful of career officers who had served at the U.S. embassy in Tokyo in the 1930s—including Captain Kai Rasmussen, who in the summer of 1941 was busy visiting Army bases interviewing Nisei soldiers as prospective students for the new school, and Major John Weckerling, who would be named the first director of the Japanese-language school at the Presidio—advocated an entirely different approach they thought would be more effective.

From the earliest ages in strict military schools, Japanese males learned Bushido, the samurai code of honor that considered surrender a disgrace. Soldiers in the Imperial Japanese Army were indoctrinated to choose between victory and a heroic death. This ancient code of conduct did not permit becoming a prisoner of one's enemy. Warriors were expected to perform *seppuku* (a ritual suicide also referred to as *harakiri*) rather than be captured. Therefore, the sons of Nippon were not taught how to conduct themselves *if* they were captured. The average Japanese soldier did not know about the Geneva Convention or its tenets regarding the treatment of POWs or that they had only to provide name, rank, and serial number.* This gap in their training could work in favor of an adroit interrogator in the field trying to get them to talk, but for the fact that a captured Japanese soldier would likely consider himself a traitor, convinced he had brought shame and dishonor on his family, his ancestors, his nation, and the emperor. He would likely expect to be tortured or killed by his captors, and a severe attitude toward him could reinforce those beliefs and make him less willing or able to cooperate.

From the six months he had spent in the 1930s embedded as an observer with the Japanese army in China, Rasmussen knew that its soldiers were badly mistreated by their superiors, who were quick to hand out caning and other severe corporal punishment for the slightest infraction. (Rasmussen came to believe that the physical abuse in their ranks, which would never be tolerated in the U.S. Army, later fostered acts of brutality by Japan's soldiers.) He thought that captured Japanese might open up to Nisei interrogators able to establish some rapport with them in their own language, emphasizing that the war was over for them and they need not die. Rasmussen believed this approach could be key to obtaining valuable intelligence.

The War Department decided the issue by approving separate foreign-language training centers, one at Camp Ritchie, Maryland, to train German-language interpreters and interrogators, and the Japanese-language school in San Francisco, where classes began on November 1, 1941, in the old hangar at Crissy Field in the Presidio. Thirty-six days later, Japan attacked Pearl Harbor. When Roosevelt signed Executive Order 9066 in February 1942 authorizing the

---

* The 1929 Geneva Convention treaty relative to the treatment of prisoners of war was ratified by forty-seven governments, including the United States and its future adversaries, Germany and Italy. Japan was not among them, nor was the Soviet Union.

Kai Rasmussen, the first
commandant of the
MISLS at Camp Savage

removal of all Japanese from the West Coast, it meant the school had to move inland, too.

When the Army decided it would be a "distracting influence" to relocate the school at an established Army post, Rasmussen undertook an extensive search for a new site. He preferred one that had existing facilities and room for expansion. Importantly, it also had to be located where Japanese Americans in U.S. Army uniforms would be accepted by the local populace, and there were many communities in the U.S. where that was not the case. After several governors flatly rejected the idea of a Japanese-language school in their states, Governor Harold Stassen of Minnesota stepped forward to offer a state-owned property that had been built up by the Civilian Conservation Corps in the 1930s.

Camp Savage was located fifteen miles from Minneapolis. It was named for a former resident of a nearby town, Marion W. Savage, who at the turn of the century owned and trained the great racing horse Dan Patch. The remote property had most recently provided indigent men with opportunities to do useful work in the camp's small cannery, mattress factory, laundry, bakery, mess hall, recreation hall, motor pool, dispensary, and utilities yard. The state leased the 132-acre property and its forty buildings to the Army for one dollar a year. The school was given a new name: the Military Intelligence Service Language School. Ironically, it was in overwhelmingly Caucasian Minnesota that the Nisei attending the MISLS found local residents willing to accept them with little animosity or racial discrimination, a novel experience for many of them, especially those from the West Coast, where far greater numbers of Japanese immigrants had settled through the years. (The 1940 census counted fifty-one Japanese living in all of Minnesota.) Rasmussen would later remark that Minnesota was an ideal location for the school because it "not only had room physically but also had room in the people's hearts."

By the summer of 1942, U.S. commanders in the Pacific were clamoring for Japanese-language teams, an early indicator of the indispensable role the Nisei were to serve in the war against Japan. The War Department directed the MISLS to produce enough Nisei teams to support an estimated fifty Army divisions expected to be fighting in the Pacific by the end of 1943.* Because there was a total ban on Nisei enlistments throughout 1942, Rasmussen had to go back to the War Department and get special authority to recruit the personnel he needed from relocation camps, which he contended was the only way they could reach the necessary level of graduates.

Washington also ordered "all necessary steps be taken to prevent publicity regarding Intelligence personnel of Japanese extraction, the Military Intelligence Service Language School, the assignment of graduates thereof or the type of work carried on by them." Japanese military officers had openly boasted before the war that their difficult language would itself constitute a complex code, keeping their orders and plans from being quickly or easily deciphered by U.S. forces in the field. Viewing this lack of communications security as extraordinary and surprising, the U.S. Army strove to take advantage of the enemy's false sense of security by keeping secret the existence of the MIS Japanese-language teams operating in the Pacific.†

Thomas "Tom" Sakamoto, who would one day witness Japan's formal surrender aboard the USS *Missouri* in Tokyo Bay, was chosen to

* Nowhere near that number of divisions ended up going to the Pacific. Of the U.S. Army's ninety-one infantry divisions that saw action in World War II, twenty-one went to the Pacific. Nearly all the rest fought in Europe. All the Army divisions (as well as several Marine Corps divisions) in the Pacific had Nisei Japanese-language teams assigned to them by late 1943.

† There were no English-language intelligence teams attached to the Imperial Japanese Army, although there were men in its ranks with the requisite linguistic ability. Several thousand Nisei who had gone to Japan before the war and were unable to return home after Pearl Harbor were subsequently drafted into Japan's military. Not only did their bilingual skills go largely unappreciated and unused, they were often ostracized and dismissed because they were Americans.

teach at Camp Savage after finishing at the top of his class at the Presidio language school in May 1942. That same month, his family arrived at the Stockton (California) Assembly Center at the San Joaquin County Fairgrounds, where more than four thousand ethnic Japanese men, women, and children—many of them American citizens—were detained prior to being sent to the Rohwer Relocation Center in Arkansas.

Two months earlier, Tom's parents, hoping to avoid internment, had packed up the family and left their rented farm in San Jose, driving one hundred miles inland to Lodi. Leaving the spring crop out in the fields, they had abandoned anything they couldn't sell or that didn't fit in their old truck, which included much of their household furnishings. Their plan was to get out of the military exclusion area and keep moving, but they didn't make it far. Shortly before they were rounded up with other Japanese in central California, Tom, on a weekend pass, found them staying in a shack in Lodi. There was no work for his parents, the kids weren't in school, and no one was making plans for tomorrow. Tom could see that his mother was taking the loss of their home and lifetime of possessions extremely hard. When they said goodbye, she broke down as if she didn't expect to ever see him again.

Tom was heartsick leaving his family in such dire straights. Possibly to save him further upset, his family did not tell him about FBI agents arriving at their farm a couple of months earlier and searching the house. At the outbreak of war, his mother had burned everything from or about Japan, including keepsakes, photographs, and letters from relatives, but she had been unable to locate the flag Tom had brought home from Japan—a parting gift from his boarding school in Kumamoto. The agents, however, found the rising sun flag neatly folded inside a trunk, and confiscated it. With suspicions raised, they questioned everyone, even removing two of Tom's brothers and a sister from their school classrooms to question them about the family's loyalty. The Sakamotos were all left shaken and confused. What they did not know was that the FBI handled background investigations for the Army, and the visit had to do with processing Tom's top-secret security clearance.

After his four years in Japan (1934–38), which had ended with his turning down an appointment as a probationary officer in the Imperial

Camp Savage instructor Tom Sakamoto

Japanese Army before his return to America (his parents had sent him a boat ticket and a new suit for the journey home), Tom read, wrote, and spoke Japanese like a native, yet he hadn't been away so long as to forget his English. Linguistically, he was the best of both worlds, fluent in Japanese but able to write cogent reports in English, the perfect combination sought by the Military Intelligence Service, which was why he was assigned to teach the top language section at Camp Savage. Even so, once classes started he was surprised to find that some of the soldiers he was teaching were even more fluent than he was in reading and writing kanji, which gives a Japanese definition to nearly half of the some fifty thousand Chinese ideographs. Other than scholars, few people in Japan had memorized the approximately twenty thousand characters in use. In fact, knowing the three thousand or so most common ideographs ensured that a person could read a newspaper without referring to a dictionary. Tom's best students were Kibei who had spent more years in Japan than he had. However, some of them had been away from the U.S. for so long that they struggled with English.

While awaiting instruction to start at the MISLS, the early arrivals helped prepare the camp for the influx of students. From drafty, rickety barracks they dragged into the open and set afire vermin-infested straw mattresses, scrubbed filthy buildings inside and out, and even pulled dandelions in front of the administration buildings. It was an inauspicious start for some of the Army's top Japanese linguists, and hard feelings festered among the young men. At night in the barracks there were loud complaints along the lines of "What the hell are we doing here being gardeners?" They had all been inducted into the Army before the war, so they were not new recruits, which made the situation sting even more. There was a war on, they were trained soldiers, they should be doing *something* other than pulling weeds. Many of them had been disarmed and held in limbo after Pearl Harbor, and their residual anger at that treatment was palpable. But overriding all of this was their unending concern about their families, most of whom were now forced to live behind barbed-wire fences in some of the most desolate regions of the country.

A few days before classes began, a senior instructor delivered a stern message that didn't go over well: "You were brought here to study, and if you don't according to our expectations, we know where your parents are!" To the young Nisei, it sounded as if they weren't trusted to be good students or soldiers without their families as hostages.

The personnel officer at Camp Savage, 1st Lieutenant Paul F. Rusch, recognizing discontent among the young soldiers, visited their barracks. With an open, smiling visage, Rusch was not a run-of-the-mill Army officer. A roly-poly, forty-five-year-old white man fluent in Japanese from his two decades in Japan as an Anglican missionary and teacher, he still possessed the zeal of a disciple converting lifelong

Paul F. Rusch, MISLS

Buddhists to Christianity. Occasionally, his tenacity came at a cost. When the entire Anglican mission left Japan in the months before the bombing of Pearl Harbor, Rusch defiantly stayed behind. His dream of peace between the two countries was shattered on December 7, 1941, and two days later he was arrested as an enemy alien. He remained interned in Japan until the summer of 1942, when he was repatriated with other foreign nationals on the Swedish exchange ship *Gripsholm*.

While he remained deeply loyal to his friends in Japan, Rusch, upon his arrival home, pledged to do whatever he could to help the U.S. win the war in the Pacific. What ailed Japan, he believed, was not its people, but its militant leaders. While he had long advocated peace over war, he believed the destruction of Japan's war machine was now the only way to liberate the country and its people, even at the cost of civilian casualties. The sooner America won, the sooner he could return to Japan and help rebuild the country he loved. Invaluable to the U.S. Army for his knowledge of Japan, Rusch was commissioned in the Army's MIS, and had been sent to bases that summer to recruit some of the Nisei soldiers now at Camp Savage.

The students thought the older lieutenant had to be the most un-officer-like officer in the entire Army. He regularly defied regulations, including the dress code—the latter best symbolized by the silver-fox fur hat he wore in cold weather to keep his bald head warm. Rusch was more father confessor than superior officer, and the men soon had a nickname for him, "Papa Paul," which he earned by caring about their feelings as much as he did their training.

Many students had received letters from their parents saying they had been told to report to the train station with one bag each, and were heading to relocation centers in other states. Their families would, they knew, be sick at losing everything they had worked for and built with many years of hard work. It was so sad and unfair.

"Look, I'm not angry with the Army," one of the students told Rusch. "The same with most of the guys here. We're just against everything that's been coming down on us and our families. We're being treated like second-class citizens."

Rusch was well aware of the anti-Japanese sentiment in America that had swept up all the Nisei and their families. "It's been difficult for you soldiers, I know. Just remember there are a lot of people watching you and counting on you. I'm sure that includes your families, and I know it includes your country. I know you guys will make us all proud. And if you need to talk to anyone, you can think of me as your friend."

Talking to the lieutenant always made everyone feel better because someone in authority listened and understood. They could only imag-ine and laugh about all the converted Christians who must be running around Japan because of Papa Paul's ability to listen and understand.

Translation practice

Classes began at Camp Savage on June 1, 1942, for 200 enlisted men, of whom 193 were Nisei and 7 Caucasian.* Twenty white officers with some background in Japanese, usually from courses they took in college, were also in the class. The all-Nisei faculty comprised seven civilians who had taught at the Presidio, and that school's ten top enlisted graduates. There were also dozens of clerical and support personnel, civilian as well as Army, working at the camp to ensure its smooth operation. It didn't take long for the students and faculty alike to get into the academic routine. Gone were the daily work details and all the complaints; there was no time for any of it. There weren't even the endless inspections and drills and formations that made for Army life elsewhere, and the uniform of the day was baggy khaki overalls with no stripes or patches or other insignias. Everything was now focused on one thing and one thing only: learning and retaining a staggering amount of material and informa-

* The June 1942 class was the last one to have only Nisei servicemen who had been in the Army prior to the war. Starting with the next class, which was twice as large, the increased number of MISLS graduates requested by the War Department were met by recruiting from relocation camps as well as from within the Army's enlisted ranks.

MISLS, Camp Savage

tion over the next six months.

Reveille was at 6 a.m., and classes were five days a week from 8 a.m. to 5 p.m., with a break for lunch, then reconvened from 7 p.m. to 9 p.m. After lights out at 10 p.m., some students studied by flashlights or even in the toilets, the only spaces that remained lighted all night. Military training took place on Wednesday afternoons, often consisting entirely of a long march. Saturdays were for examinations; Sundays were free, filled with diversions such as taking a bus into Minneapolis to eat at restaurants, go to movies and clubs, and ice-skate at an outdoor rink.

The curriculum for the first three months emphasized the study of Japanese grammar, reading, writing, and simpler translations. Those students already proficient in the language helped those who were not. Prior to the war, Japanese was taught at only a few colleges in the United States, and was regarded as a difficult language that took years to master. At the MISLS, some Nisei who hadn't gone to school in Japan struggled to keep up in the language courses, but they were helped by small class sizes, maximum contact with instructors, peer mentoring, and having grown up with Japanese spoken at home by their immigrant parents. Practical instruction was emphasized over book learning, honing their conversational Japanese for hours at a time and reading newspapers.

The fourth month and first half of the fifth were devoted to the study of Japanese military terminology, called *heigo*; the Order of Battle of the Imperial Japanese Army (its organization, armament, jargon, and tactics); military interpreting; translation of captured enemy documents; and reviewing the Japanese written styles. Students studied sorobun, a formal writing style that originated in seventeenth-century

Japan and was still in use, and sosho, a flowing shorthand that could be difficult to master even for those who had studied Japanese for years. In the last half of the fifth month, lectures were given on Japanese history, politics, and culture. In the sixth and final month, all personnel were divided into translation and interrogation teams for more practical work. They also took a hands-on course in intercepting radio and telephonic communications, which included listening to and translating live radio broadcasts from Tokyo.

The *heigo* courses were considered by most students to be among the most difficult. Their purpose was to give the students a large military vocabulary so that they could read, write, speak, and translate Japanese military terms. In the course work, they also acquired extensive knowledge that could be used to assess information developed through interrogations and translations, and to be knowledgeable sources in the field on matters pertaining to the Japanese military. The *heigo* textbook was a guide and reference constantly being revised as more information was learned about the enemy. In fact, the intelligence sent back by MIS teams in the field helped to make future editions more complete and useful for the students who followed.

Even college graduates agreed that they had never studied as hard or been required to retain as much information as at Camp Savage. The intensity of the training, the sheer volume of courses and infor-

Nisei soldiers at the Army's Japanese-language school

Hitting the books at the MISLS

mation, and the urgency of the war put immense pressure on both instructors and students. "What they were trying to do was cram down [us] within six months what would take four years in college to learn," explained one student. Those courses included:

Naganuma Reader (reading and translation)
Heigo Readers (military terms)
Sakusen Yomurei Field Manual (reading and translation)
Cyo Senjutsu Applied Tactics (reading and translation)
Interrogation and Interpretation
Captured Documents
Grammar, Japanese, Colloquial
Grammar, Japanese, Literary
Grammar, English
Sosho (Japanese shorthand)
Kanji (characters and dictation)
Japanese Geography
Heigo Military Lectures (in English and Japanese)
American Military Terms
Conversation (for students weak in Japanese conversation)
Japanese-English and English-Japanese Translation
Radio Monitoring
Intercept Messages
Lectures (Japanese society, history, and politics)

Documents from Guadalcanal and other early battles arrived in sealed cartons. Many were personal letters and diaries, usually written in sosho shorthand. Most were from friends or relatives in Japan, and likely had been removed from dead bodies. While it was real-world translation practice, it was also reading someone's personal mail, missives to young men who were probably gone and not returning home. For the Nisei soldiers, these documents, most of them written on razor-thin rice paper, represented their first intimate look at the war. Because they would be able to read the enemy's letters and diaries on the battlefields across the Pacific, they would never have the luxury of fooling themselves into thinking they were fighting anyone other than fellow human beings.

Dear Big Brother,

It has been a long while. How have you been doing since then? We are all doing well, so please do not worry about us. Time flies quickly, doesn't it? On February 24th, Big Sister's death anniversary, we collected rose-gold pussy willow and placed it at her grave. This year that flower seemed to have bloomed earlier than usual . . .

I am graduating in about twenty days. I sincerely wish to have you as my mentor upon graduation.

Please take care of yourself.

See you again.
Yasunosuke

October 3, 1942

To the Honorable Officers and Soldiers of the Imperial Army,

The leaves in the garden's trees are swaying in a soft breeze, hinting at the beginning of the fall season! Rice plants that used to grow bright green are now turning gold, adding even more beauty to it all.

How are things with you all?

As soon as the South-East Asia theatre began, you courageously stood for our Emperor, defending him with your precious lives. As we all listened to the news, we learned that our Air Force won a glorious victory! Although it brought me great joy, I could not help but feel mournful for the lives that were lost. The news reminded us of the importance of fostering a strong mental attitude.

I'm overwhelmed with feelings when I imagine what you are going through every day in maneuver training and in charging the enemy with your own bodies and your divine Yamato-damashii, Japanese spirit.

Times have changed. In particular, since December 8th, the day of the declaration of war by the United States, we have become a different people. If we had been born men, without a doubt we would go to the battlefields and commit to dying for our country! However, we are women. At the very least, we will protect our mainland.

Amid your achievements and your rigorous schedule, I understand that your operations are progressing steadily. Far away from home, fierce battles take place incessantly day and night in the foreign sky. I imagine you would not even have a second to recall your distant native home.

On the mainland, the cosmos flowers are beautiful now. Even though it may wither by the time you get this letter, I am sending you a pressed flower that bloomed in our schoolyard the other day.

Please stay strong and cheerful, and keep going.

Taki Rizaki
Ibaraki Shimodate Girls' High School

In the final weeks, MISLS students took part in mock interrogations, practicing the techniques for learning the enemy's strength, location, morale, and other conditions on the battlefield. During one lecture, the instructor said they might come across POWs who demanded to be interrogated by someone of equal or greater rank.

"If the prisoner is a sergeant," said the instructor, "borrow lieutenant bars and put them on so as to outrank the prisoner."

One student yelled from the back of the hall, "Give *us* our bars now!" He had hit on a sore point, and a hush fell over the group. There were to be no commissions given to Nisei, per the War Department. For now, the officers who graduated the MISLS and commanded the teams would all be Caucasians, although few of them had the linguistic skills to handle translations or conduct interrogations. The Army saw the white officers performing two functions: ensuring that the intelligence reports by a team were written in proper English and

Army-speak; and as buffers for the Nisei if they had to deal with racial prejudice from other officers in the field. (Some teams were to be led by Nisei sergeants since there were not enough white MISLS graduates to spread around.)

The small contingent of white officers enrolled that fall at Camp Savage did not graduate before hearing from Rusch. He implored the future leaders of Japanese American troops to treat them as individuals, not as members of an ethnic group. "Every man in your team is a human creature, with a heart and a soul like your own," said Papa Paul. "Every soldier who wears this uniform wants some visible protection from a rigid, soulless system. As his officer, you must provide this."

———

One of the students in the first class at Camp Savage was Kazuo Komoto, who had thought he was being kicked out of the Army when he was ordered to board a train with thirty other Nisei in Texas but instead arrived in Minnesota. Having been taken by his mother at age ten to Japan for schooling, and after graduating high school there before returning to America in 1938, he aced the MISLS language test and went into the top 1-A section. (Each section had about twenty students, with one instructor in charge.)

When he first heard reports of the Japanese on the West Coast being moved inland, Kazuo had been in the segregated barracks at Fort Bliss, Texas, with other Nisei soldiers. Concerned about his parents and five younger brothers, he wrote to his mother but didn't immediately hear back. He correctly guessed why. She could write only in Japanese, and was afraid to write in her native language. In fact, writing to her in Japanese had made Kazuo uneasy, too, given newly instituted mail censorship. He did not yet know whether his family had been taken from their home in Sanger, California, and if they had, to where. There was a sizable Japanese community where they lived, and Kazuo wondered if they would all be moved together. He could imagine his family's devastation at being forced from their home, but on reflection he thought that a government camp might be the safest place for them right now. There were some hostile farmers in the Sanger area long opposed to Japanese working the land, and he could only imagine how they felt now. And he had zero confidence in the local sheriff being able to protect his family. At least in camp his little brothers wouldn't be beaten up.

Kazuo found Camp Savage's head instructor, John Aiso, to be a good man, highly intelligent but also strongly opinionated. A 1941 draftee, Aiso had been discovered by Kai Rasmussen on one of his early Nisei recruiting trips to an Army base. At the time, Aiso was relegated to working in the motor pool, although he knew little about cars or engines. Born in the Los Angeles suburb of Burbank in 1909, he had graduated at the top of his Hollywood High School class in 1926. After spending a year studying Japanese at Seijo University in Tokyo, he returned to the United States and graduated cum laude from Brown University, where he captained the debate team and majored in economics. He continued his studies at Harvard Law School, receiving his jurisprudence degree in 1934, and worked in private practice in Los Angeles and New York, then from 1936 to 1940 in Japan representing U.S. and British companies. Rasmussen saw that Aiso was trans-ferred out of the motor pool and sent to teach at the MISLS, where he so distinguished himself that he was soon named its director of academic training. He quickly became the school's heart and soul, bringing not only his language and academic skills but also an under-standing of the challenges his fel-low Nisei would encounter in a war against their parents' homeland.*

When someone asked Aiso a question in class, his explanation

John Aiso, MISLS

* As a lowly Army private, Aiso couldn't serve as the MISLS's director, and with Japanese Americans prohibited at the time from receiving commissions, he was discharged from the regular Army and hired by the War Department as a civilian. In 1944, when the chief of Army intelligence visited Camp Savage, he was outraged that a civilian was in command of military personnel. Aiso was given a direct commission to major, becoming the highest-ranking Japanese American in the U.S. Army.

would often be deeper and more thought-provoking than the query required. He believed if he gave them a pat answer, they wouldn't learn as much. "By pushing you," he often said, "you're forced to get that much better." One way Aiso had of providing an extra push was telling a marginal student if he didn't study harder and improve his grades, a "letter of disapproval" would be sent to his parents at their internment camp. The mere threat of such shaming was usually more than adequate motivation.

One day, Kazuo was called into Aiso's office for something wholly unexpected: Aiso wanted to know why he wasn't buying war bonds.

"We want everyone here to buy a ten-dollar war bond every month," Aiso explained. "You have not, Komoto. Why not?"

"Mr. Aiso, I get thirty-six dollars a month. I am paying for Army insurance, I have to pay for laundry, and I want to go into Minneapolis once in a while to see a Sunday matinee. I cannot afford ten dollars a month out of my pay."

Aiso, who had a dictatorial manner that could be harsh, refused to back down. He said he wanted to see "100 percent participation" in the war bond drive. "You must buy a war bond every month to prove your loyalty to the United States."

Kazuo bristled at Aiso's reasoning. "I don't need to spend ten dollars a month to prove my loyalty. That's a bunch of baloney. I've been in the Army a year and a half and soon I'll be going overseas. I don't know whether I'm coming back or not. And you want me to give ten dollars a month to prove I'm loyal to my country?"

They stared at one another for a long moment.

"Okay," Aiso said. "You have your reasons. Keep up the good work."

Kazuo did keep up the good work, and come graduation time he was voted the valedictorian, and gave the only commencement speech in Japanese. (Another student gave a speech in English.) He spoke of his upbringing and his family, and how proud he was to be serving and defending his country in time of war. He ended on a note of what they might soon face in the Pacific, reminding his classmates of the importance of taking care of their buddies when things got rough.

In all, 117 Nisei enlisted men and 12 Caucasian officers graduated from the first MISLS class on November 3, 1942. Twenty enlisted men graduated early and had already been rushed to Australia and the South Pacific. Twenty-nine enlisted men were held over at Camp Savage for further instruction, and thirty-four students (17 percent of the entering class) failed to make the grade and were returned to their units. When the graduates received their orders, twenty students judged to possess "exceptional instructional ability" remained at Camp Savage to teach the next class. With the MISLS greatly expanding its enrollment in the second class starting in December, the faculty increased as well, from seven to fifteen civilian teachers, and from ten to thirty enlisted instructors, including Tom Sakamoto, who was retained as a senior instructor.

The graduates were given fourteen days of leave. Kazuo, knowing there was a good chance he would be sent overseas, wanted to use the time to visit his family. By then, he knew his parents and brothers and sisters were in the Gila River Relocation Center in Arizona. He and his mother were exchanging letters again; his mother had taken classes at Gila River to learn enough English to be able to write to him.

When Kazuo applied for a travel pass to buy a train ticket to Arizona, he was refused. The reason: Gila River was located inside the sprawling Western Defense Command. No Nisei—not even those in U.S. Army uniforms—were then being allowed to travel freely in the area. Kazuo went to MISLS headquarters to argue his case with a clerical sergeant who was also a Nisei. The sergeant finally threw up his hands. "Look, Komoto, that's a standing order from Washington. What can I do?"

It was clear to Kazuo that there was nothing he could do for or about his family—he couldn't even visit them to say goodbye.

Kazuo was promoted to sergeant upon graduation, and was the ranking noncom of a ten-man Nisei team. Based on input from the MISLS instructors, the teams were organized before departing Camp Savage so they consisted of a sergeant who "possessed outstanding leadership ability as well as linguistic proficiency," three interrogators, three interpreters, and three translators. While in the field these duties often proved interchangeable, there was a method to the selection process. Interrogators had to possess strong verbal skills, as they would be questioning POWs; interpreters had to be strong in Japanese-to-English explanations, and translators must possess excellent reading skills in all Japanese writing styles. Each team was balanced so some members were strong in Japanese and others excelled in English. Teams would go into the field with Japanese dictionaries, including specialized ones with military and medical terms, and each man carried a thick copy of military terms from the *heigo* text, as well as any handwritten notes from his courses that he wished to keep with him.

Kazuo and his team took the train to San Francisco, and were billeted at the Presidio in a barracks not far from the old hangar where the Army's first Japanese-language school had convened the previous year.

The night before they were to ship out for the Pacific, and after being confined to the base since arriving, Kazuo asked that his men be allowed to spend a few hours in San Francisco. When he was turned down, he went to see the captain in charge, who barely looked up from a stack of paperwork as he heard Kazuo out.

The captain then said dismissively, "Can't let you go into town, sergeant. Something might happen."

"What do you think might happen, sir?" Kazuo asked.

"You know, unfriendlies on the street, you being Japs—Japanese. Can't have you gettin' in a donnybrook night before you ship out."

Kazuo pointed out that lots of other GIs leaving in the morning were going into town. "My men have been segregated and kept on base since we got here. You're keeping us here because something might happen? Sir, do you think that's fair? We're going overseas tomorrow."

The captain looked up at Kazuo, and seemed to be considering his request. "Okay, sergeant," he said. "I'll sign your passes, but you guys stick together, and you can only go to Chinatown. Enjoy some chop suey."

That's what they did, without any trouble, and for a few hours they forgot about tomorrow and enjoyed their last night on the town.

Shortly after dawn—three days after Christmas 1942 and a year after Japan's attack on Pearl Harbor—Kazuo Komoto and his team joined a thousand GIs aboard a crowded troopship headed to the South Pacific.

Seven

SOLOMON ISLANDS

Kazuo Komoto was seasick most of the way across the Pacific, which surprised him because he recalled only smooth sailing on his boyhood voyages to and from Japan. Four days into his wartime crossing, an enemy submarine was detected. An escort vessel attacked with depth charges, and his troopship set a zigzagged course the rest of the way.

After three weeks at sea, they arrived at Suva in the Fiji Islands on January 21, 1943. Following the Pearl Harbor attack, Fiji had been seen as a likely target for a Japanese invasion; Suva had one of the finest natural harbors in the South Pacific—three miles wide and jutting inland for two miles—and one of the few concrete airstrips in the South Pacific. Had they controlled Fiji, Japanese naval and air forces could have severed the sea lanes to the Allied nations of Australia and New Zealand, cutting them off from the United States. American and New Zealand troops had rushed there in 1942 to build up its defenses, but the anticipated attack never came following Japan's loss of four aircraft carriers and hundreds of planes and pilots at Midway in June of that year. Fiji now served as a harbor for U.S. Navy ships and a staging area for Allied ground units newly arrived in the Pacific. Kazuo's ten-man MIS team was attached to the G2 Intelligence section of the 37th Infantry Division, a National Guard outfit from Ohio that had been among the first troops sent to Fiji the previous year but so far had not seen any combat. Leading the MIS team were two white officers, Captain Gilbert Ayres and Lieutenant Jerome Davis, both of whom had been in the first graduating class at Camp Savage with Kazuo, as had the Nisei enlisted members: Taro Asai, William Ishida, Dye Ogata, Seiichi Okazaki, Haruo Ota, Frank Sanwo, Kiyoto Shintaku, George Tokunaga, and Tomoyoshi Uyeda. Kazuo considered the two officers not sufficiently fluent in Japanese to translate or interrogate without a Nisei present.

Kazuo was troubled by the mantra spreading through the ranks that in close jungle fighting it was best to "shoot first and ask questions later." He recalled Kai Rasmussen's warning at Camp Savage that in the Pacific they could be shot not only by the enemy but also mistakenly by other Americans. Kazuo made sure his men spent time mingling with the other GIs, hoping they would be recognized as fellow Americans in the heat of combat. The loss of a man to friendly fire worried him even more than enemy action, especially after some U.S. Army cooks who were Chinese were mistaken for Japanese as they showered outside in broad daylight on another island and were gunned down by Marines. His men couldn't help that they had the visage of the enemy, but as a precaution Kazuo implored them to speak Japanese only during interrogations and to speak English at all other times.*

Guadalcanal in the Solomon Islands chain was the next stop for the 37th Division and Kazuo's team, although by the time they arrived in April 1943 the fighting there had ended, other than some isolated pockets of resistance. The first major island offensive against Japan was fought there from August 1942 to February 1943, when after bitter fighting and rampant diseases took a heavy toll on both sides the Japanese evacuated by barges under the cover of fog and darkness their last ten thousand men from the island. By then, they had sustained losses estimated at twenty-five thousand dead—nearly

* Typical of the xenophobia sweeping the nation following Pearl Harbor, a *Time* magazine article, "How to Tell Your Friends from the Japs," published on December 21, 1941, provided "a few rules of thumb" for telling Chinese and Japanese apart. "The Chinese expression is likely to be more placid, kindly, open; the Japanese more dogmatic, arrogant . . . Japanese are hesitant, nervous in conversation, laugh loudly at the wrong time, and walk stiffly erect, hard-heeled. Chinese, more relaxed, have an easy gait."

fifteen thousand in battle and another nine thousand from disease. Allied losses were more than seven thousand killed and four thousand wounded or sick. Prevailing against the Japanese at Guadalcanal had been a costly but significant early victory in the Pacific.

There were no prisoners remaining on Guadalcanal for Kazuo's team to interrogate, even for practice. Most of the some eight hundred POWs taken there had been Koreans conscripted into the Japanese army and shipped to the Pacific as "patriotic labor corps" after receiving limited military training; by all accounts, they saw little reason to die in combat for the emperor and welcomed surrender at the first opportunity. Kazuo was shocked to learn that only about one hundred Japanese soldiers were captured at Guadalcanal. They had already been moved to POW camps in New Caledonia and New Zealand, but a cache of unread documents remained behind. Kazuo's team began reading, paying particular attention to enemy maps and any documents containing unit identifications. More absorbing reading came from inside boxes filled with little books, many of them stained with dried blood—diaries taken from the bodies of dead Japanese soldiers. The handwriting in sosho cursive was not made with the artistry of a calligrapher but in the scrawl of soldiers writing in a jungle foxhole, and was often difficult to decipher. The Japanese at Guadalcanal who faced the first major counterattack of U.S. forces in the Pacific war were fighting not only American Marines and infantrymen but also rampant disease and hunger. In many diaries, Kazuo noted that the Japanese name for Guadalcanal was rendered with characters that meant "Starvation Island."

After six months in the Pacific, Kazuo began to feel as if he was always chasing a fight that had left him behind. Then, in July 1943, in the sweltering jungles of New Georgia, he finally caught up with the shooting war.

————————

A volcanic island two hundred miles northwest of Guadalcanal, New Georgia is one of the largest islands in the Solomons. Fifty miles long and half again as wide, this supersized South Seas isle is no tropical paradise. Its interior, swathed in unremitting heat and humidity, is an inhospitable mix of rain forest, flooded swamps, marshes choked in mangroves, and low-slung mountains, the highest of which is Mount Masse, at 2,820 feet. In the nineteenth century, the rule of the island's last chief of headhunters was ended by a British colonial army, and New Georgia was declared a British protectorate. A century later, much of its interior remained unexplored.

Landing on New Georgia early in the war, the Japanese built an airfield at Munda Point on the southwest coast and docks on the northwest shore at Bairoko Harbor. Achieving air and naval superiority were key in the South Pacific, and by summer 1943 some fourteen thousand Japanese were entrenched there under orders to hold the island at all costs.

For the Allies, driving the enemy from the Solomon Islands would end Japan's invasion threat to Australia and New Zealand, and provide a stepping stone toward the drive to liberate the Philippines. But before that happened, the capture of strategic New Georgia had to be next. While few Americans had heard of this wretched spot, it was about to see some of the most grueling fighting yet. Before it was over, what was planned as a two-week campaign involving about eight thousand men turned into a brutal month-long struggle for some twenty-five thousand U.S. soldiers and Marines. For many of them, it was a baptism by fire they would not soon forget.

Preparations for the New Georgia landings began with an amphibious assault that overwhelmed a small enemy garrison on Rendova. Only eight miles of the Blanche Channel separated Rendova and New Georgia. The 43rd Infantry Division, a National Guard unit from Connecticut, was designated the main New Georgia attack force. Like the 37th Division, which was to be held in reserve with some of its units at Rendova but most of the division remaining on Guadalcanal, the 43rd had never been in combat. The New Georgia invasion was scheduled for early July, with two regiments of the 43rd hitting the southern shore to capture the Munda airfield, and other units in the north to take Bairoko Harbor.

When advance elements of the 43rd Division landed at New Georgia's Zanana Beach, some five miles east of Munda, on July 2, they faced no opposition, and quickly set up defensive positions to allow the rest of their men, equipment, and artillery to be brought in by landing craft. The rain had not let up for a week, and in the downpour the 169th and 172nd Regiments made ready for their trek to the air-field. On a topographic map, their objective didn't look far away, but these rookie infantrymen were about to find out that an advance of any distance in the jungle against a seasoned, well-prepared foe could be a very long way.

The planners of the operation did not expect the Munda force to meet serious opposition until they neared the heavily defended air-field. The overall ground commander, Major General John Hester, whose last combat experience harked back to the Pancho Villa Expe-dition in Mexico in 1916, planned to capture the airfield on July 7. But by that date, his forces were only leaving the beachhead at Zanana and starting forward on the Munda Trail, a native footpath waist deep in places with stagnant water and thick mud. Forced to proceed single file, the men at the front hacked back overgrown bamboo vines, some of which grew a foot or more in a single day. Solid walls of vegetation reduced visibility in every direction.

Among the enemy forces waiting on the Munda Trail was the 229th Regiment, 38th Infantry Division, of the Imperial Japanese Army. It had already been a long war for this outfit, originally comprised of farmers and timbermen conscripted from the Gifu Prefecture, a landlocked region of central Japan known for its forests and arable plains. They had started with the Second Sino-Japanese War in China in the late 1930s, gone on to the conquest of Hong Kong in 1941 and then the Dutch East Indies in early 1942, followed by Guadalcanal later that year. One battalion had been sent to New Guinea, where by January 1943 it had been decimated at Buna-Gona. Its two remaining battalions were sent to work on fortifications at Japan's large mili-tary base at Rabaul in Papua New Guinea before being rushed to help defend New Georgia. While they received a substantial number of replacements before arriving, a nucleus in the regiment had seen action in China, and were tough, disciplined fighters. They set up deadly blocks along the Munda Trail with fields of fire cleared for their mortars, light machine guns, and Type 92 heavy machine guns secured in camouflaged pillboxes behind logs stacked several feet high. They placed mortars and, farther back, artillery positions to rain death and destruction down on the trail.

That first day, the GIs made it less than a half mile before walking blindly into the first ambush. The *tat-tat-tat* of a lone machine gun opened up on their right flank, immediately followed by a chorus of weapons firing from all sides. They had met the enemy on his ground and his terms, and the fight to get past this first ambush took two days, and cost six American lives and thirty wounded.

What happened at that first trail block would occur time and again as the Americans found themselves confronted by a network of well-sited and expertly prepared Japanese defensive positions. Pinned down on the narrow path by deadly fire from an enemy that was all but invisible, they were unable to spread out and attack with flanking movements by squads or platoons taught in the Army training sylla-bus. Jungle warfare was a different kind of fight, and for inexperienced infantrymen it was a confusing and terrifying introduction to combat.

From his headquarters on Rendova, far removed from the action, General Hester made a fateful decision. When he was told how slowly the two regiments were progressing through the jungle, he ordered the 172nd to turn back and proceed farther up the shoreline to secure a new beachhead at Laiana, where supplies from Rendova could be landed and brought into the jungle on a shorter route, and from which the 172nd could attack the airfield from the rear while the 169th con-tinued along the Munda Trail in a frontal assault. Splitting his forces was not textbook, and the gap left by the departing 172nd was wide open. In fact, there was soon so much jungle between the two regi-ments that the Japanese seized the opportunity to place a full bat-talion between them, cutting them off from providing or receiving any mutual support, and in position to bombard the new landings at Laiana Beach with artillery and mortars.[*]

After two days of combat and a third day traversing the jungle, there had been little opportunity for the men of the 169th to sleep. Exhausted and alone on the trail, they dug in that night without estab-lishing a perimeter defense veteran jungle fighters had learned to rely on, such as laying trip wires with tin cans that rattled when struck.

---

[*] Hester's decision to separate his two regiments would later be judged as "per-haps the worst blunder in the most unintelligently waged land campaign in the Pacific" by no less an authority than the Pulitzer Prize–winning military historian Samuel Eliot Morison.

Like a shade pulled down, darkness came quickly in the jungle. Not more than fifteen minutes later, Japanese troops commenced nighttime harassment tactics: after a barrage of mortar rounds to announce their arrival, they moved noisily in the bush, rattled their equipment, shouted in Japanese, cursed in broken English, fired rifles and machine guns, and threw grenades, all while daring the Yankees to come out and fight. Some jittery GIs responded by throwing grenades blindly in the dark that struck trees and bounced back, exploding near their own foxholes. Other men fired indiscriminately until their guns emptied.

The 169th Regiment had made little progress after five days. Its bloodied and fatigued battalions were scattered along the trail, with units passing through each other and little coordination between them. Enduring hunger and thirst, lack of sleep, an unforgiving jungle, and constant attacks by day and nonstop harassment at night, men were succumbing to what the medics diagnosed as "neurosis" in numbers no one had yet seen in the war. Many were tagged by medics as unfit to fight and sent back with other casualties.*

Admiral William Halsey, in charge of land and sea operations in the Solomon Islands, was distressed at how badly things were going on New Georgia. Not only were the two regiments of the southern force split in half and the 169th stalled on the Munda Trail, still not near their airfield objective, but the northern force had been unsuccessful in its attacks at Bairoko Harbor against strong Japanese defenses. The first remedy was for Hester to be replaced as overall ground commander of the operation by Major General Oscar Griswold, a combat veteran. Hester, whom Griswold judged "too nice for a battle soldier," was soon on his way home with what was officially described as exhaustion from combat.

* The neurotic disorder caused by the stress of war and combat was called "shell shock" in World War I, "neurosis" or "combat fatigue" in World War II, and, in recent times, post-traumatic stress disorder, or PTSD. Regardless of the era or the name, the symptoms are the same: hypersensitivity to stimuli such as noises, movements, and lights; overactive responses that include involuntary defensive jerking and jumping (startle reactions); easy irritability progressing even to acts of violence; and sleep disturbances including battle dreams, nightmares, and inability to sleep.

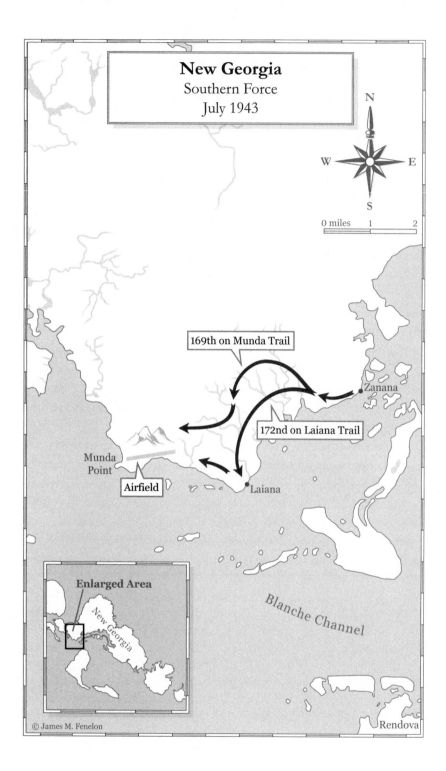

New Georgia
Southern Force
July 1943

N
W   E
S

0 miles   1   2

169th on Munda Trail

Zanana

172nd on Laiana Trail

Munda
Point

Airfield

Laiana

Blanche Channel

Enlarged Area

New Georgia

© James M. Fenelon

Rendova

Other heads rolled, too. The commander of the 169th Regiment—halted and disorganized on the Munda Trail—was sacked along with his entire staff, to be replaced by a regimental commander from the 37th Division, still sitting idle on Rendova waiting to be committed to the fight.

On Rendova in the afternoon of July 10, Colonel Temple Holland, commander of the 145th Regiment, 37th Division, gathered his staff and told them they would be going with him in the morning to New Georgia, where he was to take command of the struggling 169th Regiment.

Holland, who had spent half his life in the Army, was in his mid-forties—a "mature colonel," in Army lingo. He was a large, square-shouldered Texan who stood a helmet taller than many of his officers and men. Even his voice was outsized, in tone and volume. Holland's reputation as a hard-charger was enhanced by his customary stance, burly arms akimbo, and an unblinking glare that bore into subordinates with whom he was displeased. After a variety of assignments during the previous two decades, more recently he had held a top staff position (G4 Logistics) for Lieutenant General Robert Eichelberger during the two-division offensive at Buna-Gona on the north coast of New Guinea in January 1943, the first major Allied victory against the Imperial Japanese Army. A month later, Holland was rewarded with command of his own infantry regiment, an outfit that had been lagging badly in training at Fiji. He set out to whip them into shape. However, the tall Texan did have some crazy ideas when it came to indoctrinating men for combat. After acquiring a bunch of empty fifty-gallon drums, he had them filled with blood and guts from a local slaughterhouse. He lined up the regiment—everyone had to strip to the waist—and made the men dip their arms into the bloody offal and smear it over their chests. When word of the bizarre exercise reached the division's commanding general, he raised hell with Holland and forbade any more brutish exhibitions.

But Holland's well-known aggressiveness seemed to fit the bill for what was needed for the 169th Regiment now stalled on the Munda Trail. The situation was so dire that a complete housecleaning was

Colonel Temple Holland (far left), ordered to break the
deadly impasse on New Georgia

ordered.* Changes in field commands were commonplace, but replac-
ing all the staff officers in one unit with officers from another was
not. Yet Holland was instructed to bring his staff with him, ten officers in all—including his second-in-command, operations officer,
and intelligence officer—along with five sergeants and a dozen other
enlisted men who had manned his regimental command post. He also
requested a pair of what he called "Nisei Jap interpreters" from the
37th Division's MIS team.

When Kazuo Komoto learned the names of the two men Captain
Ayres had selected to send with Holland, he pointed out that one of

---

* The performance of the 169th Regiment during its first week on New Georgia
was so poor that the Army's inspector general conducted an investigation, which
found many deficiencies in the regiment's training: no tactical exercises in which
Japanese methods of night fighting were simulated; no exercises for spotting and
demolishing enemy jungle emplacements; no system of night defense rehearsed;
no training as a combat team. In addition, the physical condition of the National
Guard troops, whose age averaged thirty-two, had deteriorated as a result of
being used as a labor force in the tropics for nine months prior to combat.

them was expecting orders any day to return to the U.S. for a new assignment. Kazuo volunteered to go to New Georgia in his place, along with twenty-three-year-old George Tokunaga, of Kailua-Kona on the Big Island of Hawaii.

"No, I need you here," said Ayres, who was to remain with the MIS team on Rendova until the division was committed to the New Georgia fight.

"I can be of help, sir," Kazuo said, pointing out that, unlike some of the men, his Japanese and English were equally strong. As the team's leading noncom, he continued, he should be among the first to see action. "It's important I do this. How else can I tell them what to expect?"

The captain relented, and methodically went over with Kazuo what he might face on New Georgia. They had no idea if there would be as few prisoners to interrogate as there had been at Guadalcanal, but they did know it had become a common boast among GIs that they took no prisoners. There were many reasons for this attitude, starting with how much U.S. soldiers hated the Japanese for the Pearl Harbor sneak attack and for the way they were known to mistreat American and Allied POWs. Although the American public had not yet learned about the 1942 Bataan Death March in the Philippines, President Roosevelt had shocked the nation three months earlier when he announced "with the deepest horror" that three of the Doolittle Raiders who flew off an aircraft carrier and bombed Tokyo in April 1942 had been tried in a Japanese court and convicted of killing civilians, and had been executed by firing squad.

There were myriad other reasons that made the capture of Japanese soldiers by U.S. forces difficult and so far somewhat of a rarity: the ferocity with which the Japanese fought and died; their belief that surrender dishonored their emperor and their families; and the pure logistics of dealing with POWs, wounded or otherwise, in the middle of a jungle. There had been reports of Japanese soldiers who could have been brought in for interrogation being slain in the field instead. Throughout the Pacific, intelligence officers were now beseeching infantry commanders to tell their men that every time they killed an enemy soldier they could have brought back for questioning they might indirectly be killing a dozen or more of their buddies due to a loss of valuable intelligence. They were also told to let their men know they wouldn't be doing the Japanese any favors by taking them prisoner, as they preferred an honorable death in combat to the shame of capture.

Ayres reminded Kazuo that when he got to New Georgia he should spread the word about the value of bringing in not only enemy prisoners but also any documents, maps, dog tags, clothing, and anything else they came across that might help identify their units. Once he had a unit number, Kazuo could look in his Order of Battle book to ascertain the unit's strength, equipment, weaponry, and everything else U.S. intelligence knew about its capabilities. He would also attempt to pinpoint through interrogations and documents the location of enemy positions and possible targets for U.S. artillery and air strikes. One incentive when it came to collecting documents and other items that had helped elsewhere was to pass the word to the men that the interpreters would translate or identify any papers or objects brought to them, and if they had no intelligence value they would get them back as souvenirs.

At 7:00 the next morning, Holland and his party were delivered by small landing craft to Zanana Beach. They formed up, gathered their equipment, and entered the jungle. The temperature was close to 100 degrees, with the humidity hovering at 90 percent. Kazuo's first impression was that he had stepped fully clothed into a steam bath.

As they pushed up the winding trail, unable to see more than ten to twenty feet in any direction, Kazuo had the feeling they were being watched. If so, the enemy had the advantage. They could decide to fade back into the jungle or spring an ambush. His unease was heightened as they passed markers with kanji characters in black ink that had been applied with a brush on pieces of board nailed to trees or drawn onto tree trunks. They appeared to be directional and location markers.

Kazuo's thoughts leapt ahead. *Would he soon face someone he knew? Even his own brother?* His younger brother Shogo had also been sent as a boy to Japan, but unlike Kazuo he had stayed there for college. The last they heard from Shogo, who had always been a good student, he was attending an engineering college in Tokyo. Then came Pearl Harbor, and not a word since. Shogo would now be twenty-three, and might well have been drafted into the Imperial Japanese Army. Same for Kazuo's schoolmates from his ten years in Japan. Were any of them fighting here?

When they caught up with the rear elements of the 169th, Holland began issuing orders. They arrived at the regimental command post at 11 a.m. Holland quickly sized up the situation he faced, and deemed it completely out of control. The hard wire for phone communications with the regiment's three battalions had been cut by enemy patrols. The regiment was at slightly less than 50 percent strength, and he could see that the men were jittery, dispirited, and exhausted after a week of jungle fighting and little sleep. Furthermore, every morning about half of the regiment's riflemen were running supplies back and forth from the regimental depot to the forward units in the jungle. He stopped this immediately and assigned clerks and other nonessential personnel to make the morning runs to keep his fighting men ready to fight. He was told about the nightly harassment, and how patrols couldn't locate the perpetrators in the morning. Holland sent out reconnaissance patrols to serve as his eyes and ears. Advising them to stay off the trails, where they could easily be ambushed, he told them to stay out for up to a week, and send runners back to him with any vital information as to enemy positions or movements. Next, he replaced several regimental officers with his own trusted people. Then, with his handpicked staff, he worked on a new attack plan.

That night, to guard against unwanted visits by the enemy, Holland moved his battalions into a cloverleaf perimeter. He made it clear that he wanted none of his men moving around in the jungle at night, but to remain in their foxholes. Anyone in the jungle at night was fair game to be shot. To prevent the undisciplined discharge of weapons and the wasting of ammunition, he had his officers designate those riflemen on the outside perimeter and a select few crack shots inside the perimeter as the only people who would fire at night. He also had telephone wire strung outside the perimeter as trip wires, and at numerous locations they were rigged with grenades to explode on contact. He next ordered new four-man foxholes to be dug, with the men teaming up in pairs, keeping two men on guard while two slept. With their defenses newly organized and disciplined, the level of nighttime harassment diminished greatly, and the fatigued men got more rest.

To carry out his new plan of attack, Holland the next morning undertook a consolidation of the regiment, which first meant bringing
the three battalions close enough to each other that they were to operate while in contact with one another for the first time. He was explicit
in how he wanted them positioned: in a column, six hundred yards
between each battalion, and each one occupying three hundred yards
in diameter.

Holland launched his attack before dawn on July 12, but it soon
bogged down, in part because the battalions became intermingled
in the shadows of the jungle. When they disentangled and resumed
the attack, they once again faltered in the face of heavy opposition
from enemy machine guns, mortars, and artillery situated on the high
ground. Pulling his men back, Holland radioed headquarters for air
support the next day.

The question he now faced was whether he should accept his losses
and sit tight or move out in force toward the objective and let the
situation develop as they went along. It didn't take him long to make
his decision.

At 10:00 the following morning, a dozen carrier-based dive bombers dropped one-thousand-pound bombs on the enemy positions
along the ridges. The effect was not only to scatter the enemy, but
also for the explosions to thin out the jungle growth enough to permit
some visibility. After U.S. artillery opened up, Holland committed his
three battalions in a frontal assault. Infantrymen clambered over fallen
trees and shell craters to attack Japanese machine gunners in pillboxes
with only their rifles and bayonets. To anyone who had fought in the
trenches of Europe in the previous war, the scene would have been
tragically reminiscent of infantry charges on the Western Front, where
high casualties were sustained for short gains. First Battalion ran head-
on into enemy opposition and suffered so many casualties that it had
to withdraw to its original position, and 2nd Battalion limped back
after suffering serious casualties from friendly artillery fire that fell
short into their lines. But 3rd Battalion fought its way forward and
after four hours secured a ridge. Digging in to hold it, they beat off
several counterattacks. At day's end they still held the ridge, although
at a cost of more than a hundred casualties. In the morning, after a
barrage of U.S. mortars and artillery rounds zeroed in on their posi-

tions, the enemy withdrew from the opposite ridge, which 2nd Battalion quickly occupied. As a regiment, the 169th at last was making some progress on the Munda Trail.

At the regimental command post with Holland, not far from the bloody battle for the twin ridges, Kazuo and Tokunaga were eager to use their training to interrogate their first POWs, but so far no such luck. They were, however, brought captured documents to translate. There was a rough map with the disposition of static defenses and a sketch that showed a system of intersecting trails, as well as a few personal letters.*

It rained the night of July 14, all night long.

Taking directions from a veteran sergeant, Kazuo and Tokunaga used their trench shovels to dig a two-man foxhole near where Holland and his intelligence officer were dug in as they wanted to keep the interpreters close by. Even depressions as shallow as twelve inches would save lives and prevent casualties, they were told, but a depth of two to three feet provided better protection from bullets and shrapnel. They took the advice and made their foxhole three feet deep, wide enough for them and their gear, and slightly longer than their frames.

Kazuo spent his last night on New Georgia stretched out in the foxhole, not sleeping, but alternating lying on his back and sides, his only protection from the pelting rain a poncho pulled over his head. He and Tokunaga had been warned not to get up at night because they could easily be mistaken for the enemy and shot on the spot. They were told that Japanese marines, dressed in camouflage that looked a lot like what the GIs were wearing, had already been killed infiltrating their lines.

* Only about twenty Japanese soldiers were taken prisoner on New Georgia. The diary of one Japanese officer, Toshihiro Oura, a platoon leader of an antiaircraft artillery unit stationed near the Munda airfield, was recovered, and translated by Dye Ogata and Frank Sanwo of the 37th Division's MIS team. Providing a trove of intelligence, it described his unit's morale and leadership, the accuracy of U.S. aerial and ground bombardments, and the effectiveness of Japanese weaponry. Oura did not survive the fighting on the island, unlike his at times poignant writings about his family in Japan, his increasing doubts about the war, his despair and bitterness toward the Imperial General Staff, as well as his own health and the fate of some of his men.

By dawn's first light of July 15, 1943, the two Nisei were nearly sub-merged in mud. As they crawled out of the morass, the men around them were also emerging from their flooded foxholes. Rising from his own foxhole was a bedraggled Holland. Caked in mud from head to foot, the colonel and his men looked like poster boys for the infantry.

The command post was a beehive of activity that morning. Since no Japanese armored tanks had been reported, Holland ordered a redistribution of men from the regiment's antitank company to where they were most needed: sixty of them to the understrength 2nd Battalion and twenty to 1st Battalion. He received a report that 3rd Battalion continued to hold the ridge it had fought so hard to win, although it had been hit by an enemy artillery barrage after midnight that killed eight men and wounded twenty-six. Enemy snipers were harassing the route used for medical evacuations off the ridge and to bring supplies up to 3rd Battalion.

Around 11 a.m., Holland, realizing that his command post was more than five hundred yards from the fighting, decided he wanted it to be closer to the action. They packed up and made it forward about fifty yards before a machine gun opened up. No one was hit, and they scrambled back to their foxholes. The command post, Holland reluctantly decided, would stay put for now.

After the enemy gun was taken out, it went quiet.

Back in their foxhole, Kazuo and Tokunaga, neither of whom had slept since landing on New Georgia four days earlier, opened C ration tins and washed down hard sausages and crackers with warm water from their canteens. Around 2:00, Kazuo got up to stretch his legs.

Nearby stood Holland, barking more orders to underlings.

Suddenly, a hail of bullets whizzed past Kazuo's ears, some thud-ding into the earth around him. Before he could dive for cover, he was hit in the right leg, which buckled underneath him. He collapsed.

George Tokunaga dragged him back into the foxhole. At first Ka-zuo didn't realize he had been shot. But then his right leg felt like it was on fire, except for his foot, which felt like he had walked barefoot on ice. He looked down to see if his leg was intact, which it was. Someone yelled for a medic, but Tokunaga didn't wait. He tore open Kazuo's bloody trouser leg and saw an oozing hole in his knee. He ripped open an envelope of sulfa powder and sprinkled it on the wound to prevent infection.

Next, was it seconds or minutes? Kazuo realized a medic was hunched over him, tightening a tourniquet on his thigh to staunch blood loss, then injecting him with a shot. The world went fuzzy after that, but he later recalled being told they found a sniper near the command post and took care of him. Kazuo was dimly aware of being hauled through the steaming jungle on a stretcher. He then waited on the beach before eventually being loaded into an LST that had brought ashore armored vehicles and now held rows of stretcher cases.

Kazuo ended up on the USS *Tryon* (APH-1), a U.S. Navy transport with a dual mission—to support invasions by bringing in fresh troops, and to save the lives of those wounded in action by rendering expert medical attention in well-equipped facilities close to the beachhead. From a doctor aboard the *Tryon*, Kazuo received some good news. Even though he had been shot by a light machine gun, he was lucky. It had to do with the smaller caliber of the Japanese rounds; had he had been hit by a more powerful slug, such as from a U.S. machine gun or an M1 rifle, it would have shattered his patella and destroyed ligaments in the joint, crippling him. Instead, the bullet had caused a perforating wound by entering at the back of the knee and exiting in front, just missing his kneecap.

Although it didn't really matter who the sniper had been aiming for when he squeezed the trigger, Kazuo couldn't help but speculate. He had heard stories about the Japanese having highly trained snipers who waited long hours or even days to nail a good target. As a Japanese American in the U.S. Army, he knew he would be considered a traitor by soldiers of the Imperial Japanese Army, and it was possible that he had been targeted by the sniper. That risk had been pointed out at Camp Savage, and Kazuo's team had discussed it among themselves. But when he was shot he had been near Holland, the big Texan with the booming voice. *If the sniper was aiming for me*, Kazuo decided, *he was a good shot. If he was aiming for the loud-mouthed colonel, he was a lousy shot*. Either way, as the guys on the ward liked to say, his ticket home had been punched.

A week after he had been shot, Kazuo was surprised to see the commanding general of the 37th Division, Major General Robert Beightler, along with Captain Ayres, standing next to his upper-level hospital bunk. The *Tryon* had just arrived the day before off Longo Point, Guadalcanal, to pick up more patients. The general carried a small rectangular case, which he opened to reveal a Purple Heart medal, awarded to members of the military wounded or killed in action.

Kazuo had never seen a Purple Heart, and it was striking. Fastened to a satiny purple ribbon, the heart-shaped medal—also purple, with a gold border—bore the embossed profile of America's first president, George Washington. It was surprising to Kazuo that a general came to give him the award. The *Tryon* deck log told the story: "0820 Major General Beightler came aboard to decorate wounded patient." As the other beds were filled with wounded from other divisions, the commanding general of the 37th Division was indeed there for Kazuo. When Ayres told him the division was being committed to the fight on New Georgia and would be leaving in the morning, Kazuo knew Beightler would soon be awarding many more Purple Hearts.

"Sergeant, you need a shave," the general said.

"Yes, sir." Kazuo couldn't remember the last time he'd used a razor.

Ayres reached up to grasp Kazuo's hand.

Kazuo smiled wanly. He was sorry to be leaving the captain in the lurch. If he had remained with the team instead of volunteering, he would be going with them in the morning. But instead he was heading home with a hole in his knee and a Purple Heart pinned on his pajamas.

An hour after Beightler and Ayres departed, the *Tryon* was under way for New Caledonia. When they arrived three days later, Kazuo was moved to Noumea Hospital, where his injured leg was placed in a plaster of paris cast to immobilize it. Then, on July 31, he was taken back aboard the *Tryon,* which sailed for Fiji, where two days later he entered a large military hospital.

About that same time, a telegram from the adjutant general of the Army was delivered to the Gila River Relocation Center, where Kazuo's parents and younger brothers had been interned in the Arizona desert for the past year. His brother Kiyoshi, then twelve, remembered years later the day being "cloudy, sultry, no wind," and his foreboding that "something bad was going to happen." Then came the

wire that caused his mother to break down and cry like no one had
seen her cry before.

WASHINGTON DC 7-30-43

MRS. HISANO KOMOTO
 REGRET TO INFORM YOU YOUR SON SERGEANT KAZUO
KOMOTO WAS SERIOUSLY WOUNDED IN ACTION ON FIFTEEN
JULY IN THE SOUTHWEST PACIFIC AREA. YOU WILL BE ADVISED
AS SOON AS REPORTS OF CONDITION IS RECEIVED.

Kazuo heard the news in early August that the Munda airfield had
been captured and Bairoko Harbor abandoned by the Japanese defenders. In the big picture, the defeat of the Japanese at New Georgia
signaled a new phase of the war in the Pacific: the beginning of a sustained American strategic offensive, island by island. But like most
GIs, Kazuo wasn't thinking of the big picture. He only hoped that
his foxhole buddy, George Tokunaga, his captain, Gil Ayres, and the
rest of the team had made it.*

In August, Fiji had a VIP visitor from Washington, D.C.

For security reasons, there had been no public announcement
ahead of First Lady Eleanor Roosevelt's trip to the South Pacific to
visit military camps and hospitals. Wherever she showed up, it was
to the surprise of GIs, medical staffs, and patients alike. She and the
others in her party were limited to forty-four pounds of luggage each
on their four-engine Army B-24 Liberator bomber converted to a
transport. That she had arranged to travel in the field uniform of
the American Red Cross (an organization she nominally headed), she
wrote a friend, solved a potential wardrobe problem given the weight

---

* Nearly 1,100 U.S. soldiers were killed at New Georgia, and 3,900 were
wounded, although the latter figure does not include the 2,500 men diagnosed
with "war neuroses" (700 from the 169th Regiment alone). The Japanese toll was
an estimated 2,500 killed. When the battle on the island was lost, the Japanese
commander, Minoru Sasaki, whose forces were outnumbered nearly three to
one, ordered the successful nighttime evacuation by barge of more than 9,000
soldiers to fight another day.

restriction. (Ten years earlier, dress designers had chosen her as "the best dressed woman in the United States.") She also brought with her a typewriter, on which she wrote her daily column, "My Day," syndicated in ninety newspapers. Her plane departed from Hamilton Field near San Francisco on August 17, 1943, just a few days after she helped her husband entertain British Prime Minister Winston Churchill and his daughter, Mary, at the Roosevelt estate in Hyde Park. Before his wife left for the war zone, the president asked her to "see as many of the men as you can." By the time she returned to the White House five weeks later, she had logged twenty-three thousand miles and visited Australia, New Zealand, and seventeen smaller islands, including Guadalcanal, where Admiral Halsey, who initially was skeptical of her visit and thought it could be a colossal waste of time, observed her up close. He later wrote,

> When I say she inspected hospitals, I don't mean that she shook hands with the chief medical officer, glanced into a sun parlor, and left. I mean that she went into every ward, stopped at every bed, and spoke to every patient. What was his name? How did he feel? Was there anything he needed? Could she take a message home for him? I marveled at her hardihood, both physical and mental, she walked for miles, and she saw patients who were grievously and gruesomely wounded. But I marveled most at their expressions as she leaned over them. It was a sight I will never forget.

The first lady's plane landed on Fiji on August 23, and after a good night's sleep—her first on a real mattress since leaving the United States (an Army cot, she wrote a friend, "would not be my permanent choice for a bed")—she set out to tour the island's two hospitals, one with 903 patients and the other with 843, most of them battle casualties from the fighting in the Solomons but many suffering from malaria and other jungle diseases, as well as those diagnosed with severe combat fatigue.

When she arrived on Kazuo's ward, the doctor on duty—a young Army captain—made a point to bring her to his bedside for an introduction. Kazuo quickly sat up in bed. She shook his hand warmly. He

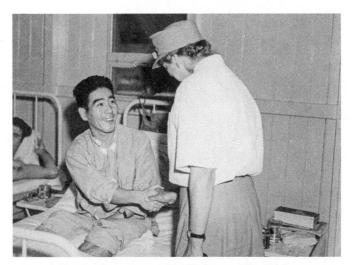

During her tour of Pacific bases, First Lady
Eleanor Roosevelt visits the bedside of the wounded
Kazuo Komoto in a Fiji hospital, August 1943.

beamed, thinking how Mrs. Roosevelt looked just like her pictures in
the newspapers and newsreels. Her blue eyes were alight with interest, and a Red Cross cap sat atop her silver hair worn in a small bun.
She asked how he was feeling, and they chatted. She put him at ease
with the little things she said in the manner of a mother and in a voice
that was high-pitched and yet soft and affectionate. When she asked
if there was any message she could take back to the president, Kazuo
screwed up his courage to tell her what was on his mind, even if he
got in trouble later. After all, he'd already been shot; what could the
brass do to him that would hurt any worse?

"Mrs. Roosevelt, my parents and little brothers are in a camp
back home because they're Japanese. And I'm out here getting shot.
Something isn't right. I wasn't even allowed to visit them before going
overseas."

It still stung that he had been refused a travel pass to visit his family after his MISLS graduation because no Japanese—not even Nisei
servicemen—were being allowed to travel on their own in the western
states.

Mrs. Roosevelt told Kazuo she had recently visited an internment
camp. "I can tell you they are being well taken care of," she said.

"But it's a raw deal," said Kazuo. "They're locked up, lost their home"—he was surprised to hear his voice cracking—"while I'm here."

"Our president is doing his best to correct any wrongs," she said, not departing from the official script, even though she had her own concerns about the mass internment policy. In fact, she was on record as favoring a new policy of releasing those individuals as jobs could be lined up for them outside the western states. While not explaining this to Kazuo, she assured him she would convey his strong feelings to the president.

Does she really mean that? He wanted to believe that she did.

The doctor spoke up forcefully. "Mrs. Roosevelt, our Nisei soldiers like the sergeant are facing two enemies. One enemy is out here shooting at them. The other one is back home."

She seemed taken aback by the doctor's bold assertion.

"Guess I better look both ways," Kazuo said, "and duck next time."

He had taken her off the hook, and Mrs. Roosevelt chuckled.

In the days that followed, Kazuo felt increasingly ashamed about putting the first lady on the spot. He should have been more respectful. He had allowed his emotions to show, and that wasn't right. She was a real lady and a good person and, yes, the president's wife. She had come all this way to tour the hospital wards and talk to the wounded, and he shouldn't have spilled out his anger about his family's situation at home.

Kazuo was sent stateside on a hospital ship in September, and spent another month rehabilitating at the new, 2,540-bed Hammond Army Hospital in Modesto, California. A little more than one hundred days after he had been shot in the jungle of New Georgia, he walked out of the hospital into the California sunshine on a crisp fall day, with some scars but no limp. Granted thirty days of medical leave, he had no trouble this time securing a train ticket to Arizona, as some of the travel restrictions had been lifted.

It had been two years since he had seen his parents and brothers— since before Pearl Harbor—and he was eager for a visit. In a letter he wrote to them in August from the hospital in Fiji, he had assured them that he was receiving wonderful medical care, and that the doctors

Anti-Japanese sign in Arizona

expected his injured leg to heal and for him to walk normally again. He told them, too, about his commanding general making a special trip to pin a Purple Heart on him.

Kazuo took the train to Phoenix. Before boarding a bus the last thirty miles to Gila River, he spotted a small grocery and went inside to use his ration stamps to buy fresh meat to take to his family in camp.

At the display counter in the back of the store, he pointed to some cuts he wanted to purchase when the butcher stopped him cold.

"I don't sell no meat to Japs!"

Kazuo stared at him. "I'm not a '*Jap.*'"

"What are you?"

"I'm an American."

"Yeah? I'm American too."

"But I'm in uniform, and you're not."

The man appeared to see the bemedaled uniform for the first time.

Kazuo had never slugged anyone—although he had come close when someone had called him a "Jap" in a Fresno pool hall before the war. He had invited that guy outside to the parking lot, and it could have gone either way; but they had talked it over, with Kazuo explaining that he had been born a few miles down the road and was as American as anyone else.

Facing the butcher now, Kazuo decided he was not going to turn around and leave empty-handed, and the butcher seemed to sense it.

"Now sell me something," Kazuo said, softly but firmly.

"Okay, okay, soldier. What'd you want?"

It was Sunday, October 31, 1943, when the bus stopped in front of the main gate of the Gila River Relocation Center and Kazuo

The Gila River Relocation Center, Arizona

stepped off with his canvas duffel bag slung over one shoulder and carrying a package wrapped in brown butcher paper. He stood rigid, staring at the sprawling encampment, home to more than thirteen thousand men, women, and children. Filled with blocks of military-style barracks, the camp had been built in the middle of nowhere. He quickly took in what he had only read about in newspapers—the armed guards, barbed wire, and gun towers—and resented it with all his might. In spite of what the residents had done to try to make it look like Main Street USA—he saw the landscaping and colorful gardens between the structures and boys playing baseball on a diamond, and heard the chatter and laughter from afar—the government had his family and other families *locked up* in the middle of the desert.

Was it for their own safety? Kazuo had read about Japanese-owned homes and businesses being burned down and Japanese residents refused service and treated like the enemy in their own hometown. He recalled an Old West story about Wyatt Earp convincing someone that the safest place when there's a lynch mob outside was locked in a jail cell.

Okay, he thought, *at least they're safe.*

Kazuo showed the Army guard at the gate his ID and leave papers, and was allowed to pass. It took him a while to find his family's block, and their tar-papered barrack. When he did, he rapped on their door.

His mother opened it and was shocked to see her soldier son standing before her, as he had not written them of his plans to visit so as not to disappoint if he was unable to make it. Three of his brothers, Susumu, Kiyoshi, and Teru, between the ages of ten and seventeen, were living with their parents and attending school at the camp taught by internee teachers, while the family's second-oldest son, twenty-two-

Kazuo Komoto visiting his family
at the Gila River Relocation Center, Arizona

Kazuo Komoto showing his Purple Heart
to his youngest brother, Susumu, at Gila River

year-old Tetsuo, had recently been able to leave Gila River for a job with Sears, Roebuck and Co. in Chicago.

The family had three small rooms separated with partitions that did not reach the ceiling, so everyone for the length of the entire barrack could hear the Komoto family's joyous reunion. Soon, neighbors poured inside; many of them Kazuo knew from home because all of the Japanese living in and around Sanger, California, had been picked up and interned together. Many hugs, handshakes, and pats on the back ensued.

Later, when they were alone on the front stoop, Kazuo's youngest brother, Susumu, asked to see where he was shot. Kazuo rolled up his pant leg. Then Susumu studied the Purple Heart medal Kazuo had brought to show the family. The boy told his big brother he was his hero.

Before he left a few days later, Kazuo was interviewed by an *Arizona Republic* reporter. An article appeared under the headline "An American Is Honored—Soldier Gets Purple Heart." It read, in part:

> Sgt. Kazuo Komoto really feels like an American now—not that he ever felt any other way, but his family was part of the 110,000 Japanese and Japanese Americans evacuated from the Pacific Coast after Pearl Harbor. Komoto visited at this relocation center last week while recuperating from a shattered knee—the work of a Jap sniper during the battle for New Georgia island.
>
> "You know," Komoto said, "getting wounded gives me an assurance that the American flag belongs to me—the red in it has been stained by my blood. And it belongs equally to countless others of many races who have shed their blood for it. Our flag is as near to our ideal of democracy as anything can be."

Before leaving, Kazuo made a couple of decisions that he didn't share with anyone. He saw how his parents lived with the upset and sadness of leaving their home and farm—his father, stoically so, his strong-willed mother more expressive in her sorrow. But neither outwardly complaining. And Kazuo concluded that there was no use in his complaining, either. Yes, his family had been treated unfairly, and he could go on about it to anyone he spoke to—as he had with Mrs. Roosevelt. No, it wasn't fair. But right now, the war had to come first.

Kazuo Komoto, the first Nisei in the Army awarded a Purple Heart for being wounded in action, would volunteer to return to the Pacific.

Eight

NORTH TO ALASKA

Nobuo Furuiye arrived in Minnesota on Thanksgiving Day 1942 for the second Military Intelligence Service Language School class at Camp Savage. Leaving behind his cushy job chauffeuring a colonel in Arkansas, Nobuo had traveled by rail with several other Nisei soldiers who had received orders to report to the school. They were among hundreds of Japanese American soldiers brought there for the next six-month class starting in December.

The train stopped a mile from the main gate, and Nobuo's group marched briskly in the dark the rest of the way, each with a heavy duffel bag slung over one shoulder. The ground was snow-packed and the temperature minus 20 degrees. It was bone-chilling for another reason: they had not been issued winter overcoats, mandatory in Minnesota but not in Arkansas, where in the dead of winter it was 50 degrees warmer.

Nobuo Furuiye

After showing their IDs and official orders, they passed through the gate and were escorted to an empty barrack, which they found was nearly as frigid inside as outside. The barrack had a single potbellied stove in the center of the room to heat the cavernous space, and they would soon discover that the bunks closest to the stove were too hot and the ones farther away too cold. The barrack was deserted, they were told, because everyone was at the mess hall for Thanksgiving dinner. Nobuo and the others hurried to join them, and made it just in time for turkey with all the trimmings.

The showers and latrines were in a building across the street, which meant running back and forth, dressed or partially undressed, in the sub-zero temperatures, as Nobuo learned in the morning. By the time he returned from his shower, his wet towel was frozen as stiff as a board.

Arriving students were given a written test to gauge their level of proficiency in Japanese. Thanks to his two years in Japan, culminating in his graduation from Kyushu Gakuin in 1938, Nobuo's score placed him in the fourth-highest-ranked class out of twenty. That meant there were three higher classes, and Nobuo soon realized how brilliant some of the students were in their command of Japanese. It did not surprise him to learn that there were GIs here with six years or more of schooling in Japan.

Classmates Nobuo Furuiye (standing, back row, far left)
and Tom Sakamoto (kneeling, middle row, far right) at
Kyushu Gakuin, one of the top high schools in Japan

Nobuo was delighted when one of his instructors turned out to be Tom Sakamoto, a good friend and classmate from his school days in Japan at Kyushu Gakuin. Tom told Nobuo about his time at the Army's first Japanese-language school that began a month before Pearl Harbor at the Presidio in San Francisco, and how after his graduation in May 1942 he had been selected to teach at Camp Savage. Nobuo's class would be Tom's second as an instructor—and his last, as it turned out.

Nobuo found the course work at Camp Savage to be a challenge. He had lost some of his proficiency in kanji characters—a clear case, he decided, of use it or lose it. At the same time, he was having to learn and retain characters representing technical military terms straight out of Imperial Japanese Army manuals recovered from battlefields. Nobuo found this kind of rote learning to be the most difficult part of the curriculum, and at times he struggled. He was a member of the unofficial "Latrine Study Group," composed of students who needed to keep studying after lights-out in the barracks. That's where Nobuo would be many nights, often until the wee hours of the morning, only reluctantly giving up his seat in a stall when someone had to use it for its intended purpose.

Given the urgency of sending more Japanese-language teams to the South Pacific, Camp Savage's second class was four times the size of its first. Nearly four hundred students, including Nobuo, graduated in June 1943, even after some sixty students washed out and were returned to their units.

After forming into ten-man teams, the new graduates awaited their orders. When they came, Nobuo found that the Army had another surprise for him. The first one had been when he didn't volunteer for the Minnesota school so he could stay in Arkansas—closer to where his fiancée, Toshie, was interned with her parents at the Jerome Relocation Center—but soon after, he received orders to Camp Savage anyway.

Now, his team wasn't going to the South Pacific as they all expected. They were headed north to Alaska.

The month before Nobuo Furuiye's Camp Savage class graduated, the only land battle of the war fought on American soil took place in May 1943 on the island of Attu, a thousand miles off the coast of Alaska.

A year earlier, the Japanese had launched a hit-and-run carrier strike against the U.S. base at Dutch Harbor on Amaknak Island, the most populated of the Aleutian Islands, a 1,200-mile chain of more than three hundred volcanic islands stretching from the Alaskan mainland to the far western edge of the Bering Sea. Japanese bombs destroyed more than a dozen Army and Navy aircraft, and left forty-three Americans dead and fifty injured, but did minimal damage to the harbor and airfield located a few hundred miles from the Alaskan mainland. Forty-eight hours later, the Japanese began landing troops on the two westernmost Aleutians: Attu and Kiska. Separated by two hundred miles of often stormy seas more typical of the North Atlantic than the Pacific, the islands averaged fewer than ten clear days a year, and most days were overcast and foggy with rain or snow, usually with high winds that occasionally reached hurricane force.

When the Imperial Japanese Army came ashore, the population of Attu was forty-five Aleuts and one white American couple, Charles and Etta Jones, a radio technician and a teacher, respectively. Charles and three Aleuts were killed in the attack, and everyone else was taken to a prison camp in Japan. Kiska was even less populated, with ten U.S. Navy sailors manning a weather station, and their pet dog, a German shepherd mix named Explosion. Two Americans were killed in that invasion, and the others were captured.

While the Japanese had no immediate plans to invade Alaska, their objective in taking the islands was to control and defend the northern perimeter of their expanding Pacific empire, to break up any offensive against their homeland by way of the Aleutians, and to prepare air bases there for future offensive action. But U.S. strategists soon ruled out striking Japan via the northern sea route as too risky and impractical, due largely to the extreme weather conditions. Thus, the far north was to become a tragic sideshow in the Pacific war, with each side sending troops to fight and die there for reasons other than military exigencies.

By spring 1943, the retaking of Attu and Kiska was at hand, after giving way for a year to higher-priority Allied operations in the South Pacific, such as the capture of Guadalcanal. The liberation of the Aleutians had been the subject of much debate among U.S. military and political leaders. Attu and Kiska might well have become a northernmost example of MacArthur's island-hopping strategy to save American lives in the South Pacific, wherein nonessential Japanese-held islands would be bypassed and cut off from resupply, the enemy troops on them left to starve. But in the Aleutians, that would have meant leaving the enemy on American soil and relatively close to the continental United States, neither of which were popular sentiments in Washington, and could erode the public's confidence and morale. The retaking of Attu came first, it was decided, because it lay at the westward end of the Aleutians (closer to Japan) and put U.S. forces in position to block any attempt to reinforce Kiska by ship from Japan.

On May 11, 1943, U.S. amphibious landings took place along the northern and eastern shores of Attu, which was approximately thirty-five miles long and fifteen miles wide. The Japanese defenders, composed of a single infantry battalion, were outnumbered four to one. In a shrewd defensive strategy, they did not oppose the initial landings. Instead, they placed their forces on higher rocky terrain, waiting for the more than twelve thousand U.S. infantrymen who landed to find them in the dense fog. As the GIs approached, the Japanese opened up with mortar, machine gun, and sniper fire from the higher ridges. When U.S. artillery and mortars zeroed in on their location, the Japanese disappeared back into the fog line, only to turn up in other nearly impregnable positions.

For the first week, the Japanese managed a coordinated defense, defending every ridge and valley, but ultimately the sheer numbers and overwhelming firepower of the U.S. forces took their toll. By the end of the second week, the Japanese had been pushed into a pocket in the mountains of northeastern Attu. Surrounded and running low on food, medical supplies, and ammunition, they faced the choice of surrendering or making a desperate counterattack. Their commander, Colonel Yasuyo Yamasaki, who had arrived on Attu a month earlier by submarine with orders to hold the island, chose the latter. He hoped that a surprise mass attack could break through the U.S. lines and seize an artillery battery and supply depot atop a prominent hill in the rear

Nobuo Furuiye in Adak, Alaska,
September 1943

area, then hold that position until reinforcements arrived by sea.

At 3:30 a.m. on May 29, every Japanese soldier who could walk set off in the dark on a silent march toward the Americans. Overpowering several sentries, they overran two U.S. command posts. A half mile from the supply depot, still in the dark, they unleashed one of the largest *banzai* charges of the war—and the only one on American soil. The human wave that swarmed uphill like cresting ocean surf was halted in desperate fighting, much of it hand-to-hand by rear-echelon personnel. Many of the attackers were killed in combat, along with Yamasaki, and most of the remaining Japanese, pushed back down the hill to the valley floor, clutched a hand grenade to their chest and blew themselves up rather than be taken prisoner. At dawn, the bodies of several hundred U.S. and Japanese soldiers lay on the hillside, and the mutilated remains of hundreds more Japanese who had committed suicide rather than surrender were scattered below on the valley floor.[*]

Attu was declared secure the next day. U.S. burial teams counted 2,351 Japanese dead. Only 28 Japanese had been taken prisoner, and some of them were not soldiers but civilian employees of the army.

For the Americans, the cost of retaking the island was nearly 4,000

---

[*] A half century earlier, Japanese soldiers became prisoners of war in the Russo-Japanese War without suffering a lifetime of disgrace when they returned home. But the generation of Japanese sent to fight in the Pacific in World War II were indoctrinated in the belief that an honorable soldier never allowed himself to be captured alive. Like on Attu, legions of Japanese soldiers throughout the Pacific exploded their last grenades against their bodies rather than become prisoners of war.

casualties, including 549 killed in action. Preparations for the invasion of Kiska, planned for August, had to be made with the presumption that its garrison, which intelligence estimated at nearly 12,000 enemy soldiers, would fight and die to the last man as all but a handful of their brethren had on Attu.

———— · ————

After taking the train from Minnesota to Seattle, Nobuo figured that he and his MIS team would soon be on a troopship bound for Alaska. But when they were driven to an airfield and put aboard a C-47 cargo plane, he knew that someone was in a hurry for them to get up north.

It was Nobuo's first flight, and one he would not forget. Shortly after takeoff, the weather turned, and suddenly they were being buffeted side to side and up and down like an amusement park roller-coaster. Ear-splitting metallic bangs and screeches convinced Nobuo that the fuselage was about to come apart at the seams. It was so cold inside the cabin, he feared that might already be happening. Strapped into a cushionless seat, Nobuo couldn't imagine that any plane could take so much punishment and stay in the air. Crashing seemed inevitable. *How in the world can we not go down?*

The rest of his team must have appeared as stricken as Nobuo because a passing crewman looked at them, grinned, and hollered to be heard over the racket, "We're riding in the safest airplane in the Army!"

"We are?" Nobuo yelled back. "Then why is it so cold and noisy?"

"No insulation!" The civilian version DC-3 has insulation, the crewman went on, but the Army had better things to spend its money on than passenger comfort! Another big smile, and he was gone.

Somehow they made it, landing at Elmendorf Field, adjacent to Fort Richardson outside of Anchorage. It was close to midnight when they stepped off the plane, but as it was summer in Alaska it was still light out, which amazed the Nisei soldiers, who had never seen daytime at night.

Nobuo recalled reading a newspaper article about the U.S. victory at Attu, but with all the studying in his final weeks at Camp Savage and the more extensive coverage given to the fighting in the South Pacific, it hadn't made much of an impression. Now, at the headquarters of the Alaska Defense Command, he met men who had fought at Attu and heard from them what a hard fight it had been, not only in terms of casualties and stiff enemy resistance but also the Arctic conditions and rough terrain.

Soon after arriving at Fort Richardson, Nobuo and his team left Anchorage aboard a crowded troopship in a convoy sailing to Adak, an island far down the Aleutians chain. When they arrived, they found thousands of soldiers and tons of materiel being assembled for Operation Cottage: the invasion of Kiska Island. The U.S. 7th Infantry Division was here, along with the 4th Infantry Regiment and the 87th Mountain Infantry Regiment, all units that had fought on Attu. They were being equipped with Arctic gear and practicing amphibious landings on the frozen, windswept shores of Adak. Planners had studied maps of Kiska and made plaster models of the island for soldiers to study. In total, the Kiska invasion force would grow to nearly thirty thousand U.S. troops.

Also joining the invasion force were 5,400 Canadians. Nobuo was astonished to find himself assigned to them because they had no Japanese-language teams. Issued a Canadian army uniform, Nobuo was sent to a battalion of the Winnipeg Grenadiers, who were quick to welcome him to their ranks. After serving peacetime garrison duty in Jamaica and Bermuda, the battalion had been sent to Hong Kong six weeks before Pearl Harbor. When the Japanese attacked Hong Kong on December 8, 1941, the Grenadiers joined British army units in defending the colony, and were virtually wiped out by the time Hong Kong fell to the Japanese on Christmas Day. Back home in Canada, the unit was reorganized in January 1942 with new volunteers, and for the past eighteen months they had been serving in a home defense role until being sent to Adak. They were untested, but eager and ready to strike back at the Imperial Japanese Army in retribution for their fallen comrades.

After the Japanese invaded the Aleutians, the U.S. built an airfield on Adak in the fall of 1942. In the past three months, U.S. fliers had made 1,454 sorties and dropped 1,255 tons of bombs on Kiska. Japanese antiaircraft gunners on the island scored occasional hits on U.S. planes, but the air campaign had continued unabated, in spite of the frequent fog and low visibility. Shortly after the fall of Attu, the U.S. Navy began a blockade of Kiska to interdict ships from Japan trying to reach the island with supplies and reinforcements. The Navy also contributed to the pre-invasion softening-up of Kiska with a bombardment on July 22 from a flotilla of two battleships, five cruisers, and nine destroyers, a powerful seaborne force given the many operations under way in the South Pacific.

Starting August 9, U.S. and Canadian troops formed long lines on Adak's docks to board their assigned transports, which once loaded moved back to their anchorage in the harbor to make room for other ships to take on troops. The loading took several days. At last, on August 13, the invasion fleet was en route to Kiska, 250 miles away.

Aboard the crowded ships, nerves were on edge, and sleep hard to come by; endless card and dice games helped infantrymen pass the time. Soldiers sharpened their bayonets and cleaned their rifles, packed and repacked what they would be carrying ashore, and studied maps of the island. When the convoy arrived off Kiska late the next day, it found typical Aleutian weather: dense fog, sheets of rain, and howling winds. That same day, ships offshore had shelled Kiska with sixty tons of explosives, and aircraft had dropped another hundred tons of bombs.

That night, Nobuo and the Winnipeg Grenadiers received a final briefing and got the lowdown on where they were to land. Nobuo's job would be to quickly quiz any Japanese prisoners, covering subjects such as locations of machine guns, mortars, and command posts, as well as troop strength, then pass along whatever he learned. As for documents, he was to also handle urgently anything having to do with codes, ciphers, and other communications, and pass the information on to field commanders. Other printed materials were to be collected and translated when time allowed.

A few hours later, they rolled out of their bunks at 3:30 a.m. for a breakfast of steak, fried potatoes, and strong coffee, although many were too nervous or seasick to eat. None of them knew or would have wanted to know the Army's official casualty estimates. Based on the bloody battle for Attu, one out of every five of them was expected to be dead by the end of the fight for Kiska.

With the invasion hour approaching, they were issued hand grenades and extra ammunition so every man had one hundred rounds for his rifle. They were also each given several days' worth of boxed

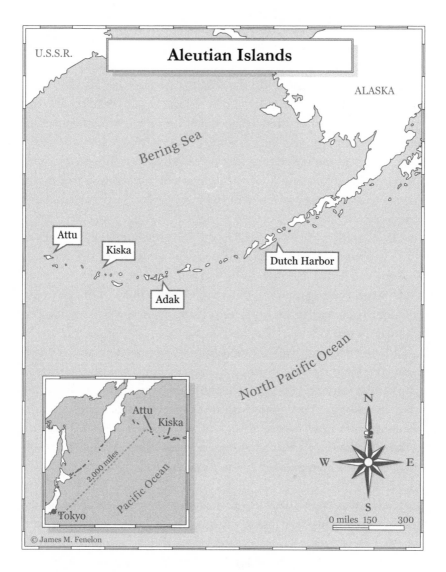

K rations, which were full meals, along with D rations for quick-energy snacks, such as chocolate bars. Then they went below for a final check of their equipment.

When they were called up onto the deck, Nobuo could see the outlines of the shore in the early dawn. As it grew lighter, the fog seemed to be lifting, and they could make out the beach, which looked empty. The small landing craft that would take them ashore were lowered over the sides. At 6 a.m., men began descending down the sides of the troopship through heavy nets, then dropped into the landing craft that motored through choppy seas to the fog-cloaked island.

The Americans landed on the southwestern shore and the Canadians a few miles to the north. To avoid the costly mistakes at Attu, the troops had been briefed to speedily seize ridges, mountain passes, and other high ground. After landing on the backside of Kiska, they were to get off the beaches as quickly as possible and fight their way inland to the opposite side of the island, where they were to capture Kiska's natural harbor that had been built up over the past year by the occupiers.

Their first surprise was that they did not come under enemy fire as they approached the beaches. The veterans of Attu spread the word that this was a trick and no one should let down their guard. It looked like Attu all over again, only this time, with so many more Japanese defenders believed to be hunkered down up in the hills, waiting to ambush them.

Nobuo's landing craft scraped bottom against a rocky reef and came to a lurching stop short of the beach. The bow ramp dropped with a thud, and they charged forward, jumping into several feet of ice-cold seawater. They waded ashore as quickly as they could, which, burdened with heavy packs and equipment, resembled a slow-motion newsreel. Then, up steep and slippery moss-covered slopes of volcanic rock, they were finally off the beach strewn with crushed black rocks.

Nobuo was taken aback by the quiet that prevailed over the beach. He only heard his own heavy panting. Every man was tense with expectation as they struggled to get off the beach, watching the men in front of them. When would the first shot ring out? And who would be the first to fall to enemy fire?

About a hundred yards up from the beach, Nobuo and the Canadians dropped their packs and looked the situation over. They couldn't see anything but hills and tundra. Patrols were sent out to probe, and they soon came across gun emplacements and dugouts overlooking the shoreline that were exceptionally well concealed, but unmanned.

For the rest of the day, landing craft chugged to and from the beaches, delivering thousands of soldiers, as well as all the equipment, artillery, and supplies that a large ground invasion required. Within half a day's time, tractors and bulldozers had cleared off swaths of beaches and transformed them into level unloading areas and supply depots.

By nightfall, a blanket of dense, gray fog came in that reduced ground-level visibility to near zero, and with it came a downpour of freezing rain. There was no shelter for the soldiers, and they only had their ponchos to throw over themselves as they dug in for the night. Taking his cue from the Canadians, Nobuo used his spade to scratch out a foot-deep foxhole in the rocky tundra, but it provided little protection from the elements and soon filled with water that he bailed out once or twice with his helmet, then gave up as it kept refilling. It was a cold, wet, sleepless night with the sound of sporadic rifle and machine gun fire along with bright tracer rounds whistling through the night like errant fireworks. Who was shooting at whom was unclear; shouts reverberated through the night, and whispered rumors circulated about Japanese sneaking around in the dark, preparing a *banzai* attack.

The next morning, fanning out into the fog in battalion columns of approach that served as three parallel lines of attack, they trudged farther inland, heading toward the eastern shore four miles away. The island was as treeless as a moonscape; its only vegetation were dwarf shrubs and grasses, with mosses and lichens covering everything.

Like everyone else, Nobuo wondered when and where the enemy would open fire. They heard occasional gunshots in the distance, but no one knew if they were patrols making contact with the enemy or false alarms. Once, Nobuo heard a faint plea for a medic. As they climbed higher into the hills, looking behind every rocky ledge and inside every dark cave, it was as if they were hunting ghosts. It got even stranger when they found abandoned positions with enemy machine guns and mortars lying in the open and empty encampments with pots of cooked rice, half-eaten meals, boxes of supplies and ammo. Scrawled on the walls of an underground bunker were messages that did not require translating.

You are dancing by follische order of Rousebelt.

We shall come again and kill Yanki-joker.

By the next day, they knew for certain what they had begun to suspect: not a single Japanese soldier, dead or alive, remained on Kiska Island. And yet, in a little more than forty-eight hours, more than thirty Americans and Canadians had been killed on the island and another fifty wounded by friendly fire. Four other fatalities and a handful of injuries came from enemy land mines and booby traps. In the fog, trigger-happy soldiers fired at anything that moved. In some cases, even after a challenge was answered correctly with the day's password, fatal shots were fired by men who believed they were shooting enemy soldiers posing as GIs or Canadians. One U.S. rifleman fired on what he thought was an enemy patrol moving toward him in the fog but were fellow GIs, who shouted desperately for him to stop. When he threw a hand grenade, they shot him dead. One Canadian soldier's spine was severed by friendly fire. Even without an enemy to fight, it had been a perilous journey through Kiska's gloomy interior, and every Nisei soldier on the trek knew just how easy it would be for him to be mistaken at any moment for the enemy.

The mystery of how thousands of Japanese troops vanished from Kiska was eventually solved, although not entirely until enemy accounts became available after the war. Following the annihilation of its Attu garrison, and recognizing the overwhelming air and naval superiority the U.S. had in the North Pacific and that isolated Kiska was no longer defensible, Japanese military commanders reluctantly decided to pull their forces out of the Aleutians. Aware of the U.S. naval blockade around Kiska, they set in motion in July 1943 an audacious plan that counted on the poor weather and summer fog to shield a mass evacuation of the island. Mother Nature obliged and gave them the lingering fog bank and reduced visibility they needed. Eleven fast surface ships slipped past U.S. patrols and into Kiska Harbor on July 29 at 1:40 p.m., and within an hour 5,183 men were hurriedly boarded. Not one member of the garrison was left behind. With no time or space to load their heavy weapons or equipment, these were abandoned or dumped in the harbor. The ships sailed back through the fog, again avoiding detection. By the time the American and Canadian troops invaded the island on August 15, the Kiska garrison was back in Japan. In fact, the only living creature found on the island was a friendly dog, which had obviously been cared for by the Japanese but was now famished. He turned out to be Explosion, the orphaned pet of the weather station sailors now in a POW camp in Japan.

For the second time in six months, U.S. military planners had been completely fooled by a Japanese evacuation. The first had been at Guadalcanal, in February 1943, when they evacuated by barges at nighttime (also under the cover of fog) their last ten thousand men from that besieged island. And now the Kiska surprise, even though radio transmissions from the island suddenly ceased after July 29, and photos showed that new bomb craters weren't being filled or repairs being made aboveground, and vehicles and barges remaining in their same positions. In analyzing this intelligence as it came in, several incorrect presumptions were made at the highest levels—among them, that the enemy must be lying low in bunkers and tunnels or had gone into the hills and were holding defensive positions in anticipation of an invasion. An enemy withdrawal from the island was deemed improbable, if not impossible, given that the Navy and Air Corps had kept the island bottled up for weeks. Also, some ranking U.S. officers held on to the belief that the Japanese placed little value on human life, and they were blinded to the possibility that the Japanese would withdraw from Kiska rather than stay and die for their emperor. One Marine officer had volunteered to take a scouting party to Kiska before the invasion to determine the enemy's strength, but that had been dismissed as unnecessary. And so, the war's largest air, sea, and land operation to invade a deserted island went ahead on schedule.

In the end, however, the Allies got what they wanted: the Japanese were out of the Aleutians and no longer on American soil. Anyone who knew combat, as the veterans of Attu certainly did, were not disappointed by the non-fight on Kiska. Had the Japanese garrison stayed to fight and die, the struggle would have been a costly one. The U.S. Army concluded that retaking Kiska could have resulted in at least seven thousand Allied casualties, including as many as five thousand killed. Still, the commanding general of the Alaska Defense Command, Major General Simon Buckner Jr., characterized the Kiska invasion as a "great, big, juicy, expensive mistake."

When Nobuo returned to Adak, he rejoined his MIS team, and together they went to work reading boxes of documents that had been left by the Japanese on Kiska. Some revealed information about various units, and there were preliminary plans for invading the mainland of Alaska. One document Nobuo read detailed how a Japanese task force had secretly sailed from Japan across the northern route and then turned south toward Hawaii for the surprise attack on Pearl Harbor.

At the bottom of one box from Kiska was a roll of undeveloped film. One of Nobuo's team members was an amateur photographer, and he developed the roll and made prints. They pictured a Japanese airfield with parked bombers on the tarmac, then the same type of aircraft in the air, and striking portraits of young crewmen inside a plane in flight. One looked to be a radioman wearing a headset and the other a navigator in front of a map. Since the Japanese hadn't yet completed the airfield they had been constructing for the past year on Kiska, Nobuo knew the pictures were taken elsewhere. But there was no indication where.

Also left on the island were diaries and letters written by Japanese soldiers. Some of the pages were moldy and the penmanship of the *sosho* cursive style difficult to read—many entries and letters appeared to have been scrawled hurriedly. A comment in one letter provided a possible clue as to the fate of the Kiska garrison. In a letter to his family that had never been sent, one soldier wrote they had been promised they would soon be rescued and sent back to Japan, and how much they were all hoping and praying it was true. *Perhaps this was a promise that had been kept?* Eager to pass along this piece of intelligence, Nobuo typed up a report and included a translation of the letter.

Some common themes in the soldiers' writings, clearly meant to be shared with loved ones and not seen by their commanders, was how much they disliked their duty on the frigid, isolated island, and how they missed their homes, farms, and families, and wished for the war to end.

Not so unlike our own complaints and longings, thought Nobuo Furuiye.

Nine

THE COUSINS

Grant Hirabayashi, who had been drafted three days before Pearl Harbor and soon thereafter found himself in "protective custody" for a month along with other Nisei soldiers, had seen his parents once since Pearl Harbor. On Sunday, December 7, 1941, after attending morning church services, they had made the thirty-mile drive to Fort Lewis near Tacoma to visit him, but with the base locked down after the attack in Hawaii they could only wave to one another through the fence.

Grant next saw them six months later, when he got a pass to go home for a few days to help his family prepare for the evacuation from their farm at White River Gardens, near Seattle. It had been heartbreaking to see how few of their possessions and keepsakes they could take with them to a relocation camp. Grant managed to sell their old Ford truck for them, but nearly everything else—from pots and pans to phonograph records—had to be given away or left behind. Soon after he returned to his clerical duties at Fort Leavenworth, his family was sent south on a two-day, thousand-mile train ride to the Pinedale Assembly Center, near Fresno, California. When they arrived, they were handed long cloth bags and instructed to fill them from a large pile of straw to make their own mattresses. Salt pills were issued upon arrival because summer temperatures often soared to 110 degrees. The family of nine plus their belongings had to fit inside a single nine-by-twelve-foot room. A month later, they were again on the move; this time, north

Grant Hirabayashi
at Camp Savage, 1943

five hundred miles to the Tule Lake Relocation Center, the largest of the ten internment camps, which at its peak held nearly nineteen thousand men, women, and children.* Later that fall, the Army sent Grant to Minnesota, where he became a member of the second Military Intelligence Service Language School class at Camp Savage. He wrote to his parents in the new year, telling them that his eight years of schooling in Japan were paying off, as he was one of the top students. After his graduation in June 1943, he was promoted to sergeant (E-4). He had some leave coming and was able to secure a travel pass to Tule Lake.

It was a long journey by rail from Minnesota to the northern California internment camp near the Oregon border. He made his final transfer in Klamath Falls, switching to a line that ran south past the camp after stopping briefly for passengers at a station near the main gate. When he stepped off the train, Grant saw a land not lush with green forests as he had been picturing but carpeted with desolate plains of tinder-dry grasses, tules, and sagebrush, with nary a tree in sight.

He showed his ID and leave papers to the gate guard.

Grant looked up to see a watchtower manned by a pair of soldiers

---

* The War Relocation Administration consistently denied that the term *concentration camps* accurately described the "relocation centers" it operated for Japanese internees. However, on October 20, 1942, President Roosevelt called them "concentration camps" during a press conference in Washington. The first use of the term dated back to the Boer-Anglo War (1899–1902), when the British concentrated noncombatants in South African camps under deplorable conditions.

The Tule Lake Relocation Center

with rifles, and next to them a machine gun set up on a tripod. He was horrified that the heavy automatic weapon was aimed inside the camp. A six-foot-high chain-link fence topped with multiple strings of barbed wire encircled the boundaries of the camp as far as he could see.

Perhaps as a courtesy to a fellow GI, one of the MPs offered to show Grant the way to his family's barrack. The camp, built on a 7,400-acre site, had agriculture and livestock operations to help feed the internees, a hospital, a sewage treatment plant, warehouses, and more than seventy blocks filled with rows of hundreds of single-story structures. After a walk in triple-digit heat, the guard pointed to a tar-papered barrack. "Good luck, sergeant," he said, then headed back.

Grant approached the squat building that looked to be about a hundred feet long and twenty feet deep. Six identical doors and a small window adjacent to each one suggested six separate units. Stenciled on the door of the end unit was the number he had been given at the gate: #5314-A.

He rapped softly, and within minutes of stepping into the stifling, two-room apartment, his parents were greeting him with hugs and wan smiles. His siblings who were at home—his youngest brother, twelve-year-old Ted (named for Theodore Roosevelt), and his seventeen-year-old sister, Ruth, a recent graduate of the camp's high school—wanted to hear about his Army life. Grant had the feeling they were all smiling on the outside and crying on the inside.

It was all so bittersweet. As pleased as he was to see his family after more than a year, Grant was shaken to see them living in such conditions. His parents had been denied their home and livelihood, and his siblings a normal childhood. He could see his parents were depressed but trying hard not to show it. Rather than talk about it, they stayed busy. His mother had sewed curtains for the two small windows, and his father had made a table and shelves. Even so, it was far from the comfortable home they had once made for the family. Their generation's stoic acceptance, he reflected, could be a strength. Like many Japanese, they were most concerned with how to cope, and they wanted to persevere without complaint. It was a time when many Issei were despondent and forlorn, but determined. At least his family had friends here, because their neighbors from home had been rounded up at the same time, with most ending up at Tule Lake. A few blocks away were their Hirabayashi cousins from White River Gardens.

Gordon Hirabayashi on steps of University of Washington

Grant had not seen his cousin Gordon since before the war, but he had been reading about him of late. As young boys, they had played together and as teenagers they drag-raced the pickup trucks their fathers used for hauling produce to market. Now, with the country at war and their families behind barbed wire, the cousins had taken divergent paths.

Gordon, who had never gone to school in Japan, entered the University of Washington before Grant returned from Japan in 1940. When he had registered for the draft, Gordon, a practicing Quaker, was granted conscientious objector status. A mathematics major at the university, he was living in a campus dormitory when Pearl Harbor was attacked. Understanding that he and his family were an ethnic minority that very likely would be grouped with the Japanese enemy, he was not concerned for himself or his siblings, all of whom had been born in America and were U.S. citizens, as much as he was for his parents, who went from immigrants to "enemy aliens" overnight. He found it difficult to believe that FDR's Executive Order 9066 authorized the internment of *all* Japanese in the western states, whether or not they were U.S. citizens. About a month before the roundups began in Seattle, a curfew was imposed that required Japanese residents to be off the streets by 8 p.m. For a week or two, Gordon rushed back to his dorm room from the school library, where he spent most evenings studying with friends. But one night he turned around when he was halfway to the dorm and went back to the library. He still had work to do, and the library stayed open until ten. He decided if his white friends could stay and study, he should be able to as well. After that, he simply ignored the mandatory curfew. When the neighborhood roundups of Japanese began, Gordon realized that since he could not abide the government curfew based on race, he could not agree to be forcibly evacuated for the same reason. Both actions, in his opinion, violated his constitutional rights. And if the Constitution and the Bill of Rights were meaningful documents in peacetime, as he believed they were, they ought to be important in wartime, too. No one had said anything to him when he openly violated the curfew, but he knew the relocation order would be different. If he was walking around Seattle as the only Japanese face in the city, sooner or later he'd be accosted or arrested. So he made arrangements with a Quaker attorney to meet him the day after the last busload of Japanese left Seattle, which made him officially in violation of the removal order, and to drive him to the FBI office so he could turn himself in. When Gordon did so on May 13, 1942, he handed over a 450-word typed statement he wrote entitled, "Why I Refuse to Register for Evacuation." It read, in part:

We have recorded in the laws of our nation certain rights for all men and certain additional rights for citizens. These fundamental moral rights and civil liberties are included in the Bill of Rights, U.S. Constitution, and other legal records. They guarantee that these fundamental rights shall not be denied without due process of law . . .

The mass evacuation of all persons of Japanese descent denies them the right to live. It forces thousands of energetic, law-abiding individuals to exist in a miserable psychological and a horrible physical atmosphere . . . Over 60 percent are American citizens, yet they are denied on a wholesale scale without due process of law the civil liberties which are theirs.

In refusing to register [for evacuation], I am well aware of the excellent qualities of the army and government personnel connected with the prosecution of this exclusion order. They are men of the finest type, and I sincerely appreciate their sympathetic and honest efforts. Nor do I intend to cast any shadow upon the Japanese and the other Nisei who have registered for evacuation. They have faced tragedy admirably. I am objecting to the principle of this order, which denies the rights of human beings, including citizens.

By that evening, Gordon was sitting in a jail cell. He remained locked up until his trial five months later, when a federal judge dismissed his legal defense on constitutional grounds and instructed the jurors to find him guilty of violating the curfew as well as the removal order, which they did after deliberating for ten minutes. Gordon was sentenced to six months behind bars. He headed off to prison convinced he had made the right stand, and still believing that as a U.S. citizen the Constitution would protect him, and that his convictions would eventually be overturned on appeal. He declined to characterize his legal challenge as strictly a "Japanese-American case," but saw it involving basic principles that affected the fundamental rights of all Americans. If these rights could be taken from one group, he believed they could be taken from another. The case of *Hirabayashi v. United States* was argued before the U.S. Supreme Court over two days in early May 1943. A month later, on June 21, 1943, the Supreme Court ruled against Gordon, upholding the lower court by a unanimous vote of 9–0, not the norm for the often-divided high court.

The Court's decision in Gordon's case made national news the week after Grant's graduation from Camp Savage. The bold headlines were eye-catching: WEST COAST JAP CURFEW HELD LEGAL BY SUPREME COURT and HIGH COURT UPHOLDS EVACUATION OF JAPS. Hundreds of local newspapers across the country picked up articles from all three major wire services (AP, UP, INS) reporting the historic decision.

> Gordon Hirabayashi, a senior in the University of Washington at the time of his arrest, was convicted in federal district court for violating the curfew order and failing to report to a control station for evacuation . . . Chief Justice Stone read the opinion, in which the high court declared: "We cannot close our eyes to the fact . . . that in time of war residents having ethnic affiliations with an invading enemy may be a greater source of danger than those of a different ancestry . . . The danger of espionage and sabotage to our military resources was imminent."

Some articles quoted Justice Frank Murphy, who wrote a separate opinion and came closest to being a dissenting voice. Murphy, who had served as U.S. attorney general before being named to the high court, stated,

> Today is the first time, as far as I am aware, that we have sustained a substantial restriction of the personal liberty of citizens of the United States based upon the accident of race or ancestry . . . no less than 70,000 American citizens have been placed under a special ban and deprived of their liberty because of their particular racial inheritance. In this sense it bears a melancholy resemblance to the treatment accorded to members of the Jewish race in Germany and in other parts of Europe . . . In my opinion this goes to the very brink of constitutional power.

But in joining the majority, Murphy concluded that it would have taken too long to make determinations as to the loyalty and dependability of individual Japanese on the West Coast, and that such delay "might have tragic consequences."*

Now, visiting Tule Lake, Grant learned from his parents that Gordon had already served his sentence and was currently living in Spokane, in eastern Washington, which was outside the exclusion area and not subject to evacuation. He worked for a Quaker group that helped to resettle people starting to be released from internment camps to work in jobs outside the western states, a program begun by the War Relocation Authority that was limited to native-born U.S. citizens who had never lived in Japan. (The Kibei, who were born in America but educated at least partly in Japan, were excluded based on the fear that they might be loyal to the emperor. This was unquestionably ironic given that Kibei were being recruited inside the camps by the Army for their language skills.)

Grant understood that his cousin had taken a courageous stand he believed in. Before the weight of the judicial system came down on him, his parents had pleaded with him to give up his legal protest and join them in camp, but even his mother's tears could not move Gordon to abandon his principles, though they did give him a sense of guilt for failing to respond as a dutiful son.

"I'd like to be with you, Mother," he had told her, "but I just can't."

There were families at Tule Lake who were proud to have sons in the U.S. Army. In fact, Grant saw walking around the camp a half-dozen other khaki-clad young men who were on furlough visiting their folks. One of them, Isamu "Ted" Noguchi, had been in Grant's

---

* As the Supreme Court was handing down its opinion, California Governor Earl Warren was in Columbus, Ohio, addressing the 35th Annual Governor's Conference. The future chief justice of the U.S. Supreme Court, who a decade later would write the Court's historic opinion on school segregation, *Brown v. Board of Education,* that began the postwar civil rights movement, told his fellow governors he opposed the return of the Japanese from relocation centers to California. He had earlier supported the mass evacuation of Japanese from the state, making no distinction between immigrants and U.S. citizens. Although not yet the liberal lion he later became, he claimed his desire to keep them out of the state was not "an appeal to race hatred, but an appeal for safety . . . We are now producing approximately half of the ships and airplanes of the country on the Pacific Coast. We don't want a second Pearl Harbor in California."

MISLS class, and two other Nisei worked in the administrative offices at Camp Savage.

But there was also support at Tule Lake for the position Gordon had taken against relocation. His mother, Suzawa, told Grant's mother, Midori, how only days after they arrived at Tule Lake two women she didn't know walked from the other side of the camp and knocked on the door to say, "Thank you for what your son is doing." The gesture helped diminish her embarrassment and shame, Suzawa confessed. At one point in Gordon's legal odyssey, she and Gordon's father had been subpoenaed to testify for the government for the purpose of proving their son's Japanese ancestry. They had to spend the night before their court appearance in jail; her husband stayed with Gordon in his cell, but Suzawa was locked up in the "women's tank" with prostitutes and petty thieves. After the unexpected thank-yous at Tule Lake, Suzawa wrote to Gordon to tell him how the supportive words from the ladies in camp had given her a big lift.

Grant had always looked up to Gordon. He was smart and had gone to college and could recite passages of the U.S. Constitution and the Bill of Rights, which most people Grant knew could not. Young Japanese Americans were not accustomed to demanding their constitutional rights; in fact, many had grown up taking certain forms of discrimination almost for granted, as had their immigrant parents before them. But not Gordon, who was steadfast in his belief that ancestry was not a crime.

Grant wondered but for different circumstances whether he would have done something similar. Had he not been in the Army when war broke out, and had he been subject to mass evacuation and relocation, would a festering anger and his own principles have steered him on another path? He would never know. He met a few young men in Tule Lake who said they were willing to enlist in the Army but only after their families were released from internment. Grant respected their position, even though he himself had already taken the oath to serve his country and was now doing so in time of war. Nothing about Gordon's stand and legal battle lessened him in any way in Grant's eyes; in fact, it was just the opposite. His cousin acted according to his conscience and fought for American values, and did so knowing the enormous cost he and his family would pay. They had both, he and Gordon, heard the same drumbeat of patriotism, and each in his own way was fighting to preserve the country he loved.

When it was time to leave Tule Lake, Grant kissed his mother and hugged his siblings, who had lined up to say goodbye. His father wanted to walk with him, so they strolled through the camp in the blistering heat.

Grant had told his parents only that he was in the Army's Military Intelligence Service because he spoke Japanese. They had known better than to ask for details he couldn't divulge. It also occurred to him that possibly they didn't want to know more. He knew they struggled daily with the shame that their beloved homeland had attacked America and started the war. And perhaps that humiliation helped them accept so stoically the rotten deal they had gotten from the U.S. government.

At the gate, a guard nodded his assent for Toshiharu to walk with his son to the train.

Their wait wasn't long. As the train came to a screeching stop, his father looked at Grant. He had been his usual quiet self and hadn't said much on the long walk from the barrack, but he clearly had something on his mind. Addressing Grant as *jiro-san* (second son), he spoke in Japanese.

These are very difficult times. You are heading toward war. I want you to take care of yourself. I want you to do your best.

Grant shook his father's hand. Nearing sixty now, Toshiharu still had a vise-like grip from all his years of farming.

Boarding the train, Grant found a straight-back, wooden seat in a middle car, and watched out the window as the train pulled away and sped up. Soon, Tule Lake was a shimmering mirage on the horizon.

Grant had known his family was interned, of course, but to see them surrounded by barbed-wire fences and armed soldiers wearing the same uniform he wore, imprisoned by the U.S. government in the high desert of northern California for no reason other than their ethnicity, had been a demoralizing blow. He had taken an oath to uphold the Constitution and fight for freedom and liberty, but at the same time his loved ones had been deprived of their own freedom and liberty.

Upon returning from leave, he was ordered to Fort Snelling, a large Army camp just south of Minneapolis and across the Mississippi River from St. Paul. Twenty miles from Camp Savage, it was here that the graduates from the most recent MISLS class awaited new orders, which for most meant assignments to units fighting in the Pacific.

Several weeks passed, and for Grant it was sheer monotony. Efforts were made to keep them busy by marching them in formation up and down the parade grounds for visiting dignitaries, and translating the same dull Japanese technical manuals over and over for practice. It all got to Grant—the war in the Pacific had been going on for nearly two years and he had yet to do a thing with his Army schooling and training.

Then the call went out for volunteers for a "hazardous mission." Although the exact nature of the mission was not revealed, two hundred men stepped forward, all of them Nisei graduates of Camp Savage's second class. Grant was one of them. He volunteered not only because he was tired of waiting around. There was a more important reason. After leaving his family behind barbed wire at the Tule Lake Relocation Center, he had something to prove, for them and for himself.

Grant Hirabayashi intended to prove that he was a loyal American.

Ten

A HAZARDOUS MISSION

The eleven new recruits from the Jerome Relocation Center in Arkansas—Roy Matsumoto among them—entered the second Military Intelligence Service Language School class at Camp Savage in December 1942. These Nisei were in the first wave of volunteers from the internment camps after the MIS received special permission from the War Department in August 1942 to recruit Japanese Americans due to the dire need for linguists in the Pacific theater.

Roy's journey had been a prolonged one since the announced relocation of all Japanese from the West Coast, when he had briefly considered packing up his car and fleeing California. After being rounded up with other Japanese residents in Los Angeles, he had been sent to the assembly center at the Santa Anita Park, where he had lived for six months in a horse stall before being moved to the Jerome Relocation Center in Arkansas. Notified of his draft reclassification from 1-A to 4-C ("unfit . . . alien exempt"), Roy, as a native-born American, had considered it the final humiliation and insult to be declared unfit to serve his country, and he'd been quick to sign up when the MISLS recruiters came to Jerome.

After arriving at Camp Savage, Roy and his younger brother, Tom, who was drafted a month before Pearl Harbor, were reunited for the first time in a year. Tom had not attended the MISLS (he would do so in 1945) but was a sergeant working in camp administration. They had last heard from the rest of the family shortly before the war; at that time, their folks and siblings, who had moved from California to

Japan in 1927, were still living in Hiroshima, where Roy and Tom had gone to high school.

Roy settled into the routine at Camp Savage. Thanks to his years in Japan and his daily use of the language while delivering groceries to Japanese customers in Los Angeles, he aced the placement test and went into the second-highest section. Although some study was required to learn Japanese military and technical terms, he sailed through most of the courses. After his graduation in June 1943, he and his classmates who hadn't yet gone through basic training were sent to Camp Shelby in Mississippi for three months.

The newly formed, all-Nisei 442nd Regimental Combat Team, with more than two thousand volunteers from Hawaii and fifteen hundred from the mainland, was also training at Camp Shelby. The MIS group from Camp Savage formed its own company, although many around Camp Shelby mistakenly assumed that they would be folded into the 442nd before it left for Europe. For security reasons, the MIS was keeping a lid on the fact that the final destination of its specially trained Nisei was the other theater of war.

Following completion of basic training, which included rifle and small-arms training, combat exercises, and night operations, Roy was sent to Camp Snelling to await new orders. His first indication that something was brewing was when the brass from Camp Savage showed up in the barracks where the recent graduates awaiting orders were billeted.

A flurry of interviews behind closed doors followed, many of them conducted by a bespectacled, studious-looking lieutenant, equally fluent in English and Japanese, who explained that the Army was seeking volunteers for what it termed a "hazardous secret mission in an active theater." The selection criteria called for men with a good command of the Japanese language and a high degree of physical ruggedness. They were questioned about their state of health and fitness, marital status, family, and educational background. The questioning was one-sided, with few details of the operation provided, other than that it was strictly voluntary and expected to involve three months of combat, after which they would be returned stateside—and that the War Department anticipated high casualties.

Roy didn't want to be sent right back to Camp Savage as an instructor, as some of the other top language students had been. He still felt the sting of being told after Pearl Harbor that he was unfit to serve his country, and the strong motivation he had to sign up for the MISLS when the recruiters came to the Arkansas relocation camp remained with him. America was at war, and he was ready to do his part. Some two hundred other Nisei waiting at Camp Snelling for orders felt the same way, and they volunteered for the mysterious mission, too. After all the interviews were completed, Roy was one of the fourteen selected. At thirty years of age, he was one of the oldest. In the interviews, he was found to be "shy, quiet, deliberate, and always thinking." Half of those selected were from Hawaii and the others from the West Coast. Roy had known several of them at Camp Savage, like the calm and meticulous Grant Hirabayashi, one of the best students in the top class, and the articulate and assertive Henry "Hank" Gosho, in the second-highest class with Roy. They had chummed around and gone into town to see a movie or to bowl on their days off.

The team's senior enlisted man and immediate supervisor was Staff Sergeant (E-5) Edward Mitsukado of Honolulu, a former court reporter; well-read, soft-spoken, always calm and confident, he was not much of a Japanese linguist but proved to be an intelligent and compassionate leader. The others answering the call for the secret mission were a varied lot. There was Thomas Tsubota of Honolulu, a Kibei with degrees from two leading universities in Tokyo, and a former champion bicycle racer whose military demeanor belied an abiding concern for the welfare of others. Herbert Miyasaki, from the tiny town of Paauilo on the Big Island, was a boisterous extrovert who never stopped advancing the cause of Hawaii statehood. Robert Honda of Wahiawa, Oahu, a graduate of the University of Hawaii with a keen mind and a photographic memory, was a man of few but well-chosen words, and a born philosopher. Roy Nakada of Honolulu was also a graduate of the University of Hawaii, glib and equally at home engaged in barracks banter or a serious intellectual discussion. Ben Sugeta of Los Angeles, a graduate of middle school in Japan, had a bigger-than-life personality and was an accomplished singer of traditional Japanese songs. Jimmy Yamaguchi, another Kibei from Los Angeles, was a skilled linguist with a flare for spouting the right proverb to fit any situation. Russel K. Kono of Hilo, Hawaii, tall and built like a football player, had been a law student at the University of Michigan. Calvin Kobata of Sacramento, California, a graduate of middle school in Japan and junior college in California, had a contagious cheerfulness that made him easy to be around. Howard Furumoto of Hilo, Hawaii, intense and impulsive but with a crooner's golden voice for show tunes, had been a student of veterinary medicine at Kansas State. Akiji Yoshimura of Colusa, California, was an Army medic at the time of Pearl Harbor. Four members of the team, including Roy, had been recruited from internment camps. The others were already in the Army when they were selected for the MISLS.

The lieutenant who interviewed them in flawless Japanese was forty-one-year-old William Laffin, who was to go overseas with the team as its officer in charge. His father, Thomas Melvin Laffin, originally from Portland, Maine, had worked his way to Japan in 1886 as a merchant seaman, and married a geisha from the Shinbashi district of Tokyo, Miyo Ishii, with whom he fathered eight children. The senior Laffin became successful in Japan, and by the time he died, at the age of sixty-nine, in 1931, he owned many valuable real estate holdings in the Yokohama area. His youngest son, William, born in Yokohama, went to school in Japan and later in America, where he acquired U.S. citizenship based on his American father. He eventually wound up in Detroit, Michigan, where he was an executive with the Ford Motor

William Laffin, intelligence officer for the Nisei team assigned to Merrill's Marauders

Company. Bill Laffin had already had an eventful war. When the Japanese attacked Pearl Harbor, he was in Tokyo on company business. Japanese authorities arrested him and held him in prison until he was repatriated six months later with more than a thousand Americans, including the U.S. ambassador to Japan, Joseph Grew, and other foreign nationals. They were taken on the Japanese liner *Asama Maru* to Portuguese East Africa (now Mozambique), where an exchange took place when the Swedish ship *Gripsholm*, sailing under the auspices of the International Red Cross, arrived from New York with a thousand Japanese citizens. Laffin returned to the U.S. in the summer of 1942 after a voyage of eighteen thousand miles, three continents, and four oceans. Within days of his arrival, he was sworn into the U.S. Army with a commission in the MIS due to his knowledge of Japan in peace and war, its people, and their language.

At Camp Snelling, Laffin and the fourteen Nisei took a train to Camp Stoneman in Pittsburg, California, which had opened the previous year to serve as a major staging area for the Pacific. A few days later they took a ferry across the bay to San Francisco and boarded the SS *Lurline*, a Matson luxury liner painted a dull gray after its conversion to an Army troopship.

Already on board were two thousand GIs who had responded to the same call for volunteers from bases in the U.S. and the Caribbean. That it was to be a dangerous mission of short duration attracted brave men looking for action, but also some rough daredevils and undisciplined malcontents willing to do anything for a change of scenery. Most of them hailed from the Midwest, New England, and the South, and many had never seen anyone Japanese, making the Nisei aboard ship a novelty.

The *Lurline* departed on the morning of September 21, 1943. As they steamed under the Golden Gate Bridge, one young GI shyly approached a Nisei with a clumsy but apparently sincere effort to be friendly.

"Say, how're things in your country?" he asked.

Without missing a beat, Akiji Yoshimura, the native Californian, who was standing at the rail gazing at the coastline he knew so well, answered, "Looks pretty good from here."

The MIS team was assigned to an upper-deck stateroom with its own shower and toilet and fitted with enough bunks to sleep sixteen— far removed from where the other troops belowdecks were in cramped berthing spaces filled with pipe-frame bunks strung with canvas.

Day after day, GIs lined the wide decks, parrying with gun butts and jabbing and slashing with fixed bayonets at a lineup of cardboard faces dangling from overhead wires. Drawn on the cutouts were cartoonish Japanese faces with closed slits for eyes and buckteeth.

Upon leaving San Francisco, the Nisei were restricted to their cabin and told to stay out of sight to avoid problems with the other men. They whiled away their time with bull sessions, reading, writing letters, and playing dice and card games. But segregating them turned out to be a mistake, as rumors spread that the ship was carrying a contingent of Japanese POWs. This resulted in boisterous threats to "throw the Japs" overboard. With all the rumors circulating, it was decided to bring the Nisei out of exile.

Laffin escorted his team to the main deck. He explained to the curious GIs crowding around them that his men had been trained by the Army as Japanese-language interpreters and interrogators, and it was their job to gather intelligence that could save the lives of U.S. soldiers.

"They're all American soldiers just like you guys," Laffin said. "Talk to them and get to know them. And fellas, protect them, because where we're going, we'll need them."

That quelled the POW rumors and threats, but not all the questions.

The one question most often asked of the Nisei for the rest of the trip was, "What do you think the Japs will do to you if they capture you?" It was a subject Roy, Grant, and the others had discussed at length among themselves while they were cooped up in their stateroom. They agreed on a best-case scenario: *Better not get caught.* In the interest of good humor, their stock answer to others was always, "Don't know what their plans are for us, but they'll have to run like hell to catch us."

One morning the men from Hawaii recognized the distinctive shape of Diamond Head on the horizon. There had been no announcement about stopping at Pearl Harbor, but as the landmark grew larger everyone talked excitedly about what they would do in Honolulu. The Nisei from Oahu saw it as an unexpected opportunity to visit their families. But the ship passed without slowing down, and they watched sadly as Diamond Head disappeared behind them.

The ship stopped a couple of weeks later at New Caledonia, then at Brisbane, Australia, to pick up more volunteers for the mission—another thousand men in all, most of them veteran jungle fighters from the Guadalcanal and New Georgia campaigns. But at neither stop were the GIs aboard ship allowed ashore. After stopping at Perth on the western coast of Australia, the *Lurline* steamed into the Indian Ocean, then headed northward into the Arabian Sea.

During the long, monotonous days at sea, the MIS team gave well-attended lectures about the enemy's weaponry—showing pictures of Japanese tanks and aircraft—and the makeup and tactics of the Imperial Japanese Army, along with some history of imperialist Japan, the rise of the militarists in the 1930s, and the customs of the Japanese people.

After forty-one days at sea, the *Lurline*'s voyage ended in Bombay on October 31, 1943. Next came a 125-mile rail trip to Deolali, where the British army ran a transient camp. Within days, the nearly three thousand volunteers were organized into three battalions of equal strength; the 1st and 2nd were made up of the men from the continental U.S. and the Caribbean, most of whom had never been in action, and the 3rd was composed of the South Pacific combat veterans. After three weeks of marching and other exercises to acclimatize them to the heat and humidity of Southeast Asia, they were again on the move in the rickety, stifling wooden coaches of the Indian Railways. For three days they traveled across more than eight hundred miles of flat central plains to arrive at the Jakhlaun Railway Station in Uttar Pradesh. From there, following a compass heading, they hiked the rest of the way to their training camp near the farming village of Deogarh, a quarter mile from the banks of the Betwa River, which wound through central India for hundreds of miles. Here, in a camp filled with tents but not a single building—close to an area suitable for jungle training as well as practicing river crossings—the real work began. And here the men at last learned the details of the secret mission for which they had volunteered.

They assembled in a sunbaked field before their senior officer, Lieutenant Colonel Charles Hunter, who had served three years in the Philippines before the war and had extensive experience in jungle warfare training. Selected by the War Department from a group of officers who volunteered for the mission, Hunter told the men they would be undertaking a long-range mission deep behind enemy lines into Burma, a British colony currently occupied by several Japanese infantry divisions. He said the concept of deep-penetration missions by a small unit into enemy-held territory to attack a larger force was not revolutionary, explaining that the U.S. Army had a long tradition of fighting "deep in hostile Indian territory." They should look at their upcoming mission into Burma in light of "the history of our Army in opening the West." Left unsaid was that the Army's history of operating in hostile territory in the West included Custer's Last Stand.

Using hit-and-run guerilla tactics against enemy forces far superior in numbers and firepower, they were to disrupt enemy supply lines and communications, and destroy their strongholds and depots in the Hukawng and Mogaung Valleys in northern Burma. At the same time, U.S.-trained Chinese forces were to attack the Japanese from other directions. Clearing northern Burma of the Japanese forces was necessary for U.S. Army engineers and laborers to complete a new road from the railhead at Ledo in the foothills of northwest India through northern Burma to link with the old Burma Road, which ran east into China for three hundred miles to the rail distribution hub at Kunming. This would open the first land route into China, over which Allied war supplies could flow from Indian seaports. It was estimated that the new Ledo Road could be used by truck convoys to move sixty-five thousand tons of supplies per month to China, then in its sixth year of fighting the occupying Japanese, greatly surpassing the tonnage being airlifted over the Himalayan peaks known as "the Hump."

Allied leaders had agreed at the Quebec Conference in mid-August 1943 to send a specially trained three-thousand-man U.S. combat unit behind Japanese lines in Burma, and two weeks later the Army had put out the call for volunteers from its ranks. They were to be the first American soldiers to fight on the continent of Asia since the Boxer Rebellion in 1900, and would operate in terrain that General George C. Marshall, the Army chief of staff, called "one of the most difficult of the war," and Winston Churchill declared "the most forbidding fighting country imaginable." The War Department anticipated 85 percent casualties—in part because while there was a detailed plan to get the U.S. troops into Burma, no plan existed to extract or reinforce them. Resupplying them would have to be done by air with parachute drops, and their medical evacuations would go out by small aircraft capable of short-field landings and takeoffs. As Lieutenant Colonel Hunter knew but did not tell the troops, the War Department understood that the small force going into Burma was expendable.

At Deogarh, an intensive six-week training cycle had been developed by one of the Army's foremost authorities on guerrilla tactics,

Colonel Francis Brink, an intelligent and meticulous officer. Brink was a former light heavyweight boxing champion at Cornell and still walked on the balls of his feet with his shoulders forward and head down, ready to counterpunch. Even before the U.S. and Japan went to war, he had been a keen observer of the Japanese army, and kept in leather notebooks his comments and sketches outlining their tactics under various conditions.

Also incorporated into the training were the combat reports of British Brigadier Orde Wingate, who had led a 3,200-man British-trained Indian army unit known as the Chindits in a deep-penetration mission into Burma six months earlier, albeit with mixed results. Wingate, who briefed Churchill and Roosevelt on deep-penetration tactics at Quebec, had learned hard lessons from the Chindits' campaign, one of them having to do with the practical limits of a man's health and endurance fighting in that region. Consequently, he was an early advocate for the U.S. mission into Burma to have a ninety-day clock, warning that their effectiveness as a fighting unit would deteriorate after that due to the unrelenting rigors of operating without replacements or reinforcements in an environment rife with diseases and deprivations.*The training was overseen by Brink, who broke down the six weeks into a forty-two-day regimen. He arranged for the training to be done by battalions; 1st Battalion practiced river crossings during Week #3, for example, while 2nd Battalion learned tactics and techniques of land mines that week and 3rd Battalion worked on platoon ambushes. Then they rotated. This was in anticipation of the battalions operating in Burma on their own most of the time. In a typical week, they made a long march with field packs, moved overland by compass, solved night problems, set ambushes and roadblocks on narrow, jungle-choked trails like those in Burma, and practiced attacking machine gun pillboxes and other fortified positions.

Brink reorganized each battalion into two combat teams, and color-

* The Chindits marched more than a thousand miles during a three-month period (February to April 1943), inflicting only moderate damage on the enemy's rail transportation and communications in Burma while incurring significant losses of their own; nearly one-third of their 3,200 men were captured, killed, or died of disease by the time they withdrew back to India.

coded them: 1st Battalion was divided into Red and White Combat Teams; 2nd Battalion, Blue and Green; 3rd Battalion, Orange and Khaki. As the battalions would often operate independently, so would the combat teams, although battalion commanders were permitted some latitude in how they deployed their two teams. Each combat team was a self-contained force of 460 enlisted men and 16 officers; a beefed-up rifle company; a heavy weapons (mortars and machine guns) platoon; an intelligence and reconnaissance platoon; a demolitions detachment; a communications element; a medical officer and medics; and sixty pack animals to haul equipment, supplies, and ammunition.

As for individual weapons, each combat team had more than three hundred riflemen armed with the M1 Garand, a semiautomatic rifle with eight-round clips and a ten-inch attachable bayonet. The Garand was a favorite of U.S. infantrymen everywhere because it had great stopping power—whatever it hit went down—and at close range in the jungle it had already proved to have a decided advantage over the Japanese five-shot Arisaka rifle, a bolt-action weapon. There was also a smattering of M1 carbines with fifteen-round clips. About fifty men in each team carried Thompson submachine guns ("Tommy guns") with twenty-round box magazines for rapid, spraying fire against a numerical-superior enemy. And about thirty men on each team packed BAR (Browning Automatic Rifle) machine guns, which at twenty pounds were the heaviest individual weapons and most often carried by the biggest men in the outfit. The BAR was favored for its rate of fire (five hundred rounds a minute) and penetrating power; its .30-06 rounds could mow down fields of tall bamboo. Although in the interest of mobility over rough terrain they had no large field artillery pieces, each combat team had eight mortars (60 mm and 81 mm) and several .30 caliber machine guns. Mortars, with a range of up to a mile and a deadly blast radius of twenty yards, were essential in defense or in an attack.

The volunteers were encouraged to get in as much practice as possible with the weapons they would be taking into Burma. The battalions seized on the opportunity to compete against one another at the firing range, and as a result the marksmanship of the troops steadily improved. When a truckload of skeet-range clay pigeons arrived, the men practiced their combat-shooting skills by placing them at intervals down a trail and up in trees. It soon became a common sight to see a sharpshooter with a Tommy gun or a BAR walking down the trail confidently firing a burst at each target, shattering every one.

This kind of practice with a purpose continued when it came to preparing and training the pack animals and their handlers, two units of Army muleskinners, many of them farmboys. Given the lack of roads and other transportation in northern Burma, the animals would be relied on to haul everything other than what the soldiers carried on their backs.

The 31st Quartermaster Pack Troop arrived on schedule by train with its nearly four hundred Missouri-bred mules. The infertile off-spring of a male donkey and a female horse, mules were more patient and hardier than horses, and less obstinate and more intelligent than donkeys. They were valued as pack animals because they had the size and ground-covering abilities of a horse but were stronger and required less food, while possessing the endurance and stolid disposition of a donkey.

The second muleskinner unit, the 33rd Pack Troop, was aboard a ship sunk en route by an enemy submarine, and while most of the men were rescued, the mules all drowned. The wranglers of the 33rd walked into the Deogarh camp dressed in odds and ends of clothing provided to the shipwrecked by the Red Cross, with none of their saddles, harnesses, or other equipment. There were no replacement mules available, but soon a herd of more than three hundred horses, originally from Australia, arrived by train from Calcutta, along with their saddles, pads, and harnesses.

A priority was placed on training the horses and mules for river crossings, of which there would be countless in northern Burma. Draining off mountains in a land that receives an average annual rainfall of two hundred inches, the rivers are often wide, deep, and swift-flowing. Where it was impossible to wade across, the men would build rope bridges or rafts, but the animals, burdened with one-third of their weight in supplies and equipment secured to the cargo packs (weighing some three hundred pounds), would have to swim across. Although mules and horses were natural-born swimmers, they often refused on their initial immersion, going under once, twice, even three times, and thrashing wildly, before trying to turn around and swim back to solid footing. It took a handler on top tugging on the reins to keep the animal's head pointed toward the far bank to convince them that was the nearest landfall, at which point they would stop struggling and swim strongly in the right direction. After a reinforcing practice run or two, they swam across without looking back.

Each man carried his personal weapon, and secured on a web belt he had a ten-pocket ammo belt with about a hundred rounds, a canteen with a metal cup, a machete for hacking away at jungle growth, and a hunting knife. Inside or tied to the outside of his standard Army haversack were enough K rations for three days (nine small meals), two light wool blankets for the cold nights in the mountains, a rain poncho, a mosquito net, a mess kit, a first-aid kit, an entrenching tool for digging foxholes, an extra pair of olive-drab underwear and socks, a second pair of jungle boots, a toothbrush, soap, and other toiletries. In addition, each man carried an individual medical kit in a canvas case that contained iodine, bandages, aspirin, the antimalarial drug Atabrine, vitamin pills, mosquito repellant, and halazone tablets for purifying water. Roy, Grant, and the other Nisei carried Japanese dictionaries and maps in chest packs, and this weight in front counterbalanced what was on their back. Few men entered Burma carrying less than forty-five pounds, and some lugged as much as seventy pounds.

The first week of January 1944, a new commanding officer arrived in camp, surprising even the two colonels, Hunter and Brink, both of whom had been giving the orders and had hoped to be in line for the combat command. But instead, the position went to Brigadier General Frank D. Merrill, who came from the staff of the China Burma India Theater commanding general, Joseph Stilwell.

Stilwell and Merrill had been together since February 1942, the former arriving in Burma ten days before Rangoon fell to Japanese troops, then in the process of overrunning Southeast Asia. With British and Chinese forces in full retreat, Stilwell led a band of about a hundred of his headquarters personnel and a surgical unit on a grueling 140-mile-long march out of Burma into India to escape capture. At one point, Merrill, an experienced horse cavalry and signal communications officer with no infantry background, collapsed and was found facedown in a river, and had to be revived. But he and everyone else kept pace with what they called the "Stilwell stride," a brisk walk of 105 steps a minute and a ten-minute break every hour, with the wiry, sixty-year-old Stilwell at the head of the column, wearing a mud-stained field jacket with no rank insignia revealing his lieutenant general's three stars, baggy khaki pants tucked into canvas leggings, and a battered campaign hat. "I claim we got a hell of a beating," Stilwell stated at a news conference in New Delhi. "We got run out of Burma, and it is humiliating as hell. I think we ought to find out what caused it, go back, and retake it." Stilwell's blunt war talk found him on the cover of *Life* the following month, and a lead editorial in *The New York Times* declared that Churchill and Roosevelt, for all their brilliant oratory, "could learn something from General Stilwell." A World War I veteran, Stilwell's caustic personality, short temper, and bawdy language had earned him the nickname "Vinegar Joe" between the wars, when a subordinate, stung by his harsh criticism, drew a well-circulated caricature of Stilwell rising out of a vinegar bottle. He had no patience for inefficiency or stuffiness, which in the China Burma India Theater often put him at odds with the Chinese army over the former and the British army for the latter.

Since his retreat from Rangoon, Stilwell, who in addition to directing U.S. military activities in the theater was also the commanding general of the Chinese army in Burma, had pushed for U.S. combat troops to be committed to Southeast Asia. He had requested at least one infantry division of ten thousand to fifteen thousand GIs, but with America's Europe-first priority in the two-front war, he had to settle for the three thousand volunteers training at Deogarh. To lead them, Stilwell, considered one of the U.S. Army's master tacticians in the war, chose Merrill, his chief of staff for Planning and Operations (G3), an officer he trusted and liked. Merrill not only knew the adversaries they would be up against, but also the jungles and mountains of Burma.

Tall and thin with a narrow chest, Merrill did not have the look of a rugged individual, even if one didn't know about his flat feet and weak heart. He was nearsighted and wore the same style of round, rimless spectacles as Stilwell. In his favor, the affable Merrill exuded a self-confidence and can-do spirit that was contagious. From the beginning, he vowed to never expose his men to more risk than he was willing to take himself. That meant a lot to foot soldiers. Possibly he felt that way because he had been one of them. Merrill enlisted in the Army as a private at the age of eighteen in 1922, and had to take the West Point entrance examination six times before being accepted to the class of 1929. Sent to Tokyo in 1938 as an assistant military attaché, he studied the language and went on maneuvers with the Japanese army to learn their structure and tactics. Steeped in the ways of Japan and its military, he was assigned to MacArthur's staff in the Philippines in 1941 as an intelligence officer. At the time of Pearl Harbor, he was on a mission to Burma and was unable to return to Manila due to the Japanese invasion of the Philippines. When Stilwell arrived in Rangoon, Merrill joined his staff and had been with him ever since. Two months before arriving at Deogarh, Merrill was promoted to brigadier general just shy of his fortieth birthday, making him one of the youngest U.S. generals since the Civil War.

In the final days of training, Merrill wanted to observe a river-crossing exercise a mile or two away. He piled into a jeep, planting himself behind the wheel, and took off in a cloud of dust with two passengers hanging on for their lives: twenty-six-year-old *Time-Life* correspondent James Shepley, who would one day become president of Time Inc.; and a visitor from the U.S. State Department, John Emmerson, whom Merrill knew from his embassy days in Tokyo. Merrill's passengers weren't sure if he was trying to prove the versatility of an Army jeep or just wanting to scare them to death by not bothering with roads or even trails and grinding through all the gears in rapid succession. They flew up embankments, in and out of muddy ditches, swerved around trees and rocks, and roared through a little village, sending the locals scattering. After watching the flawless exercise of a hundred mules and horses crossing the river single file, they took another hair-raising ride back toward camp. Along the way, Shepley mentioned that Merrill's men, as the first and only American combat troops on the mainland of Asia, deserved to be called something other than their official but forgettable designation: "5307th Composite Unit (Provisional)." One of the men he had spoken with complained that their unit name sounded "like a street address in Los Angeles." Something more colorful was needed for future press dispatches and to catch the imagination of the public back home.

"Something like 'Merrill's Marauders,'" Shepley said airily. "What do you think, general?"

Merrill made a dismissive snorting sound, but said nothing.

Nevertheless, the name stuck.* Early in the training, the fourteen Nisei were dispersed among the three battalions so each would have its own Japanese-language team. In making the assignments, an effort was made to pair up someone who was strong in Japanese with someone who was equally strong in English, so between them they could handle the interpreting and interrogations as well as writing sound intelligence reports. The three buddies from Camp Savage ended up in different battalions: Grant Hirabayashi went to 1st Battalion, Roy Matsumoto to 2nd, and Hank Gosho to 3rd.

In late January 1944, the battalions took their longest train ride yet: a full week spent in overheated passenger cars chugging through central India for more than a thousand miles to Ledo, a small town encircled by forested hills tucked into the northeastern corner of the country. Their equipment, supplies, and animals arrived by rail as well.

A forty-two-year-old second-generation American Baptist missionary, Harold Young, who was born and raised in northern Burma, was brought in to speak to the battalions. Pastor Young had grown up hunting with the indigenous tribes and had a lifetime of experience navigating the inhospitable terrain they were about to enter. He demonstrated how to get water from bamboo and banana trees, how to build shelters and insect-proof bedding in the jungle, and how to hunt and trap small game. He said Burma was home to at least forty varieties of venomous snakes, including cobras, many-banded krait, and vipers. The venom from their bites caused vomiting, abdominal pain, diarrhea, dizziness, and in severe cases led to paralysis, respiratory failure, and death by asphyxiation. Burma's snake bite mortality rate was twice as high as the world average, and in addition to snakes that could kill with their venom, Young said, there were species powerful enough to crush a man to death. Holding his audience's rapt

---

* The War Department's code name for the 5307th Composite Unit (Provisional) in reports and dispatches was "GALAHAD," but that name was so secret that it was not known to the men in its ranks but only to a few of the unit's top officers until nearly the end of the Burma campaign.

attention, he told them about the Burmese python, which could be more than twenty feet long and weigh as much as 165 pounds. He described them as opportunistic carnivores that were always hungry, and said they ate birds and mammals as large as pigs, goats, and deer. They used their sharp teeth to seize their prey, then wrapped around it to kill by constriction, and ingested whole their still-warm meal. On occasion, he added, pythons attacked and devoured humans. With that, the pastor smiled and wished them Godspeed.

Roy's 2nd Battalion broke camp early the next morning and spent the day packing. Shortly before midnight they set off on foot down the newly constructed Ledo Road, headed for Ningbyen, Burma, 140 miles away. Soon, lining both sides of the forty-foot-wide dirt road as far as Roy could see in the shimmery light of the moon were the bobbing helmets of soldiers with full packs riding high on their backs. For security reasons, the battalions made staggered, nighttime departures; 1st Battalion had left late the night before, and 3rd Battalion was to leave the following night.

The hardpack road had been hewed out of dense rain forests and

The long hike into northern Burma

solid rock masses by Army bulldozers and laborers, thousands of the latter from segregated African American units such as the 45th Engineer General Service Regiment and the 823rd Aviation Engineer Battalion. For months, these crews had toiled night and day in the heat, humidity, and monsoon rains on the new road, which when completed would bisect Burma to connect India and China by a 1,074-mile overland route. In terrain rife with steep gradients, hairpin curves, and sheer drops, the work required the removal of earth at the rate of 100,000 cubic feet per mile.

As 2nd Battalion soldiers trudged past road crews, the Army laborers stepped back, leaning on their shovels and picks to cheer, wave, and whistle, delighted to see U.S. combat troops at last moving into position between them and the enemy. For months, advance surveying parties had been harassed by Japanese patrols, and bulldozer drivers and road crews had come under fire from snipers. And for months there had been rumors of American infantrymen on their way, but nary a one until now. It was a glorious sight. One night, the soldiers were even serenaded by a band from an engineering regiment that waited hours for them to pass. The musicians played stirring renditions of "Dixie" and "God Bless America" that put a spring in the steps of the weary marchers.

But not everyone was so welcoming. Roy saw a GI filling up his canteen from a large lister bag hanging from a metal stand. A common sight on the road, the thirty-six-gallon canvas bags held fresh water for the workers. Down to a few gulps in his canteen, Roy went to fill up.

A black private stepped in front of him, blocking his way.

The five-foot-two Roy looked up at him. "Can I get some water?"

"No. Not for Japs."

Roy walked away without another word, even though as a sergeant he had more stripes on his sleeve and could have ordered the private to step aside. Roy was angry enough to have done that and more, but he held his temper. The sad irony of the encounter in the midst of a war stayed with him for a long time. *One second-class American discriminated against by another second-class American. Was there no end to it?*

The fully laden men and pack animals averaged ten miles a day. Whenever dawn approached, they stepped off the road and made camp until sundown, resting through the heat of the day. Then after sunset, they hit the road again. On the fifth night, they crossed the India-Burma border, which they only recognized thanks to a hand-painted sign in English stuck in the ground: WELCOME TO BORDERVILLE—GOD BE WITH YOU. A cold rain spattered on the sign and a U.S. flag planted next to it on the dividing line between the two countries. The snowcapped Himalayas could be plainly seen in the distance, and the awe-inspiring view during a short break took their minds off the many miles still in front of them.

The rain continued intermittently, and parts of the road became a quagmire. As they wound down mountains as high as 4,500 feet—the same ones they had so laboriously scaled on the other side—they were deflated to find that going downhill with all their heavy gear was even more difficult, and it was a struggle every step of the way to keep from losing their footing.

They came to the end of the new road about twenty miles short of Ningbyen, where Merrill's battalions were to assemble and be resupplied before advancing against the enemy in the Hukawng Valley. The hike down Ledo Road had been a long haul, but the final miles on an overgrown native trail through the jungle proved to be rougher still. As they could scarcely see in the dark, they switched to traveling in the heat of the day. Even so, the opaque light filtering through the mass of vines and banyan trees was barely enough to see more than ten to fifteen feet. Steep downgrades were followed by nearly perpendicular uphill climbs, only to be repeated, over and over again.

Roy's battalion reached Ningbyen on February 18, and by the next day all three battalions were together again. Supplies had been dropped the day before by aircraft, and the exhausted men feasted on the meals in the ten-in-one food parcels, a veritable holiday spread compared to the K rations they had been limited to on the march. Now they had coffee, pudding, evaporated milk, canned meats and vegetables, biscuits, jam, cereal, candy, salt, sugar, and valued accessories like a small can opener, and more toilet paper, soap, and water-purification tablets.

Ningbyen had been the scene of a successful Chinese attack against entrenched Japanese positions three months earlier. The debris of that battle was still everywhere, with wrecked Japanese equipment strewn about and the ruins of a Buddhist temple along with hundreds of broken clay and wooden idols scattered on the ground. Overlooking the

Merrill's Marauders and pack animals
making a river crossing in northern Burma

scars of battle, the men washed themselves and their clothes in a
nearby river, and for a few days caught up on their rest.

On February 23, 1944, when Merrill returned by jeep from a conference with Stilwell at his field headquarters a few miles away, he convened his staff, as well as battalion and combat team commanders.

"Well, gentlemen," Merrill said, grinning, "here's what we've been waiting for." He went to a large relief map on the wall. "We move in the morning with our general objective to cut the road between Jambu Bum and Shingbwiyan and get into the 18th Division Jap command sector."

The Japanese 18th Infantry Division, considered one of the ablest and best-trained divisions in the Imperial Japanese Army, were veterans of the Battle of Nanking and participants in the atrocities known as the Nanking Massacre. The division had chased Stilwell, Merrill, and the Allies out of Burma once, and they now held the main line of defense in northern Burma, charged with defending the ground they had previously won, keeping the Allies from completing their road to China, and holding the only all-weather airfield in northern Burma at Myitkyina, just thirty-five miles from the China border. Comprised of two infantry brigades, each with two regiments, as well as an anti-tank battalion, eight tank companies, and several artillery regiments, the division's total strength was estimated by U.S. intelligence at 22,200 men.

"The enemy situation is shown here," Merrill said. He tapped a pointer at each location on the map as he recited the names from memory. "The Japs are located here at Mungwan, at Taipha Ga, Kaduja Ga, Nzang Ga, Lanem Ga, Tanja Ga, and on the east bank of the Tawang Hka River. In the area around Maingkwan, Mashi Dam ferry, and

Nisei interrogators with Merrill's Marauders in Burma

General Frank Merrill, center,
with Herbert Miyasaki (far left)
and Akiji Yoshimura

at Makaw and Lalwan Ga, there is another company dug in. There is a possibility of artillery at Sina Gahtawng. The 55th Regiment of the 18th Division, the seasoned jungle fighters who took Singapore, is east of the main road and the 56th Regiment is west of the main road. All that this information does is give us the general picture. We must depend on our own resources for information on which to make our future plans. Therefore, I am taking the Intelligence and Reconnaissance Platoons from all three battalions and placing them directly under my command for our first move."

Merrill estimated that by March 2—in about a week's time—they would make contact with "sizable forces of Japanese." After a brief discussion about specific troop assignments, the meeting broke up.

The next morning, before they headed into the jungle for the combat they had all volunteered for months earlier, their last letters home were turned in to be read by Army censors. For security reasons, they would not be able to send letters home while behind enemy lines.

One private wrote his family a short note that ended with a line the censor did not cut: "My pack is on my back, my gun is oiled and loaded, and as I walk into the shadow of death, I fear no son-of-a-bitch."

Eleven

MERRILL'S MARAUDERS

Roy Matsumoto was assigned to the intelligence and reconnaissance (I&R) platoon of 2nd Battalion's Blue Combat Team.

Each of the Marauders' six combat teams had its own I&R platoon, and they all had a Nisei interpreter with them. Trained to stay at least a full day in front of their combat team, an I&R platoon picked the safest routes for the troops behind them, and found fields suitable for supplies to be dropped by parachute. Built to travel light and move fast, each I&R platoon had two pack animals: one to carry their equipment and supplies, and the other for mounted reconnaissance or to transport a messenger or casualty. Their radios consisted of SCR-300s, backpack walkie-talkies with a range of three miles for communications within the platoon, and a larger SCR-284 radio with a twenty-five-mile range. Scouting far out in front, it was likely they would make first contact with the enemy, against whom they were to fight only long enough to determine their position, strength, and weapons. After radioing a contact report, they were to meld back into the jungle.

The I&R platoons were composed of fifty men chosen for their toughness and stamina. They were the fastest and hardiest marchers, the most experienced outdoorsmen, the most skilled hand-to-hand fighters, and the best shots. During training, Roy had qualified as an expert marksman on the rifle range, which surprised him since he had never fired a gun before the Army. He had chosen to carry a semi-automatic M1 carbine over a Garand rifle because it was lighter and had fifteen-round clips; at ten pounds, the Garand was twice as heavy and used eight-round clips. While training in northern India, he had shown off to his buddies his proficiency with the M1 by aiming for a large rock in the middle of the Betwa River. From three hundred yards away, he hit what he was aiming for, but the rock turned out to be a six-foot alligator, which leapt high into the air and with a swish of its tail dove out of sight into the murky waters.

On February 23, 1944, just hours after Merrill briefed his officers following his conference with Stilwell, Roy's I&R platoon departed to begin reconnoitering the forested heights of the 4,100-foot Kumon Range, which formed the imposing eastern boundary of the Hukawng Valley, an isolated 5,585-square-mile valley ringed by steep mountains to the north, east, and west. Before they departed, Merrill had reminded the scouts of their vital role: "You're not to fight unless necessary. Your mission is purely reconnaissance." They were too few to handle a large force on their own, he told them, and he didn't want to lose his "eyes and ears."

With a map case and a sheathed machete strapped to his side, Merrill led his command group out of camp shortly after the scouts left, heading for the place Stilwell had chosen for the first battle to reconquer northern Burma. By flanking and hitting the Japanese at Walawbum, sixty miles away, the Marauders would create a second line for the enemy to defend as three Chinese divisions under Stilwell's command struck five miles north of Walawbum at Maingkwan.* To avoid detection by enemy patrols in the valley, the Marauders were to climb into the high country before turning south. In order to pull off a surprise flanking movement of the enemy, they would have to march through some of the most difficult terrain in northern Burma.

On the trail, Roy and the other scouts carried on only short, hushed

---

* Although the Chinese attack was technically a frontal assault, they were in the rear of the Marauders at Walawbum, and for most of the battles that followed in northern Burma. Many of the Chinese units had never been in combat and were neither fully trained or staffed nor supplied with adequate automatic weapons. And several of the Chinese regiments were in such poor physical condition that they often could not keep up with the pace of planned operations, and frequently arrived several days late.

conversations, but the jungle was far from quiet. Exotic bird and parrot calls, crickets chirping, frogs croaking, and the humming and buzzing of cicadas and other insects produced a rain forest symphony. Over-ripe mangos and papayas contributed to a powerful, earthy aroma. The men walked in hundred-degree heat that bore down on them, the air so humid they could practically taste it. Mostly, they went in silence; the only sounds they made were their own heavy breathing, the hacking back of overgrown vines, and the soft clopping of boots and hooves on exposed roots and dead leaves. But it was enough to frighten flocks of birds into flight. At one point, a colony of monkeys took off swinging through the trees, screeching until their chattering receded in the distance. The scouts knew their presence had been announced for miles on the jungle telegraph.

That night and every night that followed, they made a wheel-shaped camp as they had been trained, with their animals, radios, and supplies forming the protected hub in the middle, and riflemen spread out around the outer rim in two-man foxholes that allowed for one man to close his eyes for a couple of hours while the other stayed alert.

On the third day, Roy was right behind a five-man squad leading the way. As they started to enter the village of Lanem Ga, the *tat-tat-tat* of a Japanese heavy machine gun rang out from fifty yards away.

The lead scout, Private Robert Landis, was killed instantly.

Roy and the others furiously returned fire. They soon realized that they were up against an enemy platoon well dug in on high ground in the village, with several machine guns covering the spot where Landis went down. Recovering his body would be impossible.

They slowly withdrew and reported the contact by radio.

Landis was the first Marauder killed in action. Roy knew the blond, soft-spoken, always-cheerful Landis well, and seeing his shattered body on the ground was his first real shock of the war. There would be other shocks and more KIAs to come, but he would never forget the first one: smiling Bobby Landis of Youngstown, Ohio.

The next morning, the scouts discovered that the Japanese had pulled out of Lanem Ga. They found Landis where he had fallen. He had been stripped of his clothes, gun, ammo, and other gear, but otherwise untouched. After making sure the body wasn't booby-trapped, his buddies buried him with a short prayer on a grassy knoll near the village center. It would be only a temporary burial site until an Army graves registration unit could move his remains to a military cemetery. The towhead from America's heartland was the first U.S. soldier killed on the continent of Asia since the Boxer Rebellion a half century earlier.

When they stopped for the night, the platoon leader, Lieutenant William Grissom, approached Roy. Since he had been friends with Landis, the lieutenant asked, would he write the next-of-kin notification letter? "Landis is the first man I've lost," Grissom said uneasily. "Look, Roy, I was a schoolteacher back home. But I don't know how to write that letter."

Roy wanted to tell the young lieutenant that he would have other such letters of condolences to write before this thing was over, but he kept quiet and wrote to Mr. and Mrs. Landis. He told them the truth—that Bob had been well liked by all the men, would be missed by everyone, and had been bravely leading his platoon in combat when he died for his country.

In the days that followed there were more skirmishes with enemy patrols and outposts as the three battalions moved on separate but parallel routes toward Walawbum, often on trails along sharp ridge- lines with rocky gorges on one or both sides. At night, they bivouacked within about a mile of one another, with one battalion in front, one in the middle, and one in the rear, each setting up a defensive perimeter.

In a week, they were within fifteen miles of Walawbum when Mer- rill elected to schedule an airdrop of supplies for the next day, as they were running low and it might be a while before they could do so again. They encamped near the banks of the Numpyek River, and the men rested, swam, and traded for trinkets with the native Kachins from a nearby village. The Kachins had been fighting the Japanese for more than a year, and several guerrillas volunteered to serve as guides through the region. The smiling, bare-breasted women of the village were a big hit with the GIs, and the naked children, who at first were frightened by the tall, heavily armed Americans, soon had grins while munching on K ration crackers.

After the airdrop, which replenished them with five days of rations for the men and grain for the animals, plus extra ammunition, Mer- rill issued final attack orders to his commanders. Each of his battalions were to move and fight independently, as they had trained. Second Battalion was to wade across the river and cut a trail through to Kamaing Road three miles west of Walawbum, where they were to set up a block on the only motor route through the Hukawng Valley. The road was not only the enemy's main supply artery but was also the key to control of the valley. Roy's I&R platoon left right away, with the rest of 2nd Battalion to follow in the morning.

Moving through the jungle later that day, the scouts came to a winding trail. Two enemy soldiers suddenly came around a bend, chattering away until they spotted the Americans, who won the ensuing quick-draw contest. They left the dead Japanese where they fell—not a full payback for Bobby Landis, the scouts agreed, but at least a down payment. The bodies were still there when 2nd Battalion passed by the next day.

The next morning, the I&R scouts started through a field when they were fired on from the opposite side of the clearing. The lead scout dropped to the ground, and a half-dozen Japanese soldiers, likely thinking he was dead or wounded, rushed forward. At that moment the scout raised up and emptied his Tommy gun's magazine on full automatic, cutting down several of the enemy and sending the rest into full flight.

Meeting no further resistance the rest of the day, Roy's platoon emerged near dusk from the edge of a teak forest right where they planned to be on Kamaing Road, which was scarred with deep ruts left by truck tires. They felled trees and dropped them across the hardpack dirt road, then dug foxholes and settled in for a long, wakeful night.

A few miles away, it was not so quiet, as 3rd Battalion soldiers, who had set up positions across a river from Walawbum and rained mortar rounds on enemy positions to announce their arrival, were now fighting off waves of attacking Japanese troops. The GIs were shelled by enemy mortars and 75 mm field artillery that filled the air with chunks of earth and splintered tree parts. The incoming rounds kept them down in their foxholes until the next infantry charge, which came with frenzied Japanese choruses of *"Banzai!"* that were answered by the Marauders' own frenetic refrains: *"Fuuuuck you!"* At least seventy-five Japanese were known to die in the day's fighting against the loss of one man and seven wounded for the Marauders.

The next morning at the roadblock south of Walawbum, all was still quiet except for some near misses by a sniper. Looking into the surrounding trees for the shooter, Roy spotted a telephone line running through the treetops parallel to the road. Borrowing a radioman's handset, he climbed a tree. Using the razor-sharp blade of his combat knife, he exposed a section of bare wire and attached a lead from the handset with an alligator clip. At first, he didn't hear anything, and wondered if it was a dead line. But after awhile, he heard scratchy voices. The conversations weren't in standard Japanese, but Roy recognized it as a Kyushu dialect spoken in the Fukuoka Prefecture on Japan's southernmost main island. Most Japanese native speakers would only have been able to pick out a few words and phrases if they weren't familiar with the dialect. Roy had learned it not during his years living in Hiroshima, where a different dialect was spoken, but while delivering groceries in Los Angeles to immigrants from that area of Japan.

Because the Japanese soldiers were speaking a Kyushu dialect, Roy realized that he had tapped into a line belonging to the 18th Infantry Division, nicknamed the "Chrysanthemum Division," which he knew had long been garrisoned in the city of Kurume in the Fukuoka Prefecture. Like other Japanese divisions—and not unlike state National Guard units in the United States—the 18th Division's conscripts came from its home region. Roy was greatly relieved. Ever since volunteering for the Army at the internment camp in Arkansas, he had dreaded the possibility of coming face-to-face on the battlefield with one of his three younger brothers who had been in Japan when the war started and all of whom were now of draft age. If they had been conscripted into the army, Roy knew they would not be in the 18th Division; they would be in the 5th Division from Hiroshima. The same held true for his friends and classmates from the years he went to school in Hiroshima. If any of them were now in the Imperial Japanese Army, they were, of course, the enemies of his country, and he would do his duty. But he prayed to never find himself facing that. In fact, he feared that more than being killed.

Roy stayed in the tree listening to snippets of conversations even as the sporadic sniper fire continued. After a bullet smacked into his tree too close for comfort, he edged around to the opposite side, wedging himself between the limbs. The tree was barely wide enough for him to hide behind, and fortunately the sniper's rifle didn't fire rounds powerful enough to penetrate the trunk; rather, they pinged off it like an out-of-tune banjo. He stayed in his tight perch the rest of the day and well into the night, not coming down to eat or rest or stretch his legs—or even to urinate, and what did that matter? It was so hot and steamy that he was wet most of the time anyway. Whenever he heard anything of interest, he dropped a note down to a communications sergeant, who encoded a message to transmit over the long-range radio to Merrill's command post.

Static on the line made for poor reception at times, and Roy often wished he could ask someone to repeat himself. Hours of silence were punctuated by bursts of conversation between different units in the field and division headquarters, none of it in code. There was a lot of anxious chatter about *Amerikahito* attacking at different locations, so Roy knew that the assault on Walawbum was well under way. The enemy radiomen spoke in the open as if they weren't the least concerned about anyone listening to them, or if anyone was listening, understanding what they were saying. It was obvious to him the enemy had no idea there were Japanese-language operators with U.S. forces in the region.

That night, Roy heard on the line the animated voice of someone who identified himself as a sergeant in charge of an ammo dump. He explained with alarm that he had only two riflemen to guard the site, and requested reinforcements. Asked to confirm his location, the Japanese sergeant read off the map coordinates. Roy jotted them down.

It was dark when he came down from the tree. Covering his head and shoulders with his rain poncho, Roy flicked on a small light and checked the British military map the scouts were using. Burma had been under British rule for more than a hundred years, and so far they alone had surveyed this isolated region. Even the Japanese were using captured British maps. Roy marked the location of the ammo dump a few miles away, and the communications sergeant radioed the coordinates.

The next morning, a single P-51 aircraft buzzed overhead. Soon, a series of thunderous explosions were heard for miles as an 18th Division ammunitions depot blew up.

A message of congratulations from Merrill for the actionable intelligence soon came in. But by then, Roy Matsumoto was back in the tree, eavesdropping on the enemy's increasingly frantic conversations.

———·———

Walawbum fell in just a few days when Japanese forces, after incurring several hundred killed and wounded, suddenly withdrew. The rapid collapse of opposition happened so unexpectedly that when the Marauders and Chinese first encountered one another at the outskirts of Walawbum they exchanged rifle and mortar fire until a Nisei interpreter identified the opposing force as Chinese, not Japanese, and the Americans ceased fire, as did the Chinese, before anyone was killed or wounded.

The first phase of the campaign to retake northern Burma ended with the capture of Walawbum, which gave the Allies control of the only vehicular road through the Hukawng Valley. The Marauders' combat casualties were surprisingly light—eight men killed and thirty-seven wounded—but in an ominous forewarning, more than one hundred men were already sick enough with malaria, dengue fever, and other tropical illnesses to be medically evacuated from the jungle. With malaria pandemic in the region, many others in the ranks were also exhibiting symptoms of the disease: fever, shaking chills, headache, vomiting, anemia, muscle weakness.

Grant Hirabayashi, assigned to 1st Battalion's Red Combat Team, was dealing with his own maladies, and they had nothing to do with combat, as 1st Battalion had been held in reserve at Walawbum and he had yet to fire a shot in the war. In fact, his health troubles began before he stepped foot in Burma. During training maneuvers in India, he had fractured his elbow when he jumped from an incline and landed on his rifle stock, and had to convince the medics to let him continue with his arm in a sling. A short time later, he began breaking out in hives whenever he ate K rations. As the 2,830-calorie boxed meals were to be their main sustenance in Burma, his allergy was serious enough for him to be seen by the battalion medical officer. After examining him, the doctor put it bluntly: "You are unfit for frontline duty."

Grant understood that he was being offered an easy way out and a return ticket home. No one could criticize him if he grabbed it. But to end up behind a desk? The Army had trained him extensively for this job, and he had not yet done anything. And if he hightailed it back now, he wouldn't have the opportunity to prove himself to be a loyal American, as he had resolved to do the day he left his family behind the wire at Tule Lake.

Standing before the medical officer, Grant pleaded his case to stay with the Marauders, pointing out that he had spent six months at the Army's language school and another three months in India training for this assignment. His Nisei partner on the Red Combat Team, Eddie Mitsukado from Hawaii, needed his help, as he had never lived in Japan and was only a passable linguist. Grant explained how he had gone to school in Japan for eight years, and had graduated at the top of his class at the MISLS. He knew the Japanese, and their culture, military, and language, as well as or better than any of the other Nisei attached to the Marauders.

The doctor seemed to mull over Grant's logical yet emotional appeal. "Well, sergeant, you'll have to face the consequences if you stay."

Grant wanted to go as far as he could, and was willing to take whatever chances came with his decision. "Doc, I am prepared to do that."

But now, deep in enemy territory in northern Burma, Grant wasn't sure he had made the right decision. Starting with the long march down Ledo Road, then the trek through the jungles and mountains to Walawbum, he had gone a solid month on waxy, heat-resistant chocolate bars filled with so much cacao that they tasted bitter, not sweet, and whatever else he could scrounge or trade for along the way. At first, he had taken the doctor's advice and tried eliminating K ration items one by one to find the culprit. But all the preserved foods in the meal kits—canned chicken, beef, pork, eggs, and cheese—sickened him. He was perpetually hungry, and each day was a struggle for nourishment. If he gave in and ate K rations, as he occasionally did, his lips swelled, he broke out in hives, and his stomach and bowels revolted. Grant felt the pounds melting away and with them his energy and strength. He didn't know how long he could keep going.

With the approach of the monsoon season (May through October), which brought with it much of the country's sixty inches of annual rainfall, Stilwell moved swiftly to exploit the Japanese defeat at Walawbum. On March 12, the Marauders went back into the hills and mountains of the Kumon Range to make another flanking movement on an enemy stronghold. Their objective was fifty miles to the south: the Kachin village of Shaduzup.

For Grant's Red Combat Team, the first two days went well and they hiked about twenty miles. On the third day, they fought several skirmishes with small enemy patrols before being halted at a trail block manned by heavily armed enemy troops. As soon as the lead platoon was pinned down by machine gun fire, the Japanese lobbed mortar shells behind them so rapidly they could not be easily supported by other platoons moving up to help. When the Marauders got their mortars into action and finally struggled through the thick growth to flank the enemy, the Japanese quickly moved 100 to 150 yards up the trail and repeated their tactics. This was good ground for such a delaying action because the jungle was so dense and difficult to get through, and once off the trail the Americans lost sight of one another past the walls of flora.

By dusk, they had made little progress. Knowing a lengthy holdup could impact the timetable for the attack at Shaduzup, 1st Battalion commander Lieutenant Colonel William Osborne decided to cut a new trail around the Japanese. He ordered the Red Combat Team to keep contact with the enemy until the following afternoon, and he moved the rest of the battalion back a short distance down the trail, where they waited out the night. At dawn, they started chopping their own path through the jungle.

Later that day, Grant's combat team disengaged from the enemy and took the newly cut trail. Soon, it was as if the jungle had swallowed the battalion. Their rear guard confirmed that the enemy was not following them, and the Red Combat Team quickly caught up with the others.

At the front of the line, it was brutal, backbreaking work. Enlisted men and officers alike spelled each other, taking turns swinging machetes and kukris, the long, curved knives favored by the Gurkhas as a tool and weapon. Groves of bamboo as tall as telephone poles were the worst to cut through. Their thick, woody stems were so interwoven high overhead that they did not fall when lopped off at ground level and had to be hacked again six feet above the ground, turning the pathway through them into a gloomy tunnel. The soldiers chopped through fields of elephant-ear taro plants as tall as six feet, their large leaves dotted with jumbo-sized black or red leeches that dropped onto passersby and clung to clothing and exposed skin. If the bloodsuckers were pulled, picked, or sliced off, parts of them remained imbedded under the skin, leaving a painful lump that easily became infected. The shiny, parasitic worms only dropped off after they were full of blood. The men found they could get the leeches to fall off intact by placing the tip of a lighted cigarette next to them, but still they left open, bleeding sores. Conducting regular body searches, they were appalled to find blood-engorged leeches everywhere: under their trousers, shirts, socks, even inside their underwear.

Grant woke up one morning and looked over at a sleeping Edward Mitsukado. To his horror, his MIS buddy's face was covered in blood. His first thought was that Eddie had been killed. But it had been leeches feasting on him during the night. Apparently, Mitsukado swiped them off in his sleep, and the worms left behind open sores all over his face.

In two days they managed only four miles before emerging at a trail-head near the village of Kumshan Ga, in the mountains northeast of Shaduzup. They were still twenty miles away. By then, they were running out of food for the men and the animals. The best available spot was cleared for supplies to be landed by parachute and bales of grain free-dropped, and Osborne radioed for an airdrop. The next morning, the cargo planes found their location, but had to push their loads out at a higher altitude than usual because the drop zone was framed by tall ridges. Caught in the wind, some chutes floated into the hills, and search parties had to be sent out. As soon as the supplies were packed up, the battalion started out on a trail heading south, with Grant's Red Combat Team in the lead.

The next day at dusk they bivouacked within ten miles of Shaduzup. Moving out in the morning, their scouts ran into a Japanese patrol; one Marauder was killed and two wounded, although not seriously enough to be evacuated. Eleven Japanese—the entire patrol—were killed. The scouts reported enemy blocks on all the trails leading into Shaduzup.

Osborne opted to again cut their own trail to avoid further engagements with the enemy until they were ready to spring the trap. For two days they chopped and slashed through five miles of nearly impenetrable growth. All agreed that the second day, when they managed a little more than a mile in twelve hours, was their most tortuous one since entering Burma. The inclines were often too vertical for the heavily laden mules and horses. Again and again, men had to unpack the loads and haul everything to the top, then repack the animals.

By March 26, Osborne's battalion of some nine hundred Marauders was finally in position south of Shaduzup. The plan drawn up by Stilwell and Merrill called for the Marauders to catch the Japanese by surprise and block the Kamaing Road south of Shaduzup at the entrance of a corridor formed by the Mogaung Valley. They were convinced that the Japanese expected to be attacked not from the rugged Kumon Range but through the Hukawng Valley from Walawbum, the most direct route and the one for which they had likely prepared. In fact, that was the route by which Stilwell had sent the Chinese 22nd Division toward Shaduzup, while the Marauders undertook the grueling trek through the mountains to strike from the opposite direction. This was the kind of deep-penetration mission behind enemy lines for which the Marauders had trained. The maneuver itself was a classic pincer movement, or double envelopment, espoused by Sun Tzu's *The Art of War*, in which attacking forces simultaneously hit both flanks of an enemy formation.* If they succeeded at Shaduzup, the supply lines between the 18th Division's base thirty miles to the south and its forward troops would be severed, depriving them of food and ammunition and eliminating them as an effective fighting force.

Osborne learned from his scouts that the enemy held Shaduzup with at least three hundred men, and had another five hundred to six hundred troops a few miles away. Confident that the Japanese were as yet unaware of their presence, Osborne selected a place to block Kamaing Road four miles south of Shaduzup, close to where the road paralleled the meandering Mogaung River. However, his scouts also

---

* The type of irregular warfare being fought by his Marauders in Burma followed another Sun Tzu tenet. "The enemy must not know where I intend to give battle. For if he does not know where I intend to give battle he must prepare in a great many places. And when he prepares everywhere he will be weak everywhere."

reported a company-sized enemy force bivouacked on the west bank of the river near the intended block. They had seen Japanese bathing and swimming in the river, and netting fish after exploding grenades in the water. The encampment of some 150 enemy soldiers would have to be taken first.

Osborne exchanged coded radio messages with Merrill, then briefed his officers. The White Combat Team would cross the river with its flanks protected by the Red Combat Team on the river's east bank. After securing the camp, they would rapidly set up the block on the road to stop enemy troops and vehicles from entering or leaving Shaduzup. Osborne knew that the other Marauder battalions were not available to assist if he needed help, as the 2nd and 3rd Battalions had been sent deeper through the Kumon Range on a course that swung wider to the east so they could strike the enemy farther south.

At 3 a.m. on March 28, the 450 men of the White Combat Team waded across the river in silence, settling into the tall grasses and shrubbery along the west bank to await sunrise. When dawn came, they saw fires crackling in the camp and early risers moving about.

When Osborne gave the order, the waiting Marauders advanced on the unsuspecting camp without encountering a single sentry. With bayonets fixed to their rifles, they swept through the camp. The Japanese were caught completely by surprise. Naked or half-dressed, they scattered in all directions. Those with weapons fired wildly, but they were quickly killed by bayonets or bullets or grenades. Within minutes the camp was overrun by the hard-charging (and hungry) Americans, who on their way through snatched rice and fish boiling over the camp fires. When they reached Kamaing Road, they put up the roadblock, dug a defensive perimeter, and waited for an anticipated counterattack.

At midmorning Grant was ordered to cross the river to the ransacked enemy camp to monitor a phone line. To ensure that he wasn't mistaken for a Japanese soldier and shot by other GIs, two Caucasian privates were assigned to accompany him. With the rail-thin, five-foot-three Grant sandwiched between the six-footers, they began wading across. At first the water was only ankle-deep but by the time they reached the middle it was nearly up to Grant's chin. He struggled to keep his M1 carbine and a canvas pouch holding dictionaries and maps from getting wet. But as the water deepened he had a more urgent worry, as he had never learned how to swim. Once when he was a kid, he had fallen into a lake, sank like a sack of rocks, and had to be pulled to safety.

At that very moment, three rapid shots were fired—*shoo . . . shoo . . . shoo.*

They impacted with splashes in the water only a few feet away.

There was no place for Grant and his escorts to take cover, and nothing to do but keep moving with their rifles held over their heads. Fortunately, the men on the bank behind them saw the muzzle flashes in a tree across the river, and opened up with a deafening fusillade. Their combined firepower was so great that it demolished the tree, with splintered limbs and branches dropping to the ground along with a dead enemy sniper. When they entered the camp, Grant discovered that the phone line was dead, too. But his hair-raising trip was not completely futile, as he found in the deserted camp a pot of steamed rice and a can of sardines and scarfed down his first real food in more than a month.

The counterattack at the roadblock was not long in coming. Japanese infantry made a number of assaults over the next few hours, and the Marauders answered them with devastating fire. In one attack alone, their machine gunners mowed down a line of charging Japanese, dropping more than sixty of them. The biggest surprise for the Americans was when artillery shells whistled overhead from 75 mm mountain guns. These were standard field artillery for Japanese infantry divisions, but the scouts had reported seeing no enemy artillery units around Shaduzup. The combat vets among the Marauders had told the others that the one thing an infantryman never wanted to hear was the warning "Incoming!" and being on the wrong end of an artillery barrage.

Grant, in a foxhole on the riverbank, now knew the truth of that statement. The earth shook as if it would split open, and after each concussive, thunderous explosion came the unnerving pings of shrapnel whizzing through the air. He tried counting the blasts. The fifth one landed so close he was covered in a layer of dirt and shredded vegetation. After that, he lost count. During a brief lull, he quickly dug his foxhole a foot deeper, and was glad he did because the shelling continued all night. Jungle combat wasn't anything like Grant thought it would be. He quickly realized that if he was killed it would likely be by an enemy he didn't see. The best way to tell which direction the bullets were coming from in the jungle was to look up at the bamboo. Any plants that were hit splattered water away from the gun's direction. This also gave the height of the bullet's path.

By the next morning, the Marauders had repelled the last of the attacks at the roadblock and were moving in force up Kamaing Road toward Shaduzup. U.S. planes flew unchallenged overhead, bombing enemy targets on the road and in the village, and knocking out Japanese artillery batteries in the hills. At the same time, Chinese units were pushing down from the north. Caught between the two advancing forces and without their own air support or hope of reinforcements, the Japanese defenses collapsed. The remaining Japanese fled into the canopy rain forest to the west, the only path of escape open to them. The enemy had been left a way to depart the field of battle during the pincer movement; not doing so, Sun Tzu had argued two thousand years earlier, risked a defeated foe fighting more fiercely when facing annihilation.

In every way, the operation went as Stilwell and Merrill had drawn it up, and the objective was achieved with light U.S. casualties. While the enemy lost an estimated three hundred dead and most of their equipment and supplies, Osborne's 1st Battalion had eight men killed and thirty-five wounded.

While a field surgical unit treated the injured, the Americans were relieved, platoon by platoon, by Chinese soldiers. The Marauders waded across the river to where they had started in the dark at 3:00 the previous morning. Fatigued by the battle as well as the long weeks of travel and hardships they had endured to get here, many of them were weakened further by tropical illnesses. But still they sang, laughed, and celebrated even as a sudden, warm downpour drenched them. They had at last faced the enemy whom they had trained long and hard to fight here in Burma, and they had kicked their asses.

The next day, April 1, a sack of grain falling from a supply plane during an airdrop crashed into the battalion's only working long-range radio, knocking it out of operation. They had no contact with Merrill's command post until a radioman succeeded in repairing it two days later. The initial messages they received were urgent ones. A sizable

Japanese force had advanced on the other Marauder battalions from the south. Second Battalion was surrounded at a hilltop hamlet called Nhpum Ga and in danger of being overrun. Third Battalion was five miles away but was in a fight of its own. First Battalion's marching orders were to "make haste" toward Nhpum Ga to break the siege and rescue 2nd Battalion.

Osborne located Nhpum Ga on his map near the southern end of the Kumon Range, twelve miles as the crow flies, a few miles farther by native footpaths. They hurriedly packed up and started on the trails they had taken only days before in the opposite direction. Backtracking along the Chindwin River, they entered the familiar foothills, then climbed into the inhospitable mountains. When they wheeled southward, they were still several days from where the 2nd Battalion was fighting for its survival.

In the searing heat and oppressive humidity, they double-timed on the trails whenever possible. For Grant, every step of the forced march was a struggle. His body ached and he was again covered in hives. Worse, he had amoebic dysentery—as did many of the men— a parasitic infection of the colon transmitted by contaminated water or food that caused diarrhea, nausea, and weight loss. The cardinal rule was to drink only clean water, but in the heart of Burma that was not easily done. Often, they just didn't have time to drop the halazone tablets into water and wait the prescribed time for it to be purified. They all tried to siphon water from the trunks of bamboo as they had learned in jungle training, but that wasn't the volume they needed to stay hydrated in the unrelenting heat.

As the animals were hauling the battalion's supplies and equipment, every man had to carry his own pack. But by now, Grant was in such a weakened state that the battalion's medical officer, Captain John McLaughlin, took his pack from him and tied it onto the back of a mule. Grant and the other men already considered Doc McLaughlin a saint practicing medicine, but Grant was too weak to even thank him.

All he could do was listlessly follow the animal.

At one trailhead, a bull elephant poked through the brush to see what the commotion was about. Apparently, it was the first time it had seen a mule, because it roared, waved its trunk, and went on its hind legs before bolting back into the shrubbery. The whinnying and hee-hawing mule was obviously just as scared, and likely would have run off down the trail if it hadn't been so damn tired and loaded down.

Later, during a short break, the mule had enough, and dropped to its knees. The muleskinner who had been leading the animal by a rope attached to its halter offered a helmet filled with water, which it guzzled. When it was time to move out, the mule wouldn't stand up.

"Grrreup!" the muleskinner barked. "Grrreup!" But no amount of yelling, cajoling, or tugging on the halter had an effect. The muleskinner unloaded the mule to help it stand, but still the animal refused to budge.

As Grant watched the scene, his heart sank. He had reached his physical limit, and was in no shape to reclaim his heavy backpack and stay up with the column, which was moving out of sight around a bend in the trail. But remaining here on his own would be a death sentence.

The muleskinner let out a long string of curses that ended in an appeal to the mule's patriotism. "Damn it, Jethro! You volunteered for this mission, too!" Laboriously, the mule rose. After its load was again secured on its back, they started out to catch up with the column.

A few hours later they came to a steep incline. The only way Grant could make it up was by hanging on to the mule's tail and letting the animal pull him along, which it did while passing gas in his face. At one point, the poor mule turned its head and stared back at him. Grant expected a swift kick to follow, which would have sent him careening head over heels down the mountainside. But instead, he got only a mulish dirty look, and together they made it all the way to the top. Then and there, Grant decided, he owed his life to a mule named Jethro.

———

A few days earlier, with 1st Battalion still at Shaduzup, the 2nd and 3rd Battalions were slogging through the jungles and mountains to cut off the Japanese withdrawing from Walawbum toward Kamaing, the 18th Division's central base and supply depot in the Mogaung Valley.

The surprise flanking attacks by the Marauders in coordination with the Chinese frontal assaults had outfoxed one of the most experienced and ablest infantry commanders in the Japanese army: Lieutenant General Shinichi Tanaka. In the 1930s, he had been one of his army's "young Turks" advocating the takeover of China and all-out war with the Soviet Union. Now at fifty, plumper and wearing a toupee, Tanaka was a skilled military strategist who maneuvered his resources superbly and knew how to make the best use of what he had at his disposal. He had been one of the first Japanese senior officers to recognize that the U.S. invasion of Guadalcanal was more than a reconnaissance-in-force. As chief of staff of the Southern Army Area, he had vehemently objected to his country's failure to send adequate reinforcements to that key battle in the Solomons—so much so that he offended Tojo, Japan's prime minister since October 1941, and in December 1942 Tanaka was dismissed from his post. He had been in limbo until the spring of 1943, when he was given command of the 18th Infantry Division, which put him in charge of the Japanese army's main line of defense in northern Burma.

The two battalions of Marauders marched to within twenty miles of Kamaing, then set up a block. Stilwell, disappointed that he had not trapped more Japanese at Walawbum before they withdrew, hoped to spring another pincer maneuver to do just that. But now Tanaka turned the tables. When his forces unleased a surprisingly strong counterattack at Inkangahtawng, Merrill decided to pull his men back into the surrounding hills to await the arrival of the Chinese infantry and artillery. Tanaka then dispatched an attack force north to hit the approaching Chinese. To counter his move, Stilwell ordered Merrill to block the trails the Japanese would have to use to flank the Chinese. Second Battalion was sent to Nhpum Ga, a village at 2,800 feet above sea level comprised of a half-dozen huts occupied mainly during monsoon flooding. The sleepy hamlet sat at an intersection of trails astride a knobby ridge of the Kumon Range. The battalion was on the last leg of an exhausting march in the rain when enemy artillery found them. There was no place to take cover because they couldn't leave the trail running along a sharp ridgeline as there were sheer drops on either side. They could only try to quicken the pace to get out of range, but that required a nearly superhuman effort as they were ankle-deep in mud.

When the dead-tired Marauders filed into Nhpum Ga, some help-ing the wounded walk or holding them atop mules and others too drained even to speak, they were greeted by a relieved Merrill, who had just arrived at the village with his regimental command post. He was soon receiving an ominous report from 2nd Battalion officers, who described the enemy they had run into on the way here as "no patrol or small unit."

"Can Nhpum Ga be held?" Merrill asked pointedly.

"Yes, we can hold Nhpum Ga," Lieutenant Colonel George McGee Jr said. McGee was just five years out of West Point, where he had graduated in the bottom 20 percent of his class, and he had only recently been promoted to battalion commander. He made the quick declaration without the slightest hesitation, but he was young and eager and this was his first combat command. He had answered the call for volunteers while languishing in a backwater assignment in Trinidad with the 33rd Regiment, the same outfit most of the men in the Marauders' 2nd Battalion had been all too ready to leave even for a top secret "hazardous mission."

"Good," said Merrill. "Hold Nhpum Ga."

With that, Merrill and his staff left on the trail through the jungle to Hsamshingyang, several miles to the north, where 3rd Battalion was protecting a rice paddy that could be used for small planes to fly out the wounded and as a drop zone for parachuted supplies. Merrill's party took the wounded and sick with them.

The next day, McGee sent out platoons to booby-trap the trails and fight delaying actions while he set up his defenses. Nhpum Ga was situated on hills carpeted with grasses, shrubbery, and mature trees. He dispersed his men along a perimeter about five hundred by two hundred yards, shaped in a figure 8 with one loop holding the village and trailheads and the other protecting the area's only water hole at the foot of a shallow hill.

Roy Matsumoto's Blue Combat Team held the south and east lines of the perimeter. He wasn't alone in realizing they were facing a situation for which they had not trained and were ill-equipped. After their slashing attack and quick victory at Walawbum, the battle here was shaping up differently. The Marauders were built to be a fast, mobile force that used stealth and surprise, rather than digging in for a static defense against an attacking army. They did not have artillery to pound the approaching enemy, and they lacked adequate tools to make bun-

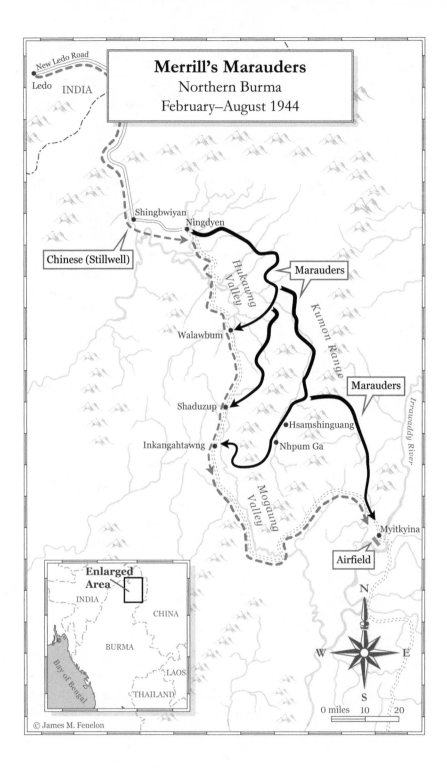

New Ledo Road

Ledo

INDIA

Merrill's Marauders
Northern Burma
February–August 1944

Shingbwiyan
Ningdyen

Chinese (Stillwell)

Hukaung Valley

Marauders

Kumon Range

Walawbum

Marauders

Shaduzup

Hsamshinguang

Inkangahtawng

Nhpum Ga

Irrawaddy River

Mogaung Valley

Myitkyina

Airfield

Enlarged Area

INDIA

CHINA

BURMA

Bay of Bengal

LAOS

THAILAND

N
W   E
S

0 miles   10   20

© James M. Fenelon

Hilltop mortar position in Burma

kers and other fortifications to defend themselves from an assault; they had only the folding spades each man carried. There was little else to do now other than dig foxholes and wait. Roy grabbed his spade and began digging.

As it turned out, their wait was a short one. The platoons sent out on the trails were forced back in a few hours, outnumbered by the pursuing enemy. A short time later, a thunderous barrage of artillery and mortar fire impacted along the southern edge of the U.S. lines, followed by an infantry attack that appeared to be a feeling-out probe. The Marauders answered back with their heavy machine guns and mortars. Sporadic mortar and artillery fire continued throughout the night. Come daylight, a new flurry of enemy shelling began, followed by another infantry attack that was repulsed, as were three more probes that day at different locations along the perimeter.

It was clear to McGee that they were up against at least one infantry battalion and an artillery company. Although his men were holding their positions for now, he worried about an extended siege against additional enemy troops. He radioed Hsamshingyang requesting that they continue to send out patrols to ensure that the trail connecting the two villages remained open, not only to evacuate the wounded but in case he had to withdraw.

Headquarters informed McGee that 2nd Battalion was on its own at Nhpum Ga, as 3rd Battalion was now also under attack at Hsamshingyang and 1st Battalion was still at Shaduzup. While the battalions had trained to operate on their own, having each one engaged in a different fight and unable to lend mutual support to the other was not how Stilwell and Merrill had envisioned using them. Having them isolated and cut off deep behind enemy lines, where they were greatly outnumbered, came with the risk of one or more of them being wiped out.

There was more bad news from headquarters. Merrill had suffered a heart attack and was awaiting medical evacuation at Hsamshingyang, although he had insisted that the other sick and wounded soldiers be flown out first aboard Stinson L-1 aircraft that could take only two passengers at a time. The news swept quickly through the ranks, and the loss of their eponymous leader rattled everyone from the most senior officers down to the lowliest enlisted men. His second-in-command, Colonel Hunter, who was presently at Hsamshingyang with 3rd Battalion, assumed overall command of the three Marauder battalions.

Roy and the others got so they knew the difference between the types of artillery hammering them at Nhpum Ga. There were the big guns, 105 mm howitzers, which they called "Big Bertha." They could hear their thirty-five-pound shells coming in from five or six miles away with a shrill whistle that gave some warning. But they most hated the high-velocity rounds of the 75 mm artillery, fired point-blank from about a thousand yards. Their muzzle blasts and impact explosions were almost simultaneous, with no time to duck and cover. But regardless of which guns fired them, the rounds landing inside the perimeter killed and maimed indiscriminately.

The fighting was taking a toll on the pack animals, too. Unable to be dug-in like the men in foxholes, the mules and horses were hitched to ropes tied between trees. About half of their two hundred animals were already dead, either killed by enemy fire or put down due to injuries. Their bodies lay unburied because snipers often opened fire at the sound of shovels striking the ground. By the second day in the hot and moist climate, the carcasses became bloated and covered with flies and maggots. The collective stench was unbearable.

McGee's radio dispatches reflected the worsening situation at Nhpum Ga.

"We have been hit on three sides."

"My rear is blocked. I cannot withdraw north."

"Casualty report today three KIA and nine WIA."

"Will need ammo tomorrow badly."

"Buried six today."

"Under heavy fire all morning."

"Situation getting critical. Took heavy artillery attack this morning. Three KIA, twelve WIA."

For 2nd Battalion, Nhpum Ga had turned into the Alamo. Whatever overarching strategy had brought them here had morphed into a single tactical imperative: Fight to stay alive. All the trails to and from the hilltop village were now blocked by the enemy, which meant that withdrawing in any direction was out of the question. They had lost the waterhole, which was now surrounded by Japanese machine gun and mortar positions. The sick and wounded cried out for water, but there was not enough even for the medics to make plaster of paris casts to set broken bones. One afternoon's rain provided barely enough water for everyone to wet their parched throats. Men were relegated to drinking from muddy puddles, but it tasted and stank so badly it could hardly be swallowed without retching. They finally received a parachute drop of ammo and three days of K rations, but more supplies landed outside the perimeter and ended up in enemy hands. Worse, they had yet to receive an airlift of potable water they had urgently requested, and were running dangerously low on medical supplies. The weary GIs understood that all the shelling and probes were likely a prelude to an all-out assault. But when and where? If their perimeter was hit with sufficient strength where they were spread thin—and there were many such spots—they could be overrun.

On April 4, one man was killed and eight wounded in all-day fighting that continued after dark, with assaults on the west, north, and east sides of the perimeter. The enemy broke through at one point, overrunning a heavy machine gun position and killing its three-man crew. The battalion log described the fighting as a "battle royal." That same day, McGee received a startling message from Hunter, in which the Marauders' acting commander advised 2nd Battalion to "fight your way out tomorrow. Destroy all excess equipment."

McGee feared that Hunter did not grasp their dire situation. Second Battalion was down from nearly a thousand men when it entered Burma two months before to barely six hundred now, an alarming rate of attrition due to KIAs, WIAs, and tropical diseases. Many of the men still in the ranks were weakened by illnesses and close to collapsing after the torturous marches in the god-awfulest terrain in the world and fighting nearly nonstop on insufficient sleep and too little food. McGee suspected that leaving their dug-in positions in the village for jungle trails and mountain passes where they would be more vulnerable was just what the enemy wanted them to do. Convinced that reinforcements were needed to break the siege, he strove to make that clear in his reply to Hunter: "I can not repeat not attack but can support any action of yours with our fire. Please hurry."

In addition to Roy, three other Nisei were assigned to 2nd Battalion, but two of them had already been medically evacuated, and Bob Honda, the taciturn University of Hawaii alum known for his few but well-chosen words, had a high fever and was so weak he could barely leave his foxhole. But still he kept up his diary even though he had begun to seriously doubt whether any of them would leave Nhpum Ga alive.

> There are Japs all around us . . . They seem to sleep all day and crawl all night, harassing us and keeping us from sleeping . . . It's hell!
>
> At 11:30 they hit us with everything they got . . . I fire and fire in sheer self-preservation. Kill, or they will kill me. My whole body shakes, uncontrollably. Scared? I don't know. I cannot stop shaking. Stupid thing to do, but I counted 64 rounds of jap artillery . . .

Holding a nose of ground that sloped downhill in the northwest corner of the perimeter was an undermanned rifle platoon led by twenty-four-year-old 1st Lieutenant Edward "Mac" McLogan, of

Flint, Michigan. This terrain had not been easy to defend for the past week, but they had fought hard to hold it to deny the high ground to the enemy. A 1942 graduate of the University of Michigan, where he had been in the ROTC program, McLogan had seen combat at Guadalcanal and New Georgia, and well understood the tactical importance of keeping the enemy off a reverse slope that would make it impossible to engage them with direct fire from the other side. In military textbooks, it was known as "denying the defilade." He just wished his platoon was at full strength—he had left India with fifty riflemen but had lost twenty of them. Of course, the other platoons were also down, and they had their own sectors to defend, as this was just one of many weak links.

About 10 p.m., McLogan and his men heard an unusual commotion in front of them. To the lieutenant it sounded like a neighborhood theater letting out back home, only everyone in this crowd was speaking Japanese. Because it had previously been noted that Japanese troops tended to become boisterous in the hours before a big attack, he reported the increased activity to the battalion commanding officer via the shortwave radio.

"I'll send Matsumoto to you," McGee replied.

When he reached McLogan's platoon, Roy found the officer's foxhole and dropped inside. He cupped his ears to try to hear better the babble of voices from across the way. After a while, he shook his head. "Can't make out much, but something's up."

Roy handed his carbine to McLogan, took off his steel helmet, and unhooked his web belt holding his ammo cartridges and other gear.

"What're you doing, Roy?" McLogan asked.

"Keep these for me, Mac. I'm gonna crawl down there closer."

Roy's left forearm was tightly wrapped due to a shrapnel wound he had received in an artillery barrage their second day at Nhpum Ga. He had ended up at the battalion aid station in one of the native huts, although he felt foolish being there for only a laceration while the doctor worked nearby on a poor guy whose guts had spilled out. A medic cleaned and bandaged Roy's wound, and he got out of there as fast as he could.

He now stuffed two grenades into his pants pockets. One was for the enemy if they closed in on him, and the other he would detonate next to his chest rather than be taken prisoner. It was a situation he and the other Nisei had talked about as far back as their voyage across the Pacific aboard the *Lurline* while cooped up in their stateroom. To outsiders, they made light of the scenario. "Better not get caught," they responded whenever someone asked what they thought the enemy would do to them if they were captured. But among themselves, they had more serious discussions. Those who had gone to school in Japan in the 1930s during the rise of the militarists warned that any U.S. Army soldiers of Japanese descent captured on the battlefield would be treated as Japanese traitors to the emperor rather than as American POWs. To a man, the Nisei had vowed they would not allow them- selves to be taken alive only to die a tortured death.

"If you hear a second grenade go off," Roy now told McLogan, "don't bother sending anyone out to look for me."

They reviewed the night's password, which Roy would have to announce upon his return to avoid being shot as an intruder. He knew the risks. So many things could go wrong. Going out, he could be killed by an enemy sentry or crawl through a minefield or trip a booby trap. Coming back, he could be gunned down by a frightened GI who saw a Japanese face. But Roy did not consider it a suicide mission; he thought he could get close enough to understand what the enemy was saying and make it back. In any case, he was the only one left who could do it. He had to try.

Roy started inching forward on his belly. It was so dark he couldn't see beyond his hands in front of him. Scared and shaking now, he said a short prayer, not remembering whether it was Christian or Buddhist, but deciding it didn't matter. An old Japanese proverb came to mind that he had learned as a schoolboy living with his grandparents in Hiroshima.

Koketsu ni irazunba koji o ezu. (If you do not go to the tiger's den, you will not catch its cub.)

He recalled its meaning. *You won't achieve anything unless you take a risk.* That's what he was doing. Heading to the tiger's den. Taking a risk.

After crawling about fifty yards, he settled into the underbrush within fifteen yards of a group of enemy soldiers. Breathing deeply and rhythmically to slow his pounding heart, he willed his body to stillness—no coughing, sneezing, or clearing his throat, any of which could be fatal.

Roy recognized the same mix of standard Japanese and the Kyushu dialect from the Fukuoka Prefecture spoken by the 18th Division troops over the phone line at Walawbum. One soldier wondered how his farm was doing without him, and another pointed out that this was the time of year rice was planted in the fields at home. They spoke of things soldiers everywhere talked about: home, girls, food. Their security discipline was nonexistent. It was no secret, after all, that they were here in force and had Nhpum Ga surrounded. And Roy knew by now that the Japanese discounted any possibility that U.S. soldiers understood their language. Blood-curdling oaths were unleashed periodically, meant to be heard by the GIs across the way. Roy listened for any clues as to what had the enemy soldiers so animated, but after a while he began to wonder if his eavesdropping would produce anything important. To that end, he planned to stay as long as he could. His only deadline was to return while it was still dark. But his timetable changed when someone boasted how their dawn attack would finally break the Americans. Several others agreed. They all sounded anxious to get on with it so they could leave and be resupplied (they were low on food and hungry, too). Their voices betrayed excitement and bravado as they spoke of sneaking up on the *Amerikahito* in the dark, attacking at sunrise, and killing them all.

This was the closest Roy had come to live enemy combatants. In spite of their training in interrogation at Camp Savage, he and the other Nisei in Burma had never questioned any Japanese soldiers. The reason was that the Marauders were not taking enemy prisoners. The order had been issued directly by General Merrill before they departed India. Due to their deep-penetration mission, the three battalions would be unable to feed or guard captured prisoners. To a man, the Marauders believed they would be treated just as harshly if they fell into enemy hands here. Roy had yet to see any Japanese waving a white flag or otherwise trying to give up, and he knew they were conditioned to fight to the death and die honorably for the emperor. They were to neither give nor receive quarter in battle.

When it became clear that the Japanese were talking about hitting the slope defended by McLogan's platoon, Roy knew he had to get right back. He turned around and began crawling uphill. It was shortly after midnight when he whispered the password and slipped back inside their lines.

Roy quickly found the lieutenant. "You're not going to like this. They'll be storming your position at dawn. Company strength, I suspect."

McLogan raised the colonel on the radio and told him what Roy had learned of the enemy's planned attack. If the Japanese succeeded, they would not only control a protected reverse slope but the high ground as well and could fire directly into the battalion's other positions.

"Booby-trap your foxholes on the slope," ordered McGee. "Then move back up the hill and dig in. I can spare you a few men if absolutely needed. Keep Matsumoto with you."

McGee passed the word, telling his men, "Let's give the Japs a surprise." After trip-wiring grenades inside their foxholes, they abandoned them and pulled back close to the crest of the hill, where they quietly dug new ones in the dark. The platoon was reinforced with some added firepower: a heavy machine gun squad and extra BAR men.

As dawn approached, after a sleepless night, everyone was in position. As the first shadows stretched across the field below, the stillness was broken with shrill cries of *"Banzai! Banzai! Banzai!"* A hail of enemy grenades landed at the bottom of the slope and exploded nearly in unison, followed by a wave of helmeted infantry sprinting out of the jungle into the open, firing their rifles. When they reached the foxholes abandoned by the Marauders hours earlier, they shot wildly into them. Those who jumped inside intending to impale U.S. soldiers with their foot-long bayonets were blown sky-high by the booby traps.

From his vantage point near the crest, Roy watched the attack unfold. The enemy appeared stunned not just by the exploding foxholes but also by the speedy occupation of what they thought would be contested ground without seeing a single U.S. soldier. With two sword-waving officers leading them, they charged up the hill like a victorious army.

So far, McLogan's men had held their fire. His orders were for the platoon to not shoot until the attackers were within fifteen yards. When that happened, all hell broke loose. The dug-in Marauders opened up with the full force of their automatic weapons—heavy and light machine guns, BARs, submachine guns, M1 rifles, carbines—as well as hand grenades. The deafening salvo cut down the advancing troops.

With a quick burst from his M1 carbine, Roy nailed one of the Japanese officers wielding a samurai sword, and the other officer was also among the first to fall. Most of the others who had made it up the slope were also down; a few were still shooting, although not for long. Roy then saw that a second wave was emerging from the jungle, although with the furious firefight up the hill they appeared to be hesitating. Should they advance or not? Some had dropped into the old foxholes and others started to turn back toward the jungle. *Of course!* They were confused because the officers leading the way were no longer giving them orders!

It was far better to take care of them now, Roy knew, than let them get away only to return when the Marauders weren't so ready for them. He had learned basic Japanese infantry tactics in compulsory military classes in high school in Japan and remembered the field commands. Rising up in his foxhole so he could be better heard over the din of gunfire, he yelled the prepare-to-charge command in perfect Japanese: *"Jūden suru junbi o suru!"*

He paused, then hollered at the top of his lungs: *"Denka! Denka! Denka!"* (Charge! Charge! Charge!)

Obediently, the second wave rose as one and blindly charged up the hill into the withering gunfire, which included Roy banging away with his carbine. As he stood fully exposed outside his foxhole, he continued to order in his most commanding voice: *"Denka! Denka! Denka!"*

The attack was repelled, and a half hour later fifty-four dead enemy soldiers were counted along with the bodies of the two officers on the slope on which they had died. Not a single American was killed.

Three days later, on an Easter Sunday the survivors of Nhpum Ga would never forget, the 1st and 3rd Battalions broke through to end the siege. That same day, the Japanese who had surrounded 2nd Battalion for ten days had enough and withdrew. Enemy dead numbered

Roy Matsumoto (far right), Burma

at least four hundred. Fifty-two Americans died at Nhpum Ga, and several hundred GIs had to be evacuated, about half with injuries and the rest due to illnesses.

Overnight, Roy Matsumoto became a legend in his own outfit.

"You know, comin' over on the ship some of us talked about throwing you guys overboard when we thought you was Jap prisoners," one gimlet-eyed Marauder admitted to Roy. "God damn good thing we didn't."

Twelve

MYITKYINA

Even with the assistance of Jethro, the patriotic mule, Grant Hirabayashi, malnourished from a near-starvation diet due to his severe allergy to K rations, was unable to make it all the way to Nhpum Ga. Seeing that he was too sick to continue, Doc McLaughlin ordered him evacuated by air on March 24. A few hours later, flushed with fever, racked with chills, and now too weak to walk, Grant was stretchered to a rice paddy, where a Stinson L-5 was waiting for him.

A length of parachute cord had been looped around the plane's tail gear and the opposite end tied to a tree. Grant was lifted into the rear of the tandem two-seater that was so thin-skinned and cramped it seemed more like a go-kart with wings. It was soon dark outside, which the pilot, sitting in front, had been waiting for so they would be less of a target. The 185-horsepower engine backfired several times before catching, then the pilot edged the throttle to full power. As the aircraft bucked at its reins like a rodeo bronc, he signaled for the tethering cord to be cut. The plane lurched forward, bouncing on uneven ground until gaining enough speed to take flight, which came just in time to clear a wall of bamboo.

For two hours they skimmed low over Burma's inky-black terrain and dove through cloud-draped passes to Ledo, India, two hundred miles away. Landing on a long, paved runway, they were met by a Red Cross van that took Grant a short distance to the U.S. Army 20th General Hospital.

It was the middle of the night when he arrived at the hospital complex that was officially rated a two-thousand-bed facility but often had
hundreds more patients at a time. Housed in large bashas, indigenous
structures made chiefly of bamboo with dirt floors and palm frond
roofs, the sprawling facilities were far from ideal. The buildings had
swinging doors that did not latch, and nurses had to drive out various
types of wildlife that wandered in. Electricity was limited and fresh
water was scarce, and the muggy heat tested everyone's physical limits. Nevertheless, staffed by 60 doctors and 120 nurses, most of them
from the University of Pennsylvania School of Medicine, along with
600 enlisted orderlies and technicians, the hospital provided standard
medical care, as well as specialized procedures such as plastic surgery,
neurosurgery, and orthopedic reconstructions. Like the other general
military hospitals in the Pacific and European theaters, it was designed
to be the end of the line for patients' medical requirements, meaning
that they convalesced to a return to duty or were sent home or died
here.* Before he was placed in a basha, Grant had his filthy fatigues
peeled off by two orderlies and tossed into a brick-lined pit, doused
with gasoline, and set afire. To further ensure that whatever bugs he
had carried from Burma went no further, he was taken into a shower
and scrubbed with a grainy, lye-based soap. Then he was shown into
a dark hut, where a female nurse took his temperature, gave him several pills to swallow, and put him to bed. It was his first solid sleep in
months, and he had to be awakened for his admission examination.
He was diagnosed with amoebic dysentery caused by the *Entamoeba
histolytica* parasite, which unchecked can spread to the heart, brain, and
lungs. He learned the medical term—urticaria—for his swollen and
painful hives, now covering much of his body. After losing 20 percent
of his body mass in three months, he weighed one hundred pounds
and had severe weakness in his limbs and crippling fatigue. He was
started on injections of emetine—then the mainstay of treatment of
amoebic dysentery—to kill the parasites lodged in his intestinal tract.

* Of the seventy-three thousand patients admitted to the 20th General Hospital
between 1943 and 1945, three hundred died, resulting in a mortality rate com-
parable to top U.S. hospitals at the time (*Two Centuries of Medicine: A History of
the School of Medicine, University of Pennsylvania*).

A diet high in calories and protein was ordered, along with plenty of liquids and bed rest.

Grant spent the next several weeks sleeping, eating, and reading. He caught up on his letter writing to his parents at Tule Lake, perused back issues of *Life* magazine, and from *Stars and Stripes* and Australian newspapers learned the latest war news. As he began to regain lost pounds, his fever abated, his hives faded, and his stamina improved. Short walks led to longer strolls on the meandering paths between the bashas. He had a setback in mid-May when he developed severe myositis in the deltoid muscle of his left shoulder and arm where he was receiving regular intramuscular injections of emetine. He was treated with anti-inflammatory drugs, and after several days the painful swelling receded. Grant had no idea what the Army would do with him next, but he was thankful to be out of Burma. His relief was short-lived, because in late May all convalescing Marauders able to fire a rifle were urgently ordered back to Burma.

Grant was one of two hundred hospitalized Marauders—some still with dressings on their wounds—flown in C-47s to the Myitkyina airfield on May 22. Doc McLaughlin was there to meet them as they deplaned. Alarmed at what he saw, he ordered the sickest flown back to Ledo. Although few were fully recovered, the others, including Grant, rejoined their old units.

The Marauders had captured the airfield five days earlier against little resistance. U.S. casualties had been light, but they had suffered a major loss. Lieutenant Bill Laffin, the Marauders' intelligence officer, was killed when the unarmed L-1 plane he had gone up in to observe enemy positions was shot down by a Japanese fighter. He and the pilot were dead when a patrol reached the wreckage. The loss of their well-liked leader was a shock to the men on the MIS teams, many of whom had been interviewed in flawless Japanese by Laffin when they volunteered for the "hazardous mission." The son of a Tokyo geisha and an American businessman, Laffin was laid to rest in a gravesite next to the airstrip he died reconnoitering.*

* William A. Laffin's remains were moved in 1950 to the National Memorial Cemetery of the Pacific (Punchbowl) Honolulu, and buried in Section P, Grave 443.

First Battalion was easy for Grant to find, as it was providing security to the airfield, while 2nd and 3rd Battalions had taken up positions near the town of Myitkyina, which had a peacetime population of seven thousand residents, many of whom had already fled. He was shocked to find his old battalion at only one-third strength. The rest were casualties of battles or a multitude of illnesses, as well as the strain of nonstop fighting and marching in impossible terrain and stifling weather on inadequate provisions. General Merrill was one of those casualties. Felled by another heart attack, he was in the hospital and not expected to return.

Grant learned of the harrowing march he missed following his medical evacuation in late March. After rescuing 2nd Battalion at Nhpum Ga and being resupplied by airdrops, the Marauders undertook the near impossible: a sixty-five-mile march over the rugged six-thousand-foot Kumon Mountains on trails considered barely passable even in the dry season. Under early but torrential monsoon rains, they climbed and descended over slippery trails and mountainsides, at times on their hands and knees. As they crested one infernal mountain after another, half of their remaining mules fell to their deaths, dropped from exhaustion, or were so weak they had to be unpacked and left behind. Supplies that could no longer be carried were abandoned; anything not absolutely necessary was discarded. On May 17, after a foul-weather trek across mile-high peaks that few military planners would have thought possible, they commenced Stilwell's attack plan, code-named "End Run." As hoped, they caught the Japanese by surprise with a three-pronged assault on the Myitkyina airfield, used since 1942 as an enemy fighter base to attack Allied aircraft flying supplies over "the Hump" between India and China. Within hours they had control of the field and its undamaged five-thousand-foot runway. The first important Japanese position to be recaptured in Southeast Asia, the victory earned a "well done" even from Winston Churchill. Although discomfited that British forces had played no part, the prime minister exalted, "The Americans by a brilliant feat of arms have landed us in Myitkyina."

The fall of the enemy-held town of Myitkyina, an important Irrawaddy River port and railway terminus two miles east of the airfield, was expected to follow rapidly. Stilwell decided that the honor should go to the Chinese. This cheered the exhausted Marauders, who expected Stilwell to keep his promise that their months-long, deep-penetration mission would end with the capture of the airfield, after which they would be replaced by Chinese troops at the front lines and flown back to India to be sent home.

But the initial assault on the town by two Chinese battalions fell into disarray when they mistook each other for Japanese and fired on their own units, killing more than two hundred of their comrades before retreating back to the airfield.* A second Chinese attack the next day by fresh troops flown in from China also failed. Stunned by the loss of the critical airfield to the Americans, the Japanese had rushed reinforcements to the town of Myitkyina, rapidly increasing their garrison from a few hundred to more than two thousand combat troops, a buildup that portended a long campaign and a potential counterattack to overrun the airfield. Within a week of the Marauders' brilliant coup at the airfield, the effort to take the heavily defended town had stalled. Due to the lack of progress by the Chinese, Stilwell decided to keep the Marauders in the fight. "Vinegar Joe" did so knowing he was pushing them past the limits of their endurance. "GALAHAD is just shot," he penned in his diary that week.

June slid into July with little progress made to break the stalemate. Between them, the Americans and Chinese now had Myitkyina blocked on three sides, leaving open only the town's shoreline along the half-mile-wide Irrawaddy River. Trying to dislodge an entrenched enemy rather than surprising a foe with their speed and stealth, the Marauders were now in a squalid war of attrition. Their rate of evacuations due to battle wounds, nonbattle injuries, and diseases and illnesses such as lethal mite or scrub typhus and severe dysentery soared. So many were falling ill that new guidelines required a temperature of at least 102 degrees for three consecutive days before a man could be medevacked. Still, the number of men requiring medical attention was

* The Chinese were often unable to tell their own troops from the enemy. Their khaki uniforms (British-supplied, lend-lease) were identical in color to the Japanese uniforms; only the helmets differed. From a distance, it was difficult to distinguish between Chinese and Japanese uniforms, especially in a forest or jungle setting.

so long on some days that as many as seventy-five soldiers were tagged by the doctors for evacuation. Transports were leaving day after day with men who could scarcely lift an arm.

At the same time, U.S. replacement troops were arriving by air to fill in the thinning ranks. Like the original Marauders, they were brave and willing volunteers. But unlike their predecessors, few had seen combat and none had trained together, for which some paid the price. One group of new arrivals ordered to join elements of a Chinese regiment south of town met on the way a patrol of fifty Asian soldiers wearing what the young American captain thought were Chinese uniforms. He didn't become suspicious until the officer leading the patrol hollered in broken English that the Americans should lay down their guns and rest before proceeding. Suspicious, the captain sounded the alarm, but it was too late. The patrol was Japanese infantry, and they opened up with Nambu light machine guns. Only a few of the green replacements managed to escape, and the young captain was not among them.

Captured Japanese documents and prisoners were brought to the airfield, where Grant and other Nisei worked on translations and conducted interrogations. As a rule, it was difficult to get frontline Chinese troops to take Japanese prisoners; because of their experiences over the years with the brutal occupiers of their country, they greatly preferred killing them. The POWs who made it to the airfield were put

Wounded Japanese POW in Burma receiving first aid

in a temporary holding pen guarded by Army MPs. The airfield was too close to the front lines to keep them there for long, and as soon as they were processed and interrogated they were sent to the rear.

One night an unconscious Japanese officer was brought in on a stretcher. The guards said he had been captured by Gurkhas who had used their kukris—the razor-sharp machetes they all carried—on him when he tried to escape. Grant saw multiple stab wounds in his arms, legs, and side. He knew that the Nepali Gurkhas, who had been fighting the Japanese alongside British and Indian soldiers for years, often found reasons to kill their prisoners, and this one looked more dead than alive.

The officer wore the insignia of a *Rikugun-Shōi* (second lieutenant) platoon leader, and he was captured with several of his men. The Japanese officers tended to be better educated and more knowledgeable than their enlisted men, but few enemy officers had yet to be caught here.

Grant told the guards to get the POW to the aid station right away, and if he lived through the night to bring him back in the morning for questioning. He was in such bad shape that Grant wasn't sure he'd see him again, but in the morning the officer was stretchered back.

The lieutenant was now fully awake and his wounds bandaged. Grant asked him a few preliminary questions.

The only response was a leveling glare, with his scowl showing only abject contempt for the U.S. soldier with the Japanese face.

Then, as if a lit charge went off: *"Uragirimono!"* (Traitor!)

Grant shook his head no. If we each cut a vein, he replied, the same blood will flow. But you are Japanese and I am American. You are fighting for your country and I am fighting for mine. I was born in the United States and will always be an American, Grant went on. Surely a native son of Nippon who loved his own country understood such loyalty?

"Anata wa uragirimonodesu!" (You are a traitor!)

Grant switched tactics. Let's get this straight, he told the officer. You fought for your country, but the war is over for you. You are now my prisoner, and you are required to answer my questions! Grant knew that Japanese soldiers weren't trained to think, but to obey. But when his bluster didn't work, he brusquely terminated the interview and sent the POW away. On a hunch, he instructed the MPs to place the officer's stretcher in the center of the holding pen with his own men. That was not normal, as Japanese officers and enlisted were usually kept separate.

The next day, Grant went to the POW pen. He was told by another interpreter that the officer was clearly unpopular among his men, who had been taking the opportunity to openly mock his haughty demeanor. When the lieutenant spotted Grant, he pleaded to be shot to save face. Grant said he didn't have a bullet to waste on him, but he could be given a captured sword so as to demonstrate disembowelment to his men. Not enthused over the offer, the officer dropped his head in shame. Without making eye contact and almost under his breath, he said, *"Tsuuyaku-san. Nanto osshaimashita ka. Koko kara dashite kudasai."* (Mr. Interpreter. I beg your pardon. Please get me out of here.)

When the officer was brought back by MPs, Grant told him he would not be returned to the enlisted pen if he cooperated, which he did.

From the interrogation of the lieutenant and other POWs, all of them from the 18th and 56th Infantry Divisions, a stark picture emerged of the enemy's situation in and around Myitkyina. The Japanese were short of food, ammo, and medical supplies, and had not received replacements or reinforcements since the first days of the siege. They had a high incidence of disease, and were unable to evacuate their sick and wounded. Corpses lay unburied, and the town reeked of death. Under the constant attacks by U.S. artillery and aircraft, morale among the Japanese troops had plummeted.

By the end of July, the fighting had moved to the streets of Myitkyina, where the Allies found the enemy garrison consisting of mostly sick and injured soldiers left behind. Hundreds of other Japanese had pulled out at nighttime and during heavy rains via the storm-swollen river on barges, rafts, and anything else that floated.

The fall of the town on August 3, 1944, produced a new harvest of some two hundred POWs. Nearly all required medical attention. Most of the wounded had filthy, bloody rags for dressings, and some had open, untreated wounds crawling with maggots. Not all of the sick could be adequately treated at the airfield and evacuation flights were arranged to take them to the 20th General Hospital in Ledo. The others, before being sent to the rear, were processed and interrogated at the airfield to gather any actionable intelligence. For the most part, they confirmed but did not change the order of battle information already known about the Japanese units at Myitkyina, although nobody seemed to know what happened to the ranking officers of the garrison, including the commanding general.

Grant developed his own style of interrogating, first offering the prisoner a cigarette, then breaking it in half and sharing it with him. Before asking anything else, he inquired as to the POW's well-being, and about his family at home. He found such simple courtesies to be wholly unexpected, and they almost always were met by a willingness to answer his questions, and not uncommonly by tears of relief when they realized they weren't going to be tortured or killed as their commanders had warned them would happen if they were captured or surrendered to the Americans.

But Grant had no idea where to start with one group of twenty POWs picked up on the outskirts of Myitkyina. Quick-thinking MPs immediately segregated them from the other prisoners before their very presence caused a riot among the GIs. The first thing Grant did was find Captain Won Loy Chan, who had been on Stilwell's intelligence staff for much of the Burma campaign and was now the officer in charge of the POW and document processing center at the airfield.

The lone Chinese American in his 1942 MISLS class at Camp Savage and his 1936 class at Stanford University, where he received an ROTC commission and a degree in economics, Chan had been called to active duty after Pearl Harbor. A native of North Bend, Oregon, where his Chinese-immigrant father ran a general store, Chan had been unable to avoid the Army nickname "Charlie," after the benevolent and heroic Chinese American detective Charlie Chan of popular books and movies.

"You aren't gonna believe this, Charlie," Grant said, "but I've got twenty female POWs, I think Korean, down at the center, and I need help."

They walked the short distance to the newly designated female holding pen. An MP guard opened the gate of a barbed-wire enclosure and let them enter. Pitched in the middle of the stockade was a large army tent with the canvas sides rolled up due to the heat. Inside were the women, sitting or squatting on makeshift mats, some in plain dresses and others wearing pants and blouses. They all appeared to be in their twenties except for an older mama-san in a Japanese kimono. Most of the women looked fearful and anxious, and some had clearly been crying.

As Grant had deduced, the young women were Korean. They spoke some Japanese but had limited vocabularies, and frequently mumbled shyly in a mish-mash of Korean and Japanese. Grant spoke Japanese more fluently than Captain Chan, but neither of them spoke Korean, so they had to ask the bilingual mama-san for assistance. Gradually, the story of what had brought the women to Burma emerged.

Ranging in age from nineteen to thirty-one, most of them were the uneducated daughters of poor farmers or peasants. They came from the same rural province in central Korea where Japanese agents had arrived in May 1942 to enlist women for war-related services in newly conquered territories in Southeast Asia. The nature of the work, which translated from the Japanese as "comfort services," was kept vague. They were told that they would be visiting the wounded in hospitals, rolling bandages, and generally making the soldiers happy. There was a financial incentive: an advance that was enough to pay off a family's debt or start life in a new exotic place like Singapore. About eight hundred women were selected, and in exchange for the initial payment of a few hundred yen (about $100), they signed contracts that bound them to the Japanese army.

The women from the province traveled to Burma in small groups with Japanese mama-san escorts. Arriving in Rangoon in southern Burma in the summer of 1942, they formed named "houses" and were sent to various parts of the country near army bases or division rest camps. Usually, four houses were assigned to an infantry division numbering thousands of men. There, they discovered what "comfort services" entailed. Settled into requisitioned homes or schoolhouses in villages and small towns, they worked six days a week as army prostitutes, some reserved for officers and others serving enlisted men. Each girl had her own room, where she lived, slept, and transacted business. The weekly schedule of customers for the Kyooi House, to which the twenty young women belonged, was as follows: Sunday,

18th Division headquarters staff; Monday, cavalry; Tuesday, engineers; Wednesday, a day off and medical exams; Thursday, medics; Friday, mountain artillery; and Saturday, transportation. Strict rules were established that called for each session to last twenty to thirty minutes, and lines formed outside, with military police standing guard to keep order. The men paid a nominal fee equal to one or two yen. Half the money went to the mama-san for safekeeping, and the rest was spent by the women, who were charged for food and clothing.

Grant had heard rumors about Japanese troops having their own female camp followers serving as prostitutes—not Japanese women, but those from occupied lands. He hadn't been sure it was true, but here they were in Burma, young country girls from Korea sold or tricked into prostitution in a strange land far from their families and homes.

The captain had photographs of some top Japanese officers. He had Grant pass them around to see if the women could identify any of them. One was quickly recognized as Colonel Fusayasu Maruyama, a regimental commander in the 18th Division and in charge of the Myitkyina garrison. They described him as "hard and selfish," with no consideration for his men. He was a regular customer of Kyooi House

Grant Hirabayashi, far right, and Captain Won Loy Chan, far left, interrogating Korean "comfort women" at Myitkyina, Burma, 1944

and always arrived drunk. As to his whereabouts, he had left in a small boat a week before the town fell, taking two comfort women with him.

Another photo was identified as the commanding general of the 56th Division, Genzu Mizukami, who after the initial attack on the airfield arrived in town with two regiments of reinforcements. The women described him as a "good and kind man." In the final days, he had ordered the abandonment of Myitkyina to save many of his men. He was never a customer of the comfort women, and they did not know his fate.*

In truth, the women had little information of military value, which surprised Grant and Chan, both of whom thought the soldiers might have their guard down during sex. But the women explained that from the lowliest privates to the ranking officers the Japanese generally refrained from discussing military matters in bed. And if a woman innocently asked about something deemed inappropriate, they were chastised for doing so.

Reaching a lull in conversation, it grew quiet in the tent. One woman spoke in hushed tones to the mama-san, and soon they were all chattering excitedly. Mama-san silenced them and turned to Grant. She said they were anxious to know what was going to happen to them now.

Grant looked at the captain.

"Tell them their confinement here is only temporary," Chan said. "As soon as it can be arranged they will be flown to India. Eventually they will be returned to Korea."

Grant relayed the message in Japanese to the mama-san, who repeated it in Korean. The women seemed to relax for the first time.

Chan noticed something that Grant had picked up on as well. The mama-san's obi, the traditional sash worn around her waist, seemed too full in front for her petite figure, unless she was pregnant, which didn't seem likely given her age. The captain wanted Grant to ask her about it.

Grant felt ridiculous questioning a woman about her bloated stom-

---

* After he ordered the town abandoned on August 1, Major General Genzu Mizukami, to fulfill his orders to "defend Myitkyina to the death," but unwilling to sacrifice his troops, wrote an apology to the emperor and committed suicide.

ach. But what if she was hiding something important? He finally worked up the nerve. Speaking as deferentially as he would to his mother or aunt about such a delicate matter, he asked if she was hiding anything.

Mama-san smiled at his obvious discomfort. She slowly began to unwind the obi. As she did, she explained that being responsible for the girls also meant protecting their savings. Before they fled Myitkyina, she had collected all the money and had been keeping it safely on her person. Bundles of bills wrapped with ribbon dropped onto the floor.

Grant picked up a bundle, still warm from her body heat. It was 10 rupee notes of Japanese invasion money, which was a promise by Japan's government to pay at some unspecified date that amount of Burmese rupees. It looked like real money; each note had Japanese characters at the bottom that read "Government of Great Imperial Japan" and was stamped with the official seal of Japan's minister of finance. But he knew that the defeat of the Imperial Japanese Army in Burma rendered the bills nothing more than worthless paper.

Grant looked at the captain, who nodded. "Better tell them."

Grant told the mama-san that the Allies were kicking the Japanese out of the country. As gently as possible, he explained that the money the young women had saved and she had scrupulously guarded had no value now.

She looked at Grant, then at Chan, in disbelief, her mouth agape but no words coming out. One by one, she picked up the bundles and carefully secured them back inside her obi, which she rewrapped around her waist. She then turned and broke the news to the women— some shrieked, some cried, but most just stared in shock.

It broke Grant's heart knowing what the women had endured to earn this useless scrip. He told the mama-san he could try to exchange some of it for cigarettes, food, and whatever they needed. She handed him a bundle of the worthless bills. He would find the supplies or buy them himself, and Charlie Chan would chip in. It was the least they could do.

The night before the women were to leave for Ledo, Grant went to say goodbye. He brought along Bob Honda and Howard Furumoto; the latter came with his guitar and crooner's voice. The Nisei belted out show tunes and Hawaiian songs. The women clapped and cheered during the songfest, and Grant realized how grand it was to see Shin, Kim, Chun, Koke, Yon, Opu, Oki, all of them, smiling and enjoying themselves.

Before the Nisei left, Mama-san said the girls wished to sing a Korean song to the American soldiers who had treated them so well.

After the lightness of their own renditions, Grant was struck by the haunting beauty of the song the women sang to them. Even without knowing all the words, he understood it was about love and loss.

As their twenty voices soared a cappella, their tears fell.

Arirang, Arirang, Arariyo,
Arirang gogaero neomeoganda.
Nareul beorigo gasineun nimeun . . .

(Arirang, Arirang, Arariyo
You are going over Arirang Pass.
The one who leaves me,
Shall not walk three miles before his feet hurt.
Just as there are many stars in the clear sky,
There are also many dreams in our heart.
There, over there, that mountain is the Baekdusan Mountain,
Where, even in the middle of winter days, flowers bloom.
Arirang, Arirang Arariyo,
You are going over Arirang Pass.)

———

The battle of Myitkyina marked the end of Merrill's Marauders.

The seizure of the airfield allowed the Allies to move ever-increasing amounts of supplies from India into China, and was the springboard for ending the Japanese occupation of Burma.

In five months of combat, the Marauders marched 750 miles— nearly the distance between New York City and Chicago—through some of the harshest terrain in the world, fought five major engagements and thirty-two skirmishes, and won two conventional defensive battles for which they were neither intended nor equipped. When the unit was officially disbanded on August 10, 1944, fewer than three hundred of the three thousand men who had volunteered for the secret "hazardous mission" remained fit for duty. The rest had been killed, wounded, or medically evacuated with illnesses.

Merrill's Marauders were never defeated in battle.

They just wore out.

Thirteen

THE ADMIRALTIES

B ack at Camp Savage, Tom Sakamoto was tired of teaching and correcting school papers. Since being drafted into the peacetime Army in 1941, he had been either a student or an instructor for nearly two years—first attending the language school at the Presidio in San Francisco and then sent straight to Minnesota to teach others. Impatient to get overseas with the war in its third calendar year, he had lobbied anyone in authority for a transfer to the Pacific, even making his case to a colonel seated in the adjacent chair at the base barber shop one afternoon.

Then, suddenly, Tom had a good reason not to go anywhere. Her name was Sadie Shoga, and she was a beautiful, smart, and gracious twenty-three-year-old Nisei. She had recently been hired by the War Department as a civilian linguist, and came to Camp Savage in June 1943 for a two-week orientation. They met in a classroom, started dating, and after knowing each other only a month, eloped. It was the most spontaneous thing either of them had ever done, and all the more uncharacteristic because neither told their families until they were wed. After returning from a weekend honeymoon, Tom learned that his transfer to the Pacific had come through. Now wasn't that just like the Army?

Born in Seattle in 1920, Sadie was eight years old when she moved with her widowed father to his hometown in Japan. After middle school, she entered the prefectural high school for girls, where she excelled academically and was an outstanding athlete. When her father moved back to America, Sadie stayed behind with relatives to graduate from high school, after which she joined him in Los Angeles in 1938. The same well-to-do family that employed her father as a gardener hired Sadie as a "house girl," and that's what she was doing when Japan bombed Pearl Harbor. Six months later, she and her father were among the first internees to walk through the front gate of the Manzanar Relocation Center, built on a hot, dusty plateau at a four thousand foot elevation in California's Owens Valley near Death Valley. When Kai Rasmussen visited the camp to recruit Nisei for Camp Savage, he met Sadie working in administration and was impressed with her knowledge of Japan and fluency in the language. He recommended her for the Army Map Service being formed by the War Department to prepare and distribute the military maps required by the armed forces. She saw it not only as her ticket out of Manzanar, but also as a way to aid in the war effort.

The newlyweds departed Camp Savage separately a week after they were married—Tom aboard a Liberty ship bound for Australia, taking with him sixty new graduates, and Sadie on a train for Cleveland, where she reported to work at the Army's top-secret Cartographic and Translation Unit in an unmarked office above a Greyhound Bus station. With a high-level security clearance and a GS-7 civil service rating that usually required a college degree or extensive experience in the field, she would help produce topographic maps of an enemy land she knew well. Assigned to start compiling a list of targets for a future bombing campaign aimed at the Japanese homeland— prioritizing military and industrial facilities and avoiding religious, historical, and cultural sites—she hoped for Japan to be defeated with a strategy that

Sadie Sakamoto

avoided mass destruction of the country and indiscriminate killing of civilians.

Sadie's younger sister was still in Japan—living in Hiroshima.

———————

When Tom Sakamoto arrived at the Allied Translator and Interpreter Section (ATIS), housed in brick-and-timber structures on a five-acre estate outside Brisbane—Australia's third-largest city located halfway up its eastern coast—he found an old classmate running things.

Major David Swift, one of only two Caucasian graduates out of fifty-eight students in Tom's class at the Presidio, had been sent there following their May 1942 graduation with eight Nisei classmates to establish ATIS, a centralized U.S.-Australian intelligence unit for the translation of Japanese documents and communications. Born and raised in Japan, Swift was the tall, blond son of an English professor at Tokyo Imperial University. David left Japan to attend college in the U.S., and after graduating worked for an oil company in China. Upon returning to America in the 1930s, he went to work for the U.S. Immigration Service and received an Army Reserve commission. He was called to active duty two months before Pearl Harbor, and three weeks after America declared war on Japan he was ordered to the Presidio language school.

Swift was pleased to see Tom arrive with the contingent of new MISLS graduates, as there was a serious shortage in Australia of Japanese translators. At the same time, there had been a titanic increase in the volume of captured papers pouring in from the Pacific battle-fields. At that moment, ATIS had literally thousands of canvas sacks full of enemy documents not yet processed due to the shortage of translators. Surely, vital intelligence was being missed just because it wasn't being read.

Tom and the other new arrivals went to work on the backlog of documents, many of which were soldiers' diaries and letters. They were amazed at how much military information was in the handwritten diaries. (The U.S. Army forbade its soldiers from keeping diaries in case their writings fell into enemy hands.) Dates, locations, battles, unit designations, names of officers and commanders, types of weapons—much of it was there in the diaries for anyone who could read *sosho* and *kanji*. There were also troves of information in their letters home. Large bundles of mail from a captured enemy post office in New Guinea ended up at ATIS, and the missives of the Japanese troops provided similar details, sans censorship. (Letters written by GIs were subjected to review by official censors, and any sensitive information was snipped out before they were mailed.) Tom could only conclude the obvious: the higher-ups in the Japanese military believed that there were no U.S. soldiers in the Pacific war capable of reading Japanese. Surprise, surprise.

Whenever they came across essential elements of information (EEIs, as they are known in the intelligence field), a detailed report was sent up the chain of command that ended at MacArthur's Southwest Pacific Area General Headquarters, which had taken over the nine-story AMP Building at 229 Queen Street in downtown Brisbane. Depending on the need to know by various commands, the translations and original documents were forwarded to Pearl Harbor or Washington, D.C., for additional analysis by experts in the military intelligence community.*

To beef up the language pool Down Under, the armed forces of several Allied nations were sending soldiers who spoke Japanese to ATIS. As their levels of fluency varied widely, Swift started a refresher

---

* In April 1944, an official-looking document inside a briefcase recovered from a Japanese military plane crash off the coast of the Philippines was taken by U.S. submarine to Darwin, Australia, then flown to Brisbane. The document, in standard Japanese text rather than code or cipher, was translated on an urgent basis at ATIS by a five-man team that included two Nisei, Yoshikazu Yamada and George Sankey Yamashiro, both from Hawaii. It revealed the tactics and strategy for Japan's top-secret "Operation Z," a planned all-out attack on the U.S. fleet intended to change the course of the war. A copy of the twenty-two-page translation was rushed to MacArthur, who forwarded it to the headquarters of the U.S. Pacific Fleet at Pearl Harbor, which distributed copies to every fleet admiral in the Pacific. With the specifics of the enemy's plan known in advance, U.S. ships, planes, and submarines dealt a devastating blow two months later to Japanese naval and air forces in the Battle of the Philippine Sea, the largest aircraft carrier battle in history and one of the decisive battles of the Pacific war. Today, many Japanese and American historians agree that the "Z Plan" was among the most significant intelligence documents seized during the war.

course for those who needed it, and he decided that Tom, as an experienced MISLS instructor, would be ideal to teach the class. But Tom had other ideas. In fact, since arriving in Brisbane, he had already put in for combat duty.

"The language pool here needs more training, and you could teach them," said Swift, hoping to change Tom's mind. "Stay and help me."

A teaching assignment would likely mean his remaining in Australia for the duration—a tempting proposition for many GIs, especially married soldiers like Tom. But he told his old friend he had been in enough classrooms to last him for two wars, and he was ready to "see some action at the front."

Teams of Nisei interpreters regularly left ATIS for combat units in the Pacific. When Tom's transfer came through in February 1944, he was surprised not to be part of a team but headed on his own to join the 1st Cavalry Division near Oro Bay, New Guinea. The division, formed shortly after the First World War and long garrisoned at Fort Bliss, Texas, had retired its steeds in February 1943 and converted from horse cavalry to infantry several months prior to leaving for the Pacific. But the division's mascot was still Trigger, cowboy star Roy Rogers's palomino horse, and its ranks were filled with real-life cowpokes. When Tom learned that he would be the first Nisei in the outfit, he had an uneasy feeling. He couldn't imagine there were many Japanese Americans in Texas, and knowing the racial animosity that existed in California and elsewhere, especially since Pearl Harbor, he was wary. But his concerns proved groundless, as the soldiers he met upon his arrival were welcoming, if a bit curious about him.

The 1st Cavalry had spent the early years of the war guarding the Mexican border and was as yet untested in combat. It was composed of two brigades, each with about three thousand men. Tom was assigned to the 1st Brigade, commanded by a new brigadier general, William C. Chase. A graduate of Brown University, Chase had been an officer on the Western Front in the waning days of the First World War, and between wars attended and later taught at the Command and General Staff College, where the Army's best and brightest were schooled.

On February 25, 1944, Chase, who nearing fifty was still trim with

Brigadier General William Chase, commander of the understrength brigade landing at Los Negros

boyish features and sported a thin Errol Flynn mustache, was summoned by 1st Cavalry Division Commander Major General Innis P. Swift. Chase was informed that his brigade would make the initial landings in the enemy-held Admiralty Islands, a group of eighteen rain-forest-covered islands 150 miles north of New Guinea. They were to make an amphibious assault at Los Negros, the second-largest island in the chain. That they were to see action after months of training was welcome news to Chase, but he was stunned to learn that they would be departing in two days and making the landing two days after that. Assault troops usually had weeks to plan and practice such an operation. Worse yet: due to limited shipping available to transport his troops, Chase had to leave behind two-thirds of his men.

The hurry-up operation had been ordered by MacArthur after receiving a report the day before of a flyover by a B-25 bomber that passed over Los Negros at treetop level without seeing any signs of enemy troops or gun positions. An airstrip on the island looked dilapidated, with no aircraft visible. The capture of the Admiralties had been planned for April, but if the Japanese had already withdrawn, why wait two months? Since being seized from Germany in World War I, the islands and their indigenous population of Melanesians had been governed by Australia until Japanese troops had landed twenty-two months earlier, in April 1942. Situated between the west coast of Los Negros and the eastern shore of the largest island, Manus, was horseshoe-shaped Seeadler Harbor, one of the finest natural anchorages in the South Pacific, and at six miles across and 120 feet deep, capable of sheltering a fleet at anchorage. If the Japanese had abandoned Los Negros, work could start right away expanding its airstrip for use by U.S. bombers, as well as new harbor facilities for the fleet. In the larger scope of the Pacific war, a foothold here would provide forward bases to support MacArthur's drive to the Philippines, greatly reducing the strategic value of the enemy's major base at Rabaul, New Britain, and cutting off from resupply tens of thousands of Japanese troops on other islands.

MacArthur had ordered a "reconnaissance-in-force" to probe Los Negros, a coral island some ten miles long and five miles at its widest. Its shores were ragged, with irregularly shaped inlets on both sides, and its interior, flat and low, was covered with swamps, jungle, and palm trees. If it was found to be undefended, more troops, as well as engineers and supplies for the occupation, could rapidly follow. In the event of significant enemy opposition, the reconnaissance force would be on their own until they could be withdrawn.

The speed with which this first amphibious assault of a key island group came together was highly unusual not only for the soldiers who were to hit the beaches in a few days but also for the Navy that had to deliver them across three hundred miles of ocean for the February 29 landing stipulated in MacArthur's expedited schedule. Regular troopships were too slow, and only destroyers were fast enough to make that date. The Navy had a dozen destroyers available for the operation, but these smaller ships, with a crew of 250 men, had limited space belowdecks for extra personnel. They could handle only about 80 soldiers per ship, which was why Chase was limited to taking only a third of his brigade.

Tom was among those chosen to make the Los Negros landing. The night before they departed, he wrote to Sadie in Cleveland. He could not tell her where he was or that he was about to see action at last, but that day, February 26, 1944, was a special day for a couple of other reasons.

My dearest wife,

Today is our 8 month anniversary. It is regrettable that we have to spend lonely hours apart . . . but you are very close to me in my thoughts . . . Today also marks my full 3 years in the Army. Indeed much has happened since I first put on my oversized khakis. When I

*return I will have many interesting tales to tell you . . . Everything will
be all right, so you mustn't worry, darling.*

Love, Tommy

The convoy of destroyers was scheduled to leave from Cape Sud-est near Oro Bay the next day after sundown to avoid detection and enemy air attacks. They made the deadline after a great deal of rushing around on their final day to ensure that the assault troops were supplied with everything they needed, especially plenty of ammunition.

At a final conference ashore, Chase was taken aback when the Sixth Army commander, Lieutenant General Walter Krueger, said he believed that Los Negros would likely be heavily defended and that Chase and his men could have "a real fight" on their hands. Krueger told Chase that a six-man patrol of the Alamo Scouts, a newly formed special jungle reconnaissance unit, had been landed by a seaplane off Los Negros that morning to go ashore and look for signs of enemy activity. They had not yet reported in by radio.

Tom boarded the destroyer USS *Reid* (DD-369) with Chase's headquarters section. No sooner had everyone stowed their gear than the destroyer was away at flank speed. Deep rumblings and jarring vibrations from the steam-turbine-propelled twin shafts generating 45,000 horsepower shook the 1,500-ton ship to its rivets.

Heading north into a pitch-black night that soon turned stormy, the ship bucked up and down and sideways like a runaway roller-coaster. Tom became seasick, as did many of the foot soldiers hitching a ride. A sailor took pity on Tom and brought him a bucket, which he hugged all night. By the next day, he began to find his sea legs and felt better when the weather allowed the troops to go topside for some fresh air.

As they passed through the Vitiaz Strait toward the Bismarck Sea, a radio message caught up with Chase. The Alamo Scouts had been exfiltrated from Los Negros after twenty-four hours. They reported that the island was "lousy with Japs." Less vague was a new intelligence estimate that Los Negros was defended by two infantry battalions, a transportation regiment, and naval and artillery units, most of which was well camouflaged and not easily spotted from the air. The latest intelligence estimate now put enemy strength on Manus and Los Negros at 3,250 men—three times more than the 1,026 U.S. soldiers packed in the destroyers. For not the last time, Chase lamented having had to leave behind 2,000 infantrymen.

MacArthur was so concerned about the operation even before the report from the scouts that he had decided to observe it personally to determine whether it should continue or be aborted. The news about the enemy strength on the island reached him en route to Los Negros aboard the light cruiser USS *Phoenix*, which had sped through the Bismarck Sea to catch up with the invasion fleet. Believing that the benefits of the attack outweighed the risks, he decided against canceling the landing.

D-day, February 29, dawned gray and murky with low cloud cover as the convoy arrived off the eastern shore of Los Negros. A pre-invasion bombardment began with all the warships firing thunderous, broadside salvos that left the island partly obscured by columns of smoke. A single enemy artillery battery answered with a few rounds that landed harmlessly in the ocean, and was promptly silenced.

Shortly after the shelling ended, Chase received a message from MacArthur aboard the *Phoenix* asking when the best time would be to come ashore and visit the troops. *What?* MacArthur was *here?* It came as a shock to Chase and everyone else. But any uneasiness Chase had at the specter of the top general in the Pacific observing the landing was offset by his pride in having MacArthur present for his men's first combat.

Assigned to go ashore in the third wave with Chase and his staff, Tom waited on deck with other soldiers for the call to man the landing craft. A few jokesters cracked wise, but most of the men stood silent and wide-eyed. They had slept little, and before dawn partook of what the sailors said was their usual "battle breakfast" of steak, eggs, potatoes, hotcakes, bread, butter, jam, and coffee. It was difficult not to think of it as the Last Supper, but after days of being too sick to even look at food, Tom ate with gusto. They then gathered their gear and went topside.

The troops of the first wave, a total of 138 infantrymen, were taken ashore in four shallow-draft landing craft through a narrow channel into Hyane Harbor, a crescent-shaped inlet about a mile across on the eastern shore of Los Negros. They could be seen hitting the beach and moving rapidly toward the airfield a few hundred yards away.

Just five minutes later, the boats in the second wave had a rougher time reaching shore. The Japanese defenders either crawled out of their bunkers or got some of their guns pointed in the right direction, because from a hill overlooking the inlet they poured rounds from 20 mm artillery, forcing the incoming landing craft to reverse course and circle outside the channel for a time. After the fire was suppressed by a barrage of shelling from Navy ships, the troop-laden boats landed.

When it was time for the third wave, Tom climbed down a rope cargo net and stepped into a waiting launch, which soon was filled with soldiers in full combat gear.

"Sergeant Yokohama," a voice behind him called out.

It was not his name, but Tom Sakamoto knew it was meant for him and turned around. The summons had come from General Chase.

"Sir?" Tom replied.

"You stay with me after we land," Chase said.

The unusual command sent Tom's thoughts spinning. The general wanted him close at hand—in case anything needed translating? Or because he was Japanese American and they were about to land on an island crawling with Japanese? He suspected the latter, but the general's order still caught him off guard. Most of the time Tom felt like any other GI, but he had just been reminded that he wasn't like the rest.

With a growl from its diesel engine, the landing craft moved slowly away in the surprisingly calm seas and swung toward the island. As they neared the channel, the sailors manning the boat hollered for everyone to keep their heads down or get them blown off. Sure enough, as they entered the channel a hail of bullets whizzed overhead. Several rounds went through the hull above the water line, leaving silver-dollar-sized holes. Returning the enemy fire, the sailors hammered away with bursts from the .30 caliber machine guns mounted behind armored plates on both sides of the landing craft. When the personnel ramp in front slammed down on a sandbar, the troops jumped off into shallow waters and ran onto the beach, where they immediately came under fire from snipers shooting from a distant line of palm trees.

Once ashore, Chase saw that the men in the first waves had over-run the runway and were advancing into the jungle. The airfield was the only flat and open terrain on the island. Elsewhere, it was rugged, with razorback hills covered by dense rain forests and jungle growth filled with wide streams and lagoons, and devoid of roads for motor vehicles. By nature a commander who erred on the side of caution rather than recklessness, Chase ordered a pullback so as not to overextend his forces. He knew if the latest intelligence estimate was correct, the enemy had a sizable numerical advantage. Already an abandoned battalion headquarters had been found, as well as field kitchens and a supply warehouse. But so far his men had encountered light resistance, which led Chase to believe that the Japanese might stage a strong counterattack.

After several hours, the unloading of the troops from the ships was completed, most of it in a heavy rain. Lacking barbed wire to make a proper defensive perimeter, the men and weapons had to be spaced close together for nighttime security. With backbreaking effort, the GIs began digging foxholes and trenches in soil heavy with coral and rocks.

Chase set up his command post toward the center of their triangu-lar perimeter behind a wooden barricade. Tom was there as well, along with his newly appointed guardian, a former New York City street cop named Mike Gerrity. Upon landing, Chase had personally given Ger-rity the assignment of staying with Tom at all times to ensure that he wasn't mistaken for an enemy soldier and shot by their own men.

"For your safety, sergeant," Chase explained to Tom.

Tom understood the general's concern, and he knew it doubtless had to do with not wanting to lose the brigade's only Japanese transla-tor. But still, it was an awkward situation for Tom. How many enlisted men went to war with their own bodyguard? But Gerrity, a big, smiling Irishman full of blarney, made the situation easier for them by acting as if it was the most natural thing in the world. From then on, they were inseparable. They got busy digging their own two-man foxhole.

At 3 p.m., MacArthur came ashore, delivered by a landing craft in which he stood erect in the bow like a heroic-sized sculpture, wear-ing his cap with the gold-braided scrambled eggs embroidered on the visor, pressed khaki trousers, and a West Point–gray trench coat. Accompanying him were his staff aides and a gaggle of correspondents. A photographer snapped pictures as the general pinned the Army's second-highest award for valor, the Distinguished Service Cross, on

MacArthur pinning medal on
Lieutenant Marvin Henshaw

the first man ashore that morning: a tall, strapping platoon leader in a rain-soaked poncho, thirty-one-year-old 2nd Lieutenant Marvin "Preacher" Henshaw, one of six Henshaw brothers from Haskell County, Texas, serving in the armed forces.

In a drizzling rain, MacArthur set out with Chase on foot to inspect the four-thousand-foot airstrip. It obviously had not been used for some time, as they found it overgrown with weeds, pockmarked with muddy craters, and strewn with rusting fuselages, a broken-down truck, and a sorry-looking Japanese bulldozer. Knowing that the inspection party made a tempting target, Chase warned that snipers were active, but MacArthur said nothing and continued on. As they surveyed the perimeter defenses, Chase saw the stirring effect MacArthur's presence had on his men. Here was the supreme allied commander in the Pacific, only hours after an amphibious landing on an enemy-held island, walking around exposing himself to possible enemy fire. He did not have to be here and could have stayed in Australia or New Guinea to monitor the operation, but the men who were digging in for a long night and a battle they knew would soon come clearly appreciated his showing up at the front lines.

Returning to the beach and the landing craft to take him back, MacArthur placed a hand on Chase's shoulder before departing. "Your men have performed marvelously. Hold what you have taken, no matter against what odds. You have your teeth in them now. Don't let go."

With that, MacArthur was gone, and with him the armada of warships except for two destroyers left behind to provide fire support to the troops ashore. That meant there was no evacuation possible for the outnumbered U.S. infantrymen on Los Negros. Before he left, MacArthur told Chase he could expect to start receiving the rest of his men he had left in New Guinea, plus engineers to start repairs on the airstrip, in two days. In a real sense, the reconnaissance-in-force was already a success. They had found Los Negros far from abandoned, but had landed a thousand men with only light casualties and were staying put, with more GIs on the way. But for now, Chase's men had to keep their foothold.

The best way for a small force to hold a large perimeter at night in a forested or jungle terrain against an infiltrating enemy was for everyone to stay in their foxholes and fire at anything that moved. But such indiscriminate shooting made it dangerous to move around in the dark for any reason, including seeking medical aid or even relieving themselves, which the GIs did in their foxholes using their helmets.

Japanese troops could be heard moving and chattering in the dark—close enough to lob hand grenades at the Americans. At times, the best defense was to not return fire, as muzzle flashes gave away one's position. Some enemy soldiers dropped into U.S. foxholes and fought hand-to-hand with the occupants. Only in the brilliant flashes from explosions did the Americans clearly see their attackers, who in those split seconds were eerily frozen in ghostly silhouette. It was a long night of fighting and dying and frayed nerves.

In the morning, sixty-six dead Japanese were counted, most of them outside the perimeter. Seven GIs were killed and fifteen wounded, some seriously. With no way as yet to evacuate casualties from the island, they were taken to a portable surgical unit set up in tents, where doctors performed emergency operations illuminated by lanterns and flashlights.

Patrols sent to probe to the west and north were stopped by stiff resistance after four hundred yards, and had to be recalled. With the Japanese so close and their intentions uncertain, defense of his position was foremost in Chase's mind. He did not have enough men to hold the entire airstrip, which was not operational in any case until work could be done and the island secured, so he pulled his men back and established a tighter defensive perimeter to await the arrival of the reinforcements. After dark, groups of Japanese probed and attacked the new U.S. lines all night.

In the morning, a runner taking a message to Chase took a short-cut. As he hurried through tall jungle grass, he noticed movement about seventy-five yards from the general's command post, which he reported upon arriving.

Chase ordered his intelligence officer to round up a few men, then turned to Tom. "You come with us, Sergeant Yokohama. If they're Japs, I want you to get them to surrender so you can interrogate them."

The general clearly had a mental block about his surname, but Tom didn't take offense, because, well, he liked the general.

When they reached the grassy area, Tom shouted in Japanese: *"Soko ni iru no wa dare da? Ima no uchi ni kousan shiro!"* (Who's there? Surrender, while you have a chance!)

When there was no response, he stepped closer, repeating his demand and adding that it was futile to continue fighting. There was a sudden rustling in the brush, and for a moment he thought someone was heeding his advice. But instead, a shot rang out, just missing Chase, who was not wearing his general's star on either his helmet or collar but, wearing a .45 sidearm and barking orders, exuded a commanding presence.

The Americans opened up with guns blazing; the intelligence officer with his submachine gun, Tom with his carbine on full automatic, Mike Gerrity and several other GIs with their M1 rifles, and even the general, rapid-firing his pistol like Wyatt Earp at the O.K. Corral. Whenever something moved in the underbrush, they poured lead in that direction.

At the sound of sharp metallic clicks, they knew what they were: Japanese grenades, detonated by pulling out the safety fork and hitting the steel striker bar against a hard surface like a rock or a helmet. They took cover, but the explosions were oddly muffled. They found seventeen dead Japanese, several of whom had committed suicide by detonating the grenades against their bodies. Some of the deceased were officers with samurai swords strapped to their sides.

The bloody corpses were searched for papers. Tom established from the ID carried by one captain that he was the commanding officer of the battalion they had been fighting for two days. Found inside a notebook he carried was an order signed by a colonel, directing an assault on the U.S. command post to "kill or capture ranking enemy officers." The order ended with: *"Ten'nō no tame ni anata no inochi o gisei ni suru koto o ketsui shi, hokaku ga sashisematte iru baai ni jisatsu suru."* (Be resolute in your determination to sacrifice your life for the emperor and prepare yourself to commit suicide if capture is imminent.)

Tom knew from his high school years in Japan about the wartime culture in that country, and the rigid obeyance that was instilled in boys, who were taught that it was an honor to die in battle. Still, it was sobering to see soldiers follow orders to kill themselves. These young men hoped for a glorious death in battle, but what mother would rather learn of her son's death on a faraway field than see his smiling face again?

At daybreak on March 2, after two days and nights of steady combat, the exhausted GIs were heartened to see more U.S. ships. A half-dozen LSTs, each carrying more than two hundred troops along with tanks and tractors, motored through the channel and beached themselves. Their ramps cranked down, and loading platforms were put into place to reach solid ground above the beach. For five hours, some one thousand infantrymen came ashore, along with hundreds of Seabees with bulldozers and ditchdiggers from a naval construction battalion.

Wasting no time using his increased strength to expand his perimeter, Chase sent a newly arrived regiment to reoccupy the airfield so the Seabees could start leveling and grading the runway. They were able to do so without firing a shot, as the Japanese had pulled back into the jungle with the arrival of the new U.S. troops.

With still no enemy prisoners to interrogate, Tom worked on translating documents, and they were now coming in at a rapid clip, some found in abandoned bunkers and buildings and others on dead Japanese before they went into mass graves. He prioritized the materials based on those most likely to yield timely intelligence so he could work on them first. One document went to the top of the stack as soon as he saw it, because he recognized it as an operation order. It had been found that morning on a Japanese officer leading a scouting party that had landed by small boat. The platoon guarding the coast allowed them to reach the beach, then opened fire. The officer had fallen dead in the surf, and the paper was soaked.

The Japanese wrote their orders and most everything else on thin

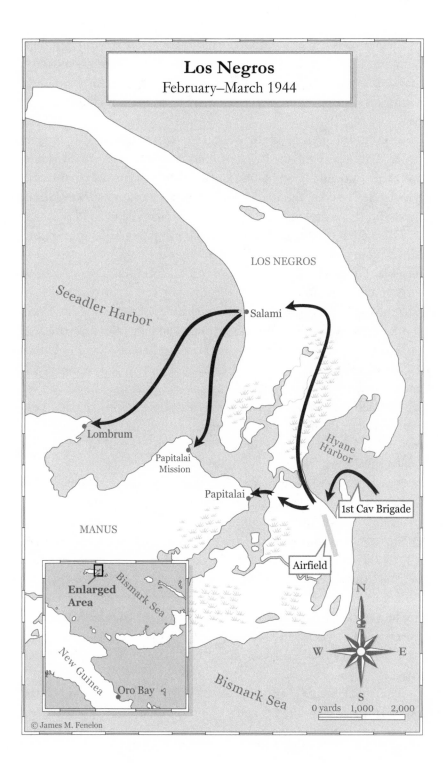

Los Negros
February–March 1944

Seeadler Harbor

LOS NEGROS

Salami

Lombrum

Papitalai
Mission

Papitalai

Hyane
Harbor

1st Cav Brigade

MANUS

Airfield

Enlarged
Area

Bismark Sea

New Guinea

Oro Bay

Bismark Sea

N
W — E
S

0 yards   1,000   2,000

© James M. Fenelon

rice paper. When the pages were wet or even just damp from high humidity, they tended to stick together. Tom had already discovered that separating them was like pulling apart wet tissues. Also, any extra dampness on a page could cause the ink to soak through to the next page.

Tom let the general know right away what had fallen into their hands. The order contained a list of units, including some from Manus and other outlying islands, being staged to "annihilate the enemy who have landed." So far, the attacks against the Americans had been piece-meal. But the order outlined a major, coordinated attack.

Even as cautiously as Tom turned the wet pages, some ripped and others were so smeared with black ink that the kanji characters were illegible. Given the urgency of the information, rather than taking time to write out a translation as he normally would, he read out loud what he could decipher, with the intelligence officer taking notes. As some pages were ruined once he turned the page, the pressure was on to get the translation right the first time—there was no going back to reread anything. A map of the attack was included in the order, and it showed where the assault troops would stage, the directions from which they would attack, and at what times. Those details were transferred by the intelligence officer onto a map of the island divided into a system of numbered and lettered grids formed by horizontal and vertical lines.

Before Tom even finished reading the order, Chase, who had been listening to the translation, got on the radio to the naval commander to arrange fire support, and request a barge-hunting mission to stop enemy reinforcements en route to Los Negros from other islands.

"Good work, Sakamoto," said the general, who was no longer having any trouble remembering Tom's name.

Within hours, Chase had every available man in the front lines, holding back no reserves as he normally would to send forward in the event of an enemy breakthrough. He massed the heaviest mortars near the center of the airfield, and other mortars closer to the front lines.

The attack started right on schedule that night according to the order Tom had translated. Enemy troops poured out of the northern part of Los Negros down a narrow causeway used by natives to pass from one end of the island to the other. By the light of yellow flares they shot into the sky, they came.

The GIs were prepared across their entire front, waiting where they knew the attacks would come. Everyone was awake and alert, with extra ammo at the ready. Patiently, they sat tight in their foxholes and trenches for the enemy to come closer, then began dropping them with accurate rifle and machine gun fire.

The Navy was also primed to provide gunfire support. One after another, destroyers steamed up to the harbor entrance and delivered withering fire on the enemy from their deck guns as infantry officers ashore radioed the latest coordinates of their moving targets.

Near the airfield, a wave of enemy troops broke through the first line of defense, but were unable to advance any farther. In the wee hours, the GIs pushed forward across a battlefield now littered with enemy dead, restoring their line well before daylight.

By morning's light, the ground was covered with hundreds of enemy dead. American casualties in the attack were 61 dead and 244 wounded.

The failure of their last-ditch, coordinated attack meant that the Japanese were no longer strong enough to push the Americans off Los Negros, although there would be much more fighting and dying before the island was secured five days later.[*]

On March 6, the 12th Cavalry Regiment arrived, and that same day U.S. forces reached the west coast of Los Negros. That afternoon, the first American plane, a B-25 bomber, landed at the repaired airfield amid the cheers, shouts, and whistles of soldiers lining both sides of the runway.

That same day, in the waters off the other side of the island, Lieutenant Henshaw, the first man ashore who had received a medal for gallantry from MacArthur, drowned when a small boat he was in swamped and sank. He was a good swimmer himself, but gallant to the end, he was last seen attempting to tow several non-swimmers ashore.

---

[*] After more fighting on Manus and other islands, the Admiralty Islands campaign was declared ended on May 18, 1944. The final cost was 290 Americans killed, and nearly 1,000 wounded. More than 3,300 Japanese were killed, and only a handful captured.

Ten days after landing on Los Negros, Tom finally had a POW to interrogate. The fact that it had taken that long to capture an enemy soldier alive was remarkable in itself, evidence not only of the ferocity with which both sides had fought but also of the mind-set of the Japanese.

He found the prisoner lying on a cot in a tent guarded by two MPs. Badly wounded, his chest was wrapped with wide swaths of sterile gauze, from which blood and other fluid oozed. He had obviously been wounded several days earlier, as his exposed skin was black and purplish from gangrene. His eyes were shut, although Tom couldn't tell if he was in a coma or sleeping or faking it. He pulled up a stool and sat next to the cot.

His wait wasn't long.

When the prisoner stirred and saw Tom, his eyes popped open in surprise. He jerked upward but then fell back with a loud moan.

Tom started speaking Japanese but was cut off.

"Anata wa nihonjindesu! Anata wa uragirimonodesu ka?" (You are Japanese! Are you a traitor?)

Tom said he was a Japanese American in the United States Army.

"Kono yarō!" (You bastard!)

Keeping his voice steady and reassuring, Tom told the man that he was now a prisoner of war, and was receiving medical treatment.

"Koroshite, koroshite! Mō ikitakunai." (Kill me, kill me! I don't want to live anymore.)

The POW soon got his wish, succumbing to his wounds.

It had certainly not gone as Tom had learned or taught prisoner interrogations, yet he understood the psyche of the enemy soldier who had died in front of him. As fervently as Japanese believed it an honor to die in battle, they believed just as strongly that being captured brought great dishonor to themselves, their families, and their emperor. In fact, after a few more interrogations, Tom realized that Japanese POWs had no desire to be liberated by their own side. Most were so ashamed at being captured that they felt they could never go home and face their families. They did not want their names on any lists of POWs compiled by the Red Cross. It was better for everyone if they were reported as killed in battle.

11 Mar '44
1st Brig. 1st Cav Div

My dearest wife,

Just now I find myself in a tent alone. The tent has a crude desk and a bench. I also have 2 cots in here. This, darling, is my office. Many things happened the first week here, but now it has quieted down considerably.

The climate is very hot here . . . I guess you'd never dream where I am, but I am in the midst of the new developments taking place in this theater of war. As for the dangerousness, well darling, it is all over now, and once again is it a very quiet place. What a place! The scenery is beautiful. The coconut trees swaying in the breeze and the blue green ocean sending waves of white foam to the shore with a sound like a concert.

Last night there was a beautiful full moon. The moon out here in the South Seas is simply magnificent. However, I must say that the moon looked sad. The orange moon was half way up shining against some coconut trees wrecked by bombardments and machine gun holes all over—quite a sight. As I sat outside my tent, I was wondering what my Sadie was doing. Here everything of home seems so distant. I guess I won't be getting your letters for awhile yet. I do hope everything is all right with you and that you are waiting patiently for your hubby to return. My only consolation is when I look at your picture.

You know, Sadie, out here you see a lot of things. Many are unpleasant but yet there are things to remember for the rest of your life. Boy—I've seen enough of this war. When I return I will tell you many interesting stories. One thing is certain though—if I ever get back, I'll never leave my wife again.

Just know I'm in best of condition. I have a greater appetite than when I was in Australia. That is a good sign, isn't it? Everything is all right, so don't worry. Okay!

Your hubby, Tommy

Within a month, Tom Sakamoto was flying back to New Guinea to take part in another invasion. He would have been amazed to know that same week, Sadie was reading all about him in *The Cleveland Press*,

and his parents and siblings were also proudly reading about him in
The Rohwer Outpost, published at the Rohwer Relocation Center in
Arkansas.

CALIFORNIA JAPANESE AMERICAN SERGEANT CITED FOR ACTION IN BATTLE FOR LOS NEGROS ISLAND

Chicago Tribune Press Service—A 26-year-old Japanese-
American, Sgt. Tom Sakamoto of San Jose, Calif., was credited
with helping save the life of an American general in combat
against Japanese forces in the South Pacific.

Sgt. Sakamoto, whose wife is a civil service employee of the
War Department in Cleveland, is the first Japanese American
to be individually cited in press dispatches for participation in
the Admiralty campaign in the southwest Pacific.

He saw action on Los Negros Island . . .

HEADQUARTERS 1ST CAVALRY BRIGADE

Subject: Commendation
14 June 1944

To: Headquarters, Sixth Army
   *During the first three days of the campaign following the invasion
of Los Negros Island, S/Sgt. Thomas Sakamoto promptly and
correctly interpreted captured enemy maps and documents. He submitted
valuable reports to me on enemy unit identifications, strength of units,
commanders' names, unit sectors, and the plans and intentions of enemy
units. One document was a field order to attack our perimeter. We were
able to smother this attack with naval gun fire, artillery support, and
concentrated mortar and machine gun fire against the enemy . . . Such
prompt translation service was of great tactical value to us.*
   I recommend the award of Bronze Star to S/Sgt. Sakamoto.

Wm. C. Chase,
Brig. Gen., U.S. Army

Fourteen

SULPHUR ISLAND

After the botched invasion of Kiska Island, where thirty-five
thousand Allied soldiers hit Alaska's frigid shores only to discover that the Japanese had withdrawn weeks earlier, Nobuo Furuiye
returned to Minnesota and Camp Savage in the summer of 1943 just
as a new MISLS class with some seven hundred Japanese American
soldiers had begun.

Reporting to the personnel office, Nobuo learned that he had thirty
days of leave coming. Since he had already been overseas, he was told
he would remain statewide for "six to ten months," and there was
even a possibility of his being assigned to the faculty at Camp Savage. Excited by the promising news, he hurriedly wrote to his fiancée,
Toshie, still interned with her parents in Arkansas, suggesting they get
married right away.

He had been courting her ever since they first met aboard ship in
1938 when they were both returning from Japan, she to visit relatives
and he after two years at the Kyushu Gakuin school in Kumamoto.
Toshie was twenty-three at the time, three years older than he was.
The age difference had initially concerned her, but not Nobuo. He
was besotted with her grace, beauty, and quiet strength. In truth, their
personalities were complete opposites, and his boldness, so unlike her
shy demeanor, put her off at first. But his quick smile was the feature
of his face; outgoing and enthusiastic, he was the warmest of hand-
shakers and huggers, and never knew a stranger for long. On a crusade
to win her heart, Nobuo made regular bus trips from his home in

Colorado to Los Angeles, where she lived with her family before the war, and they continued to write one another even after she spurned his first marriage proposal. Disappointed but undeterred, he refused to give up. He had declined to volunteer for the MISLS in the fall of 1942 when recruiters came to his Army camp in Arkansas. How could he leave the state with Toshie within visiting distance, a hundred miles away at the Jerome Relocation Center? But the Army soon sent him to Camp Savage anyway. Now, he was thrilled when she wrote back with the answer he hoped to hear.

After arranging through government channels to have Toshie released from Jerome so they could be married, Nobuo took a train to Arkansas to pick her up. Together they arrived arm in arm at the Denver train station, where his parents, Daijiro and Tamaye, met them. They drove twenty miles to the family's farm near Lafayette, where Nobuo was born and which his father still worked, hauling his vegetables to the produce market every week. A few days later, the young couple were married by a Buddhist priest in Denver. After two weeks, they took the train back to Arkansas. Even though Toshie would have been allowed to live with her husband in Minnesota, she decided—with Nobuo's blessing—that her place was with her parents in camp as they were on their own since her younger brother, Toshiake, had been able to relocate to Salt Lake City to work in a defense plant. Her older brother, Hitoshi—in the Army since before Pearl Harbor—was with the 442nd Regimental Combat Team training in Mississippi.

Newlyweds Nobuo and
Toshie Furuiye, 1944

When he returned from leave, Nobuo reported to the Camp Savage administrator who handed out the new assignments.

"Got a good deal for you, Nobby. You've made staff sergeant."

Nobuo beamed. Now that he

was married, he could use the extra money that came with the promotion as he intended to set up a monthly allotment for Toshie to
save for their nest egg. But he had been in the Army long enough to
know that whenever they had a "good deal" for you, it was smart
to watch out for what came next.

"Is there a catch?" Nobuo said, only half in jest.

Turns out, there was.

He was one of three Nisei back from the Alaskan campaign who
were being promoted and given their own ten-man MIS team.

"Your team will be leaving immediately for Pearl Harbor."

"What about my six months stateside?" Nobuo asked.

"You didn't really believe that, did you?"

Right. He should have known better.

Heading off to gather up his team, Nobuo could think only of
Toshie. Leaving his new bride in the internment camp had been difficult, but now he was very glad she was there with her parents. With
him leaving, she would have been left in Minnesota with no friends
or family. Would he have proposed if he had known he was going
overseas so soon? His head said no; it would have been best to wait
until they could be together. But his heart screamed yes; she was now
his wife at long last, and he had her to return to from the war.

After six days and nights on a jam-packed, smoke-filled troop train
to California, Nobuo managed to get passes for his men to sightsee in
San Francisco, now a major port of embarkation for soldiers, Marines,
and sailors headed to war in the Pacific. When it was their turn to go,
they boarded a gray-camo troopship for an uneventful crossing to
Hawaii.

They were met at the pier by an intelligence officer, who escorted
them to their new quarters, not on one of Oahu's more than two
dozen military bases as they had anticipated but in a nondescript two-
story building on Kapiolani Boulevard in an older business section
of Honolulu. A large sign in front read STATE HOME FURNISHINGS.
There was a display of furniture in the window facing the street, but
in the same window was a small sign saying the store was temporarily closed. It was all about security and obfuscation for a top-secret
operation, although the neighbors were not deceived for long. On the
bottom floor were dormitory-style living spaces complete with shower

facilities, and the top floor was lined with rows of metal tables, all topped with identical Underwood typewriters. It was here, next door to a cushion factory operated by an all-female workforce and across the street from a popular luncheonette, that the newly arrived Nisei became part of the second-largest language intelligence nerve center in the Pacific theater of war.

Created as the Joint Intelligence Center Pacific Ocean Area (JICPOA) in the fall of 1943, only the Army's Allied Translator and Interpreter Section (ATIS) in Australia was larger. JICPOA was the intelligence arm of Admiral Chester Nimitz's naval, air, and land forces within his vast Pacific Ocean Areas command, which encompassed the whole of the central Pacific. Responsible for preparing weekly estimates of Japanese naval, air, and land forces, JICPOA produced and disseminated maps, charts, and other data from captured documents.

Since Japan's surprise attack on the fleet at Pearl Harbor, naval officials at all levels had remained suspicious of any persons of Japanese ancestry, and the Navy forbade the enlistments of Nisei, a policy that would not be reversed until after the war. For its Japanese-language capabilities, JICPOA had been relying on Caucasian graduates of the fourteen-month-long Japanese-language programs established by the Navy at a number of universities, including Harvard, the University of California at Berkeley, and the University of Colorado at Boulder. But by the spring of 1944, with U.S. forces island-hopping their way closer to Japan, the volume of enemy documents arriving at Pearl Harbor could be measured in tons, overwhelming JICPOA's ability to evaluate which ones were routine or highly technical or had any strategic value. The Navy accepted the War Department's offer to provide JICPOA with a contingent of the Army's Nisei linguists, who had proved their value translating captured documents at the front lines and at ATIS in Australia. However, the Navy refused to relax its post–Pearl Harbor security rules prohibiting anyone of Japanese ancestry on the U.S. Naval Base. This applied not only to immigrants but to U.S. citizens and soldiers as well. As a result, Nobuo and the other Nisei could not work in JICPOA headquarters at Pearl Harbor, where more than a hundred intelligence specialists conducted a range of operations. They were unable to sleep in the base's barracks or eat in its mess halls or show up at sick bay when ill. Among themselves, the Nisei groused about being discriminated against by the Navy even as their linguistic skills were needed. But they soon realized that there were distinct advantages to being on their own. They were paid a per diem to eat at restaurants, and those men with family in Hawaii could go home at night. Rather than reporting to a military base every day, they worked at the faux furniture store, officially designated the "JICPOA Annex."

The Nisei at the Annex—particularly the Kibei like Nobuo—could decipher sosho cursive and handwritten kanji in diaries, letters, and notebooks faster and more accurately than anyone who had learned the language in classrooms. The hurried scrawl of a soldier hunkered down in a jungle foxhole was more difficult to read than printed orders and technical manuals. That said, there were Caucasians at JICPOA who were fluent in conversational as well as written Japanese. One of them was the commanding officer of the Annex: Major Glen Bruner, who had been a missionary in Nagasaki in the 1920s, and later worked for the U.S. Foreign Service in Japan. Bruner knew Japanese as well as any educated citizen of Japan.

The naval liaison officer for Nobuo's team, Lieutenant Donald Keene, also excelled in Japanese, having studied it at Columbia University, which he entered at the age of sixteen. Now twenty-two, he had never been to Japan, but his strong aptitude for the language was combined with a photographic memory. He had memorized the *Rose-Innes Dictionary*, a book of common Chinese-Japanese kanji characters, abbreviations, and variants. Nobuo was amazed that Keene not only knew the definitions by heart but also knew the pages they were on. He spoke of his desire to visit Japan after the war, and said reading the captured diaries and letters had given him his first insight into the emotional lives of the Japanese people.[*]

---

[*] Donald Keene's fascination with Japan, its language, and its people continued after the war. His translations of Japanese literature into English and his own academic work at Columbia University, where he taught Japanese for many years, made him a celebrity in both countries. He published some twenty-five books in English and many more in Japanese. After retiring from Columbia, which established the Donald Keene Center of Japanese Culture in his honor, he moved to Japan. He died in Tokyo in 2019, at the age of ninety-six.

Enemy documents arrived from island battlefields stuffed inside wooden crates and canvas seabags. When they were unpacked, many gave off a strange stench that Nobuo associated with the odor of death. It permeated everything around them, and stuck to their clothing. Some papers were so stained with dried blood and God knows what else that they had to be gently wiped off with rubber erasers before they could be read.

Decisions were made about newly arriving documents as to which might contain valuable intelligence so they could be translated first. The rest were set aside until there was time to work on them. While orders and other official documents often provided useful information, the Annex translators found that the handwritten diaries and notebooks of Japanese soldiers were among the best primary sources of intelligence.

One of the most important documents to arrive at the Annex was also the lengthiest: a multivolume industrial directory for Japan's four major home islands that took months to translate in its entirety, and which would later be used to plan strategic bombing raids on war production targets ranging from aircraft plants to ball-bearing factories.

In addition to keeping a complement of fifty Nisei at the JICPOA Annex, the War Department dispatched 230 MIS-trained Nisei to Marine or Army divisions conducting amphibious assaults in the summer and fall of 1944 at places like Saipan (June), Tinian (July), Guam (July), Peleliu (September)—once-obscure Pacific islands most Americans never heard of until they were in newspaper headlines at home.

Nisei from the Annex were periodically rushed to locales where their language skills were urgently needed. Most returned in a month or two with sunburned faces and exciting accounts of action on far-away islands, which enthralled those men stuck behind desks, since the only break from their daily monotony was gazing out the second-floor windows of the furniture store at water buffalo pulling plows across nearby fields. They knew they were luckier than the infantrymen fighting in jungles, yet they tired of the office routine—long, mundane days and nights reading, translating, and typing up intelligence estimates. Blurry-eyed from all the paper pushing, they found it impossible to quantify how much of what they were doing was helping in the war against Japan.

After a new promotion to technical sergeant made him the Annex's senior enlisted man, Nobuo figured he would remain here for the rest of the war. But he was mistaken, as he was soon headed to Saipan on a temporary assignment, arriving shortly after the fighting ended in July 1944. For several weeks, he was the lone Japanese linguist working in civil affairs for the new military government set up to aid a populace that had greatly suffered. Tragically, more than a third of the island's population had died in the three weeks of fighting, slain by the bullets, artillery shells, land mines, and bombs of one side or the other, although in the last days of the battle as many as two thousand civilians committed suicide in the face of intense anti-American propaganda warning of the savagery of U.S. soldiers. The toughest cases for Nobuo were the orphans looking for their parents, reunions that in many cases did not take place because their loved ones were buried in mass graves.

By mid-August, Nobuo was back in Honolulu, where new letters from Toshie awaited him. Only then did he learn that he would be a father by December. Thrilled with her announcement, he wondered how old the baby would be before he made it home. He learned that Toshie and her parents were no longer in Arkansas, as Jerome had been turned into a German POW camp. They were now interned at Gila River in Arizona. He hated that they had been uprooted again, especially with Toshie expecting.

As Toshie's due date approached, her letters stopped for several weeks, and Nobuo fretted. Finally, a short note arrived, and Toshie wrote that she and baby Carol were doing just fine. The news prompted a celebration, and Nobuo handed out cigars. His buddies had lobbied for a girl to be named Carol, since her birth would be during the holiday caroling season, and Nobuo had sent their suggestion to Toshie. Now, with much back-slapping and handshaking, the men acted like proud uncles.

Nobuo didn't have long to savor the news, as he was soon sent packing to the 5th Marine Division. He knew that could mean just one thing. The Marines did not serve as occupational troops after a battle had been fought, but were the tip of the spear in the central Pacific. It was likely that he would finally catch up to the fighting. The irony of it happening now when he was married and a new father wasn't lost on him. He had once wondered how old the baby would be before he made it home, but now he had to consider the possibility that he might never see his daughter. Such unfairnesses happened in war, and he knew when your number came up it didn't matter who you were or who was waiting at home. But Nobuo believed that his wife and their new baby ensured he would leave behind a vital part of himself if he didn't make it back, and that gave him some peace of mind.

The 5th Marine Division had been formed at Camp Pendleton in California ten months earlier. There was an urgency surrounding the activation of the new division and rapid recruiting and training of large numbers of new Marines due to the staunch resistance of the Japanese soldiers on island after island, leading to soaring Marine casualties. Unlike the four older Marine divisions in the Pacific, the 5th had yet to see action, although many of its senior officers and leading noncoms were combat veterans. Since arriving in Hawaii in October, the division had been undergoing combat training at an isolated camp on the Big Island between the twin fourteen-thousand-foot peaks of Mauna Kea, and thirty-five miles away, Mauna Loa, the biggest volcano on earth and one of the most active.

Nobuo took with him an MIS team from the Annex. After a boat trip to Hilo and a winding sixty-mile truck ride across the island through lush foothills and desolate scrublands, they reached Camp Tarawa. Opened in December 1943 for another Marine division to rest, recuperate, and train replacements after suffering several thousand casualties at Tarawa, the camp lay at 2,600 feet above sea level in a cool clime known for its harsh, dusty conditions.

Given his rank, Nobuo was assigned to share quarters in a sprawling regimental tent camp with a master gunnery sergeant known to officers and enlisted men alike as "Gunny," or to those select few he allowed to address him more personally, "Big Mike." After thirty-three years in the Marines, he talked, slept, and breathed his beloved Corps. He had fought in Haiti and Nicaragua during the Banana Wars, and in the trenches in the First World War. In the 1930s, he was among the

Marines who helped develop the amphibious-assault operations now being used in the Pacific.[*]

Big Mike graciously took Nobuo under his wing, but he was less solicitous to recruits or replacements until they proved their mettle. Whenever the company received newbies, he lined them up at attention and lectured them in a growl that grew in menace.

"Think you're already Marines? You're wrong! I'll show you what a Marine is. If you can't keep up with me, you're not gonna be here long."

That was just the warm-up. Then came the heart of his message: "If the man next to you can't depend on you for his life, then you'll never make a Marine. And you won't be in my outfit 'cause I won't have someone I can't depend on." This proved not to be an idle threat.

In the weeks remaining before they left Camp Tarawa, the men of the new division were tested to their physical limits: scaling steep slopes, firing weapons on the small-arms ranges, training in hand-to-hand combat, making practice amphibious landings at Hapuna Beach, and much more. The nearby Parker Ranch provided excellent ground for troops destined to fight in mountainous terrain. Inexplicably, not far from camp they even had their own small volcano, nicknamed "Buster Brown" after a pint-sized comic strip character. But the Marines found nothing funny about the near-vertical climb up the rocky slopes to the flat-nosed six-hundred-foot peak, a man-breaker they scaled in full battle gear. Through it all, Nobuo lugged a rifle and a field pack like everyone else. By the time they broke camp, he had counted fifteen new recruits or replacements who failed to make the grade and were sent elsewhere. Tough old Gunny had kept his word.

By the third week of January, the division was ready to practice a full-scale amphibious assault. On the western shore of Maui near Maalaea Bay, waves of landing craft hit the beaches one after the other, disgorging combat teams that dashed ashore and fanned out as if under fire. All that day and night and into the next day they conducted

* There were 126 U.S. amphibious invasions by the Marines and Army in the Pacific theater during World War II; the first one was at Guadalcanal on August 7, 1942, and the final one at Sarangani Bay in the Philippines on July 12, 1945.

small- and large-unit maneuvers. On the third day, the exhausted men boarded ships that took them back to Oahu. While the division was resupplied for what came next, the men enjoyed a few days of liberty. After completing their battle training, the Marines of the 5th Division were in excellent physical condition, their morale was high, and they were ready for the real thing. Nobuo, who seldom drank alcohol, went into town with Mike one night and was amazed by the copious amounts the big Marine imbibed and that he was still able to rise before dawn looking crisp and sharp. Because Nobuo was with Mike, who had eight red stripes known as "hash marks" down his left sleeve—each represented a four-year stint—the guards at the gate had given Nobuo no trouble when passing him through.

But the next day several Nisei returning to base were not so lucky. "No Japs allowed!" said a Marine guard at Pearl Harbor's main gate, even though they were in uniform and had military ID.

"Screw 'em!" said one Nisei, infuriated at being called the hated J-word and denied entry when they were about to go into combat with a Marine division. "Let the sons-a-bitches sail without interpreters!"

After some heated discussion, a compromise was reached, but the Nisei soldiers were only allowed back on base when a passing Navy officer volunteered to escort them all the way to their barracks.

When the 5th Division sailed from Oahu in a troop convoy, its strength was 17,856 men. Their destination was a well-kept secret, but that soon changed. Two days out, briefings were held on crowded decks. Only then did the Marines learn they were on their way to invade an enemy island just 350 miles from Japan, the closest to the enemy's homeland U.S. assault forces had yet struck. Taking the island, they were told, would increase the effectiveness of the bombing campaign against Japan, likely shortening the war. The island had three existing airfields, and P-51 fighters could be based there to escort B-29 Superfortress bombers all the way to Japan. Presently, due to the distances involved from the closest U.S.-held islands in the Marianas where the B-29s were based, they were making 3,000-mile, fourteen-hour round trips without escorts, which left them easy prey for enemy fighters as they approached Japan. Once captured, the island could also serve as an emergency landing field for damaged B-29s as well as a base for air-sea rescue operations to save aircrews forced to ditch at sea.

Intricate plaster models and raised relief maps of the target island were brought out for the troops to inspect up close. They were briefed on the plan of attack, which called for the 4th and 5th Marine Divisions to land abreast of one another on a 3,500-yard invasion beach on the southeast coast of the island, with the 3rd Marine Division held in reserve aboard ships until needed. For the first time in the war, the assault force comprised three full Marine divisions, totaling more than seventy thousand men. The enemy's estimated strength was put at fifteen thousand to twenty thousand men, many of whom were believed to have been there for as long as a year preparing its defenses. Even so, the planners predicted that the island could be captured in a week at most. After all, it was only five miles long and two and half miles wide at its widest point—eight square miles of mostly flat and barren terrain that had been saturated for months with naval and air bombardments in the longest preinvasion "softening up" in the Pacific.

The name of the island didn't mean anything to the Marines. It was just another in a string of obscure Pacific islands unfamiliar to most Americans. First charted in 1779 by the English explorer James Cook as Sulphur Island, it was so named due to abundant sulfuric deposits from a small but still active volcano. In Japanese, the name of the island was Iwō-tō. The rest of the world soon knew it by another name: Iwo Jima.

------·------

D-day eve fell on Sunday, February 18, 1945.

Aboard the troopships carrying the 5th Marine Division, well-attended church services were held in wardrooms, galleys, and berthing spaces. Afterward, men wrote letters home, then checked and rechecked their battle gear until lights-out. A few hours later, a jarring middle-of-the-night reveille followed by a send-off breakfast of pan-fried steaks and scrambled powdered eggs climaxed weeks of heightened tensions as the hour approached when they would step onto a contested beachhead.

The anticipation among the Marines was palpable. Those who had never been in combat were left to face in their own way any doubts they had about measuring up in battle. Some did so mutely, others boisterously, but it mostly came from the same place. Less than half of the division had seen action, and the combat vets were spread throughout the regiments and battalions to provide a stabilizing element. They had earned a degree of swagger, yet those who had seen buddies cut down knew better than anyone how swiftly war maimed and killed.

Shortly after sunrise, Nobuo went up on the deck of the troopship, which had anchored in the dark a few hours earlier off the southern shore of Iwo Jima. He wore freshly laundered olive-drab utilities with "USMC" emblazoned on the left breast pocket above the Marines' globe-and-anchor insignia, and carried a carbine, a canteen, a gas mask, a rolled blanket, a poncho, and a heavy knapsack with extra gear, including a change of socks and dungarees, toilet supplies, a few old letters from Toshie and his parents, and two Japanese dictionaries. So attired, the Army sergeant looked like any of the Marine riflemen on deck except for one incontrovertible feature: his face. The same face as the enemy.

The Marines had been warned to be on the lookout once ashore for infiltrators because Japanese soldiers were known to strip the battle dress off dead Americans and put it on themselves to raise havoc behind U.S. lines. Nobuo understood how easily he could be mistaken for the enemy, especially since the Marines were not drafting or enlisting Japanese Americans into their own ranks. In fact, one reason given for the Marine Corps' ban on Nisei was the concern that they could be killed in battle due to mistaken identity. His battalion commander shared that worry, and as insurance against losing his Japanese linguist to friendly fire he assigned a newly promoted sergeant, Anthony J. Raymondo, to shadow Nobuo. An Italian Catholic from Knoxville, Tennessee, Raymondo wasn't the least bit upset with an assignment that others might have resented. "Call me Tony," he said amiably, pumping Nobuo's hand when they met. At five foot five, he was two inches shorter than Nobuo but outweighed him by thirty pounds, most of it muscle. Raymondo became Nobuo's constant companion. For anyone to get to Nobuo they would have to go through this fireplug of a Marine first.

From where he stood on deck, Nobuo saw ships of all sizes and shapes in every direction. Mixed in among the myriad troop transports were destroyers, light cruisers, heavy cruisers, and battleships. As the warships had been doing for much of the past three days, their deck guns were slamming away at the island, now obscured by orange shell bursts and dark funnels of heavy smoke and thick dust swirling into the skyscape. Nobuo had learned that about a third of the island was covered in concrete runways and revetments, a third consisted of old cane fields and scrub growth, and the rest was barren. But from two miles away, Iwo Jima's most discernable feature was the volcano on its southern tip. The volcano's base was several times wider than its height, giving it the appearance of a mountain that should be taller but had been ingloriously hacked off. On the invasion maps, the volcano was code-named "Hot Rocks," but by now Nobuo knew its real name and dimensions. Mt. Suribachi, at a height of 554 feet, was shorter than Buster Brown by only the length of a telephone pole. It struck him as astonishing that they had practiced for weeks at Camp Tarawa on a volcano almost exactly the same elevation and shape, especially given his battalion's assignment that morning. They were to land on the far left of the invasion beaches, at the base of Suribachi. While other units turned right (north) toward the airfields, they were to wheel left to the volcano, cut it off from the rest of the island, clear out enemy positions, and secure the volcano's slopes and peak.

The morning's sea was mostly smooth, and overhead a light wind floated cumulus clouds across an azure sky. There was little surf on the beaches, which was a lucky break for the landing forces. In fact, it was ideal weather for an amphibious assault, something the Marines at Guadalcanal and Saipan had not had, and it seemed like a good omen.

"All hands! Man your debarkation stations!"

As they had drilled during the two-week, five-thousand-mile voyage here, the Marines went quickly to their assigned stations and awaited the command to swing into the cargo nets and drop down to the coffin-shaped landing craft idling alongside to take them ashore. The order wasn't long in coming. Soon, the small boats filled with Marines were pulling away into a crowded sea, circling in designated lanes like rush-hour traffic as an expanding fleet of assault boats.

When the rolling thunder of the naval bombardment ceased, it turned eerily quiet. Nobuo thought, *Here we go.* He and Raymondo were squeezed inside the crowded boat with two dozen other 2nd Battalion, 28th Marines. They were scheduled for a D+15 landing, meaning his battalion was to constitute the second wave fifteen min-utes after the first wave (1st Battalion) landed at Green Beach. But rather than starting toward the island now, all the boats kept circling.

Nobuo soon saw why, as the sky filled with Corsairs launched from nearby aircraft carriers. The navy pilots raked the island with napalm bombs, striking along the boulder-strewn base and steep slopes of Suribachi, sending up smoldering balls of flame and black clouds. When they finished, a formation of long-range air force B-24 Lib-erators approached, their metallic fuselages glinting in the early sun. Flying in from their base on Saipan seven hundred miles away, they each carried nearly three tons of general purpose bombs, most of them five-hundred-pounders filled with TNT and effective against airfields, vehicles, and all types of construction. As the B-24s overflew the island, they released their payloads, and the bombs blew sand, dirt, rocks, and whatever else they hit hundreds of feet in the air. When the air strikes ended, the ships resumed their broadside, aiming the final salvos at the stretch of invasion beaches.

The boats of the first assault wave at last bore down on Iwo Jima.

At 9:02 a.m., more than a thousand Marines spilled onto hostile shores. The second wave headed for the beach a few minutes later.

Nobuo had been standing in the packed landing craft for nearly two hours when they at last turned for shore. A stiffening wind now scalloped the surrounding seas. Most of the men were nauseous from all the zigzagging and exhaust fumes that blew back whenever they turned downwind. Normal conversation was impossible over the loud rumble of the engine, but no one had much to say anyway. Men alter-nated between tight-lipped grins and grimaces. Some held their heads up so they could see where they were going, and others kept heads bowed so they didn't have to look.

Nobuo could see that the beach was filled with Marines who had landed ahead of them. Were they pinned down? At the moment, he was less concerned about being shot than drowning. He was a weak swimmer, and weighted down with his pack he knew he'd sink like a sack of stones if he fell into deep water.

They jolted to a stop fifty feet from shore and bounded as one from the landing craft. Nobuo found himself wading through shallow water, but he soon sank to mid-calf in a black sand mixed with an ashy soil from volcanic cinders, a viscid combination that sucked at his boots like wet concrete. The tanks and amtracs that had landed before them were bogged down in the sand, some stuck midway up on berms as high as twenty feet. The bulldozers that would have to carve paths through the sand had yet to arrive. For now, the beached war machines were of little help, and the men slogged past them. This is not the way their practice assaults had gone in Hawaii. They were trained to quickly get off the beach, where they were most vulnerable, and to make room for the next assault waves, but their efforts to do so now looked like a Movietone newsreel at slow speed.

Nobuo was surprised to hear no shooting. They had been warned to expect heavy fire, as the Japanese had attempted to halt invasions at the beachheads on other islands, but all he heard was Marines grunting and swearing and engines grinding. Had the naval bombardments and air strikes broken the enemy? Maybe Iwo Jima *would* be a cakewalk.

The 28th Regiment's commanding officer, Colonel Harry Liversedge, a former track star nicknamed "Harry the Horse" after he won a bronze medal in the shotput at the 1920 Olympics, radioed his first report from Green Beach at 9:19 a.m. "Troops ashore and moving to isolate volcano." Initial reports from the other invasion beaches reflected similar optimism. "Casualties unexpectedly light." "Moving inland." "Bogged down in heavy sand and steep terraces but conditions generally favorable."

Shortly after 10 a.m., all hell broke loose. From earthen mounds overlooking the beaches, enemy machine guns fired from barely visible slits, and artillery and mortar rounds exploded in a near-blinding kaleidoscope of ear-splitting blasts. From the north end of the island and the heights of Suribachi, Japanese coastal defense and antiaircraft guns that had been silent now zeroed in on the congested beaches.

The Marines, with scant places to take cover, were cut down by volleys of bullets or blown into the air by blasts that left their bodies in twisted, bloody heaps, with missing limbs and viscera exposed. Cries of *Corpsman! Corpsman!* for the Navy medics to treat the grievously wounded echoed across the killing field. Shell-shocked men clawed at the sand with rifle butts and bare hands trying to dig foxholes for protection, but the slipping sand caved in as fast as they shoveled. Urgent calls went out for sandbags. Desperate, some men leapt into smoldering shell holes.

Nobuo and Raymondo hugged the ground, holding their steel helmets tightly over their heads. The damnable sand that reeked strongly of sulfur reminded Nobuo of the volcanic beaches on Kiska, where men and vehicles had also struggled in terrible footing. But that was where the similarities ended between his two assault landings a year and a half apart. Kiska had been deserted by the enemy weeks earlier. But with ample time to prepare their defenses, they were making a stand here.

Three years after enlisting, Nobuo was finally in the shooting war. The first enemy shots that whizzed past him weren't loud reports like at a gun range but insipid *ping-ping*s. Marines hit by them fell flat, as if suddenly losing their battle with gravity rather than being thrown theatrically backward or off to one side like in cowboy movies Nobuo had seen. As the intensity of the enemy fire increased, the reality of combat became more horrific than anything he could have conjured. There was the dreaded *pop-pop-pop* of mortar rounds propelled from tube dischargers and the sharp crack and whine of artillery shells arriving like of a speeding locomotive and detonating in concussive waves that sucked the air from the chest and burst the eardrums. The ground gave no sanctuary, and every blast threatened to crack open the earth. In no time, the dead and the dying and the screams of agony were all around him.

At 10:46 a.m., Colonel Liversedge, who had won a Navy Cross for heroism at New Georgia, broadcast over the radio circuit monitored by the invasion commander aboard his flagship. Speaking over the crackle of static and the cacophony of the incoming fire, the combat veteran gave a bleaker picture than his earlier report: "Taking heavy fire and forward movement stopped. Machine gun and artillery fire heaviest ever seen."

But the 28th Regiment did not stay stopped for long. Advance units headed for the island's opposite shore, jumping from one shell hole to another as they fought across the volcanic moonscape a few yards at a time, destroying pillboxes, blockhouses, and dugouts as they went. Enemy artillery and mortar rounds rained down on them, their deadly accuracy seldom wavering as spotters on Suribachi reported their every move to gun crews. The crossing of the island's narrowest neck of land—less than a mile across—cost hundreds of Marine casualties. While the regiment fell short of its D-day objective of securing the volcano, they had cut the island in half and isolated Suribachi. And in heavy fighting to the north, other regiments captured the first of the three enemy airfields.

By late that afternoon, Nobuo and Raymondo were settled in a foxhole reinforced with sandbags about three hundred yards up from where they had landed on Green Beach. Situated at the extreme left of the beachhead, closest to Suribachi, they were now in volcanic terrain dotted with rocks and stones. All headquarters personnel were ordered "not to stick your heads out of your foxholes," as the beaches were still receiving enemy fire. When the sun set, it turned bitterly cold and downpoured.

The next morning, bulldozers carved out corridors for tanks and other vehicles to get off the beaches while working parties offloaded supplies, vehicles, and heavy equipment from newly arrived LSTs. At the same time, thousands of fresh Marines were streaming ashore from the 3rd Division, held in reserve off the coast until needed, which was now.

Casualties were stretchered back to the beachhead, where they waited to be triaged off the island to hospital ships and transports with medical facilities. Already it was clear that there were no rear areas; every inch of ground on the small island was on the front lines. In fact, many luckless casualties awaiting evacuation were hit a second time. And medical personnel were not spared: the regimental surgeon Daniel McCarthy of Savannah, Georgia, was killed by a mortar round as he treated the wounded on Green Beach.

The 28th Regiment's initial assault on Suribachi was halted by a wall of withering fire from a honeycomb of defensive positions. More air strikes and naval gunfire were requested, and for the rest of the day Suribachi was plastered anew. As formidable as any of the volcano's other defenses was its hidden network of caves. There were miles

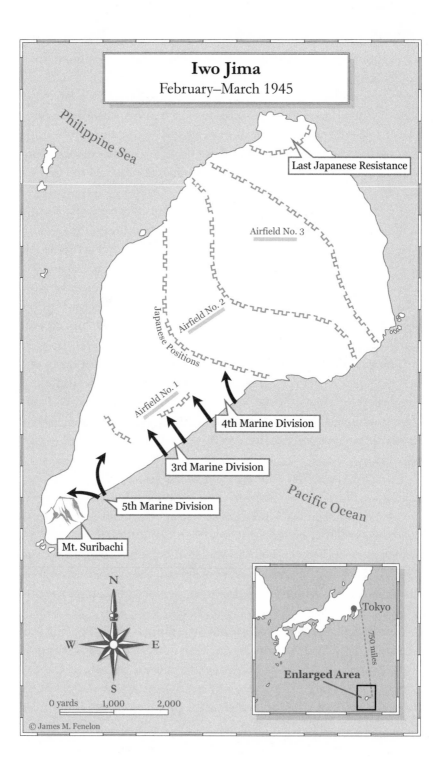

Iwo Jima
February–March 1945

Philippine Sea

Last Japanese Resistance

Airfield No. 3

Airfield No. 2

Japanese Positions

Airfield No. 1

4th Marine Division

3rd Marine Division

Pacific Ocean

5th Marine Division

Mt. Suribachi

N
W   E
S

0 yards   1,000   2,000

© James M. Fenelon

Tokyo

750 miles

Enlarged Area

and miles of them, both natural and manmade. Many had from two to five entrances and tunnels that went deep inside the mountain to larger caverns that were ventilated by air shafts and fitted out with spartan living quarters stocked with food, water, and ammunition. Used as subterranean routes to move troops and supplies, the thick-walled caves made excellent air raid shelters, which explained why so many Japanese defenders had survived the preinvasion air strikes and bombardments.

In the morning, three combat teams attacked enemy positions around the volcano. It was close-in fighting in steep terrain—unsuited for tanks and artillery—against tenacious, well-prepared defenders. One by one, enemy caves and bunkers were located, blasted by gre-nades and flame-throwers, and sealed up by powerful demolition charges. By nightfall, the Marines had tightened the noose around Suribachi in preparation for securing and occupying the summit of the volcano.

"Tomorrow," Liversedge told his men, "we climb."

The next day, February 23, 1945, was D-day plus four.

That morning, a short distance up from Green Beach, the first dead were brought to an open field newly designated as the 5th Divi-sion cemetery. (The other divisions had their own cemeteries farther north.) Up to now, the dead were left where they fell, as there had been no safe way to collect the bodies from the field of battle. But leaving remains unburied raised health concerns and was bad for morale, so the division's 75-man Graves Registration Unit had begun the grim work for which they were trained: collecting, identifying, and tagging bodies for burial. Given the numbers involved—before leaving Iwo Jima after a month of combat, the 5th Division buried 2,280 Marines—burials had to be mass interments. Bulldozers cut trenches eight feet deep and thirty yards long, and GI blankets or ponchos were used as shrouds. The graves were listed on a location chart by name, rank, and serial number. Some remains were so burned or mutilated or just fragments of flesh and bones that they could not be identified. In those cases, tattoos, scars, and birthmarks were noted. Pre-manufactured crosses and markers were placed at the head of each grave. Chaplains went row by row, grave by grave, blessing the young men who were the sons of mothers and the husbands of wives but whose lives had been cut short on a squalid enemy island in the Pacific.*

Newly assigned to regimental headquarters, Nobuo was seated on an overturned crate in a tent pouring over a cache of captured enemy documents, separating out the documents of immediate tactical value. Anything pertaining to the enemy's order of battle—specific units and their strengths—or current defenses in the field he translated first. That information was sent forward to combat units. Anything else went to the division's large translation team, which worked on the documents themselves or bundled them in seabags to be flown to JICPOA in Hawaii.

So focused on his work, Nobuo likely would have missed what happened at 10:30 a.m. that morning had it not been for the thunderous cheers of thousands of Marines along the beaches and hundreds of ships blowing their sirens, bells, and horns. He stepped outside to see who or what was receiving such a spontaneous and boisterous reception.

And there it was—

Atop Suribachi a U.S. flag fluttered from a long pole. Everyone surely knew there was more fighting and dying to be done here, but Old Glory flying at the summit of the volcano was an inspiring sight. The U.S. Marines had made it to the top, and they would triumph. *Semper Fi.*

Nobuo joined in the cheering. He would never again see an American flag without remembering this moment on this island.

His first enemy interrogation took place as the prisoner lay on a stretcher at the regimental aid station. The man had been badly burned by a flamethrower, and patches of his skin looked like a rack of barbecued ribs. A corpsman said the lining of his lungs were likely charred. At first Nobuo couldn't tell if he was still breathing, but when he

---

* The remains of 5,394 U.S. Marines buried in the three cemeteries on Iwo Jima were disinterred in 1947 and removed to a new mausoleum on Saipan. Their families had the option of burying their loved ones in a national cemetery near their homes at government expense, in a private cemetery with the government contributing $50, or in a permanent American military cemetery overseas.

The first flag raised at the top of Suribachi at about 10:30 a.m. on February 23, 1945. Later, this flag was replaced by a larger flag, a moment captured in an iconic image by the photographer Joe Rosenthal.

spoke to him in Japanese the man opened his eyes and asked for water. His hands were heavily bandaged, so Nobuo held a canteen to his lips.

Unwrapping a Hershey bar, Nobuo broke off a chunk and slipped it pass the man's lips. The chocolate melting in his mouth seemed to soothe him. He spoke only haltingly, but Nobuo was able to glean from him his name, rank, and unit, and that he'd been assigned to a blockhouse near Suribachi. When he faded suddenly, Nobuo thought he was a goner. But then he reawakened with a start, anxiously pointing at something.

Nearby was a filthy Japanese field jacket, its sleeves seared like the man's arms. He nodded when Nobuo motioned to the jacket.

"*Moji,*" he whispered hoarsely. "*Moji.*"

Nobuo found the letter in an inside pocket.

As the man's voice grew weaker, Nobuo had to lean closer. The letter was addressed to his parents in Tokyo, the prisoner explained. Looking up with pleading eyes, he asked if Nobuo would mail it.

Nobuo said he would.

"*Arigatō.*" The POW shut his eyes and died.

Nobuo was astounded at how peacefully and quickly the man went.

He slipped the rice paper missive into his breast pocket. It couldn't be mailed during the war, of course, but maybe afterward. Nobuo knew how his own parents in Colorado would feel if the situation were reversed.

The next day Nobuo went with a psychological warfare team to a cave entrance that was surrounded by a squad of Marines. With the frontline units being exhorted by intelligence officers to take prisoners, the enemy soldiers holed up inside would be given an opportunity to surrender. The team set up a speaker near the cave entrance. For half an hour Nobuo tried to convince them to come out, promising food and medical attention. He told them not only was the battle here lost but the war was over for them and there was no reason to die. But no one came out. Then, echoing from deep inside came the sound of a grenade exploding. Nobuo handed back the microphone, and the technicians packed up their equipment. Nobuo accompanied several Marines into the cave, where they found the eviscerated bodies of two dead Japanese soldiers.

Nobuo understood that the Marines who would have had to fight these enemy soldiers preferred this outcome, but he felt differently. The job for which he had been trained was to persuade the enemy to surrender so they could be interrogated for intelligence that might save American lives, and that had not happened. There was another reason, which he kept to himself because he didn't expect many combat Marines to understand. He well remembered his classmates in Kumamoto who hated the fanatical army types and the Kenpeitai secret police as much as he did, and how they had no desire to die in a foreign war, which at that time Japan was waging in Manchuria and China. How many of them had been drafted into the Japanese army, and were now being led by zealots who preached suicide in a cave as the only way for a warrior to uphold his honor in defeat? It saddened him to think of those boys he had known being sacrificed. If they had fought honorably, there was no reason for shame and no need to die to prove their courage. He would have liked to tell them, "You fought your hardest and did your best," and that good men would be needed after the war to rebuild a defeated Japan.

One of the few enemy prisoners brought in by the 28th Regiment had no problem ignoring the cultural taboo against surrender. Stepping out from a hillside cavern, an usually tall Japanese soldier appeared with his hands high in the air, waving a white rag. The Marines kept their rifles trained on him as he came forward in case it was a trick. In perfect, unaccented English, the Japanese soldier yelled, "I don't go for this hari-kari shit!" It turned out he was a Japanese American raised in Chicago who had been visiting his grandparents in Japan when war broke out. He had been forced to join the army or face incarceration. Much to his later regret, the young Nisei told Nobuo, he chose the army over a prison cell.

By the end of the first week, Nobuo's regiment had taken only a half-dozen prisoners, and similarly low numbers were reported by the other Marine regiments and divisions.* The daily interrogation reports showed that little actionable intelligence had been gained from POWs on Iwo Jima. This did not seem to have to do with any general unwillingness to cooperate, as once they realized they weren't going to be tortured or killed by the Americans the majority expressed gratitude at being spared and were willing to tell interrogators what they knew. But in most cases that wasn't much. Intelligence officers attributed the dearth of information to their isolated existence as they manned

---

* In a month of fighting on Iwo Jima, the 28th Regiment took only 16 POWs; in the same period, the three Marine divisions captured a total of 216 Japanese. By the war's end, only about 35,000 Japanese soldiers had been taken prisoner by Allied forces, a fraction of the 945,000 German and 490,000 Italian POWs captured in the war.

the island's defenses. Most of them did not know what was going on outside their own caves and tunnels.

Nobuo came across one notable exception. During the third week of the campaign, a notebook taken from a captured Japanese sergeant caught his attention. While he had interrogated only a handful of prisoners, he had by then read hundreds of Japanese documents, most of them containing little of any military value. But the notebook looked more promising, and he went to question the sergeant, whom he found with several prisoners inside a guarded enclosure near the invasion beaches. The sergeant confirmed Nobuo's hunch that he was a "code man," or cryptographer, and volunteered that he had decrypted communications with Tokyo for the island's commanding general. Nobuo knew that a cooperative code man might help U.S. codebreakers working on Japan's military ciphers. But codes were changed often, so it was vital to have him debriefed quickly by U.S. cryptographers who knew the right technical questions to ask to get the most important information.

Nobuo reported their prized catch to the division's intelligence officer. "I think we get him out of here, sir, and back to Pearl."

The major agreed, and the POW was whisked off the island.

By March 26, the heaviest fighting was over and the island was declared secured. That week, an Army infantry regiment landed to relieve the Marines and conduct mop-up operations. It would take them another three months to root out the remaining Japanese, most of them near starvation, from all the tunnels and caves.

The bloodiest campaign in the Pacific to date and the costliest one in Marine Corps history, the thirty-six-day battle resulted in 25,851 casualties, including more than 6,800 dead and 17,000 wounded. Every third Marine who landed on Iwo Jima was either killed or wounded in the fighting. Japanese losses were difficult to estimate at the time due to all the caves sealed up with the dead as well as the living inside, and compounded by the enemy's practice of removing their dead from the battlefield at night and taking them away to be cremated in large pyres. But later estimates put the number at 20,000 Japanese killed in the fighting on Iwo Jima.

Nobuo left the day after Iwo Jima was officially secured, saying goodbye and thanks to his loyal companion, Tony Raymondo, and

Big Mike, the gunnery sergeant who had kept close tabs on him since Camp Tarawa. Along with several other Nisei heading back to JICPOA, he boarded a Navy cargo ship for Pearl Harbor, four thousand miles away. Loaded with equipment and other gear the Marines were sending back to Hawaii, the ship had taken aboard only two dozen passengers. Nobuo and the others, thankful to be off the god-forsaken island and back on the open sea, sunned on the deck by day and played cards in their berthing compartment at night. Nobuo reckoned it was as relaxing an ocean cruise as one could hope for in wartime—that is, right up until April 12, 1945.

That afternoon, all the ships of the U.S. Pacific Fleet received the same uncoded broadcast in their radio shacks. Aboard the freighter, the staggering news was piped over the loudspeaker system.

"Attention! Attention! All hands! President Roosevelt is dead. Repeat, our Supreme Commander, President Roosevelt, is dead."

A hush fell over the ship. Few of the men said anything, or even looked at one another. Everyone began drifting apart, as if instinctively wanting to be alone at this time. What could any of them say?

Nobuo was stunned and confused. He didn't recall a time in his life when someone other than Roosevelt was president. He was barely in his teens when FDR was first elected in 1932, and when he returned from Japan in 1938 Roosevelt was still president. And when he voted for the first time in 1940, Nobuo had cast his ballot for the leader whose New Deal had helped farmers like his father get through the Great Depression.

Nobuo had heard FDR's address to Congress on the radio with his parents the day after Pearl Harbor was attacked. That "day of infamy" was such a traumatic event for the country, yet the president's inspirational words had dispensed great hope. "No matter how long it will take us," he promised, Americans would "win absolute victory . . . With confidence in our armed forces, with the unbounding determination of our people, we will gain the inevitable triumph—so help us God."

That promise and that dose of Roosevelt optimism propelled millions of Americans into action, including Nobuo, who immediately asked that his agricultural draft exemption be canceled so he could enlist. His feelings about Roosevelt became more complicated with the president's executive order in early 1942 authorizing the forced removal of Japanese Americans in the western states to internment camps. While his own family was exempt from the order because they lived in Colorado, Toshie and her family had been among those who lost their jobs, homes, world possessions, and freedom. Nobuo understood that FDR's legacy had to include the fact that tens of thousands of Americans were forced to live in relocation camps for no reason other than their race.

Nobuo found himself at the fantail, mesmerized by the ship's wake.

He turned and looked up. Flying high atop the main mast was the U.S. flag, already half-masted in a salute to the lost president. Seeing it reminded him of FDR's promise to the nation more than three years ago.

First things first, Nobuo decided. And the war had to come first.

Then he would go home and work to rebuild his trust in the "land of liberty," where his own little girl had been born behind barbed wire.

Fifteen

THE LAST INVASION

The convoy that departed Oahu in September 1944 taking the 96th Infantry Division to war—along with Takejiro Higa, his brother, Warren, and their ten-man MIS team—was en route to invade the enemy-held Caroline Islands when it was decided to bypass those small coral islands north of New Guinea in favor of liberating the Philippines, which had been occupied by the Japanese for nearly three years. The fully loaded troopships put in at the Admiralties, where plans for the new operation were finalized, then sailed for Leyte, 1,750 miles away.

One of the largest islands in the Philippines, Leyte sat in the heart of that archipelagic country, well situated from which to strike enemy positions on the other islands, including Luzon, and the capital of Manila. Heavily forested with steep mountains and waist-deep swamps, Leyte averaged 250 inches of rain annually. The island where it rained nearly daily had close to a million residents, many of whom were fishermen or farmers growing coconuts, bananas, and sugarcane.

On the morning of October 20, 1944, the still-untested 96th Division, now part of the powerful Sixth Army under the overall command of General Douglas MacArthur, landed near the coastal town of Dulag on Leyte's eastern shore. The first to hit the beach was a regiment of infantry reinforced with amphibious tanks. As they dashed across the sands onto solid ground, sporadic enemy mortar and artillery fire from a nearby 1,400-foot hilltop killed and injured

several men, but U.S. casualties were
light compared to the invasion beaches
of other Pacific atolls and islands.

Takejiro and Warren were spectators
for the first hours of the invasion, peering through binoculars from the deck
of a combat transport along with two
members of their team, Herbert Yanamura and Takeo Nonaka. As the senior
enlisted man, Warren was in charge of
the ten-man 314th Headquarters Intelligence Detachment, all of whom hailed
from Hawaii or California. He had dispersed six men to the division's three
infantry regiments: Fred Fukushima and

Takejiro Higa,
MISLS graduation

Rudy Kawahara to the 381st; Thomas Masui and Ernest Kawana to
the 382nd, and Osamu Yamamoto and Akira Ohori to the 383rd.
Warren made sure that one of each pair was strong in Japanese and
the other in English for report writing. Their main job was to evaluate captured documents and translate those that were important to
battlefield tactics, such as the location of mortars, machine guns, and
other weaponry. They would also question any prisoners captured
by their regiment, but likewise limit the interrogations to matters of
similar tactical importance. All captured papers and prisoners were to
then be sent to division headquarters, where operational orders dated
within the last month were to be translated and prisoners interrogated
for any useful intelligence. Warren had attended a Japanese school
in Hawaii for a few years but had a limited Japanese vocabulary. He
kept Takejiro with him at division not because they were brothers but
because he was their top Japanese linguist.

The three regiments had all gone ashore while Takejiro, Warren,
Yanamura, and Nonaka were still watching the action from the ship.
It had been quite a show. As the morning mist lifted, they saw the
hills behind the beach and beyond them the dark, ominous mountain-
tops. They watched as hundreds of small boats beached, disgorging
thousands of infantrymen. They saw columns of smoke from the
impact of artillery rounds, heard the muffled explosions, and inhaled

Brigadier General Claudius Easley personally
oversaw the marksmanship of his men.

the pungent scent of gunpowder. Just as Takejiro began to think they
had been forgotten, they were ordered to board a waiting landing craft.

When they reached the beachhead, it was congested with troops,
vehicles, and supplies. They hiked through a dense coconut plantation to the division command post (CP), where the assistant division
commander, Brigadier General Claudius Easley, was already in charge.
(The division commander, Major General James Bradley, wasn't due
ashore until the next day, which allowed him to retain clear command and control channels from offshore if things went badly on
the beaches.) Easley had been with the division since it was formed
in 1942. He arrived with a reputation as a competitive sharpshooter
and a skilled rifle and pistol coach, and supervised their marksmanship training, which progressed so well that the 96th was now called
the "Deadeye Division."

A row of spacious, ten-foot-tall tents had gone up, and engineers
had dug nearby bomb shelters using coconut logs for the roofs, on
which they piled mounds of dirt. Finding a suitable spot in a small
clearing, the four Nisei unpacked their gear—including typewriters
and a box of leather-bound dictionaries—and set up a large tent to
serve as their workspace with turned-over crates for seats and tables.
They were no sooner settled when the first batch of enemy documents

arrived for translation. There were maps and operational orders—both took top priority—along with pay records, notebooks, diaries, and letters. Nothing indicated where this cache had been found, but it was clearly from an enemy stronghold.

After dusk, Takejiro and the others were startled to hear shouting in Japanese: *"Tenno heika banzai!"* Although it came from a distance, they understood the words and what they portended. Rapid shots popped off like strings of firecrackers on July 4, followed by a fusillade of machine gun and mortar fire. A *banzai* attack was hitting U.S. lines not far away!

Takejiro could only imagine how terrifying it must be for young GIs in their first combat facing a human wave of jacked-up diehards charging from the shadows at them. The gunfight lasted only a short while, and when it stopped the night turned eerily quiet. When Takejiro learned details of the incident the next day, it was obvious that the enemy chose the wrong place and time to attack. About a hundred Japanese hit a heavy weapons company that had just set into position their nighttime perimeter defense, consisting of a circle of evenly spaced foxholes to prevent anyone from infiltrating in the dark. Their automatic weapons and fields of fire were perfectly placed to cut down the attackers before they got near enough to do real damage. Reports from the field told of so many enemy dead that their bodies had landed atop one another like fallen timber. Not a single American was killed, and only two were slightly wounded. Lessons were learned from successfully repelling this first *banzai* attack, and the word spread among the troops. Set your defenses before dark. Don't let the yelling and screaming unsettle you. Remain calm and keep low. Hold your fire until they are in the open. Recognizing that *banzai* attacks gave them the chance to kill large numbers of the enemy with minimal losses of their own, the sharpshooters of the Deadeye Division began to welcome them.

For the next several days the front lines remained close to the command post, and they were shelled daily by enemy artillery. One strike killed three men and wounded nine, including the colonel in charge of the division's logistics and planning. After that, the fighting moved farther inland, much of it on steep, wet mountain trails and in the grasping mud of swamps.

Stacks of enemy documents arrived daily for the linguists to read and translate. Before long, the Sixth Army's MIS teams had pieced together the identities of the enemy units operating on Leyte. Their efforts were later commended by the officer in charge of the Order of Battle Section for providing "a missing piece in the jigsaw puzzle. We [soon] had the complete layout of Japanese forces."*

No interrogations were taking place, however, as Japanese soldiers were not surrendering, and if any were trying to give up, they weren't being brought in alive. Intelligence officers pleaded with field commanders to impress upon their men the importance of interrogating enemy prisoners. As an inducement, some outfits instituted bounties of extra cigarettes and beer rations for bringing in POWs. Still, it was two weeks before the first one arrived at division, and he came on a stretcher.

A medic worked on him as Takejiro and Yanamura stood by. When a filthy bandage was removed, live maggots could be seen inside a deep wound. The worm infestation was a shock to the Nisei. Why had the POW allowed the maggots to be on him? they wanted to know.

He answered quietly, *"Yoi uji."* (Good maggots.)

After the medic scooped out the worms, cleaned the site, and treated it with an ointment, then wrapped it in a new sterile dressing, he announced that it was free of infection, adding that the maggots eating away the dead tissue had likely prevented gangrene from setting in.

Takejiro handed the injured man a Lucky Strike and gave him a light. The prisoner nodded his thanks and drew deeply on what was likely his first American smoke. But when he was offered something to eat, he looked stricken.

"Dame dame dame! Onaka suitenai." (No, no, no! Not hungry.)

That was hard to believe, given his emaciated appearance. Yanamura opened a can of C ration meat, ate a spoonful, then handed the tin to the POW. Now convinced that it wasn't poisoned, the man

---

* Approximately 120 Nisei served in MIS language teams on Leyte. Some came from JICPOA in Hawaii and ATIS in Brisbane, and others fresh from graduating from MISLS.

Nisei interrogating POW

gulped it down. The proffered cigarette and food had the desired effect, and soon he was answering their questions and chatting easily about himself and his unit.

As more prisoners trickled in over the next couple of weeks—and later in droves as the Japanese were being routed in the mountains—Takejiro found most of them similarly ready to cooperate. No physical coercion or threats were used against them. Rather, they were fed and given cigarettes, and their injuries were treated. Takejiro soon saw that establishing rapport with a prisoner was the most effective method of interrogation. One of the first things he noticed was their genuine surprise at facing an ethnic Japanese in a U.S. Army uniform. None of them dreamed that the American Army had such men in its ranks. When spoken to by a fellow Asian in their own language, many seemed to relax for the first time. Takejiro was amazed how openly they spoke once they started talking, which he attributed to their being uninformed as to their rights under international law, unlike U.S. soldiers who were instructed to reveal only "name, rank, and serial number."

At 6 p.m. on December 7, what first sounded like the persistent hum of an approaching bee swarm grew steadily louder until it turned into the quaking rumble of a large formation of low-flying aircraft.

Stepping outside, Takejiro saw that the planes weren't the U.S. carrier-based fighters that had been buzzing Leyte for several weeks.

The last time he had seen so many planes bearing the rising sun insignia was three years ago to the day, when the Japanese attacked Pearl Harbor and he had watched in disbelief from the rooftop of the YMCA cafeteria in downtown Honolulu as the bombs fell.

The din was so loud now, cries of warning were barely audible.

"Enemy aircraft!" "Jap transports!" "Paratroopers!"

Paratroopers? Takejiro now saw them leaping from the rear exits of a dozen planes overhead. They floated down under billowing white canopies. As they neared the ground, they disappeared behind the forest canopy. They looked to be jumping on the Burauen airfield, which the Japanese had built and U.S. aircraft were now using. It was only a mile away.

With the front lines having moved farther into the hills, the MIS team hadn't had any reason to use their foxholes. But now, grabbing their rifles and ammo, they dropped into the holes for a long night, alert to every sound and fleeting shadow around them.

Inside the division CP tents, plans were drawn up for a counterattack at first light. When sunrise finally came, a battalion from the 382nd Regiment—joined by elements of the 11th Airborne Division bivouacked in the area—was sent out to find the enemy paratroopers. Many of them had come down beyond the airstrip in an area of tall trees, the bane of parachutists everywhere. One planeload had jumped to their deaths when the aircraft's anchor line designed to pull open their chutes failed. Some of the paratroopers managed to destroy a few light aircraft on the ground and torch some stores of aviation fuel before withdrawing into the woods. But the majority who survived the jump were hopelessly scattered, and were easily hunted down with few U.S. casualties.

One wounded Japanese paratrooper was brought in to be interrogated. He told of having taken off from the island of Cebu, sixty miles west of Leyte, and how the attack was to be coordinated with their remaining ground forces in eastern Leyte. He provided details of the operation, which dovetailed with what MIS interpreter Tom Masui had learned two days earlier in his interrogation of a Japanese soldier, who told of the planned assault on the Burauen airfield involving a parachute brigade on *Pāruhābā no hi* (Pearl Harbor day). Masui immediately turned in his Interrogation of Prisoner of War (IPW) report with all the pertinent information. He was surprised that no alert went out to the troops in the area. In retrospect, the intelligence was dead-on accurate, and the opportunity to forewarn U.S. soldiers of the airborne assault squandered.

Masui was upset about it. "That was our chance to show our stuff," he grumbled to the team. "How come that got screwed up?"

None of them knew the answer and could only speculate. Either Masui's IPW report hit a bottleneck on its way up the chain of command or it *had* reached the top, where someone decided the intelligence wasn't credible. Whatever the case, it was disheartening, because it was the kind of vital information they were trained to acquire in order to save American lives on the battlefield. It was lucky for everyone from the top brass on down—especially the U.S. infantrymen on the ground—that the attack from the sky was a debacle for the enemy when the link-up with their ground forces failed to materialize since most of them had been pushed westward into the mountains.

A few nights later, the MIS team gathered in the division's radio section for an hour of music and news, compliments of Tokyo Rose, whose playlists included tunes by big bands and torch singers meant to make GIs homesick, which they often did. But she was less demoralizing than she was entertaining, and the "war news" read theatrically by the sultry voice always got plenty of laughs. Tonight, Takejiro and the other Nisei found one of her breathless bulletins especially comical.

"Brave Japanese paratroopers, in coordination with our courageous troops on Leyte, successfully forced all American troops off the island. Leyte is once again completely under Japan's control!"

Three weeks later, organized resistance on Leyte officially ended on Christmas Day. Credited with killing 7,700 of the enemy, the 96th Division's losses were 376 killed, 1,289 wounded, and some 2,500 victims of illnesses or nonbattle injuries. Ordered to remain on the island to mop up Japanese holdouts and perform security duty, the division was to start receiving new equipment and training replacements for whatever came next.

There was still dangerous work to be done on Leyte as American troops fanned out to destroy isolated pockets of Japanese or persuade them to surrender. A Nisei interpreter with the 7th Infantry Division, twenty-four-year-old Frank Hachiya, went into the field on New Year's

Frank Hachiya,
of Hood River, Oregon

Eve to speak to a group of Japanese holdouts in the hills. As he was returning to U.S. lines, he was shot in the stomach, either by an enemy sniper or friendly fire. Hachiya, a native of Hood River, a quiet little town on Oregon's Columbia River, died in a field hospital four days later without knowing that his town's American Legion post had weeks earlier removed from its "Roll of Honor" the names of the sixteen local Japanese Americans serving in the military. The same month Hachiya died on Leyte, the county clerk and chamber of commerce manager published a letter in the local newspaper. It was titled: "So Sorry Please, Japs Are Not Wanted in Hood River."*

There was much speculation among the men of the 96th Division as to their next assignment, especially when the attack on Luzon was launched in January 1945 without their participation. Takejiro was among the few who knew what the Army had planned for them, and he had been losing sleep over it. But sworn to secrecy, he couldn't tell a soul.

———

It all started for Takejiro when he was called to the G2 tent and the division's intelligence officer, Colonel Adrian Lindsey, ordered him to report to Corps headquarters. He would have a driver and jeep to take him there.

---

* Frank Tadakazu Hachiya, a December 1942 graduate of the MISLS at Camp Savage, was posthumously awarded the Silver Star for "conspicuous gallantry and intrepidity in action." In April 1945, after critical coverage in some of the national press, the American Legion post restored to its "Roll of Honor" the names of all the local Nisei servicemen. Hachiya's remains were returned from the Philippines in 1948 and reinterred in Hood River's Idlewilde Cemetery.

As Takejiro mumbled, "Yes—sir," his mind raced.

What the hell?

XXIV Corps was a high-level command headed by Major General John Hodge, a decorated division commander at Guadalcanal and Bougainville who now controlled four infantry divisions on Leyte, totaling some 100,000 men. Takejiro could think of no reason for his being ordered to the headquarters of the two-star general. He dared not ask the colonel why, but ruminated the entire way before deciding that the summons from headquarters could not be anything good. He must be in big trouble, but for what?

When they arrived, he was taken to a windowless room humming with activity as officers and enlisted specialists worked at desks and tables strewn with aerial photos and maps. His gaze was drawn to a large, raised-relief map on one wall of an island he knew well.

Okinawa!

In that instant, Takejiro understood why he was there.

Okinawa had been the only home he knew after his mother took him there as a baby. He hadn't returned to Hawaii, his place of birth, until he was sixteen years old, in 1939. In early 1943, Takejiro tried to join the all-Nisei infantry unit then forming in Hawaii to fight in Europe but hadn't scored well enough on the English proficiency exam. A few months later, when the Army wanted to recruit him for his fluency in Japanese, which he had learned in school on Okinawa, he agonized over it before volunteering because he understood that he would likely be sent to the Pacific, where he could even end up fighting on Okinawa.

A bespectacled captain looked over at Takejiro.

"Higa? I hear you lived in Okinawa."

Staring transfixed at the big map, Takejiro nodded vacantly.

He was handed photographs of flattened buildings and scorched wreckage he didn't immediately recognize as aerial views of Okinawa's capital, Naha, even though he knew the city as a boy from delivering sugar and oranges by horse-drawn cart to its docks. But Naha looked much different since it had been bombed two months before by hundreds of planes from a dozen Navy carriers. Docks, airfields, and other targets across Okinawa were hit, leaving twenty cargo ships and a score of enemy warships sunk in the harbors, and nearly a hundred aircraft destroyed on the ground. Because most of the island's structures were wooden, incendiary bombs were used, and the fires burned until they ran out of fuel, destroying entire villages and cities. Since that all-day raid, reconnaissance planes had crossed over Okinawa taking thousands of high- and low-level and oblique-angle photos of the island.

In one photo, Takejiro finally spotted a structure he recognized. He knew it had been a school in downtown Naha. Now roofless and gutted, only its concrete walls were still standing. If the bombs fell during the day, the classrooms would have been filled with students and teachers. He couldn't fathom how many lives had been lost in the ruined city.[*]

"Show us where you lived," said the captain.

Takejiro went to the map and pointed to the village of Shimabuku, the birthplace of his parents and generations of ancestors. Shown an oversized photo of several images pieced together for a wider perspective, he recognized their village. Had it been bombed like the capital? He knew there had never been any industry there, and doubted its military value. But he could say the same about the school in Naha.

Handed a magnifying loupe, he studied the village closely. Seeing no visible damage, he finger-traced his way along the countryside to his aunt and uncle's farm. He was greatly relieved to see it looked unscathed.

Takejiro was shown several photos of deserted coastlines. He studied them through the loupe but saw only empty beaches. When he finished, he looked at the officer, shrugged, and shook his head.

"God damn it, look carefully!" ordered the captain.

What had he missed? Takejiro looked again.

"We're worried about all those fortifications above the beaches where the troops will be landing," the captain said. "See them?"

What Takejiro saw was that the intelligence analysts needed a crash course in Okinawan culture.

---

[*] An estimated five hundred Japanese soldiers and twice as many civilians were killed or wounded in the October 10, 1944, air strikes. Thousands of homes and buildings were destroyed or damaged, most by fire, on Okinawa and a half-dozen smaller islands.

"These aren't fortifications, sir," he said. "They're *haka*."

"*Ha-ka*? What's that?"

"Burial tombs. Okinawans view their tombs as their final home. They'll spend more money on them than on their houses. They build them on hillsides to have a view of the ocean."

Other photos were placed before him.

"And what about all these crater-like holes in the fields?" asked the captain. "We think they're machine gun nests."

Takejiro bent low over the photos, studying them. He straightened up with a sly grin, which he quickly wiped away before anyone noticed.

"You see how they're located in the corners of fields, sir? They're not machine gun nests, but manure-composting pits used by farmers."

The captain nodded curtly. He had made his decision. "Higa, you're going to report here every morning to assist with invasion planning."

Takejiro was speechless. He had saved some tombs and piles of manure, and now he was going to help plan the invasion of Okinawa?

"What you see and hear in this room is strictly need to know," the captain said sternly. "You're not authorized to discuss it with anyone."

314th Headquarters MIS team, 96th Division, on Leyte, November 1944. Left to right: front row, Thomas Masui, Warren Higa, and Rudy Kawahara; middle row, Fred Nonaka, Osamu Yamamoto, and Haruo Kawana; back row, Fred Fukushima, Akira Ohori, Herbert Yanamura, and Takejiro Higa.

Takejiro returned to his team shaken by the images he had seen and what had transpired. When Warren saw him he started to say something, but Takejiro cut him off. "Don't ask me what happened," he told his older brother. "I've been ordered not to say a damn word."

His daily routine varied little over the next few months. At corps headquarters he pored over photos and maps and answered endless questions. The size and complexity of the invasion plan with the counterintuitive code name Operation Iceberg stretched from long-range projections to the anticipated daily movements of individual units, all to be precisely coordinated with the timing of naval and air support. Eight infantry divisions were to take part in the massive operation, with two Army divisions and two Marine divisions the first to land on an eight-mile stretch of Okinawa's southwestern shore. Their objective was to split the island as rapidly as possible, with the Marines sweeping north and the Army turning south. Plans were drawn up for the processing, interrogating, and securing of enemy POWs, and for the handling of many thousands of displaced civilians. The entire operation was expected to take two months to secure the island. But Okinawa wasn't just another Pacific island. It was the closest one yet to Japan, only 330 miles from Kyushu, the southernmost home island, and airfields and harbors could be used there for a buildup of U.S. forces to invade Japan.*

When Takejiro returned to his division each night, he rejoined the team in the tent lit by bare bulbs strung from above. There was usually much discussion about the latest rumors, ranging from receiving thirty days' leave to their being stuck in the Philippines for the duration. But such benign prospects were not in the cards for them, and Takejiro

* The U.S. Tenth Army, the newest and last of the Army-level commands activated in the Pacific—composed of XXIV Corps (Army) and III Amphibious Corps (Marines)—was formed for the Okinawa campaign and the anticipated ground invasion of Japan to follow. Commanded by General Simon Buckner Jr., the Tenth Army landed 160,000 troops in the first ten days of the Okinawa campaign, and more than a half million before the island was secured three months later. Typical of military campaigns elsewhere in the war, only about one-third of the GIs in the invasion force were combat troops; the rest were legions of soldiers working in logistics, supplies, engineering, transportation, and other support positions.

knew it. The 96th Division was one of the Army divisions chosen to spearhead the amphibious assault on Okinawa, but he could not say a thing about it to the trusted members of his intelligence team, or even to his own brother.

For weeks, Takejiro slept fitfully. The images and maps he studied by day had him dreaming of Okinawa at night. The meandering country roads, the sweet-scented orange groves, the muddy rice paddy ditches and leafy taro patches where he had played. His grandparents and aunt and uncle came to him, and the laughing faces of his cousins and schoolmates, still young as he had once been. Yet every morning he reported to Corps to help plan the invasion of the island he loved.

Takejiro's opinion was sought as to what could be expected of the local residents after U.S. troops landed on the island. He told them of the Japanese education system and assimilation program that had mostly succeeded in turning Okinawans into loyal subjects of the emperor. Although Okinawans considered themselves a race apart from Japanese "mainlanders," who in turn did not consider Okinawans to be true Japanese citizens and looked down on them as an inferior race, he cautioned that Okinawa was not the Philippines. A majority of Filipinos supported liberation from their hated Japanese occupiers, and guerrilla forces had fought them for years. But the Okinawans had long looked to the Imperial Japanese Army as their protectors, Takejiro explained. He had no doubt that the thousands of Okinawan conscripts in the Japanese army would defend their homeland.

But he emphasized that most of the half-million residents of Okinawa—about two-thirds lived in the southern one-third of the island—were poor peasants and farmers with no interest in global politics or the war. Few residents read the island's daily newspaper (filled with pro-Japan propaganda) or owned radios, and, in any case, most were uninterested in what went on outside their village. They worked hard to eke out a living on the land or from the sea, feed their families, raise their children, and care for their elderly. Having been one of them for most of his life, Takejiro knew how frightened and vulnerable they would be caught in the crossfire of the two powerful armies. He was deeply troubled about massive civilian casualties, and for the safety of his own family and friends, none of whom had any idea of the juggernaut headed their way.

On March 25, 1945, troopships carrying assault infantry weighed anchor from Leyte Gulf, and the balance of the invasion fleet left two days later. The divisions placed on alert for Okinawa had been relieved of their duties on Leyte in early February to spend six weeks preparing for the operation. Never in the war did such a large force have a shorter time to get ready for a major campaign. They jammed into their training of new replacements the complicated business of loading and offloading ships, tank-infantry drills, and demolitions work. Even after the convoy left port, however, their destination remained a mystery to the troops until the second day at sea, when it was announced over the loudspeakers.

Takejiro found his brother on the main deck of their transport.

"Warren, now I can tell you what I was doing."

"Yeah?" his brother said, grinning. "I knew it had to be Okinawa."

Months earlier, Warren had picked up a book titled *Ryukyu* off the desk of the division sergeant major. Complete with maps and photos, it was a history of the chain of more than 150 Ryukyu Islands stretching from Japan to Taiwan, with Okinawa the largest. A few hours later, the sergeant major rushed into the MIS tent to retrieve the book, and ordered Warren not to say anything about it for security reasons. Taking a wild guess, Warren took him aside and said, "Sarge, if we're going to Okinawa next, maybe my kid brother can help. He lived there for fourteen years." Days later, Takejiro was called to headquarters. The Higa brothers had known about the upcoming invasion for months, but sworn to secrecy, hadn't spoken of it, even to each other. Now, they were going back as U.S. soldiers to their ancestral land for the biggest battle in the Pacific war.

Warren didn't share Takejiro's strong emotional ties to Okinawa, however. Their mother had taken him there at the age of five along with two-year-old Takejiro and their sister, but his father soon brought Warren and his sister back to Honolulu. For Warren, Hawaii was home, not Okinawa.

During the six days the task force steamed for Okinawa, briefings were held aboard the ships. The troops were told by their commanders that they faced a tough enemy who would fight fiercely to defend

Japanese soil. The early assault waves were expected to come under intense machine gun, mortar, and artillery fire from the moment they landed. Some units were told casualties might run 80 percent before they got off the beach, and that the landings could be "worse than Iwo Jima."

D-day dawned on Easter morning, April 1, 1945. It was the usual preinvasion routine for the steely-eyed veterans dispersed throughout units filled with fresh-faced replacements recently arrived from the states. Reveille hours before sunrise, long lines at the heads, more lines for the customary steak and eggs, then back to the berthing compartments for final checks of their weapons and gear.

In addition to their M1 carbines and standard kit, Takejiro and the other linguists toted gear essential to their work. Each man carried his own pocket dictionaries, and they divvied up among themselves weighty tomes of Japanese nautical, aeronautical, and military terms, kanji characters, and compounds, all to assist with translations, and a *Webster's* dictionary for their reports. Completing their haul: a typewriter, magnifying glasses, stationery, rulers, paper clips, pencils, pens, staplers.

Topside, Takejiro found the steel deck lined with infantrymen, who said little and bantered less than usual. Most stood speechless, staring out at the East China Sea overflowing with ships, many of which were firing their deck guns in a chorus of muffled booms and distant flashes. The invasion convoy had grown exponentially overnight, turning into a vast flotilla of more than a thousand ships of all types and tonnage. It was the largest Allied fleet ever to put to sea in the Pacific. Nearly every amphibious operation in the Pacific theater had been larger than the one preceding it, and the invasion of Okinawa dwarfed them all.

In the fleet were the heavy, dreadnought battleships *Tennessee* (BB-43), which had been moored in Battleship Row when the Japanese attacked Pearl Harbor but had not been seriously damaged, and *Idaho* (BB-42), transferred from service in the Atlantic to the Pacific early in the war. They were joined by the *Missouri* (BB-63), in action for less than a year and the last of the great battleships to be built by the United States. They were joined by smaller, faster battlewagons like the *South Dakota* (BB-57). The light cruiser *Birmingham* (CL-62),

named after the most populous city in Alabama, was there to join
in providing fire support for the assault forces, along with countless
destroyers, such as the *Paul Hamilton* (DD-590), *Ault* (DD-698), and
Mannert L. Abele (DD-733). The warships jockeyed for position in
the crowded seas along with troop transports and supply ships, some
known as "reefers" because they carried fresh and frozen provisions.
Other vessels remained farther out at sea, like the aircraft carriers *Savo
Island* and *Anzio*, both named to memorialize earlier battles and whose
planes were flying sorties over Okinawa as well as providing air protection for the fleet against enemy aircraft; the fleet oilers *Severn* (AO-61)
and *Ocklawaha* (AO-84); and the all-white hospital ships *Comfort* and
Bountiful—manned by Navy crews and Army medical personnel—
which stood out to sea seventy-five miles away, ready to treat wounded
evacuated from the beachhead.

From three miles away, Takejiro gazed across the cobalt-blue sea to
the island he recognized. Six years ago, he had been relieved to depart
its shores to avoid being forced into the Manchurian Youth Corps, but
he had also left behind the only life he knew. After a difficult year in
Hawaii and struggling to learn English, he would have gone back in
1940 had his sister not pleaded with him to give it another year. Had
he returned to Okinawa, he surely would have been drafted into the
ranks of the Japanese army even though he was a U.S. citizen.[*]

It was a beautiful, crystal-clear morning, and from the ship's railing
he could make out the stretch of shore assigned to the 96th Division
at the southernmost sector of the invasion beachhead. They were
to land near the coastal town of Chatan, an area he knew well. The
lowlands along the shore gave way to rolling, terraced hills in the east,
and much of it was *taa-bukkwa*, an Okinawan term for "large area of
rice paddies." Three miles inland lay Shimabuku, and from there it was
another mile to his uncle's little farm. Here, he had come of age, and
Okinawa still felt more like home than Hawaii. He recalled an old saying: *Mitsugo no tamashi hyaka made* (the spirit of a three-year-old will last
a hundred years). He was that young when his mother brought him

* Anyone born in Hawaii, a Territory of the United States, on or after April
30, 1900, was a U.S. citizen by birth. Hawaii was admitted to the Union as the
fiftieth state in 1959.

here, and he grew up not far from where he was to land as a soldier. His worlds were about to collide. His was not a conflict of loyalties, but a conflict of emotions. He loved the Uchinanchu (Okinawan) people, who had long been treated as second-class citizens by Imperial Japan. He knew how frightened they would be with a foreign armada offshore and bombs falling and a major ground battle looming. Caught between the warring armies, how many would die? Takejiro, his vision blurred by tears, turned away, and he joined a stream of GIs silently heading to where they would climb down a cargo net into the waiting landing craft.

Given his familiarity with the island's geography, and as the only member of the MIS team fluent in Okinawan, Takejiro was chosen to accompany an advance team from division headquarters in the second assault wave. He was handpicked for the job by Easley, who called him "Junior" because he was the younger Higa brother and the general found his first name hard to pronounce. As he had at Leyte, the assistant division commander and his staff were to land on D-day to set up a command post and have it operational when the commanding general arrived the next day. "You stick with me, Junior," the affable Easley had told Takejiro, "and make sure I don't get lost."

At one minute past 8 a.m., the landing craft carrying the first assault waves pushed away from the troopships. On schedule at 8:30 a.m., they arrived off Chatan beach, its sparkling white sands made brighter by the sun rising in the eastern sky. Tense and nervous to a man, the troops were steeled to face anything that morning. But what greeted them on the sands of Okinawa was not the expected sharp crack of gunfire or howl of mortar and artillery rounds. It was so tranquil the first sounds Takejiro heard were the rhythmic lapping of waves and the backwash of frothy water returning to the sea. Then came the revving of engines, the grinding of gears, the commands of officers, the loud cursing of sergeants, and his own labored breathing as he crossed the beach, weighed down with so much gear that his boots left deep indentions in the sand.

The troops swiftly cleared a ten-foot seawall using folding ladders. Soon, amphibious tanks armed with .50 caliber machine guns or 4.2-inch mortars crawled through openings blasted in the wall by demolition charges. Supported by the tanks, the troops fanned out, heading toward their first objective: Kadena airfield, a mile away. As yet, not a shot had been fired. The ease with which the GIs came ashore was so contrary to the expectations of the men in the early waves as to be ominous, and led to their cautious probing in anticipation of an ambush at any moment.

Advancing along a twisting road in the hills behind the beaches, the headquarters group with Takejiro entered checkerboard farmlands already deeply scarred by war. Farmhouses were flattened, burned out, or ablaze, and the carcasses of cows, goats, and horses lay in barnyards and fields. The ruined countryside was a heartbreaking sight for Takejiro. After a solid week of preinvasion softening-up along the coast by naval guns and bombing sorties, he feared a similar fate for his relatives' farm. There were no locals to be seen, which gave him some hope that the residents had been able to safely evacuate to other parts of the island. But few would have homes to which they could return.

A sudden movement in a roadside ditch startled Takejiro. He swung his carbine around and shouted, *"Dette Koi!"* (Come out!)

There was no response to his order in Japanese.

He knew of the division between younger Okinawans, who learned standard Japanese in school, and the older, less educated islanders who spoke Okinawan, so he repeated his order in the local dialect.

Still no response.

With the safety off, he slipped an index finger inside the trigger guard. On semiautomatic, he could empty the carbine's fifteen-round clip in under ten seconds, firing a .30 caliber round with each trigger pull. If he didn't kill or incapacitate with the first shot, he had fourteen more chances.

One final warning: *"Anata ga daredeare, dete kinasai! Detekuru!"* (Come out, whoever you are! Come out!)

There was increased thrashing in the ditch.

Takejiro knew he could wait no longer. But a second before he raked the ditch with gunfire, he saw a scrawny leg and next to it a child's small foot sticking out from the weeds. Civilians were hiding in the ditch!

Shifting exclusively to Okinawan, he urged them to come out from hiding, promising they wouldn't be hurt. His pleas took on a softer lilt.

"Njiti mensoree." (Come out, please.)

At last an older woman crawled from the ditch. A girl, five or
six years old, crept out behind her. Having responded to Takejiro's
entreaties in flawless Okinawan, the woman seemed shocked they
were spoken by an American soldier. He handed them a canteen of
water, which they shared. The old lady did not take her eyes off him
for a second, and finally asked a question that was clearly on her mind.
Was he Uchinanchu? Takejiro said yes, explaining that he had grown
up in Shimabuku, where he still had many relatives. The old lady
looked relieved. She told him that the rest of her family had escaped
into the hills but she hadn't been able to join them because she had
weak legs, and her granddaughter had stayed to hide out with her.

Takejiro knew she meant they were hiding from the Americans.
He asked if she had seen Japanese troops. Grandma, with her new-
found trust in him, reported *"ufusan Yamatunchu hiitai"*—many Japanese soldiers—going by on foot and in vehicles. When he asked which
way they went, she pointed to the south—the same direction the 96th
was headed.

He made arrangements for the woman and girl to be taken to a
civilian refugee camp being set up near the coast. He gave them a pass
showing they had been questioned, and warned them not to hide again
but to wait by the road to be picked up.

Takejiro thought he had likely questioned and processed the division's first Okinawan refugees. But he had also almost killed them,
which unnerved him. Still amped up from the landing and expecting
imminent contact with the enemy, he had nearly shot blindly into the
ditch. Thank God he had seen them in time. The grandmother, conditioned by years of Japanese propaganda portraying Americans as
rapists and murderers, would not have knowingly surrendered herself
and her granddaughter to U.S. troops; she only came out because he
spoke Okinawan. If he hadn't come along when he did, any passing
GI might have shot them.

By noontime, the advance command post was humming under
Easley, who initiated a slew of radio messages coordinating the arrival
of the 96th's third infantry regiment held in reserve on troopships
and the rest of their armor, artillery, and engineers. The Kadena airfield was secured that morning without a fight, and so light were the

division's D-day casualties that
not a single man was medically
evacuated off the beach.

In fact, the landing that first
day, of nearly sixty thousand
troops, took place against negli-
gible resistance, with only brief
delaying actions by small pockets
of enemy soldiers. By nightfall,
assault forces had secured the
entire beachhead, advanced three
miles inland, and seized their
first-day objectives: the Kadena
as well as Yontan airfields, already being readied for U.S. aircraft. Upbeat rumors circulated

Brigadier General Easley (left)
at the front lines

that Japan's generals must have guessed wrong about the location of
the next U.S. amphibious assault and moved their forces to another
island, such as Formosa.

Some captured documents and maps were rushed to headquarters that first afternoon. By then, Warren, Yanamura, and Nonaka
had rejoined Takejiro. Realizing the urgency to translate the materials,
Takejiro went to investigate a *haka* he had seen from the road as a possible place to work that night without their lights drawing sniper fire.

He found the burial tomb on a windswept incline with a panoramic
view of the sea. Having explored many *kamebōbaka* (turtleback burial
tombs) as a boy, he was amazed by this one's size. It was the biggest
tomb he had ever seen, and must have belonged to a family of some
wealth. He knew from his school days that the design originated in
China, and the roof was dome shaped like a tortoise because they
were known for their longevity (up to 150 years), which the Chinese
believed promised a long life to the descendants of the deceased.
Okinawans saw something else in the omega-shaped tombs, believing
they represented a woman's womb, with the entrance being the birth
canal, thereby enabling departed loved ones to return to their source.

The front walls of the big tomb were chiseled with elaborate etchings, some with names, drawings, and poems. His own family tomb on a hillside outside of Shimabuku was smaller and not as ornate, but no less sacred to his family. Unlike in Japan, Buddhism and Shintoism did not have a great influence in Okinawa. In their place was a strong native belief in ancestor worship, which Takejiro considered his own true religion. He was here on earth, he believed, not because of God or Buddha but thanks to those who came before him. And the *hakas*, so numerous on coastal hillsides, were how Okinawans honored their ancestors, rather than praying to icons in temples or shrines. He thought back to his first day at Corps when he was shown aerial photos believed to be enemy coastal fortifications that were, in fact, *hakas*. If he hadn't been there to explain, how many old family tombs would have been destroyed?

The upward-sloping turtle-back roof was bordered on three sides by a concrete rim, which according to the principles of feng shui protected the tomb from ill winds. Several steps led up to the entrance, an opening only a few feet high. Reaching the top step, Takejiro switched on a flashlight and crawled through a narrow passage, checking for snakes as he went. Inside, the ceiling rose to about six feet, and he was able to stand and walk around. His beam of light shone on an open coffin. He was relieved to see it was empty. He knew about the traditional burial ritual, during which the body of a loved one was allowed to decay in a coffin for up to seven years. The skeletal remains were then removed and cleaned by female relatives, and placed feetfirst into a tall earthenware pot. The bone containers, or *jūshigāmi*, some artfully decorated, were lined up in rows according to the seniority of their occupants.

By the time Takejiro returned, it was dusk. He told the others there was room inside the big tomb to set up a temporary workspace. Not everyone was keen on the idea of spending the night inside the crypt. He agreed it would be "spooky" and "eerie," but asked if that wasn't preferable to being shot by a sniper. That settled the matter.

"Plus," Takejiro grinned, "it's real quiet in there."

The team packed up, bringing with them a mobile field desk, lanterns, and their dictionaries. For the next forty-eight hours, they worked in the *haka* translating Japanese. They painstakingly copied from a captured artillery map elevations, coordinates, latitude, longitude, and topographic features such as roads, rivers, lakes, and towns. U.S. military maps of the island, based mostly on aerial photos, had only rough features, with large swaths of terrain uncharted. A new, detailed English-language map was flown to Pearl Harbor for reproduction, and seventy-two hours later thousands were delivered back to Okinawa to be distributed.

On April 4, the four Nisei and other headquarters personnel piled into jeeps and drove inland to the town of Futenma, taking over buildings at the prefectural Agricultural Experiment Station, where researchers for the past twenty years had developed many contributions to local agriculture, including new varieties of sweet potatoes, paddy field rice, and sugarcane. The MIS team was still unpacking when incoming artillery rounds shrieked overhead. They dove for cover as loud explosions shook the ground and rattled the walls and windows, making it difficult for any of them to be comforted by the old infantry axiom, "As long as you hear the artillery shell, you're safe." In fact, they soon had lots of practice diving for cover at the sound of incoming rounds.

Two miles away, a regiment of "Deadeyes" approached Kakazu Ridge, which they had to pass over to reach the southern end of Okinawa. At a height of a few hundred feet, it did not appear to be a daunting barrier. But its north face rose from a deep gorge and could be scaled only with difficulty. As the GIs were about to find out, the reception the enemy had prepared for them at the top was multilayered and lethal.

Months of planning by the command staff of the Japanese 32nd Army—formed in March 1944 expressly to defend Okinawa—had proceeded on the assumption that its three infantry divisions, several mixed brigades, and local draftees would be insufficient to throw back into the sea a large-scale U.S. invasion force.[*] Rather, their strategy was to deny the Americans use of the island for as long as possible

---

[*] Japanese forces on the island numbered seventy-five thousand troops (about half were combat infantrymen), plus some twenty thousand Okinawan conscripts in militia and labor battalions.

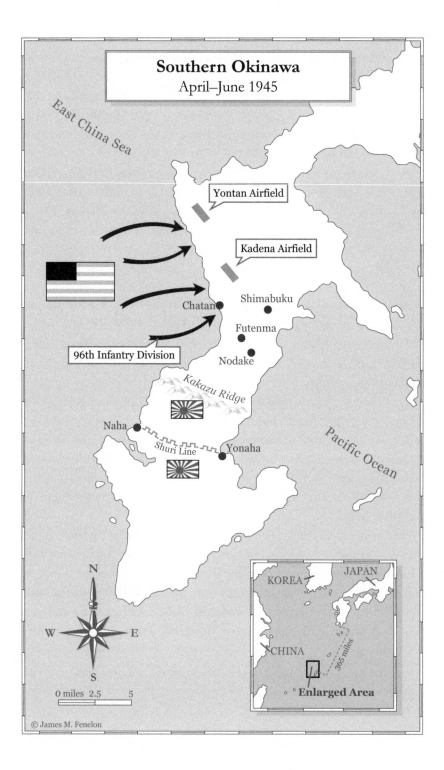

Southern Okinawa
April–June 1945

East China Sea

Yontan Airfield

Kadena Airfield

Shimabuku

Chatan

Futenma

96th Infantry Division

Nodake

Kakazu Ridge

Naha

Shuri Line

Yonaha

Pacific Ocean

N

W   E

S

0 miles 2.5   5

© James M. Fenelon

KOREA   JAPAN

CHINA

365 miles

Enlarged Area

while inflicting maximum casualties. Importantly, a long battle here gave their home islands more time to prepare for the expected invasion of Japan.

Evacuation from Okinawa was not an option for the Japanese troops waiting on Kakazu Ridge in pillboxes, tunnels, and caves, their machine guns and other weapons covering all approaches to the top. Embedded on its reverse slopes were 81 mm mortars ready to launch seven-pound, TNT-filled shells. South of the ridge were camouflaged artillery batteries: 75 mm and 120 mm field guns, and the larger 150 mm howitzers, all mounted on rubber-shod, wooden wheels for mobility.

The 96th Division's initial attempt to cross the ridge began under the cover of predawn darkness on April 9. By midmorning, about two hundred infantrymen had worked their way up to the crest when the enemy trap was sprung. A lone pillbox opened fire first, followed by the furious *tat-tat-tat* of multiple Japanese machine guns, then incoming mortar and artillery rounds in a cacophony of concussive, ear-splitting explosions. Japanese charged forth from caves, hurling grenades. The GIs on the ridge fought off waves of attackers, but outnumbered and outflanked, they were in danger of being cut off and wiped out. The U.S. commander at the top radioed for a smoke barrage to cover their withdrawal, but the first smoke rounds fired by artillery landed on the other side of the ridge. When they were at last able to pull back, they did so under fire and only a few men at a time. Leaving their dead behind so as to carry out the wounded, the shell-shocked survivors straggled into U.S. lines well after dark, half walking, half crawling, carrying the seriously wounded in litters fashioned from ponchos. When a casualty count was taken of the men who went to the top that morning, fifteen GIs were listed as killed in action, seventy-five missing and presumed dead, fifty wounded, and only forty-six still able-bodied. The rapid advances and light casualties that marked their first days on Okinawa were at an end.

Cracking the rock-ribbed defenses at Kakazu Ridge took three weeks of bitter fighting and the greatest land attack in the Pacific war: a thunderous assault by three U.S. divisions (96th, 27th, and 7th) abreast, supported by the combined firepower of artillery, warships, and aircraft.

The 96th Division's casualties at Kakazu Ridge totaled 603 killed and 1,401 wounded. The division killed an estimated 4,600 Japanese. But shockingly, the bloodied ridge was only the outermost perimeter of the enemy's five-mile-long "Shuri Line," which started at the capital of Naha on the west coast and went through the Shuri district— site of a castle that for four hundred years was the palace of the Ryukyu Kingdom—to the Yonabaru harbor on the eastern shore. The concentration of enemy positions in caves, tunnels, and bunkers ran three to four miles deep. The worst was yet to come for both warring sides, and above all for the people of Okinawa.

The Americans took scant enemy prisoners during the early weeks of fighting along the fortified Shuri Line, and most of them were so badly wounded they didn't last long enough to be questioned. But volumes of captured documents continued to flow into 96th Division headquarters, and the MIS team worked day and night prioritizing and translating them.

Takejiro and his team found the most common of documents among the most revealing: the diaries of individual soldiers. It seemed as if every Japanese kept one, and they contained not only personal

Cave blasting

Cave flushing on Okinawa

details but also useful military information. These first-person accounts also helped to gauge enemy morale. A common complaint among Japanese troops on Okinawa questioned why they looked out to the sea and saw only American ships. To them, the Imperial Navy was the most powerful in the world, and they knew of no foreign navy its equal. So where was their navy when they needed supplies and reinforcements? They also wrote about the difference in the power of the invading force compared to their own. *If we fire one mortar shell toward the enemy, at least ten will come back in response*, wrote one dejected diarist.

The first POW to arrive at headquarters for interrogation was an older sergeant. The first statement he made to the interpreters was a simple one: *"Koroshite kudasai."* (Please kill me.)

He made his request quietly, without drama or jingoistic fervor.

Asked why he wanted to die, he related this story: He had been serving as company commander because all their officers were dead and he was the ranking enlisted man. There were about thirty-five men left in his company, and nearly all were sick or injured, many seriously. They had been in a cave for weeks and had run out of food and water. When he heard a voice at the entrance hollering in fractured Japanese, *"Dete koi,"* he knew the Americans had arrived. He stepped outside with his hands up to tell them that his men wanted to surrender, but found that none of the Americans spoke Japanese other than that single phrase—"Come out"—they were taught to say when clearing a cave. As he tried to make them understand about his men in the cave, the American soldiers set off a loud detonation. The explosion loosed huge rocks and boulders that sealed the entrance to the cave, burying his men alive.

The sergeant looked at Takejiro and Yanamura seated across from him. Because he had failed to bring his men safely out of the cave, he said, he had no right to go on living. He bowed his head and repeated his plea.

"Koroshite kudasai."

Yanamura told him they could not grant his request.

Takejiro knew how differently things could have gone had there been an interpreter with the GIs at the cave. A surrender could have been arranged, and the MIS team would have had an influx of prisoners to interrogate, the dearth of which had been the subject of a recent order by the division commander to capture more of the enemy for the purpose of acquiring actionable intelligence.

The narrow roads of central Okinawa were congested with streams of refugees of all ages, most of whom were trudging northward. Destitute and homeless, with nowhere to go, they carried on their backs and in two-wheeled pushcarts their worldly possessions. Some of them had left their homes weeks earlier during the preinvasion bombing, but thousands more were fleeing the fighting in the south.[*]

Those displaced persons who poured into U.S. lines were taken to civilian camps a safe distance from the action, where they were fed and received medical attention. Initially, the camps were intended only as a temporary solution, and in the first few weeks families were trucked to villages that had escaped destruction, where they had freedom of movement within boundaries established by the military police.

Many of their countrymen, however, were unwilling to seek or ex-

[*] Against weaker opposition in the north, the Marines had cornered a few thousand Japanese troops on the Motobu Peninsula by April 13. After several days of fighting in mountainous and wooded terrain, the north end of Okinawa was declared secure a week later. The heavy fighting in the south would continue for two more months.

Nisei soldier sharing his water with a child on Okinawa

pect humanitarian assistance from the foreign invaders, believing the wild tales of cruelty promulgated for years by the Japanese—that the Americans would slaughter their children, rape their women, and behead their men. Too many opted instead for suicide with their loved ones. In that way, they believed their spirits would be inseparable for eternity. Eyewitness reports from the Chatan coast told of mothers leading young children to the edge of high cliffs and leaping to their deaths on the rocks below. These turned out not to be isolated incidents. As civilians were encouraged by the Japanese army to commit acts of group suicide rather than surrender, the first mass suicide took place in a cave not far from Futenma, where a large number of Okinawans were buried when explosives went off inside.

When Takejiro responded to an urgent call for an interpreter just down the road from headquarters, he found several GIs standing next to a brick-lined well. They told him a woman had climbed over and jumped inside.

"She had a baby with her," said one soldier.

Peering inside, Takejiro saw the woman in the shadows about ten feet below, partly submerged in muddy water. When he spoke to her in Japanese, she looked up in surprise. Did she want help getting out?

"Hai! Watashi no akachan." (Yes! My baby.)

They lowered one end of a rope to her, and she tied it around her waist as instructed. Carefully, they hoisted her up. The baby was still secured to her back by an obi belt, a broad sash that went around her upper torso. The woman had only a few cuts, but the baby had drowned.

Takejiro was sad and furious at the same time. The woman set out to kill herself and her baby, then changed her mind. But it was too late for the baby. How could she live with that? Or how long before she could not?

While endeavoring to care for Okinawa's refugees, the U.S. Army rigorously attempted to expose enemy soldiers hiding among them. Because of his fluency in both languages, Takejiro was sent in early May to a civilian compound on the coast to catch possible imposters.

His first interrogation was of a thirtysomething man. Perhaps his well-conditioned physique or the way he comported himself had aroused suspicion, because a tag had been placed around his neck indicating that he should be questioned further. He had given an Oki-nawan name.

After a few preliminaries, Takejiro asked where he was from.

"Chīsana mura." (A small village.)

Which one? Takejiro asked nonchalantly.

The man studied Takejiro, as if considering for the first time the possibility that he was speaking not just to a U.S. Army interpreter but to someone who knew the island. He waited a beat too long before answering, then said Yamauchi, which was such a small village few

Americans would know it. But his choice was an unlucky one for him, because it was less than three miles from Shimabuku, and Takejiro knew it well. After a few inconsistencies in his story, Takejiro decided that the man had not lived in Yamauchi. He abruptly switched from Japanese to the Okinawan dialect, and reeled off a series of rapid questions.

The man looked thunderstruck. He didn't understand what Takejiro had said!

"Omae wa ittai dareda?" Takejiro demanded in Japanese. (Who the hell are you?)

At first, silence.

Then: *"Ah, shimatta! Hitochigai!"* (Oh, damn it! Wrong person!)

Yes, Takejiro was definitely the wrong person to bluff about being Okinawan.

Only then did the man confess—a little shamefaced, at first. He had pretended to be a civilian to receive better treatment than he would in a POW camp. Rapidly recovering his pride, he announced he was a *Rikugun-Chūsa* (lieutenant colonel) in the Imperial Japanese Army.

Because the prisoner was a high-ranking military officer, Takejiro ended the session and made arrangements for him to be sent to Tenth Army headquarters for interrogation. A lieutenant colonel could have

Warren Higa interrogating POW at Okinawa

commanded a battalion or even a regiment, and might have vital information about Japanese forces and defenses.

Before being escorted away, the colonel wanted Takejiro to know
something. He had found the Americans to be *"hijō ni jindōteki"*
(extremely humane), he said—much different than what he had
expected. He was impressed by how they treated the wounded, even
the Japanese, and the considerate gestures like handing out cigarettes
and candies. It was a strange ending to a session during which Takejiro
exposed an enemy field grade officer. Strange because the Japanese
colonel had unwittingly reminded Takejiro how proud he was to be
an American.

After a full day of interviews, Takejiro was about to return to Futenma when an MP sergeant told him there was another person to interrogate. The man had been picked up in a field scurrying about in the
dark digging up potatoes, as starving Japanese soldiers, slipping from
caves at night to gather food, were doing in droves. He was in civilian
clothes, but in spite of his insistence that he was a schoolteacher he
was suspected of being an enemy deserter and had been segregated
from other civilians; he was scheduled to be sent to a military POW
camp.

When the man entered the room Takejiro recognized his teacher
instantly.

Reverently, Takejiro murmured, *"Sensei."*

"Ah, kimi ka!" came the surprised reply. (Oh, it's you!)

Standing before him was Shunsho Nakamura, his middle school
teacher and so much more; he had been a father figure to a young,
parentless Takejiro. Under his tutelage, Takejiro had learned standard
Japanese as well as any educated native of Japan. Mr. Nakamura had
also been his basketball coach and took their overachieving team to
the district championship in Naha one year. His sensei had been a
positive role model during his formative years, and Takejiro owed
him so much.

Nonetheless, it was his job to question his teacher about his activities. They talked for the better part of an hour. Nakamura explained
that he had been head of the local chapter of a citizen's league supporting the government, and was listed as a rural officer on standby
but had never been called up by the army. For a while after the in-

vasion, he and his family had stayed at their home, a mile inland from the Chatan beaches. When American soldiers and tanks began rolling through the countryside, he had taken his wife, children, and in-laws farther into the countryside for safety. Their empty stomachs could not be ignored, and between bombings he went into the fields to dig up sweet potatoes. Returning from one forage with his young daughter, they found the rest of the family being rounded up by U.S. soldiers. Fearful of what might happen to his daughter, he hid out with her rather than surrender. Splitting up the family had been a mistake, Nakamura now knew. He and the girl had been picked up a few days later anyway, and the Americans turned out not to be beasts after all.

Toward the end of the session, Takejiro asked about his own relatives in Shimabuku, but Nakamura had no news about them. When Takejiro was finished, he turned to the MP standing nearby.

"This gentleman, Mr. Nakamura, was my schoolteacher here in Okinawa before the war," he explained. "Do not send him to a POW camp. He needs to be reunited with his family as soon as possible."

Takejiro and his teacher said their goodbyes, shaking hands warmly. They had been astonished to find one another in the midst of the war, and they had no idea if they would ever see each other again.

Upon learning months before that his division would take part in the Okinawa invasion, Takejiro had dreaded his two worlds colliding. But as he watched his sensei being led away, he was grateful that he was here to help someone who had been so important in his life.

Takejiro was more concerned than ever about his aunt, uncle, and cousins. Were they still in Shimabuku? Or in a refugee camp? For weeks now, the division headquarters at Futenma had been located only a few miles south of where he grew up, but he hadn't felt right about asking for permission to look for his family. As it turned out, he did not have to ask.

After the Shuri Line finally fell in May, the 96th stood down for a few days before joining other divisions in the final push southward. As they prepared to move headquarters away from Futenma—ten miles farther from his village—General Easley came into the G2 section looking for Takejiro.

"Junior, you have relatives in Shimabuku, four klicks north, yes?"

"Yes sir, I do."

"Go visit them. Take Captain Fernandez with you. Two hours."

The captain, in charge of the counterintelligence section, rounded up a driver and jeep. They made the short trip on winding, rutted roads lined with fewer refugees than they expected. It turned out that Shimabuku had escaped destruction, and the houses looked exactly as they had when Takejiro had left seven years earlier. The residents appeared to be going about their daily lives as if there were no war. But when they reached his aunt and uncle's farm on the outskirts, Takejiro was in for a big surprise.

The farm where five people once lived was crammed inside and out with a hundred or more people who had laid down straw sleeping mats everywhere. Even the barn and pig shed were packed. Every pair of eyes bore into the three American soldiers as they approached.

Takejiro noticed that the captain had unholstered his .45 pistol and was holding it down at his side. Seeing all the unfamiliar faces, even Takejiro hesitated on the porch of his childhood home before stepping inside. The captain was right to be uneasy, because who knew if there were any enemy soldiers or deserters in the mix? Takejiro, his M1 carbine slung on his shoulder, led the way into the house. Their driver, packing his own carbine, watched their backs as they moved through the throng. Had Takejiro known any of the squatters, he could have explained that he was a nephew come to visit, but they were all strangers. Where were his relatives?

At last he saw a face he knew. His auntie hurried toward him through the crush of people, her arms already outstretched for an embrace, his beaming uncle right behind her. She was his mother's sister, and their resemblance was remarkable. She had raised him as one of her own after his mother and grandparents died. Shocked to see her nephew standing before her in a U.S. Army uniform, she hugged him tightly and landed kisses on his cheek.

Speaking in Okinawan, Takejiro caught them up on how he and Warren were translators and interrogators serving in the same unit. He asked about his cousin Hiroshi, who had been like a big brother to Takejiro. He knew Hiroshi was studying to be a doctor, but he now learned he had been drafted into the Japanese army medical corps. The last his parents had heard, he was working at a military hospital in the Philippines. Takejiro assured them that the Americans did not bomb hospitals. He told them the fighting there had ended, and Hiroshi was most likely in a POW camp in the Philippines.

Takejiro asked about all the strangers. His aunt said their farm, untouched by the war, had been designated an evacuation center, and they came from hamlets and villages less fortunate. Takejiro had to smile at that; his big-hearted aunt who opened her home to an orphaned boy years ago was now taking in entire hamlets and villages. Many of them hid for days in their family *hakas* to escape the bombing, she went on, and emerged to find that their homes had been destroyed.

The division headquarters soon moved south to Yonaha, three miles east of the ruined capital of Naha, newly captured following a vicious forty-eight-hour battle that left the few buildings still standing a mass of rubble. They had to walk there because the dirt roads were impassable due to monsoon rains that had turned them into mud-choked gulches. That meant the graves registration details were unable to complete their work, and the MIS team passed dozens of dead GIs lying side by side awaiting burial. The patches on their shoulders identified them as fellow Deadeyes. As they passed the lifeless forms sprawled in the mud, everyone went mute. Their somber silence lasted for miles, as if in a funeral procession.

One of the first days at Yonaha, two Japanese POWs in tattered army khakis were brought to Takejiro. He was told they had dug their way out of a collapsed bunker with their bare hands. Judging by their scarecrow looks, he figured they hadn't eaten for a long while and offered D ration chocolates, but neither accepted.

"Dō shimashita ka?" he asked. (What's wrong?)

"Doku," came the barely audible reply. (Poison.)

"Bakayaro!" exclaimed Takejiro. (Idiots!)

He unwrapped a bar and took several bites.

The prisoners eyed the remaining two bars with renewed interest, then wolfed them down while chugging from a canteen of water.

Early in the interrogation, the prisoners confirmed Takejiro's initial impression that they were local conscripts in a labor battalion. Claiming to have done nothing more than dig out trenches, shelters, and caves, they said they had been given only shovels and picks, no weapons or any military training. Takejiro knew that many Okinawan laborers, caught in the wrong place at the wrong time, had already been killed.

More questions followed, and as they conversed in Japanese, Takejiro began to think the men looked familiar. Their faces were dirty and it had been a long time, but—had they all been schoolmates?

Did you go to Kishaba school? Takejiro finally asked.

The men looked at each other in surprise. How did he know?

Their names hadn't registered at first, but now Takejiro was certain. Did they have a teacher named Shunsho Nakamura? he asked.

Now they were flabbergasted. *You know about sensei too?*

Takejiro next asked if they knew what had become of a classmate named Takejiro Higa. All they knew was that he had moved to Hawaii.

Would they recognize him?

Well, er—*it's been many years.*

Takejiro now switched from Japanese to Okinawan.

Don't you recognize your own classmate? he laughed.

The realization that the American soldier speaking to them in perfect Okinawan was their old classmate hit them simultaneously. Without uttering a word, the two men burst into tears.

Takejiro did not expect that. Why were they crying?

Because now we know we're not going to die, they answered. All along they had feared that after the questioning was over and no one had any more use for them, they would be taken out and shot. But with Takejiro on the other side, they knew their lives would be spared.

"Shiawasedakara naiteru." (We're crying because we're happy.)

While their tears were joyful ones, Takejiro felt a deep regret. As boys, they had gone to the same school, learned and played together. Yet as grown men, the war had turned them into enemies. *We cannot ever have another war.* Never had he been so sure of anything in his life.

With a full-scale humanitarian crisis taking place on the island, Takejiro and other Nisei interpreters were rushed at all hours and in all weather to the rock-strewn entrances of caves in an effort to save lives. Takejiro's first cave was near the village of Nodake. When he arrived, he was told that some two hundred civilians—including many families with children—were inside. It was not known if they had explosives inside and whether they intended to kill themselves, or whether there were Japanese soldiers intent on suicide mixed in with all the civilians.

Takejiro knew that most Okinawans did not trust Americans—not after being convinced by the Japanese about the savagery of the Americans, and certainly not after all the bombs, fires, and destruction they had brought to the once-peaceful island. But to be desperate enough to jump off a cliff holding a baby? Or blow up one's family in a cave? It was incomprehensible. His deepest heartache was for the children. They wore no uniform and bore no responsibility for the war yet carried the cruelest burden of all: lives tragically cut short.

Takejiro knelt near the entrance. Using a bullhorn, he projected a message of hope over despair. His voice echoed calmly into the cavernous dungeon, first in Japanese, then Okinawan.

My name is Takejiro Higa. I am an Okinawan son. I grew up in Shimabuku. My family is still here and I just saw them. They are fine. I am an American soldier now. I can tell you Americans are not savages. They are good people. You will not be mistreated. We have food and water. If you are hurt or sick, we will care for you. Don't waste your life. Please save yourselves.

Again and again, he delivered the same message of life over death. In a scene repeated myriad times in the coming weeks, the voice coming from outside the cave and the message it delivered was *heard*. Again and again—a hundred times or more—Okinawans listened, and with their loved ones came out of the darkness into the sunlight, trusting the American soldier who had lived among them and spoke their language.

Okinawa was declared secured on June 22, 1945.

In the last two weeks of that final month, an estimated 80,000 Okinawan civilians, many of them wounded or sick, emerged from caves on the southern end of the island. In long columns, women, children, the very old, and scant few able-bodied men strode wearily toward crowded refugee camps. The bodies of thousands of other civilians lay bloated in ditches, in fields, or in the rubble of their homes and villages, or were sealed inside caves. The precise number of civilian casualties may never be known, but according to the Okinawan prefectural government nearly 100,000 civilians—about one-fourth of the island's wartime population—perished during the three months of the cruelest battle of the Pacific.*

* The final toll of American casualties on Okinawa was the highest of any campaign in the Pacific during World War II. Total U.S. casualties (including naval, air, and ground) totaled more than 12,000 killed or missing and 36,000 wounded. Another 26,000 Americans were "nonbattle" casualties (disease, fatigue, and "combat neurosis"). Of an estimated 75,000 Imperial Japanese Army troops believed to be on the island at the time of the invasion, some 7,400 were taken prisoner and the remainder were killed or missing. Of the estimated 20,000 Okinawan conscripts manning Japanese service and labor battalions, a few thousand were taken prisoner and the rest were killed or missing.

Sixteen

CHINA

The Army had trouble finding Hiroshi "Roy" Matsumoto to pin a medal on him. He had been on the last planeload of Merrill's Marauders to leave Myitkyina when that battle ended and the force was disbanded in August 1944. Those fit for duty went to Camp Landis in northern Burma to receive new assignments. But a wound on Roy's arm became infected, landing him in a hospital in Ledo, India. He was there for three weeks—long enough to receive a bedside visit from the English playwright Noël Coward on a USO tour.

Hospital patient Roy Matsumoto visited
by the English playwright Noël Coward

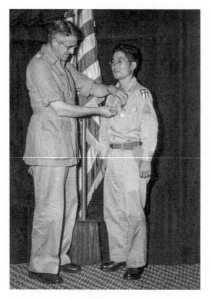

Frank Merrill pinning
the Legion of Merit on
Roy Matsumoto in India

After his hospital discharge, Roy was loaned to the Royal Air Force (RAF), which needed Japanese-language interpreters.

Credited with the destruction of a major ammunition depot as a result of his monitoring enemy communications round the clock from a treetop at Walawbum, Roy was to receive the Legion of Merit. After the Army located him in New Delhi, the ceremony took place there in November. He was surprised to see Frank Merrill there to give him the medal. Standing a head taller than Roy, the general, bespectacled and trim, with the sleeves of his fatigue jacket rolled to above his elbows, appeared rested and relaxed. The man who had led them through northern Burma looked fully recovered from his last heart attack months earlier.

Standing before a U.S. flag hung from a staff, Merrill pinned the Legion of Merit on Roy as an Army photographer snapped pictures. The medal, a five-armed, blue-and-white cross attached to a crimson ribbon, was bestowed for "services rendered in a clearly exceptional manner."*

Befitting his immersion in the language while serving as a military attaché in prewar Tokyo, Merrill congratulated Roy in Japanese.

---

* Roy Matsumoto also received a Bronze Star for his "heroic actions" in saving his battalion by misdirecting waves of charging Japanese troops on a hillside at Nhpum Ga. Every member of Merrill's Marauders received a Combat Infantry Badge for being under fire during ground combat in northern Burma and a Bronze Star for "meritorious service," and all were entitled to wear a Presidential Unit Citation ribbon for their "extraordinary heroism in action against the enemy."

"Yoku yatta, gunsō." (Job well done, sergeant.)

Roy smiled shyly. *"Arigatōgozai-masu."* (Thank you, sir.)

Working at RAF headquarters alongside Roy was another former Marauder, Grant Hirabayashi. The MISLS classmates agreed that it was good duty at headquarters; they weren't hiking up mountains or dodging incoming rounds. Since the Army had not kept its promise to send the Marauders home after the mission for which they had volunteered, the prospects of spending the rest of the war in a backwater office in New Delhi was fine with Roy and Grant.

Roy Matsumoto wearing the Legion of Merit medal

But it wasn't to be. Strolling down a street one day, they passed a British army general dressed in khaki shorts and knee socks. In the Marauders, they had learned not to salute an officer in the field because it was a sure way to get him shot by an enemy sniper looking to target officers. Some habits forged by combat weren't easy to change.

"Soldiers!" came the angry reproach.

Roy and Grant turned around.

"You didn't salute me!" said the general, waving his swagger stick.

They raised belated salutes.

"Too late! Names and serial numbers!"

What should have been a minor flap became a major incident when the aggrieved general filed a report that a pair of Japanese American soldiers had disrespected his rank and should be court-martialed. While the U.S. colonel in charge of MIS personnel in New Delhi said he thought the "limey general" had overreacted to the lapse in etiquette, he told Roy and Grant they would be brought up on charges if they stayed in India. On the other hand, the colonel went on, if they were to be suddenly transferred out of the country, the whole thing would "just go away."

That's how Roy and Grant ended up on a C-46 flying over "the

Hump" to China one stormy Christmas Eve. The two-engine plane was configured for cargo, not passengers, so there were no seats in the unheated and unpressurized compartment. They sat on top of boxes of ammunition for six hours, holding on as the plane was buffeted from side to side by howling crosswinds, dropped precariously in downdrafts, only to make sudden ascents in updrafts as they overflew fifteen-thousand-foot mountains in the snow, sleet, and fog. Hundreds of aircraft and more than a thousand crewmen had been lost flying this route to deliver critically needed supplies to China. There had been so many crashes it was dubbed the "Skyway to Hell" and the "Aluminum Trail."

They landed safely in Kunming, which had been a quiet resort town in the mountains until it became one of the busiest airports in the world as the main terminus for materiel arriving from India over the Hump. When the fuselage door opened, a U.S. enlisted man peered inside at the two shaken passengers. Clearly surprised, he said, "Oh, you guys made it!" The plane before them was missing and presumed down, he told them, and everyone thought the two Nisei servicemen had been on that flight.

Roy and Grant soon found themselves on another plane headed farther into China, to Chungking, since 1937 the provisional capital of Generalissimo Chiang Kai-shek's Nationalist Chinese government. They were assigned to the Sino Translation and Interrogation Section (SINTIC). In no time, Roy was back in hot water. During an early interrogation, he asked the Japanese soldier how long he had been a POW, and was shocked by his answer. *Eight years.* There was no military value in interrogating someone who had been out of the war since 1936!

"You're wasting my time," Roy told the officer in charge.

The officer said he figured Roy "needed the practice."

"I don't need the practice! I've been in combat. Have you?"

That angered the officer. He told Roy it could be arranged for him to be sent *back* to combat. That was fine with Roy. Better to do something in the war than waste his time here. He was soon on his way to southern China, where he joined OSS Detachment 202, operating behind enemy lines near the French-Indochina border—blowing up bridges and rail lines, disrupting communications, and capturing prisoners in support of Chinese forces attempting to tie down as many Japanese troops as possible. Back in the war, Roy felt right at home.

Grant found Chungking trying for different reasons. At first he worked exclusively on document translations. The workdays were long—sunrise to midnight—and the stacks of documents never-ending. But no one was shooting at him, and he had only to recall the unforgiving jungles of Burma and the mule that saved his life on a steep mountain trail.

Grant Hirabayashi

After a few months, he caught a break when he was put in charge of interrogating Japanese Army Air Force (JAAF) prisoners in Chungking. He figured someone at headquarters found out he had been an Army Air Corps flight clerk before attending the MISLS. Now able to set his own schedule, he would spend a solid week questioning prisoners at the POW compound and the next week at a hot springs resort where he lodged, typing up his reports.

The JAAF, whose planes had dominated the skies over China for years, and many of the Pacific battlefields early in the war, was now decimated. Due to the strategic bombing of Japan's manufacturing sector, the country's aircraft factories were unable to meet wartime production demands. The lack of replacement aircraft was compounded by the loss of experienced pilots. (Japan's naval air wing was weakened for similar reasons, as well as the fact that most of its aircraft carriers had been sunk.) Since late 1944, and in desperation as the Allies drew closer to Japan's home islands, the JAAF had been sending waves of kamikaze against U.S. ships, mass suicide attacks that would have been an unthinkable waste of pilots and planes earlier in the war.

In April 1945, Grant interrogated a recently captured JAAF lieutenant who seemed misplaced in the military. Not a pilot, he looked more like an academic, in rimless spectacles magnifying his weak eyes. In fact, he claimed to have an engineering degree from Tokyo Imperial

University, Japan's most prestigious university and one of the oldest. He proclaimed rather airily that were it not for the disruption of the war, he would be teaching at his alma mater.

The statement struck Grant as pompous, and he couldn't help himself. Yes, and if not for the war, he said, he'd be teaching at Harvard.

Grant's sarcasm seemed to provoke the man to prove himself. With a patronizing smile, he pushed a box of wooden matches across the table. Without fanfare, he said, *"Watashitachi wa toshi o hakai suru kono saizu no bakudan ni torikundimasu."* (We're working on a bomb this size that will destroy a city.)

Grant shook his head. He knew when his leg was being pulled.

But the POW insisted, *"Īe, sore wa hontō desu."* (No, that's true.)

To keep him talking, Grant decided to feign interest and feed the man's air of intellectual superiority. Soon, the would-be professor was lecturing his uninformed American student about the secret research in Japan to make a new, powerful weapon he called *"genshi bakudan."*

It was a strange term, Grant thought. *Bakudan* meant "bomb," and the English word for *genshi* was "atom." He recalled from high school chemistry that atoms were the smallest unit of matter, and every atom is composed of a nucleus and one or more electrons. But how could atoms be used in a bomb? The engineer explained that when a hollow uranium projectile was driven into a target cylinder inside the bomb, it triggered a nuclear explosion. As he listened, Grant took detailed notes, and was glad he did because the terms thrown around by the engineering major were many and mindboggling. Who knew if any of it was *true*, but what a story!

The lieutenant said the research was under way at three locations in Japan. First, at his own school, Tokyo Imperial University, under the direction of Professor Yoshio Nishina, an internationally known physicist who had been asked by Japanese army officials a year before Pearl Harbor to investigate the possibility of creating an atomic bomb. Nishina began studying the military applications of fission, building in his laboratory a large cyclotron that was now nearly operational. The prisoner said he knew this because he had worked on the army-sponsored research being done in Nishina's lab. The Imperial Navy was sponsoring another group of researchers at Kyoto University to work on the bomb, he continued, and still other scientists were doing similar work at Osaka University.

"Saikurotoron to wa?" Grant asked. (What is a cyclotron?)

A machine that accelerates charged subatomic particles to high speeds using a strong magnetic field, said the lieutenant. He went on to explain that a main obstacle to building a fission-based bomb is the difficulty of separating the uranium isotope U-235, which is needed to sustain a fission chain reaction, from the isotope U-238. They are chemically identical but have different masses. The lighter isotope, U-235, is deflected more by the magnetic field of the cyclotron than the heavier U-238, and this results in two streams that can be separately collected.

Grant was lost. His notes were filled with words and terms he did not fully understand. At one point, he excused himself to go into another room and consult his Japanese-English dictionaries, but they were of little help. Many of the words were not in any dictionary, even those with technical and military terms. By now, he had an idea that his informant knew of what he spoke, even though much of the information defied comprehension and belief. A bomb with an explosive, radioactive core the size of a box of matches capable of destroying a city? It sounded like comic-book fiction.

Grant went away that day with his head spinning. The next morning, he happened to be introduced to a pair of college graduates who had recently completed Officer Candidate School and had just arrived from the States. Grant figured they might be up on the latest.

"Have you heard of an atomic bomb that can destroy a city?"

The two officers looked at each other and shrugged.

"Never heard of anything like that," one of them said.

The other officer said flat out, "No such thing."

Grant shared a few more details, which were met with rolling eyes. He got the impression that they thought he had been overseas too long.

He worked on writing up his interrogation report, realizing how unbelievable it was going to sound. As he feared, the science proved challenging. Not only was it impossible for him to explain all the technical terms, but the idea of a single bomb unleashing such devastation seemed implausible. Wanting some guidance from higher-ups, he sought out Major John Burden, in charge of SINTIC.

Burden, fluent in Japanese, was a legendary figure in the MIS. Born to American missionary parents in Tokyo in 1900, he was sent to the U.S. as a teenager to continue his education. He earned a medical degree in 1936, and was working as a doctor in Hawaii when Pearl Harbor was attacked. Having already been granted an Army reserve commission, he was placed on active duty a week later and ordered to the Army's Japanese-language school at the Presidio in San Francisco—one of two white men (David Swift was the other) alongside the fifty-eight Japanese Americans in the first class, which had started a month before he arrived. Soon after he graduated in May 1942, Burden shipped out to the Pacific in command of a ten-man team, which at Guadalcanal became the first Nisei linguist team to be used for translations and interrogations in an active combat zone.*

Grant made an appointment to see Burden at his Chungking headquarters. When he entered his office, the tall major was standing behind his desk next to a window, reading a document. He didn't look up, so Grant stood silently in front of the desk, waiting to be acknowledged.

When Burden finally looked his way, Grant took that as his cue, saluted, and began summarizing what he had been told by the Japa-

---

* In July 1943, John Burden sent a twenty-two-page report to Army officials in Washington. He wrote, in part, "A great deal of prejudice existed regarding the use of Nisei in the combat zone . . . This prejudice was based on two factors: 1) A general distrust of all persons of Japanese extraction. 2) A fear that due to the attitude of U.S. troops toward Japanese, the lives of the Nisei would be endangered in the combat zone. The first argument is the result of the national hysteria which resulted following the attack on Pearl Harbor. Distrust of the Nisei is unfounded inasmuch as each man engaged in this work has been thoroughly investigated by the FBI and his loyalty has been unquestionably proved. The second argument is not applicable . . . The small amount of prejudice that still exists is wiped out as soon as an individual becomes acquainted with the Nisei. They have made a splendid showing in the combat zone . . . It has been proven that the use of Nisei . . . is essential in obtaining information. I am glad to say that those who opposed the use of Nisei the most are now their most enthusiastic advocates."

nese air force lieutenant, even as the major returned to his reading. When he got to the part about one bomb being able to destroy a city, Burden looked over at him with upraised eyebrows, but then turned back to his document, which Grant could see was in Japanese.

When Grant finished, the major was still reading. He didn't look up again, and never said a word. Grant stood in the silence for maybe sixty seconds, but it seemed like a long time. Then he saluted, turned, and left.

Two tries, two misses. The recent OCS graduates had dismissed him out of hand, and his commanding officer had made no comment. Had the major already heard about the atomic bomb research taking place in Japan? Or did he judge the intelligence so bizarre as not to be credible? Grant would never know, but he had come away from the interrogation believing that there was some truth in what the prisoner was reporting. He wouldn't have taken it all the way up to the major had he felt otherwise. However, Grant now had to seriously consider whether he had screwed up. Had he misjudged the POW? Had he allowed himself to be taken in by a wild story spun by a pretentious academic who enjoyed talking circles around people? Anyway, the hell with it. He wasn't going to turn in anything about a so-called atomic bomb that no one took seriously.

When he returned to his desk, he threw away the report.

———

Three months passed, and Grant didn't think anything more about atomic bombs or his interrogation of the Japanese lieutenant with the vaunted engineering degree. It was as if it had never happened.

Then, on August 6, 1945, alerted to breaking war news, he flipped on the radio in time to catch the middle of a CBS news flash. "... There is reason to believe that the Japanese city of Hiroshima, approximately the size of Memphis or Seattle or Rochester, no longer exists. To all questions as to how the new atomic bomb was carried, how large it was and from what altitude it was dropped, the military was uncommunicative."

Grant could barely breathe. *We dropped an atomic bomb on Japan? We were conducting atomic bomb research all along?* Yet when he had stumbled onto a prisoner who warned about Japan's own research program, the idea of an atomic bomb was so preposterous no one believed him! Then came some hard questions that gave him the chills. *How close was Japan to having an atomic bomb? What if they had built one first?**

That night—around midnight in China—a statement by President Truman was broadcast from the cruiser *Augusta* mid-Atlantic as he returned from the Potsdam Conference, where he had met with Churchill and Stalin to decide how to divide up a defeated Germany, which had surrendered three months earlier, ending the war in Europe.

> [Today] an American plane dropped one bomb on Hiroshima . . . That bomb had more power than 20,000 tons of T.N.T. . . . The Japanese began the war from the air at Pearl Harbor. They have been repaid many fold, and the end is not yet . . . It is an atomic bomb. It is a harnessing of the basic power of the universe . . . Before 1939, it was the accepted belief of scientists that it was theoretically possible to release atomic energy. But no one knew any practical method of doing it . . . We have now won the battle of the laboratories . . . We are now prepared to destroy, more rapidly and completely, every productive enterprise the Japanese have in any city. We shall destroy their docks, their factories,

---

* In answer to a similar question from the audience while on a speaking tour of the United States in 1969, the retired Japanese naval aviator Minoru Genda, who helped plan the surprise attack on Pearl Harbor, said, "If we had the atomic bomb in 1945, we would have dropped it on you." But Japan's atomic bomb project never reached the stage of controlled nuclear fusion reaction, and they were not close to developing a nuclear bomb. The Japanese, as well as the Germans, who had their own atomic bomb project, were impeded by a lack of sufficient high-quality uranium, which the U.S. was able to purchase in large quantities from mining operators in the Belgian Congo (3.4 million pounds in 1944), and lesser amounts from American and Canadian mining companies. The Hiroshima bomb, code-named "Little Boy," used Congolese uranium. Inside the ten-foot-long, five-ton bomb were stacks of U-235 rings fired on a solid cylindrical U-235 target measuring about seven inches long by four inches in diameter, which formed the bomb's explosive core and was the approximate size of the box of wooden matches the Japanese lieutenant pointed to during his interrogation by Grant Hirabayashi.

and their communications. Let there be no mistake, we shall completely destroy Japan's power to make war.

Grant hopped in a jeep and raced through the darkness to the POW compound. He waited for the MPs to find the Japanese lieutenant and bring him into a well-lit interrogation room.

When they were alone, Grant told him about Hiroshima. "Oh—ohh." The man lifted his hands to his face, hiding it.

When he brought them back down, his eyes were filled with tears. Oddly, he didn't ask about casualties.

But he didn't have to ask, Grant realized. The lieutenant knew what happened when an atomic bomb was dropped on a major city.

"Sensō wa owatta ni chigainai." (The war must be over.)

Not yet, Grant Hirabayashi replied. *"Shikashi sugu ni."* (But soon.)

Seventeen

RETURN TO JAPAN

When the war ended, 2nd Lieutenant Tom Sakamoto was in the Philippines. After helping save his general's life at Los Negros, followed by combat in New Guinea and a stint at ATIS in Brisbane, Tom had received his commission and was assigned to MacArthur's Manila headquarters.

First word of Japan's surrender came in a surprise radio address on August 15, 1945, by Emperor Hirohito, who had succeeded to the Chrysanthemum Throne more than sixteen years before upon his father's death. Yet, it was the first time he had spoken publicly, and until that moment his 100 million subjects had never heard his reedy, high-pitched voice. From the Imperial Palace in the heart of Tokyo, Hirohito addressed his "good and loyal subjects" nine days after Hiroshima was leveled and six days after a second atomic bomb destroyed Nagasaki, attacks that hastened the war's end, as he acknowledged in his short speech:

Lieutenant Tom Sakamoto

The enemy has begun to employ a new and most cruel bomb, the power of which to do damage is, indeed, incalculable, taking

the toll of many innocent lives. Should we continue to fight . . .
it [would] result in an ultimate collapse and obliteration of the
Japanese nation . . .

Hirohito warned of more difficult days ahead for Japan.

The hardships and sufferings to which our nation is to be subjected hereafter will be certainly great . . . We have resolved to
pave the way for a grand peace for all the generations to come
by enduring the unendurable . . .

As Tom listened to the speech it was clear to him that the emperor
was preparing his country for a military occupation to follow. Known
in Japan as *Gyokuon-hōsō* (Jewel Voice Broadcast), the emperor's talk
lasted four minutes and thirty-six seconds. He spoke in a formal,
archaic Japanese comprised of Chinese-origin characters and pronun-
ciations best understood by the well educated, not by the country's
millions of commoners. Tom noted that Hirohito didn't once use the
word *kōfuku* (surrender). Rather, he said the government was "resort-
ing to an extraordinary measure" in accepting the "provisions of a
joint declaration" by the Allied powers. But the Japanese press had not
reported on the declaration from the Potsdam Conference weeks earlier demanding that Japan unconditionally surrender or face "prompt
and utter destruction." Many Japanese citizens would have been left
confused by the words and meaning of the emperor's historic radio
message had not an announcer clarified after the speech that Japan
was surrendering.

Planning the invasion of Japan had been going on for months at
MacArthur's headquarters. "Operation Downfall" was to begin in November 1945, with fourteen Army divisions—supported by twenty-
four battleships, forty-two aircraft carriers, and four hundred other
ships—landing on thirty-five invasion beaches on the southern home
island of Kyushu. Then, in March 1946, another twenty-five Army
divisions were to land on Honshu, the largest home island. Tom had
seen casualty estimates of more than a million Americans, and several

million Japanese. Now, two atomic bombs later, the invasion to end all invasions was off.*

Overnight, planning for peace replaced war planning. MacArthur's staff immediately began drafting the "Instrument of Surrender" to be signed by the representatives of Japan and the Allied nations. When a delegation from Tokyo arrived to discuss the surrender terms, Tom and other linguists interpreted for them and translated documents. After the final wording of the eight-paragraph surrender instrument was approved by the War Department and President Truman, the question became on what to print the historic document given the limited resources in war-torn Manila. An enterprising staffer found a cache of rare parchment paper in the basement of a monastery, and it was delivered to a printer. Comparing the covers of the two documents left no doubt as to which side had prevailed. The English version was bound in leather and gold lining with the official seals of both countries on the front, and the Japanese edition was in a rough, lightweight canvas left blank on the front.

Tom soon had his next assignment: to serve as escort and inter-preter for nearly thirty correspondents from U.S. newspapers and wire services going to Tokyo for the surrender ceremony. Seven years after graduating high school in Kumamoto on the island of Kyushu and returning to America, he was headed back to his parents' homeland.

The fast pace of events continued, with Tom and the newsmen hurrying to board a four-engine C-54 transport along with paratroop-ers of the 11th Airborne Division, which was chosen by MacArthur to escort him into Japan and spearhead the occupation. Four hours later they landed in Okinawa, where headstones filled the hills overlooking the blue-green waters of the Pacific, stark testimony to the ferocity

* Had Japan not surrendered, a third atomic bomb would have been dropped as soon as August 19. Possible targets: Niigata, the largest city on the west coast of Honshu; Kokura, an ancient castle town guarding the straits between Honshu and Kyushu; and Tokyo itself. The U.S. had an inventory of six additional atomic bombs that could have been dropped in September and October. There were also discussions at the War Department as to the tactical use of atomic bombs after U.S. forces invaded Japan, targeting concentrations of enemy troops and weaponry. It was believed that American troops would have to be at least six miles away from a nuclear blast to be safe.

of the recent battle. Tom had never seen anything like it. "One look upon it," he wrote to his wife, Sadie, "gave me a lump in my throat." He thought the rows of white crosses made it seem as if the soldiers who had fallen were still in formation.

The reporters pressed Army officials to get them into Japan without delay, arguing that they needed to be in-country before MacArthur so they could report and photograph his arrival. That landed on receptive ears. With MacArthur due to land in Japan the next morning, and planeloads of paratroopers leaving Okinawa for Japan every ten minutes, Tom and the newsmen were allowed to board a flight that took off at 2 a.m. for Tokyo, seven hundred miles away. As they flew through the black of the night, most of the young paratroopers slept easily in their seats, knowing they weren't heading to war but to peace. Tom, however, did not sleep. He was returning, he knew, to a far different Japan than the one he had left.

As a milky overcast began to lift at dawn, Tom saw in the distance a looming shadow that came into view between cloud banks. It was Mount Fuji, Japan's tallest peak, sixty miles southwest of Tokyo. Since ancient times, *Fujisan* had been considered holy and sacred. The 12,390-foot volcano had long inspired artists and poets and been the object of pilgrimages. Tom had made his own trek in the summer of 1937. He and a school friend took a train to the resort area at the northern base of the mountain, camped for the night, and the next day hiked a trail to the top. Exhilarated by their feat, they stacked stones inside the crater to mark their climb. He had always pictured it as the same majestic, snow-capped peak, but today it looked different. Shrouded by storm clouds, it was a dark, ghostly figure—reflecting, he thought, the mood of a defeated land.

Passing over neatly laid out patterns of rice fields and a landscape dotted with thatched farmhouses, they began a bumpy descent through pockets of air turbulence for a straight-in approach to a runway at Atsugi Airdrome. The large Imperial Japanese Navy airfield thirty miles from Tokyo was the base of the 302nd Naval Aviation Corps, whose Zeroes and twin-engine Nakajima Gekkō night fighters had been Tokyo's frontline air defenses against U.S. bombers. Only a dozen planes were still parked in revetments, and most looked to have been stripped for parts.

For the next two hours, Tom and the newsmen waited for MacArthur to arrive. They were joined by a group of Japanese reporters and interpreters in khaki uniforms complete with white armbands. Tom recognized one of the interpreters. He was James Wada, a fellow Nisei whose parents had sent him to Japan for high school. He and Tom had been classmates at the Kyushu Gakuin boarding school in Kumamoto. But instead of returning to America after their 1938 graduation as Tom had done, Wada, always a top student, stayed on after being accepted to one of the best universities in Japan, Meiji University in Tokyo. Wada was just as surprised to see Tom, and the two men serving on opposite sides of the war greeted one another like long-lost friends. Tom had heard that Wada hadn't made it back home before the outbreak of war, and always wondered what happened to him. Wada said the Imperial Navy found him at university, and put him to work as an English translator, although because he was an American he was never fully trusted and was kept under close scrutiny by the military police as a possible spy. Wada explained that this had been the fate of thousands of Nisei "who missed the last boat out of Japan before Pearl Harbor." Stuck in a country that didn't want them, they had difficulty finding work to support themselves or even acquiring ration coupons once the severe food shortages hit Japan.

The newsmen, Americans and Japanese, were tightly grouped on the tarmac when the five-star general, a long corncob pipe clenched in his jaw and wearing aviator dark glasses, stepped from his plane. MacArthur paused dramatically at the top of a stairway that had been rolled into place for him, holding for several beats a sweeping gaze to his left, then, as camera shutters clicked, in the opposite direction. At that moment, Tom realized that everything he had heard about MacArthur was true. The general hadn't just paused—he had struck a Napoleonic pose for pictures, and only then did he come down to earth to answer the reporters' questions.

As yet unable to enter Tokyo, Sakamoto and the newsmen headed twenty-five miles south to the coastal city of Yokohama. They rode in several of the vehicles waiting in a long line at the airfield with local drivers to transport U.S. occupation personnel. En route, Japanese soldiers stood rigidly at attention, evenly spaced along the shoulder of the road, their backs to the traffic. For what reason, Tom didn't

MacArthur speaks to reporters on the tarmac upon his
arrival in Japan on March 30, 1945. Tom Sakamoto can
be seen in upper right corner.

know, but it seemed a gesture of obedience rather than defiance. The
civilians they passed looked expressionless, even shell-shocked. The
somber drive was broken only by scattered groups of children smiling
and waving at the caravan.

Yokohama was a shell of the thriving port city Tom remembered.
Entire blocks had been razed, and tall piles of rubble from collapsed
buildings were on every street. From bomb damage assessments he
had seen at headquarters, Tom knew that half of the city's structures
were destroyed and thousands of people killed in a single raid on the
morning of May 29, 1945, when hundreds of B-29s dropped more
than two thousand tons of incendiary bombs. Japan's cities were vital
to its war effort, as manufacturing was widely dispersed to prevent
precision attacks on major production centers. With so many wooden
structures, towns and factories were vulnerable to incendiary attacks,
and far more buildings were destroyed and people killed by fires than
by exploding bombs. Tom found it inconceivable that this state of

devastation, which he knew was repeated throughout the country and had left hundreds of thousands dead and millions homeless, had not been enough to convince Japan's leaders to surrender months ago before the two atomic bombs.

As a schoolboy in Japan, he had seen firsthand the fervent nationalistic movement in the mid-1930s, and knew how the ruling militarists had eagerly committed the country to faraway wars that not all Japanese understood or wanted. He recalled the questions he and other students had back then, such as why conquering China was important to the defense of Japan. But they had to be careful, for fear of being labeled a traitor. In Japanese society, independent thinking and expression were limited. In American schools, students were encouraged to speak up when they didn't understand something or saw things they thought were wrong. That was not the case in Japan, where the moral ethics taught in school and at home centered around loyalty to the emperor, to the country, and to one's parents—in that order.

As they drove into the ruined metropolis, Sakamoto reflected bitterly on what all the years of fighting and dying had accomplished other than taking the country to the brink of collapse. He understood *Yamato-damashī*, the spirit of the people, and the centuries-old *Bushido,* the "way of the warrior" he had learned firsthand competing on his school's kendo team, a traditional martial art. He wondered if those prideful terms would mean anything again. Knowing the people here as he did, and based on what he now saw in their faces, he expected that they would be living with contrition and shame for years.

Tom and the newsmen checked into an inn that was among the few original buildings still standing on the block. It featured tatami-matted rooms, *shoji* sliding doors, and a communal dining area serving traditional dishes that included local specialties and raw fish.

When Tom came down the next morning, a kimono-clad server looked at him shyly with an expression he had seen many times already, and one he would continue to see as the Japanese reacted to someone in a U.S. Army uniform who looked like them.

Something else had caught the young woman's eye.

"Naze anata wa jū o motte iru no desu ka?" she asked. (Why do you have a gun?)

The question surprised Tom, who was wearing his .45 sidearm.

"Watashitachi wa anata to tatakatte imasen, sensei," she said shyly. (We are not fighting you, sir.)

Yes, the war is over, he agreed. He took off his pistol belt before sitting down for breakfast.

Three days later, Tom and the reporters gathered at 5 a.m. on a Yokohama pier to board a U.S. destroyer that took them into Tokyo Bay to the anchored U.S. battleship *Missouri*. The date was September 2, 1945.

THE NEW YORK TIMES
JAPAN SURRENDERS TO ALLIES,
SIGNS RIGID TERMS ON WARSHIP;
TRUMAN SETS TODAY AS V-J DAY
WAR COMES TO END

. . .

MacARTHUR SEES PEACE

. . .

Emperor Orders Subjects
To Obey All Commands
Issued by General

. . .

By The Associated Press.

ABOARD THE USS *MISSOURI* in Tokyo Bay, Sunday, Sept. 2—Japan surrendered formally and unconditionally to the Allies today in a twenty-minute ceremony which ended just as the sun burst through low-hanging clouds as a shining symbol to a ravaged world now done with war . . .

The day after attending the surrender ceremony in Tokyo Bay, Tom and the newsmen flew from Tokyo to Hiroshima on an Army C-47. During the four-hundred-mile flight, the reporters talked animatedly about being the first Western reporters to cover "the greatest story of the century." They weren't referring to the previous day's surrender ceremony, although it had been big news, of course, and they had all filed stories. But nothing would beat reporting from ground zero of the world's first atomic bomb blast.

"We have a terrific responsibility to report this story," said one reporter. Everyone agreed, and their excitement was palpable.

Tom was frankly surprised that the Army had approved a press junket to Hiroshima only a month after the bombing. But he assumed that it was safe or they wouldn't be making the trip, and the reporters felt the same way. Just before they left, the Army announced that a survey team had entered Hiroshima and found "no measurable radio-activity at the point of detonation or elsewhere." Up until then, all the talk by U.S. officials had been about the explosive power of the atomic bomb equaling fifteen thousand tons of TNT, which one reporter calculated would fill four trains of seventy-five boxcars.

Approaching a coastal airstrip shorter than the plane usually required, they skimmed so low over Hiroshima Bay that the wheels touched ground as soon as they were over dry land. They bounced once, then skidded over a surface pockmarked with bomb craters. The pilot braked hard and they stopped fifty feet from the end of the runway.

They had arrived at Kure Naval Base, a sprawling installation some twenty miles south of Hiroshima. It had been Japan's largest naval base, fuel depot, and arsenal, as well as one of its principal shipyards. Its ways and dry docks had spawned many of the ships that fought and died in the Pacific, including the largest battleship ever built, the seventy-two-thousand-ton *Yamato*, sent to the bottom by U.S. aircraft five months before off Okinawa. Now, another battleship, the *Haruna*, bombed at its mooring six weeks ago, listed drunkenly in the harbor. *Haruna* and a dozen old destroyers tied up at buoys and docks, and the wrecked hulks of other ships farther out in the bay, were the only visible remnants of Japan's navy, once the world's third-largest fleet but now consisting of only forty combat vessels in the entire Pacific, many of them damaged and unseaworthy.

The Americans bunked in an empty barrack through which the wind howled all night because the windows had been blown out. The reporters included Leo M. Litz of *The Indianapolis News*, Vern Haug-

Vice Admiral Kanazawa Masao
of the Imperial Japanese Navy

land of the Associated Press, Robert Brumby and Clark Lee of the International News Service, and James McGlincy of the United Press, familiar bylines to newspaper readers at home for their coverage of the war.

In the morning, the correspondents requested an interview with a top Japanese officer before leaving for Hiroshima. They were escorted to the home of the Kure naval commander. When they arrived, Tom quietly suggested that they remove their shoes in the *genkan*, an entryway where pairs of oxfords and house slippers were neatly lined up, explaining it was a centuries-old cultural tradition before entering a Japanese home.

"We won the war!" howled one reporter. "The hell with it!"

The reporters charged across the straw tatami in their army-issued boots.

Vice Admiral Kanazawa Masao, who spoke passable English, greeted them on a spacious portico where folding chairs had been set up for the visitors. The stocky, grinning admiral was not at all the pompous, Tojo-esque enemy the American reporters expected. Courteous and composed, he deftly answered their sharp, rapid-fire queries with degrees of bluntness and humor, mostly in broken English but occasionally pausing for Tom to translate questions or his own lengthy answers that he preferred to give in Japanese.

Following many years of sea duty that culminated in his command of the battleship *Kirishima*, the admiral had been his country's naval spokesman until 1939. After that he headed the navy's bureau of personnel, then was naval attaché to the puppet government in China until shortly after Pearl Harbor, when he was assigned to the staff of the South Seas Fleet (4th Fleet), responsible for defending the Marshall, Carolina, and Mariana Islands, former territories of the German colonial empire given to Japan under a League of Nations mandate following World War I.* After December 1942, he spent the remainder of the war in Japan, serving first as head of the naval facilities command, and, since May 1945, as commander of the 2nd Naval District at Kure.

"Was this Japan's greatest naval base?" asked a reporter.

"It was," Kanazawa said, chuckling and gesturing toward the nearly empty harbor. "But there are no big ships left." Most of the sailors at Kure had been demobilized and sent home, he said, adding that the Japanese people "went into this war on orders and stopped fighting on orders. It is all finished. It is good. Now we can play tennis together again."

Asked what the turning point of the war had been, the admiral did not hesitate. It came at Guadalcanal, he said. After the U.S. victory there in early 1943, "Japan was on the defensive," and it had been impossible for his country to successfully fight a defensive war in the Pacific because "there was too much to defend and too little to do it with." He looked as if he wanted to say more. "Japan made very many strategical mistakes," he added, "but the biggest mistake of all was starting the war with America."

There had been discussions at the highest levels in Tokyo about landing troops in Hawaii at the time of the Pearl Harbor attack, said the admiral, who opined that a landing "would have been easy," but it was not done because they doubted that they could maintain supply lines across four thousand miles of ocean. More thought was given to invading Hawaii after their planned capture of Midway in June 1942, but Japan's crushing defeat in a sea battle there (four aircraft carriers were sunk) ended that talk. He confirmed that Japan had plans at one time to invade Australia, but denied that any consideration had been given to landing troops in the continental United States. The admiral ticked off other blows he said had been costly to Japan. The loss of

---

* Japan entered World War I on the side of the Allies in 1914, primarily with the hope of making territorial gains among Germany's scattered island holdings in the Pacific, which it accomplished. Japan's troops did little fighting, but after the war the country was a signatory to the Treaty of Versailles and gained entry to the League of Nations.

the Philippines, a source of vital supplies and materials; the capture of Saipan and Okinawa, which cut Japan's military empire in two; and the long-range bombing of the home islands beginning in late 1944 that destroyed war production factories.

To the disbelief of the reporters, Kanazawa stated that Japan did not really lose the war. The military was willing to carry on, he explained, and the Japanese people would have fought to the last.

"But, admiral, how do you figure that?" asked a reporter. "Look at your factories and docks, look at all your battleships and carriers sunk. How would you fight on?"

"That is the difference between the Japanese and other people," he said. "We would have carried on."

"In spite of the atomic bomb?" asked another skeptic.

"Hai. Watashi no kotae wa onajidesu." (Yes. My answer is the same.)

"We were all willing to die," an impassive Kanazawa continued in English, "but the emperor told us to stop fighting."

Tom knew better than the reporters that whether it was the congenial admiral or the hated Tojo, the military men leading Japan came from the same samurai stock. They were ready to fight and die for the emperor and their honor, and expected everyone else, military or civilian and regardless of age or gender, to be just as willing. And Tom did not doubt that millions of Japan's citizens of all ages would have died if the war had gone on.

Kanazawa now seemed to contemplate the possibility that he had been misunderstood. "Please take word back to your headquarters. Everything will be delivered peacefully. I promise my whole area of Japan, which includes the coastal defenses of Honshu, will be orderly. There were thousands of kamikaze pilots based here, but they have been sent home. Even the schoolchildren have been instructed to behave themselves."

The admiral signaled to a white-jacketed houseboy, who briefly left, then returned with a tray of etched Kimura glassware and a tall bottle of Suntory whisky. When the glasses were passed out and the liquor poured, the admiral proposed a toast.

"Gentlemen, you beat us at war," he said, his affable nature back on full display, "but next time I see you I'll beat you on the golf course."

Tom realized that the admiral had diplomatically ended the session on a drink and a joke. Everyone laughed, and threw back the smooth, spicy Japanese whisky the reporters agreed tasted something like Scotch. As a parting gift, three bottles of Suntory were given to them for their trip.

For the drive to Hiroshima, the correspondents were given use of a charcoal-burning bus that had seen better decades, and a local driver. He was a young sailor they dubbed "Kamikaze Kid" for his erratic driving on the winding road. Heading up the coast, they saw white clouds and fleecy wisps of fog floating among the mountain peaks above Hiroshima.

It was their last beautiful sight of the day.

After being one of three Japanese Americans at the surrender ceremonies aboard the *Missouri*, Tom knew he would likely be the first Nisei soldier to set foot in Hiroshima after the atomic bomb. He had a personal connection to the city through Sadie. His wife's twenty-year-old sister, Toshiko, born in Seattle but taken back to Japan as a young girl by their father, lived there. (Their father, a widower, had returned on his own to California before the war.) Prior to leaving Yokohama, Tom had written Sadie and told her of his upcoming trip. "Dearest . . . Hiroshima was pretty badly hit, but I'll see if I can get some information regarding your sister."

It took them nearly an hour to reach the outskirts of the shattered city. They passed rows of crushed and collapsed frame houses. Those that were still upright were stripped of their roofs and furnishings, and looked like empty dollhouses. On deserted streets they drove past and around the torched hulls of streetcars, trucks, and automobiles. Some of the fire damage was similar to what they had seen in Yokohama, but with fewer heaps of rubble on the streets. The reporters decided that whatever debris wasn't flattened or dispersed by the speed-of-sound windblast must have disintegrated in the roiling fireball of the nuclear blast. People, birds, dragonflies, grass, trees, anything in the city that could burn had burned. Buddha statues melted, granite stones disintegrated, roof tiles fused, telephone poles carbonized into charcoal-like posts. The only remaining vegetation were a few charred trees, shorn of their branches, standing like sentries unwilling to leave their doomed posts.

In the center of Hiroshima was the Aioi Bridge, which had been lifted a few feet by the blast and set back down. The steel girders of the hundred-yard concrete bridge were heavily damaged and the walkways had collapsed. Because its shape was easily recognized from the air, this T-shaped span over two rivers had been the aiming point for the atomic bomb released at thirty-one thousand feet by a B-29 that its pilot, Colonel Paul Tibbets, named *Enola Gay* after his mother. After falling six miles in forty-six seconds, the 9,700-pound bomb was off target by three hundred yards when it exploded at 8:16 a.m. some two thousand feet above Shima Hospital, a low-cost clinic known for its high standard of treatment, whose medical staff and patients, about eighty in all, died instantly. A large quantity of bleached bones was found at the bottom of a debris pile; the victims had been instantly skeletonized.

The solitary building in the vicinity of the bridge—and it was only a roofless concrete shell—was Honkawa Elementary School, where about four hundred first and second graders who arrived for class that Monday morning, and ten of their teachers, disappeared from the face of the earth.

There was no bomb crater, which surprised Tom and some of the newsmen. One reporter explained that there was no crater because the atomic bomb had been an "air blast," not a surface detonation;

Hiroshima, near ground zero

the latter causes a crater as well as extensive localized ground radiation, while the former disperses the radiation at higher elevations over larger areas.

Their bus rattled to a stop at the Yorozuyo Bridge, a half mile from the hypocenter of the blast. Though extensively damaged, the bridge was open to foot and bicycle traffic. When they stepped off the bus, Tom was struck by the total silence. There were no city sounds—no vehicles, no horns, no voices. It was, he thought, like stepping into a silent movie.

They all strolled onto the span. The asphalt was scorched black except for a row of whitish shadows. As they drew closer, they realized they were looking at the etched outlines of nine human beings. Not shadows, but the detritus of adults and children of varying heights, shapes, and strides, who had been crossing the bridge during the peak of the morning rush hour and were instantly vaporized.

When they returned to their bus, the reporters wanted to be taken to police headquarters. It wasn't far. One of the few structures near downtown that escaped the full force of the withering blast and superheated fire, the building's windows were shattered and every wall blackened with soot, but the heavy masonry structure was intact.

With Tom translating, the deputy police commissioner, Hayashi Fuyufume, related what it had been like on the morning of August 6. His was the first atomic survivor story the newsmen had heard, and they listened intently and took copious notes. He had just arrived at his office that morning when there was a terrific white flash, followed a split second later by a tremendous roar. He was knocked out, and when he came to he was lying in a heavy, black dust that made it impossible to see more than a few inches and very difficult to breathe. Ten people in the building survived—*"motto ōku wa shimasendeshita"* (many more did not)—and Fuyufume was the only one uninjured. The city sustained extensive damage up to three miles from the blast, he said, and fires were ignited as far away as four miles. For three days and three nights Hiroshima burned. Seventy percent of the buildings were destroyed or damaged. Basic infrastructure such as electricity, telephones, railways, sewers, and municipal water no longer existed, and there was a critical shortage of food, water, and medical supplies.

Asked about military targets—in his August 6 announcement President Truman described Hiroshima as "a military base"—the commissioner said the city had been the longtime home of the 5th Division, but it had left for Manchuria a few months earlier. The headquarters of the Second General Army, an army group responsible for the defense of all of southern Japan, was destroyed, along with its command staff, communications center, storage depots, and some troops garrisoned in Hiroshima. The commissioner estimated that about 10 percent of the casualties in the city that had never before been bombed were military.

"How many people died here?" asked Litz of *The Indianapolis News*.

The police commissioner said the current estimate was seventy thousand dead. Many thousands of victims were hospitalized with grievous injuries and burns, however, and the death toll was expected to rise.*

The reporters' next stop was the Sekijuuji (Red Cross) hospital. Although only a mile from the hypocenter of the blast, it was one of the city's few medical facilities still in operation. In all, sixty staff members and patients had died in the bombing. Fast-acting bucket brigades drained water from storage tanks to save the main building, but an adjacent wooden dormitory filled with student nurses just off the night shift burned to the ground, hopelessly trapping many of them.

Tom led the way through the entrance, and before they went more than a few steps the smell hit them. It was the odor of decay. Inside, lying in every available space were not soldiers, but women, children, and the elderly. The stench was overpowering, and the blowflies, born

---

* The commissioner was right. In the months and years that followed, many more died from their injuries or delayed radiation illnesses. The final Hiroshima death toll is estimated at 135,000, more than half of the city's population of 255,000. Three days after Hiroshima, a plutonium bomb equal to twenty-two thousand tons of TNT was dropped on Nagasaki, which made the nuclear target list for its shipyards, and steel and ordnance plants. The detonation instantly killed some 24,000 residents. The final Nagasaki toll is estimated at 74,000 dead, more than a third of that city's population. Several thousand Nisei children, visiting from America, were staying with relatives in their parents' hometowns of Hiroshima and Nagasaki at the time of the attacks, and became casualties. Those residents of the two targeted cities who survived are known as *hibakusha,* which translates to "atomic bomb victims."

of maggot larvae, were thick and determined in their hunt. They fed on the open wounds and pus-filled burns of the unconscious or those just too weak or too tired to shoo them away. Some of the victims had their bodies so disfigured by the radiated heat and fire that their skin had melted off, exposing raw gashes. One boy who looked up at Tom had no discernable face, just eyeballs protruding from flesh and bones. Another burn victim, a young woman, had imprinted on her arms and back the pattern from the kimono she was wearing at the moment of the bomb's brilliant flash.

Moving among the wounded and dying, even the veteran war correspondents recoiled. By unspoken assent, they all soon retreated to the bus. They had seen enough. On the drive back to Kure, no one said anything. And on that night's long flight back to Tokyo, few words were exchanged. All the earlier enthusiasm for covering the "story of the century" was gone, replaced by silent reflection on what they had seen.

Tom was equally shaken. He had fought in the Admiralties and the jungles of New Guinea against the Japanese army, which is what soldiers did in war. But the hospital was filled with suffering and dying kids, women, and elders—few young men, because most were off to war. He didn't know if Hell existed, but if it did he couldn't imagine it being more hellish than Hiroshima. He had had no time to find out about Sadie's sister, but based on what he had seen, he feared the worst for her.

He thought back to Admiral Kanazawa pulling him aside after the press conference, and saying softly, *"Gambatte ne"* (Do your best). At the time, Tom had nodded but said nothing. What did the old admiral mean? Did he think it was difficult for Tom to escort such a throng of reporters—and it could be trying—or rough for him as a Japanese American to be here as a U.S. soldier? The latter was not difficult. His parents were Japanese, he was American. Japan was their homeland, not his.

What *was* difficult was seeing the death and destruction that it took for Japan to give up. What *was* difficult was hearing the admiral say they had surrendered *too early*, and that the people would have fought on. Not changing the outcome, but lengthening the war and increasing the anguish and dying on both sides. For that, he blamed Japan's leaders.

They could have and should have capitulated earlier, but they didn't have the will or courage to do so. Yes, the U.S. dropped the atomic bombs, and they were horrible nontactical weapons that killed innocent people. Tom saw that decision as one based not on a bloodthirst to kill more Japanese people but to save American lives by ending the war Imperial Japan brought to Asia in the 1930s and extended to the United States. Had the Japanese continued to fight on, and had the ground invasion of their homeland gone forward, the result would have been the annihilation of Japan and millions more dead. He realized there was a moral question as to whether using the atomic bombs on Japan was necessary and right—one that he suspected would long be debated.

The only thing Tom Sakamoto knew for certain was that no one who walked through the Hiroshima Red Cross hospital in September 1945 could advocate using a nuclear bomb on human beings ever again.

———·———

Nobuo Furuiye arrived in Japan on the "noisiest, coldest, slowest flying machine" ever built: a PBY Catalina. He figured a seagull could have flown from Guam faster than the twelve hours it took the lumbering seaplane. Landing in central Japan only long enough to refuel, they took off on the last leg of the longest flight of his life, heading for the southernmost home island of Kyushu, eight hundred miles away, another seven hours in the air.

After Nobuo returned to Honolulu in April 1945, following the Battle of Iwo Jima, he had again found himself the senior enlisted man among the Nisei interpreters and translators at the JICPOA Annex. In August, a week after Japan's capitulation, he boarded a destroyer with an admiral and his staff to Marcus Island (Minami-Torishima), an isolated Japanese atoll in the northwestern Pacific, to negotiate the surrender of the 2,500-man garrison. Nobuo worked on the bilingual surrender document, which was signed by the admiral and a Japanese general aboard ship.

What now brought Nobuo back to Japan seven years after graduating from the Kyushu Gakuin school in Kumamoto (with his Nisei classmate Tom Sakamoto) was his assignment to a new research group,

Nobuo Furuiye, second from right, at Japanese surrender
on Marcus Island, August 1945

NAVTECJAP (Naval Technical Mission to Japan), to be headquar-
tered at Sasebo, an Imperial Japanese Navy base and shipyard the U.S.
Navy was taking over. Drawing personnel from technical and language
specialties, their mission was to uncover and report on advanced Japanese naval technologies. Such as: How did the design and construction
of their warships compare with ours? What range and power did their
guns have? How heavy was their armor, and what was its metallurgy?
Were they ahead of us in electronics? The Navy wanted answers to
a thousand such technical questions, and quickly, as documents and
equipment had to be seized before they were destroyed and key Japanese interviewed before they dispersed.

When he arrived at Sasebo, Nobuo felt his first pangs of nostalgia.
He had come here often as a teenager to visit an aunt who was married
to a chief petty officer in the Japanese navy. A deep bay protected by
a narrow, dogleg entrance surrounded by forested hilly peninsulas,
Sasebo was a prime location for a fleet anchorage and shipyard that
employed at its wartime peak some fifty thousand workers building
and refitting warships. As familiar as the area was to him, Nobuo's

initial visit to town was unsettling. At first he couldn't figure out what was wrong, then it hit him.

He asked an elderly man passing by, *"Subete no josei to kodomo-tachi wa doko ni imasu ka?"* (Where are all the women and children?)

Clearly startled to hear Japanese spoken by an American soldier, the old man stopped, and squinted hard from behind thick eyeglasses. It wasn't until he got a good look at Nobuo that he answered: *"Yama ni kakurete imasu. Watashitachi wa Roshiahito ga kuru to omotta."* (Hiding in the mountains. We thought the Russians were coming.)

They didn't have to worry about that, Nobuo said.

"Amerikahito dake," he added. *"Roshiahito wa imasen."* (Only Americans. No Russians.)

Within a week, the women and children began to return home.

Nobuo settled into reading technical materials and conducting interviews, but that routine was short lived. Given his years living in Kumamoto—ninety miles from Sasebo—he joined a small team leaving for the prefecture capital on the other side of the Ariake Sea, a giant tidal flat he and his father's cousin had fished for mudskippers and tonguefish.

When they arrived, they reported to headquarters near the ancient Kumamoto Castle, a large, well-fortified hilltop castle that had survived many historic sieges. The team's priority was collecting and inventorying the flood of weapons—rifles, handguns, swords, knives, *take yari* (bamboo spears), and so on—being turned in by the military, police, and civilians alike. From what Nobuo saw, there was scant resentment by ordinary Japanese at the mandatory disarmament. The people who expected to die defending their homeland were visibly relieved that the war was over.

After a couple of weeks, Nobuo asked his officer in charge if he could have time off to visit his relatives who lived twenty miles out of town.

"Sure, Nobby," said the young Marine captain. "Take my jeep. I'll get another one from the motor pool."

Nobuo left the next morning. Determined not to arrive at his relatives emptyhanded, he took bags of white rice, tins of K rations, and canned bacon. It wasn't much, but knowing the extent of the country's food shortages, he collected whatever he could buy or barter for, even throwing in a bottle of sake he had been saving for a special occasion.

Because Nobuo had no way of getting word to them, his uncle and cousins were astonished when he pulled up to their small farm in an Army jeep. It wasn't until they went inside that his uncle told him the sad news about his aunt, who had been like a second mother to Nobuo during his years in Kumamoto. She had become sick and died a year ago.

Nobuo spent the night on the farm, and the next morning visited the Sugitani family, old friends of his parents and former neighbors in Colorado, who now lived on a small plot of land in Kumamoto. Born in Japan, the couple had migrated to America shortly after their marriage, then a few years before the war moved back to their homeland with their teenage sons, Yoshinori and Mutsuhio. The old neighbors were delighted to see Nobuo, but he saw they had aged terribly and looked to be carrying a heavy burden. He soon learned why. Their sons, who were born in Colorado and had dual American and Japanese citizenship, had been drafted into the Japanese army and sent overseas. They had both been killed, one on Java in the Dutch East Indies and the other in the Philippines. Their father blamed himself.

"We should never have moved here," he said quietly. "We should have stayed in America. Japan was our country, not theirs."

Nobuo didn't know what to say. He had gone to the same redbrick elementary schoolhouse in Lafayette, Colorado, with the boys, and they had all played summer-league baseball together. He remembered Yoshi and Mutsu as all-American types who hated their Japanese-language lessons. It seemed so strange that they had died on the opposite side of the war.

Back at Sasebo, it was announced in November that MIS enlisted men with enough points accumulated for time in service and overseas could go home. The MIS Nisei working there were asked how many wanted to return right away. "Every damn one of us!" someone quipped.

There was still something Nobuo had to do before leaving. He found the letter he had been carrying since his first interrogation on Iwo Jima of the badly burned enemy soldier who died so quietly in front of him. As the man grew weaker, he had Nobuo reach in his pocket for the letter addressed to his parents in Tokyo, and asked him to mail it. Nobuo said he would. Then the man died, just like that. Nobuo now kept his promise, posting the rice paper missive, and hoping the parents would receive it.

Nobuo was among the last of the Nisei at Sasebo to board a troopship sailing for Honolulu. Docking the day before Thanksgiving, they were taken to a barrack at Fort Shafter to await flights home. Each morning Nobuo checked to see if his name was on a list for a flight, and on the fourth day he found it. After crossing the Pacific, they landed in Oakland, California. Nobuo and three other GIs from Colorado flew on to Denver, reporting to Fort Logan, eight miles southwest of the city. It was the same place Nobuo had been inducted into the Army nearly four years ago to the day. He called his parents' farm in nearby Lafayette to tell them he was close by and would be home soon.

The next afternoon, the paperwork for his discharge done, Nobuo phoned for his younger brother to come get him. An hour later, Yukio, wearing a faded baseball cap and a big smile, pulled up to the main gate in his old pickup.

"Hey, big brother! Hope you're hungry. Big feast for you tonight."

They were soon out of the city, driving northward through gently undulating hills covered by a heavy snowpack. Last month had broken records, Yukio said, for the wettest and snowiest November of all time.

"Forty-three inches!" he exclaimed. "Double the 1929 record."

Nobuo smiled. He had forgotten how farmers talked about the weather. Though there was something familiar and normal about it, he had an idea it would take some time for him to adjust to the mundane.

There was no sign of precipitation now, only a few cotton balls crossing steel-blue skies above. The road ran past humble farmhouses, but there were no people to be seen outside in the freezing cold, and the only sign of habitation was smoke drifting from chimneys. Beef cattle and dairy cows fed on grain and hay dropped by truck or tractor across frozen fields that had no vegetation for winter grazing. Huge clay-tiled silos as high as fifty feet dotted the landscape, standing tall to preserve enough oats, corn, and wheat for the livestock to get through the winter.

Yukio told how he and their father had taken the train to Arizona as the Gila River Relocation Center was closing down after Japan surrendered, and brought back to Colorado Toshie, her parents, and the baby. They had all been living on the farm since then.

The pickup turned off the highway onto the long driveway to the house, passing the now-frozen fields Nobuo knew well because he had spent many days of his youth working them. In a few months, the snow would be gone, and his father would again plant oats, corn, and wheat to sell to the large farmers' cooperative at negotiated prices, along with beets, tomatoes, lettuce, cabbage, cucumbers, and other vegetables to sell to produce houses.

Nobuo guessed that come spring, he'd be out there with his father and brothers hoeing and planting again. Maybe talking about the weather and the soil and crop prices, thinking about all those normal things that might help him forget about the killing fields and caves of Iwo Jima.

Yukio started blasting the horn a hundred feet from the house. *Honk, honk, honk.* Like the Cadillac convertible carrying the mayor in a parade.

When they pulled to a stop, the front door flew open.

And there she was. Toshie. Running out into the bitter cold without a jacket or sweater, determined to be the first one. He rushed for her, too. She flew into his arms. They held each other tightly, afraid to let go. They had been married just shy of two years, but had only spent their first month together. They could now start their married life. He kissed and kissed her sweet face, tasting her tears.

Inside the house, he saw their baby for the first time—the little girl born behind barbed wire in the desert internment camp and whose name had been suggested by his Nisei buddies since she was arriving close to the holiday caroling season. She was swaddled in a soft, pink blanket, and he held her as if she might break. Here was his child he had once feared he might not live to see. She was tiny, wide awake, and beautiful.

Today, December 2, 1945, was Carol's first birthday.

The perfect day for Nobuo Furuiye to come home from war.

EPILOGUE

Three weeks shy of his seventy-second birthday, Takejiro Higa, still lean and limber but with graying hair and now wearing bifocals, returned to the island of his youth for the fiftieth-anniversary ceremony memorializing those who died in the bloodiest and costliest battle of the Pacific war.

Soon after his arrival in Okinawa, Takejiro was interviewed by a reporter from the *Ryūkyū Shimpō*, the island's largest daily newspaper. In a story for the next edition, Takejiro related his experiences in the battle, describing how he used his fluency in the Okinawan dialect as well as Japanese to coax civilians from the caves where so many went to die. His MIS team was credited with saving thousands of lives, but Takejiro could not say how many caves he went to as "there were too many to count."

He explained how he crawled close to the entrance and used a bullhorn to amplify his voice. "Every cave I went to, first thing I did was introduce myself: I am Takejiro Higa. My parents come from Okinawa. I was born in Hawaii as a Nisei, son of Japanese immigrants, but grew up in Okinawa from age two to sixteen and went to school here. And how I still have family in Shimabuku. Then I'd say, 'Believe me, Americans are not savages like you've been told. Come out while you still can.' I repeated the same thing in both languages, and kept repeating it." Often, he said, he could spend only ten minutes at a cave before rushing off to another one, leaving without knowing how many people answered his pleas.

On April 1, 1995, Takejiro attended services at the All Souls Church in Chatan. It had been an Easter Sunday fifty years before to the day, on the nearby and now peaceful beaches, that Takejiro had landed with the assault troops of the 96th Infantry Division. The bishop of the church was an ex-kamikaze pilot who never made his final flight, and the reverend was a Japanese American who as a boy was interned with his family in the U.S. Now, Okinawans, Japanese, and Americans alike came to pray for the departed souls of those who died in the months-long battle.

Later that day, Takejiro attended a ceremony of remembrance held at the entrance to a large cave a short distance from town. As he approached the welcoming tent, he was offered tea, which he accepted but found he was unable to drink because his throat was knotted with emotion. He took a narrow path up a rocky grade toward the mouth of the cave. He didn't know if he had been here before, but there had been so many caves it wasn't likely he'd recognize it. The line of people was long—locals as well as military veterans of the battle—and he could not get very close. The prayerful ceremony began in Okinawan, then switched to Japanese and English. Even for those who didn't understand every word, there was no mistaking the feelings present, and tears were shed.

Takejiro had long despaired all the lives they hadn't been able to save. More Okinawans were killed or died by their own hand than the combined battle deaths of both sides. If only the people hadn't been so programmed to distrust the GIs—if there had been a hundred more interpreters to cover a thousand more caves—his list of what-ifs was long. After leaving Okinawa, his division returned to the Philippines, and was preparing to take part in the invasion of Japan when the war ended. He volunteered to go back to Okinawa to assist in the ongoing effort to clear caves and coax frightened civilians out of danger. But instead of helping to save more lives, he was sent to Korea to interrogate Japanese POWs.

Before returning home to Hawaii, Takejiro was contacted by the reporter who had written the story about him. She had received a call from a woman named Toyo Tawada who read the article and wanted to see him. They arranged a meeting at a Kentucky Fried Chicken restaurant.

Takejiro arrived first, and was alone in a booth when two women walked in. One was a grandmotherly type, and she was with a younger woman. His picture had appeared in the paper, so when they saw him they came right over and introduced themselves. The older woman was Toyo, and she was with her daughter. They sat down across from him.

"I wanted to meet you, Mr. Higa, because my life was saved by you," Toyo said. "I saw your name in the paper. I recognized it."

Takejiro was too astounded to comment.

She took a deep breath to steady herself.

"I was in a cave with two hundred other people. Near Nodake. We were told so many terrible things. Everyone was ready to blow themselves up. It seemed better that way. Then we heard your voice outside. You introduced yourself, said you were an Uchinaa [Okinawan] boy. Some of the young people, me included, thought it was a trick. I felt strongly against Americans. Thought you were the enemy. I am sorry."

She bowed her head, and wiped her eyes with the back of a hand.

"Some wanted to believe you, but many of us didn't. We refused to go out. One elder told us young people not to throw our lives away. 'There's a Uchinaa boy out there waiting for you. He ain't going to lie to you. Go out. Be safe.' So we did. Young and old. Everyone walked out."

This cave he remembered! It was his first as a "cave flusher." When he arrived he was told there were two hundred civilians inside, and many families.

"And I wasn't there when you came out?" Takejiro said softly.

She shook her head. "No. I threw some strong words against you and the other Americans. Thinking it *was* a trick. I am truly sorry."

"I went to another cave." He felt he owed her an explanation.

She nodded understandingly. "We received medical attention and food. We were so scared and hungry."

She smiled for the first time, and locked eyes with him.

"Mr. Higa, I owe you for the life I enjoy today."

Takejiro took off his glasses, and wiped his eyes with a napkin.

"I came here to thank you," she said.

The daughter now spoke for the first time. "I want to thank you, too, Mr. Higa. Because of you, I am here, and my children are here."

"Thank you—both," Takejiro said, barely getting out the words.

He flew back to Honolulu the next day.

Fifty years did not seem that long ago. It was still so fresh, his stepping on the beach with the landing forces and carrying so many mixed emotions. He had wanted to do his duty as a U.S. soldier, and at the same time he hoped to help the people with whom he had once lived.

Meeting the two women was a powerful reminder that he had somehow done both. He had not fired a single shot from his rifle in the war; rather, he had used his dictionaries, a bullhorn, and languages to save them.

DRAMATIS PERSONAE

NOBUO FURUIYE, *Aleutians and Iwo Jima.* His first year back from the war, Nobuo helped his father farm in Lafayette, Colorado. For several months he had vivid nightmares from which he awakened screaming, kicking, and bathed in sweat. The horrific visions were always death masks frozen in agony. Like so many of the dead he had seen on Iwo Jima.

By the end of 1946, Nobuo and Toshie had moved to Denver and he was working at a grocery store. Three years later, they relocated to San Pedro, California, where Nobuo started a gardening business.

In June 1950, seventy-five thousand North Korean troops poured across the border with the pro-Western Republic of Korea, and the U.S. was in a new war only five years after the last one. A member of the Army Reserves, Nobuo was recalled to active duty and assigned as a Japanese-language instructor to the Defense Language Institute at the Presidio of Monterey, which traced its roots back to the Army's first Japanese-language school at the San Francisco Presidio. Toshie and Carol, then six, joined him, and they lived in family quarters at nearby Fort Ord. Fourteen months later, when his enlistment was up, Nobuo wasn't sure about reenlisting, but Toshie was more certain about Army life. "No more!" she proclaimed. They returned to Denver in the fall of 1951, and Nobuo worked for a supermarket chain, rising to assistant manager. Like many returning vets, he used his GI home loan to buy their first house. Hired by the U.S. Postal Service, he delivered mail for fifteen years before taking an early retirement, which he soon found boring. His last job was with Hertz Rental Cars.

In 1991, when he turned seventy-three, Nobuo retired for good, and began volunteering for groups like the Lions Club. A member of Denver's all-Nisei American Legion Post 185, he cofounded the Rocky Mountain MIS Veterans Club, which grew to more than fifty members.

Nobuo lived to see his grandson, Craig Yamamoto (Carol's son), leave for Japan to teach English at a school in Kumamoto, the same prefecture where he had ventured sixty years earlier to study Japanese. Be proud of your heritage, Nobuo counseled, but never forget you are an American. It was the same advice Nobuo's father had given him.

Nobuo died in 2004, at the age of eighty-six.

TAKEJIRO HIGA, *Leyte and Okinawa.* Discharged from the Army in January 1946, Takejiro returned to Honolulu's Farrington High School at the age of twenty-three, determined to finally get his diploma. After graduating the following year, he attended the University of Hawaii on the GI Bill, majoring in business and accounting. He dropped out after a year to work for his grocer brother-in-law, who had to replace an experienced butcher about to retire. Takejiro attended an eight-week course at the National School of Meat Cutting in Toledo, Ohio, to learn the trade.

In 1953, he married Ruby Fumie Miyasato; like him, she was a Hawaii-born Okinawan. Ruby helped out at the store on weekends, and one day she asked her husband if he was "planning to be a butcher" all his life. If he wanted to go back to college to get his degree, she said, they would be able to "keep food on the table" with her salary as an elementary school teacher. So encouraged by his wife, Nobuo returned to school full-time. Given the long layoff, he had to study hard his first year to keep up, but he earned academic scholarships his last two years. After graduating in 1960 with a bachelor's degree in accounting, he was hired by the Internal Revenue Service in Honolulu as a tax examiner. He was an IRS agent for the next thirty years. Takejiro died in 2017 at the age of ninety-four.

Takejiro's older brother, Warren, with whom he served on the same MIS team throughout the war, also resumed his education upon returning home to Hawaii. After graduating from college, Warren began a long career in banking, eventually rising to vice president at Central Pacific Bank. He was also a director of the Honolulu Community Action Program, a nonprofit organization on Oahu delivering human services to "enable low-income individuals or families to achieve self-reliance." Warren died in 2015 at the age of ninety-five.

GRANT HIRABAYASHI, *Merrill's Marauders, Burma and China.* Six weeks after Japan surrendered, Grant caught a Liberty ship out of Calcutta with a few hundred other soldiers rotating home. They steamed through the Suez Canal, the Mediterranean, the Atlantic, and slipped into New York Harbor past the Statue of Liberty. Dockside, a waiting band struck up "Sentimental Journey." It occurred to Grant that the government had sent him on an all-expenses-paid trip around the world that lasted twenty-six months. He just wished he had known during those darkest days in Burma that he was holding a round-trip ticket. He took the train to Wisconsin to be discharged at Camp McCoy, then a bus to Minneapolis, where his parents had settled near friends who sponsored their release from internment. His father was working as a hotel clerk and his mother as a seamstress.*

Grant applied to the University of Minnesota, but was told he'd have to wait a semester. So he went to visit Army buddies at the MISLS, which had moved from Camp Savage to the larger Fort Snelling a few miles from Minneapolis. The new Japanese-language classes were as large as the wartime classes due to the urgent need for interpreters and translators in occupied Japan, but the school was short of instructors. Grant was offered a position as a civilian instructor, which he accepted. He soon met a California-born Nisei nursing student, twenty-year-old Ester Tamaki Nakamura, who was attending the University of Minneapolis, and they married in July 1947.

When the MISLS relocated to the Presidio at Monterey, Grant taught at the renamed Army Language School for a year. He then accepted a transfer to the legal section of the supreme commander for the Allied powers in Tokyo to serve as interpreter, interrogator, and court monitor for war crimes trials taking place in Yokohama. Ester was able to join him, and the couple lived in Japan for nearly four years until deciding it was time to return home. Grant enrolled at the University of Southern California, where he received his bachelor's and master's degrees in international relations. In 1959, he was hired by the Department of Defense, and became a linguist/analyst for the National Security Agency in Washington. Upon his retirement in 1990, he proved to be a popular speaker relating his wartime experiences to a variety of audiences locally, as well as out of state. In his remarks, he always said he hoped the Nisei soldiers had conveyed "that

---

* Grant's parents, Toshiharu and Midori, never returned to White River Gardens or Washington State, which, in deference to powerful agricultural interests that viewed Japanese growers as an economic threat to white farmers, had confiscated their fertile farmlands twenty years earlier. Dispossessed of their other possessions after internment, they started over in Minneapolis, where they lived the rest of their lives.

Americanism has nothing to do with place of origin or color of skin and everything to do with spirit and conviction and love of freedom." The true definition of patriotism, Grant believed, was a citizen fulfilling his right and responsibility. "Our Constitution is vulnerable," he cautioned. "We have to be very vigilant and protect our liberty and freedom." Grant died in 2011 at the age of ninety-one.

After the war, Gordon Hirabayashi, Grant's cousin, with whom he grew up at White River Gardens, returned to the University of Washington, earning a doctorate in sociology. He taught at the American University in Beirut and later Cairo, and at Canada's University of Alberta. In the mid-1980s, he was contacted by the California attorney Peter Irons, who, through a Freedom of Information Act request, uncovered evidence showing that the Justice Department purposely withheld documents that would have helped Gordon's Supreme Court case. The papers included intelligence reports stating that Japanese Americans posed no threat to the U.S. during the war. With the new evidence, Gordon's case was reopened, and advanced to the U.S. Court of Appeals for the 9th Circuit, where a three-judge panel ruled unanimously in his favor, vacating his convictions. "Although this has been a forty-year crusade," Gordon said after the verdict, "I never lost faith in the legal system. I feel today that justice has been served. The court has recognized the injustice committed against Japanese Americans during World War II." Gordon died in 2012 at the age of ninety-three.

KAZUO KOMOTO, *Guadalcanal, New Georgia, and Burma.* Following his three-month convalescence—during which he was visited bedside in a Fiji military hospital by Eleanor Roosevelt—and visit to the Gila River Relocation Center to see his family, Kazuo received orders to join the 442nd Infantry Regiment at Camp Shelby, where it was preparing for Europe. Since he was specially trained for intelligence work in the Pacific, he called John Aiso, the influential director of academics at the MISLS, to see what could be done about getting him back in the war with Japan. Aiso had him temporarily assigned to the Camp Savage faculty, and three months later Kazuo headed back to the Pacific with his own ten-man team.

Upon arriving in the China Burma India Theater, his team was attached to the 475th Infantry Regiment, which, combined with a second U.S. regiment, was designated the MARS Task Force. Their mission was similar to that of Merrill's Marauders, disbanded months earlier after the fall of Myitkyina: to operate behind enemy lines in Burma, cut off their supplies and reinforcements, and help open the Allied supply route into China.

Kazuo was in Kunming, China, when the war ended. He turned down a direct commission because he didn't want to stay in the Army. Discharged in the fall of 1945, he returned home to Sanger, California, and opened a nursery. He later worked for an insurance company and became a real estate broker. He married Chikako "Rose" Kimoto, a California Nisei, in 1948.

Like many members of his generation, Kazuo, the first Nisei soldier to be awarded the Purple Heart for being wounded in combat, was unassuming, modest, and not given to talking much about the war. But he quietly passed down to his children and four grandchildren the importance of being willing to make sacrifices to "keep our country free."

Kazuo died in 2018, three weeks after turning one hundred years of age.

HIROSHI "ROY" MATSUMOTO, *Merrill's Marauders, Burma and China.* Roy was in southern China with OSS Detachment 202 blowing up enemy bridges and rail lines when news broke of the bombing of Hiroshima. As the soldiers around him rejoiced, rightly assuming that the war would soon end, Roy thought of his family. He had been the only one to return to the U.S. after they moved to Hiroshima in 1927. The last he had heard, his parents, three brothers, and two sisters were living above his father's photography studio two blocks from the Aioi Bridge in downtown Hiroshima. Hearing reports of the city flattened by the nuclear blast and tens of thousands killed, he was certain his entire family had perished.

Two months after the war ended, Roy was transferred to the 701st Military Police Detachment in Shanghai, where thousands of Japanese soldiers were held in POW camps. Assigned to a JAG legal office, he scoured long lists of prisoners, searching for those believed responsible for war crimes so they could be interrogated and held for trial in a military court. The rest were to be repatriated to Japan. On one list of POWs about to return to Japan, Roy saw the name of his cousin, Yoro "Harry" Omoto, who had lived with him in Los Angeles while going to UCLA. After his junior year, Harry, a Nisei working in a grocery to pay for school, accepted a full scholarship from the Japanese government.

Roy had his cousin brought to an interview room. When the door opened, Harry, wearing a Japanese army uniform, broke into a wide grin.

"Hiroshi ni-san!"

The two cousins had much to catch up on. Harry told how he had been tricked by the scholarship offer. Once he arrived in Japan, he was sent to an industrial school in Manchuria, not a top university in Tokyo as promised.

Then he was drafted into the army when the war started. It dawned on Harry that he had not yet told Roy something very important.

"Hiroshima no mono inaka ni itteru kara daijobu." (Your people in Hiroshima went into the country, so they are well.)

His family moved in 1942 from the city to Jigozen, ten miles away, to be near the grandparents, said Harry, who knew this because he had corresponded with them. For months Roy had been thinking they were dead, only to learn now that they weren't even in Hiroshima when it was bombed.

More good news followed a few days later when Roy found the name of his youngest brother, Isao, on another list of POWs to be returned to Japan. Isao was now twenty-four years old, and Roy would not have recognized him when he was brought to the interrogation room. His brother had been only six years old when he last saw him. A private in the army, Isao said he had been a clerk at a division headquarters in central China. He told Roy their other brothers had been drafted, too, even though they were all born in America and none of them had denounced their U.S. citizenship. "I was never promoted," Isao said, "and always watched carefully." Their brother Noboru had been at Guadalcanal but was evacuated to a hospital back in Japan due to contracting beriberi and suffering loss of muscle function, and Takeshi, a brilliant student, was put to work as a civilian engineer at the Kure Naval Base. Counting Tom in the U.S. Army, the five Matsumoto brothers had all survived the war. After all the killing and dying he had seen on both sides, Roy knew just how lucky his family had been.

Roy reenlisted in the Army. From Shanghai, he was sent to Tokyo and Counter Intelligence School, then assigned to MacArthur's headquarters. In Tokyo, he met twenty-six-year-old Kimiko Mochizuki, a native of Shiuoka, Japan, who was teaching high school economics. They married in 1947, and soon had two daughters. Roy brought his growing family home when he was assigned to Sixth Army Headquarters at the Presidio in San Francisco. They next spent five years in Virginia, where he was in charge of the Army Post Office at Fort Story. He retired from the Army as a master sergeant in 1963. They returned to the Bay Area and Roy opened a home repair service in Berkeley. When he retired again, they moved one last time, to San Juan Island, Washington.

Celebrated at reunions of Merrill's Marauders as "the hero of Nhpum Ga" for saving his battalion from annihilation, Roy admitted to a newspaper reporter in 1997 to a lingering anger at being classified "an enemy alien" and sent to "concentration camps." The pain he carried in his heart at having his loyalty to America questioned never went away.

Roy died in 2014, a week shy of his 101st birthday.

TOM SAKAMOTO, *The Admiralties, Los Negros and New Guinea.* Two months after escorting the newsmen into a devastated Hiroshima, Tom returned to the U.S. and his wife. By then, he could tell Sadie that her sister who lived in Hiroshima was alive, as he had learned she was visiting relatives elsewhere in Japan on the day the atomic bomb was dropped.

After his promotion to first lieutenant in January 1946, and with the prospect of interesting travel and assignments, Tom decided to stay in the Army. He and Sadie moved to Japan, where he worked in MacArthur's occupational government for two years. Not long after they returned home, war broke out in Korea, and Tom served there as an intelligence officer with the 25th Infantry Division, overseeing MIS teams. He was later sent to Panmunjom, where the peace treaty was negotiated and signed in 1953. When he returned for a second tour to Japan, Sadie joined him once again. For three years he worked as a foreign intelligence officer developing contacts in Japan's national government, police, and military. Transferred to Okinawa in 1958, he was military aide to the high commissioner of the Ryukyu Islands. When President Dwight Eisenhower arrived in Okinawa on a Far East tour, Tom became his chief interpreter, and read the president's major speech in Japanese on live television.

Promoted to lieutenant colonel, Tom became chief of security of the Sixth Army at the Presidio of San Francisco in 1964. It was the same post that helped orchestrate the mass exclusion and removal of Japanese Americans from the western states two decades earlier. Rising up the ranks of Army intelligence, Tom was one of only a few high-ranking Japanese Americans at that time entrusted with the nation's secrets and security.

After a thirty-year career in the Army and serving in three wars—his last post as chief of the Army's counterintelligence in Vietnam—Tom retired as a colonel in 1970. He became a banker, rising to senior vice president of the Sumitomo Bank in San Jose, California, and a respected civic leader. A popular guest speaker at Rotary Clubs throughout northern California, he was introduced at one luncheon as a "retired army colonel," to which an audience member loudly asked, "Which army? What side did he fight on?" Even after stating he had been born in the United States, he would often get questions like, "You speak good English. Where did you learn it?" Steadfast and disciplined, Tom never bit on racist bait. But he once explained, "This is the reason I am active in community service. Because of that ignorance in the American public, we need to speak out. The United States is a country of diversity, and that is our strength."

As president of the San Francisco–based National Japanese American Historical Society in the 1990s, Tom led the organization to raise local, state, and national awareness of the MIS Nisei story, and helped secure public and private funding to develop the site of what is now the MIS Historic Learning Center in Building 640 at Crissy Field, where he and fifty-seven other Japanese American soldiers attended the Army's first Japanese-language school at the Presidio. At the age of ninety-five, Tom passed away in 2013, two weeks shy of the MIS Center's grand opening. The restored original classroom was dedicated in his honor.

AFTERWORD

My Nisei parents, Ted and Constance Yamada, were born in the small Japanese immigrant community of Florin, California, not far from Sacramento. They both came from farm families. They married in 1940. Two years later, they were given ten days to report for evacuation. They could only bring what they could carry, and they sold or gave away almost everything else. (Some of the belongings and wedding gifts that they stored in my grandparents' barn were stolen during their years in camp.) They were bused to an assembly center at the Fresno Fairgrounds and housed with thousands of other Japanese internees for months. Then they were transported by rail to Arkansas and interned at Jerome Relocation Center, where I was born in 1944.

After the war, my family returned to Florin. My father went into the grocery business, starting with a trailer on a flatbed truck he drove to outlying areas to sell produce and canned goods. Then my parents opened a mom-and-pop store. Eventually, my father cofounded a two-store supermarket chain in Lodi, thirty miles to the south. With a single exception, neither of them talked about what they experienced during the war. Only later did I learn that an unwillingness to speak of that time was commonplace among Japanese Americans of that era.

The one time my father shared something about their internment years was on April 7, 1956. He had returned from the hospital in the late evening and woke me up, asking that I come into the kitchen. We sat down next to each other, and he lit a cigar. It was an unusual sight, since I knew him to be a nonsmoker. He announced that my mother had just given birth to a boy they named Kenneth. I already had a sister, Linda, three years younger

than me. "When a son is born, the father needs to smoke a cigar to celebrate," he explained. After a few puffs, he became quiet, and seemed deep
in thought. "You're not our oldest son," he finally said. "Mom was pregnant
when we went to Arkansas. Living in camp was hard on her. The baby was
born dead." He told me they named the baby Katsumi by combining their
Japanese middle names, Katsuji and Miyoko.

Years after my parents died, I examined their War Relocation files at the
National Archives in Washington, D.C. From my mother's records, I discovered that my stillborn brother was delivered on April 5. The closeness
of that date to Kenny's April 7 birthday is likely why my father was reflec-
tive that night. He never again spoke to me of Katsumi, the son they lost.
After my father passed away in 1979, my mother had the baby disinterred
and brought home to Lodi, where his little coffin was buried atop my
father's. She never talked to me about losing the baby. In 2005, I offered to
take her to Jerome, as I had it in mind to walk the land and touch the earth
where I was born, and see where our family was interned. She declined.
"Without Dad, I don't want to go back there." My mother died in 2007,
and we had her buried next to my father and their firstborn son.

What my father told me that night stayed with me, although I didn't
fully grasp the depth of the anguish they must have felt until I became
a father. (And yes, I smoked a cigar to celebrate the birth of each of our
three children.) My parents' painful loss, the death of a brother I never
knew, and my entire family's internment have been ample motivation over
the years for me to be active in groups supporting the Japanese American
community. It seems the least I can do.

My parents had many reasons to be bitter and resentful. Wartime internment had cost them everything: their home, their possessions, and their
first child. Instead, they returned to their hometown and set about rebuild-
ing their lives, which they did with optimism and much hard work. They
believed in America and its opportunities. This same faith was shared by
many internees from the camps, and also by those young, patriotic Nisei
who joined the U.S. Army during World War II.

The Japanese American soldiers who served as Military Intelligence Service interpreters, translators, and interrogators in the war against Japan had
the added pressure of being in the fight to defeat their ancestral homeland.
In so doing, they ran the risk of being branded as "traitors" by others in the
internment camps, in their local communities, and even within their own
families. Unfortunately, much of what the MIS did during the war remained
long classified, and is still little known to many Americans.

I have long felt that the Nisei who fought in the Pacific did not get the full measure of recognition they deserved. I have tried to do my part, as president of the Japanese American Veterans Association (JAVA), to honor their significant contributions. When the House of Representatives passed legislation authorizing the Congressional Gold Medal—Congress's highest expression of national appreciation—for the Nisei servicemen of World War II, it initially included only those who served in Europe with the 442nd Regimental Combat Team and 100th Infantry Battalion. At the time, I was on the committee monitoring Senate support for the bill and preparing to organize the award ceremony. I was one of the advocates who pushed for the Nisei soldiers who served in the Pacific to be included, and as a result of our efforts, the legislation Congress approved was amended to honor the MIS veterans as well.

I was pleased to be asked by Bruce Henderson to write this piece. I accepted because *Bridge to the Sun* is the first comprehensive and penetrating look at the Japanese Americans who fought in the war against Japan. Bruce's meticulous research into the individuals and events gives us a moving and in-depth account of the invaluable contributions made by the MIS Nisei in the Pacific, just as he did in his *New York Times* best seller, *Sons and Soldiers*, for the MIS Ritchie Boys, many of them German-born Jews who served in Europe during World War II.

Not incidentally, and for the benefit of the veterans and their families, published herein is the first roster of more than three thousand U.S. Army Japanese Americans who served in the Pacific—a list compiled for *Bridge to the Sun* by JAVA member and volunteer researcher Roger Eaton over the course of two years. Also, fittingly, the names of Nisei soldiers who lost their lives in that theater of war.

As my parents taught me, I look to the future with optimism, not bitterness. It is my hope that this inspiring story will encourage others to keep faith in our country and its bedrock values—just as the Japanese American soldiers of World War II did in those difficult times—and help our society overcome the hatred and prejudice that too often divides us.

Gerald H. Yamada
Vienna, Virginia

Gerald Yamada is president and past general counsel of the Japanese American Veterans Association (JAVA); national coordinator and chief strategist for the National Japanese Heritage Coalition; founder and treasurer of the National Japanese American Political Action Committee; cofounder and first cochair of the Asian Pacific American Heritage Council; past executive director and general counsel of the National Japanese American Memorial Foundation; past governor of the Japanese American National Museum; and past president of the Washington, D.C., chapter of the Japanese American Citizens League.

ACKNOWLEDGMENTS

In a work of narrative nonfiction that spans the entirety of World War II, the facts of history must come before any attempts at compelling prose. In my own deep dive for this project—seeking details, details, and more details to enrich the telling—I had the able assistance of military researcher Steve Goodell, of Washington, D.C. I was also greatly assisted by Lori Miller of Redbird Research at the National Archives, St. Louis; Ruth Quinn, historical researcher at the U.S. Army Intelligence Center, Fort Huachuca; and Tyler Chisman and Cameron Binkley at the Defense Language Institute, Monterey, California.

Others who were most helpful and patiently answered my endless questions: Rosalyn Tonai of the National Japanese American Historical Society, San Francisco; Terry Shima, retired executive director of the Japanese American Veterans Association (JAVA); documentarian gayle k. yamada; military historian James McNaughton; genealogist Pat Dupes-Matsumoto; translator Sonya Johnson; historian Mark Matsunaga; Tom Ikeda of Densho; producer Lucy Ostrander; Brian Shiroyama; Yoshi Minegishi; Dale Kaku; Neet Ford; Metta Tanikawa; Yoshi Minegishi; Shigeko Koyama in Japan; Roger Eaton; Max Nihei; Seiki Oshiro; Jeff Morita, and physicist Ronald Mallett.

My heartfelt thanks to all the family members who shared memorabilia and recollections of their loved ones. These included: Karen Matsumoto; Jim Sakamoto; Nelson Higa; Jeffrey Komoto; Carol Yamamoto; Dawn Ehrlich; Tina Chan; Carol Hirabayashi; Calvin Ninomiya; Lynn Bettencourt; Carol Gosho; Merrill Gosho; Larry Kubo; John Tagami; and Marion Sumihiro and Don Sumihiro.

I am grateful to my Knopf editor, Victoria Wilson, who grasped my initial vision for this book and let me write it without worrying about such trivial matters as contracted delivery dates. And to my literary agent, Dan Conaway of Writers House, for his friendship and sage advice.

And once again, to Laura Jason—friend, lover, muse.

SOURCES

Complete book publication details are supplied in the bibliography. U.S. Army records such as unit histories, action reports, war diaries, and field interrogations are at the National Archives II, College Park, Maryland. Military personnel records are at the National Archives at St. Louis, Missouri. Records and personal papers pertaining to the service of Japanese American soldiers in the Military Intelligence Service in the Pacific are available at the National Japanese American Historical Society in San Francisco, California. Thoughts, feelings, and dialogue attributed to individuals in this book come from interviews, oral histories, published and unpublished memoirs, and contemporaneous correspondence. Other direct quotes are from official reports and documented sources. On occasion, italics are used for translated dialogue between two individuals when the original conversation took place in Japanese. For continuity, the Western format is used for Japanese names (given name first, family name last).

PROLOGUE: TOKYO BAY, SEPTEMBER 2, 1945

Time, September 10, 1945; Adm. Stuart S. Murray, U.S. Naval Institute Oral History (1974); Thomas Sakamoto, biographical statement (undated); Thomas Sakamoto interviewed by gayle k. yamada (1999, 2001); Thomas Sakamoto, Hanashi Oral History (2001); Thomas Sakamoto, MIS Oral History (1989); Thomas T. Sakamoto, "Witness to Surrender," *Nikkei Heritage* (Winter 2003); Thomas Sakamoto interviewed by David Swift, *First Class* (2006); Mamoru Shigemitsu, *Japan and Her Destiny*; Douglas MacArthur, *Reminiscences*; Charles A. Willoughby, *MacArthur*; Lyn Crost, *Honor by Fire*; *New York Times* (February 23, 1945).

ONE: THE TYPE OF SOLDIER WE WANT

Kazuo Komoto interviewed by author (2018); Kazuo Komoto, Hanashi Oral History (2005); Kazuo Komoto interviewed by gayle k. yamada (2000); Kazuo Komoto, NJAHS Oral History (1996); Kai Rasmussen, "Growing Up in Denmark" (1977).

TWO: "HARM THEM . . . HARM ME"

Nobuo Furuiye, Hanashi Oral History (2000); Nobuo Furuiye, NJAHS Oral History (1996); Nobuo Furuiye and Clarke M. Brandt, *I Am MIS* (1999); William Wei, *Asians in Colorado* (2016); Adam Schrager, *The Principled Politician* (2008); Gordon Prange, *At Dawn We Slept* (1981).

THREE: "WHERE IS PEARL HARBOR?"

Calvin Ninomiya, *Patriots/2* (2012); Grant Hirabayashi interviewed by Tom Ikeda, Densho Virtual History Collection (2006); Grant Hirabayashi, MIS Oral History (1997); Grant Hirabayashi, Hanashi Oral History (1999); Grant Hirabayashi interviewed by gayle k. yamada (2000); Grant Hirabayashi interviewed by John de Chadenedes (2008); Grant Hirabayashi interviewed by Terry Shima, Veterans History Project (2005); Grant Hirabayashi, Merrill's Marauders Association speech (2001); Stan Flewelling, *Shirakawa* (2002); James A. Hirabayashi, "Four Hirabayashi Cousins," *Nikkei in the Northwest* (2005); Gordon K. Hirabayashi, *A Principled Stand* (2013); Gary Iwamoto, "Rise & Fall of an Empire Furuya," *International Examiner* (August 29, 2005); Hugh Byas, *Government by Assassination* (1942); Eugene Soviak, ed., *A Diary of Darkness* (1980); Daniel B. Moskowitz, "Jeanette Rankin: The Congresswoman Who Voted NO to WWII," *World War II* magazine (2016).

FOUR: EXECUTIVE ORDER 9066

Karen Matsumoto interviewed by author (2018); *Honor & Sacrifice: The Roy Matsumoto Story*, a documentary film produced by Stourwater Pictures (2013); Roy Matsumoto, NJAHS Oral History (1996); Roy Matsumoto interviewed by gayle k. yamada (2000); Roy Matsumoto interviewed by Craig Yahata, Hanashi Oral History (2001); Roy Matsumoto interviewed by Alice Ito and Tom Ikeda, Densho Virtual History Collection (2003); Roy Matsumoto interviewed by Terry Shima, Library of Congress Veterans History Project (2005); Roy Matsumoto interviewed by John de Chadenedes (2008); Roy Matsumoto interviewed by Tom Ikeda (2008); Peter Irons, *Justice at War* (1983); Maisie and Richard Conrat, *Executive Order 9066* (1992); Commission on Wartime Relocation and Internment of Civilians, *Personal Justice Denied*

(1997); John Hersey, "Behind Barbed Wire," *New York Times* (September 11, 1988); Roger Daniels, *Concentration Camps USA* (1971); George Takei, *To the Stars* (1994); C. Calvin Smith, "The Response of Arkansans to Prisoners of War and Japanese Americans in Arkansas 1942–1945," *Arkansas Historical Quarterly* (1994); Russell Bearden, "Life Inside Arkansas' Japanese-American Relocation Centers" (1989) and "The False Rumor of Tuesday: Arkansas' Internment of Japanese-Americans" (1982); "Army Empowered to Move Persons From Military Areas," Palladium-Item, Richmond, IN, February 21, 1942; Henry McLemore, "This Is War! Stop Worrying About Hurting Jap Feelings," *Seattle Times*, January 30, 1942; Walter Lippmann, "The Fifth Column on the Coast," *New York Tribune*, February 12, 1942; Anthony L. Lehman, *Birthright of Barbed Wire* (1970).

FIVE: ROPE IN THE OPEN SEA

Takejiro Higa interviewed by James McNaughton (1994); Takejiro Higa, Hanashi Oral History (1999); Takejiro Higa interviewed by Warren Nichimoto and Michi Kodama-Nishimoto (2005); Takejiro Higa interviewed by gayle k. yamada (2000); Takejiro Higa interviewed by Gena Hamamoto (2006); Takejiro Higa, "Takejiro Higa," *The Hawai'i Nisei Story* (2005); Hawaii Nikkei History Editorial Board, "Takejiro Higa," *Japanese Eyes, American Heart* (1998); Clarence W. Hall, "The Missionary Whom No One Remembers," *Young Ladies' Journal* (Summer 2012); Ted T. Tsukiyama, "Nisei Military Experience During World War II," in *Remembering the Pacific War*, edited by Geoffrey M. White (1991); Henry L. Stimson letter to John W. McCormack (July 8, 1942); Wallace Carroll, "Some of Japanese Fliers Shot Down at Hawaii Wore Ring of Honolulu High Schools and Oregon State," United Press (December 30, 1941); "Myths and Facts About the Japanese Americans," Department of the Interior (April 1945).

SIX: CAMP SAVAGE

John Weckerling, "Confusing Early Days," in *Japanese Americans Play Vital Role in U.S. Intelligence Service* (1946); John Weckerling, "Nisei in War: A Treatise Prepared by Brigadier General John Weckerling" (1948); John Weckerling letter to Lt. Col. C. C. Dusenbury, December 31, 1941; "Japanese Language School," Memorandum for the Chief of Staff (April 3, 1942); "Publicity Regarding Intelligence," Confidential Memorandum, Adjutant General's Office (August 14, 1943); Thomas Sakamoto, Hanashi Oral History (2001); Thomas Sakamoto interviewed by gayle k. yamada (2001, 2007); Thomas Sakamoto interviewed by author (2018); Thomas Sakamoto, biographical statement (undated); Paul S. Sakamoto, REgenerations Oral History (1998);

Col. Kai Rasmussen, "History and Description of the Military Intelligence Service Language School" (1944); Yuki Kikuchi, "The Pacific War of the Nisei in Hawaii" (1995); Kan Tagami, Japanese Cultural Center of Hawaii Oral History (1994); Kan Tagami interviewed by James McNaughton (1994); Kan Tagami, Hanashi Oral History (1984, 1999); Kan Tagami interviewed by gayle k. yamada (2000, 2001); Andrew T. McDonald and Verlaine Stoner McDonald, *Paul Rusch in Postwar Japan* (2018); James C. McNaughton, *Nisei Linguists* (2006); Tad Ichinokuchi, *John Aiso and the M.I.S.* (1988); Donald M. Richardson, "Random Recollections" (1991); Kelli Y. Nakamura, "They Are Our Human Secret Weapons," *Historian* (Spring 2008); Irwin and Carole Slesnick, *Kanji & Codes* (2006); Kazuo Komoto, Hanashi Oral History (2005); Kazuo Komoto interviewed by gayle k. yamada (2000); Kazuo Komoto, NJAHS Oral History (1996); Kazuo Komoto interviewed by author (2018).

SEVEN: SOLOMON ISLANDS

Kazuo Komoto interviewed by author (2018); Kiyoshi Komoto interviewed by author (2019); Kazuo Komoto, NJAHS Oral History (1996); Kazuo Komoto, Hanashi Oral History (2005); Kazuo Komoto interviewed by gayle k. yamada (2000); James C. McNaughton, *Nisei Linguists* (2006); Donald Keene, *On Familiar Terms* (1994); "Japanese Tells of Pacific War at Rivers [Gila River] Camp," *Baltimore Sun* (November 20, 1943); John Miller Jr., *United States Army in World War II* (1959); John J. Higgins, *A History of the First Connecticut Regiment* (1963); Joseph Zimmer, *The History of the 43rd Infantry Division 1941–1945* (2012); Samuel Eliot Morison, *Breaking the Bismarcks Barrier* (2001); Robert J. Conrad, "Battle Experience Filled With Confusion," *Hartford Courant* (July 26, 1993); Stephen J. Lofgren, *Northern Solomons: The U.S. Army Campaigns of World War II* (2015); Joseph P. Lash, *Eleanor and Franklin* (1971); J. William T. Youngs, *Eleanor Roosevelt* (1985); William F. Halsey and J. Bryan III, *Admiral Halsey's Story* (1947); Audrie Girdner and Anne Loftis, *The Great Betrayal* (1969); "An American Is Honored: Soldier Gets Purple Heart," *Arizona Republic* (November 11, 1943).

EIGHT: NORTH TO ALASKA

Nobuo Furuiye, Hanashi Oral History (2000); Nobuo Furuiye, NJAHS Oral History (1996); Nobuo Furuiye and Clarke M. Brandt, *I Am MIS* (1999); "Summary of Student Personnel 1941–1946," MISLS Training History (1946); Samuel Eliot Morison, *Aleutians, Gilberts and Marshalls* (2001); Samuel Eliot Morison, *The Struggle for Guadalcanal* (2001); "Short History of the Battle of Attu," Intelligence and Operations Sections, Camp Earle (1945); Del C. Kostka, "Operation Cottage: A Cautionary Tale of Assumption and Perceptual Bias," *Joint Force Quarterly* 76 (1st quarter 2015); Galen Roger Perras, *Stepping Stones to Nowhere* (2003); Brian Garfield, *The Thousand-Mile War* (1969).

NINE: THE COUSINS

Grant Hirabayashi: Hirabayashi interviewed by Tom Ikeda, Densho Virtual History Collection (2006); Hirabayashi, MIS Oral History (1997); Hirabayashi, Hanashi Oral History (1999); Hirabayashi interviewed by gayle k. yamada (2000); Hirabayashi interviewed by John de Chadenedes (2008); Hirabayashi interviewed by Terry Shima, Veterans History Project (2005); Calvin Ninomiya, *Patriots/2* (2012); Hirabayashi, Merrill's Marauders Association speech (2001); Jeffery F. Burton, Mary M. Farrell, Florence B. Lord, and Richard W. Lord, *Confinement and Ethnicity* (1999); Harold Stanley Jacoby, *Tule Lake* (1996).

Gordon Hirabayashi: Hirabayashi interviewed by James Hirabayashi (1983); Hirabayashi interviewed by Becky Fukuda and Tom Ikeda (1999); Hirabayashi interviewed by Tom Ikeda (2000); Hirabayashi interviewed by Tom Ikeda and Alice Ito (2000); *A Personal Matter:* Gordon Hirabayashi vs. The United States, a film directed by John de Graaf (1992); James Hirabayashi, "Four Hirabayashi Cousins," *Nikkei in the Northwest* (2005); Gordon K. Hirabayashi, *A Principled Stand* (2013); "High Court Upholds Evacuation of Japs," *Santa Rosa* (CA) *Press Democrat* (June 22, 1943); "West Coast Jap Curfew Held Legal By Supreme Court," *San Francisco* (CA) *Examiner* (June 22, 1943); "Army Safety Regulations, Challenge by Japanese, Upheld by U.S. Supreme Court," *Oakland* (CA) *Tribune* (June 22, 1943); U.S. Supreme Court, *Koyoshi Hirabayashi v. United States* (June 21, 1943); Ed Cray, *Chief Justice* (1997).

TEN: A HAZARDOUS MISSION

Roy Matsumoto interviewed by Alice Ito and Tom Ikeda, Densho Digital Archive (2003); Roy Matsumoto interviewed by Tom Ikeda (2008); Roy Matsumoto, NJAHS Oral History (1996); Roy Matsumoto interviewed by gayle k. yamada (2000); Roy Matsumoto interviewed by Craig Yahata, Hanashi Oral History (2001); Roy Matsumoto interviewed by Alice Ito and Tom Ikeda, Densho Virtual History Collection (2003); Roy Matsumoto interviewed by Terry Shima, Library of Congress Veterans History Project (2005); Roy Matsumoto interviewed by John de Chadenedes (2008); Akiji Yoshimura, "14 Nisei and the Marauders: Saga of the Merrill's Marauders," *Pacific Sun Holiday Issue* (1959); Thomas Tsubota, "Thomas Tsubota" (1993); Barbara W. Tuchman, *Stilwell and the American Experience in China 1911–1945* (1970); Lyn Crost, *Honor by Fire* (1994); Richard Reeves, *Infamy* (2015); Col. Francis G. Brink, "Summary of Organization and Training of the 5307th Composite Unit

(Provisional)," Fort Benning, GA (April 4, 1944); Col. Charles N. Hunter, "Report of Overseas Observations," Fort Benning, GA (February 17, 1945); Capt. John M. Jones, *The War Diary of the 5307 Composite Unit (Provisional)* (2012); Col. Charles Newton Hunter, *Galahad* (1963); Charlton Ogburn Jr., *The Marauders* (1956); Lt. Col. Henry L. Kinnison, "The Deeds of Valiant Men: A Study in Leadership; the Marauders in North Burma, 1944" (1993); Gerald Astor, *The Jungle War* (2004); John K. Emmerson, *The Japanese Thread* (1978); Fred O. Lyons, "Merrill's Marauders in Burma: Here's What Really Happened" (1969); *Merrill's Marauders: February–May 1944* (1945); Donovan Webster, *The Burma Road* (2003); Edward Young, *Merrill's Marauders* (2009).

ELEVEN: MERRILL'S MARAUDERS

Roy Matsumoto: Capt. John M. Jones, *The War Diary of the 5307 Composite Unit (Provisional)* (2012); Donovan Webster, *The Burma Road* (2003); *Merrill's Marauders: February–May 1944* (1945); Matsumoto, NJAHS Oral History (1996); Matsumoto interviewed by gayle k. yamada (2000); Matsumoto interviewed by Tom Ikeda (2008); Matsumoto interviewed by Craig Yahata, Hanashi Oral History (2001); Henry L. Kinnison IV, "The Deeds of Valiant Men" (1993); Charlton Ogburn Jr., *The Marauders* (1956); Barbara Tuchman, *Stilwell and the American Experience in China 1911–1945* (1970); Lyn Crost, *Honor by Fire* (1994); Ronald H. Spector, *Eagle Against the Sun* (1985); Matsumoto interviewed by John de Chadenedes (2008); Edward A. McLogan letter to U.S. Army Intelligence Center (June 17, 1996); Gavin Mortimer, *Merrill's Marauders* (2015).

Grant Hirabayashi: Capt. John M. Jones, *The War Diary of the 5307 Composite Unit (Provisional)* (2012); *Merrill's Marauders: February–May 1944* (1945); Hirabayashi interviewed by Craig Yahata, Hanashi Oral History (1999); Hirabayashi interviewed by Tom Ikeda, Densho Virtual History Collection (2006); Hirabayashi interviewed by gayle k. yamada (2000); Hirabayashi interviewed by Dye Ogata, MIS Association, NorCal (1997); Henry L. Kinnison IV, "The Deeds of Valiant Men" (1993); Donovan Webster, *The Burma Road* (2003); Hirabayashi interviewed by Joseph Harrington (1977).

TWELVE: MYITKYINA

Grant Hirabayashi interviewed by Craig Yahata, Hanashi Oral History (1999); Grant Hirabayashi interviewed by Tom Ikeda, Densho Virtual History Collection (2006); Grant Hirabayashi interviewed by gayle k. yamada (2000); James H. Stone, *Crisis Fleeting*, "Marauders and Microbes" (1969); Edward Young, *Merrill's Marauders* (2009); Christopher Magoon, "The 20th General Hospital," *The Pharos* (Autumn 2016); Patrick K. O'Donnell, *Into the*

Rising Sun (2002); Grant Hirabayashi interviewed by Terry Shima, Veterans History Project (2005); Grant Hirabayashi interviewed by John de Chadenedes (2008); Calvin Ninomiya, *Patriots/2* (2012); Barbara Tuchman, *Stilwell and the American Experience in China 1911–1945* (1970); James E. T. Hopkins, *Spearhead* (1999); Joseph W. Stilwell, *The Stilwell Papers* (1948); Won-loy Chan, *Burma* (1986); John K. Emmerson, *The Japanese Thread* (1978); "Japanese Prisoner of War Interrogation Report No. 49," Psychological Warfare Team, India-Burma Theater (August 1945).

THIRTEEN: THE ADMIRALTIES

Thomas Sakamoto, biographical statement (1996); Thomas Sakamoto, biographical notes (undated); Thomas Sakamoto interviewed by gayle k. yamada (1999, 2001); Thomas Sakamoto, Hanashi Oral History (2001); Thomas Sakamoto, MIS Oral History (1989); Thomas Sakamoto, Go for Broke Oral History (2010); "Japanese Americans Who Fought Against Japan," NHK Documentary (2006); James C. McNaughton, *Nisei Linguists* (2006); David W. Swift Jr., *First Class* (2006); Joseph D. Harrington, *Yankee Samurai* (1979); Historical Division, War Department, *The Admiralties* (1990); Samuel Eliot Morison, *Breaking the Bismarcks Barrier* (2001); William C. Chase, *Front Line General* (1975); John Toland, *The Rising Sun* (1970); Thomas Sakamoto letters to Sadie Sakamoto (February 26, March 11, 1944); Leo P. Hirrel, "Bismarck Archipelago," *U.S. Army Campaigns of World War II* (1994); Bertram C. Wright, ed., *The 1st Cavalry Division in World War II* (1947); Edward G. Miller, "Action in the Admiralties" (Fall 2017); Gordon L. Rottman, *World War II Pacific Island Guide* (2002); Stephen Taaffe, *MacArthur's Jungle* (1998).

FOURTEEN: SULPHUR ISLAND

Nobuo Furuiye, Hanashi Oral History (2000); Nobuo Furuiye, NJAHS Oral History (1986); Nobuo Furuiye and Clarke M. Brandt, *I Am MIS* (1999); John C. Chapin, "The Fifth Marine Division in World War II," Historical Division, U.S. Marine Corps (August 1945); Gordon L. Rottman, *World War II Pacific Island Guide* (2002); James C. McNaughton, *Nisei Linguists* (2006); Donald Keene, *On Familiar Terms* (1994); Robert O'Neill, ed., *The Road to Victory* (2011); Dan King, *A Tomb Called Iwo Jima* (2020); Samuel Eliot Morison, *Victory in the Pacific 1945* (2001); Lee Mandel, *Unlikely Warrior* (2015); Joseph D. Harrington, *Yankee Samurai* (1979); Whitman S. Bartley, *Iwo Jima: Amphibious Epic* (1954); Bill D. Ross, *Iwo Jima* (1985); Alexander Astroth, *Mass Suicides on Saipan and Tinian, 1944* (2019); Howard M. Conner, *The Spearhead* (1950); Richard F. Newcomb, *Iwo Jima* (1983); Donald L. Miller, *D-Days in the Pacific* (2005); Fred Haynes and James A. Warren, *The Lions of Iwo Jima* (2008).

FIFTEEN: THE LAST INVASION

Takejiro Higa interviewed by James McNaughton (1994); Takejiro Higa, Hanashi Oral History (1999); Takejiro Higa interviewed by Warren Nichimoto and Michi Kodama-Nishimoto (2005); Takejiro Higa interviewed by gayle k. yamada (2000); Takejiro Higa intterviewed by Gena Hamamoto (2006); Takejiro Higa, "Takejiro Higa," *The Hawai'i Nisei Story* (2005); Herbert Kiyoto Yanamura Oral History Interview by Ted Tsukiyama (1998); Orlando Davidson, J. Carl Willems, and Joseph A. Kohl, *The Deadeyes* (1947); Samuel Eliot Morison, *Leyte, June 1944–January 1945* (2001); James C. McNaughton, *Nisei Linguists* (2006); David W. Swift Jr., *First Class* (2006); Bruce Henderson, *Rescue at Los Baños* (2015); Seiji Horie, *Aru Okinawa Hawai Imin no Shinjuwan* (1991); Samuel Eliot Morison, *Victory in the Pacific 1945* (2001); Hawaii Nikkei History Editorial Board, "Takejiro Higa," *Japanese Eyes, American Heart* (1998); Ian W. Toll, *Twilight of the Gods* (2020); Joseph D. Harrington, *Yankee Samurai* (1979); Ray E. Boomhower, *Dispatches from the Pacific* (2017); Mitsugu Sakihara, *Okinawan-English Wordbook* (2006); Clarence Glacken, *The Great Loochoo* (1955); Roy E. Appleman, James M. Burns, Russell A. Gugeler, and John Stevens. *Okinawa* (1948); Ted T. Tsukiyama, "The Battle of Okinawa Revisited"; Aniya Masaaki, "Compulsory Mass Suicides, the Battle of Okinawa, and Japan's Textbook Controversy" (2008); Tad Ichinokuchi, *John Aiso and the M.I.S.* (1988); Karleen Chinen, "Takejiro Higa: An Okinawan Caught in the Battle of Okinawa," *Hawaii Herald* (July 2, 1993).

SIXTEEN: CHINA

Roy Matsumoto: Matsumoto interviewed by Craig Yahata, Hanashi Oral History (2001); Matsumoto interviewed by Alice Ito and Tom Ikeda, Densho Virtual History Collection (2003); Matsumoto interviewed by Terry Shima, Library of Congress Veterans History Project (2005); Matsumoto interviewed by John de Chadenedes (2008); Matsumoto interviewed by Tom Ikeda (2008); Matsumoto, NJAHS Oral History (1996).

Grant Hirabayashi: Calvin Ninomiya, *Patriots/2* (2012); Hirabayashi interviewed by Joseph Harrington (1977); Harrington notes of Hirabayashi interview (1977); Hirabayashi interviewed by Tom Ikeda (2006); Hirabayashi interviewed by John de Chadenedes (2008); Hirabayashi interviewed by Dye Ogata (1997); Hirabayashi interviewed by Craig Yahata (1999); Hirabayashi interviewed by gayle k. yamada (2000); Deborah Shapley, "Nuclear Weapons History: Japan's Wartime Bomb Projects Revealed," *Science* (January 13, 1978); "Interrogation of Japanese Prisoners in the Southwest Pacific, Intelligence Memo No. 4" (November 10, 1943); John Hersey, *Hiroshima* (1985).

SEVENTEEN: RETURN TO JAPAN

Thomas Sakamoto: Sakamoto, biographical statement (undated); Sakamoto interviewed by gayle k. yamada (1999+, 2001); Sakamoto, video interview, National Japanese American Historical Society (1995); Sakamoto, Go for Broke Oral History (2010); Sakamoto, Hanashi Oral History (2001); Sakamoto interviewed by David W. Swift Jr., in *First Class* (2006); Thomas Sakamoto, "News of the Century: Japan's Surrender & Hiroshima," *Nikkei-Heritage: National Japanese American Historical Society* 7, no. 3 (11) (1995); Rinjiro Sodei, *Were We the Enemy?* (1998); "The United States Strategic Bombing Survey: The Effects of Atomic Bombs on Hiroshima and Nagasaki," U.S. Government Printing Office (June 30, 1946); Tom Sakamoto letters to Sadie Sakamoto (August 30 and 31, 1945).

Nobuo Furuiye: Furuiye, biographical statement (undated); Furuiye, Hanashi Oral History (2000); Furuiye, NJAHS Oral History (1986); Nobuo Furuiye and Charles M. Brandt, *I Am MIS* (1999).

EPILOGUE: OKINAWA, SPRING 1995

Takejiro Higa interviewed by Warren Nichimoto and Michi Kodama-Nishimoto (2005); Takejiro Higa interviewed by gayle k. yamada (2000); Takejiro Higa, Hanashi Oral History (1999); Takejiro Higa, "Takejiro Higa," *The Hawai'i Nisei Story* (2005); Hawaii Nikkei History Editorial Board, "Takejiro Higa," *Japanese Eyes, American Heart* (1998); Karleen Chinen, "The Battle of Okinawa: 50 Years Later," *Hawaii Herald* (August 8, 1995); George Lince, *Too Young the Heroes: A World War II Marine's Account of Facing a Veteran Enemy at Guadalcanal, the Solomons and Okinawa* (1997).

ROSTER OF NISEI VETERANS
OF THE PACIFIC

Abe, Akira
Abe, James Kiyoshi
Abe, Kiyoshi
Abe, Leonard Hubert
Abe, Masao
Abe, Roy Y.
Abe, Toshio William
Abe, Victor Hiroshi
Abe, Yoshii Jerry
Aburamen, Edward Hisao
Adachi, Isamu
Adachi, James Shogo
Adachi, Jiro
Adachi, Warren Genichi
Adaniya, Terry Hiroshi
Agari, Junsuke
Aiba, Kenichi Ken
Aiso, Daniel Iwao
Aiso, James Kazuo
Aiso, John Fujio
Ajari, Choji Phil
Ajimine, George Hideo
Aka, Yoshimori Roy
Akaba, George Yutaka
Akaba, Jimmie Fujio
Akagi, Hideo

Akahoshi, Ralph Kazuo
Akama, Karl Tooru
Akamine, Kisei Conrad
Akase, Matsuyoshi Ray
Akisada, Mark Mitsuhiko
Akitake, Harry Hiroyuki
Akitake, Haruo Harry
Akiyama, Joe S.
Akiyama, Joseph Stuart
Akiyama, Kenichi
Akiyama, Kenji
Akiyama, Saburo
Akiyoshi, Roy Hisashi
Akune, Harry Masami
Akune, Kenjiro
Amaki, Seichi Joe
Amano, Masao
Amemiya, Minoru
Amioka, Shiro
Amioka, Wallace Shuzo
Ando, Tomomi
Andow, Harry Katsuto
Aoi, Yoshio
Aoki, Barney Toshiharu
Aoki, George Masatomo
Aotaki, Masao

Aoyagi, Stanley Tadao
Aoyama, Shoji
Aoyama, Tsugio
Aragaki, Masatsugu Henry
Arai, Kazuyoshi
Arai, Ryo
Arakaki, Jiro
Arakaki, Takejiro Paul
Araki, Harry T.
Araki, James Jitsuo
Araki, James Takehiro
Araki, Masaichi Mac
Arase, Paul
Arashiro, Richard Kiyoshi
Arashiro, Yonemitsu
Arida, Edward S.
Arita, Harry S.
Arita, Katsuki
Arita, Ken
Ariyasu, George Joji
Ariyasu, Masaru Jim
Ariyoshi, Koji
Asada, Shiichi
Asahi, Kyosuke
Asai, George T.
Asai, Taro
Asakawa, Hisao
Asaki, Goro
Asakura, Meme
Asano, Fujio F.
Asano, Toshio Terry
Asano, Wakichi M.
Asari, Iwao
Asato, Seisuke
Ashida, Frank Fukumi
Ashida, Haruo James
Ashikawa, James K.
Ashizawa, Roy Yoshio
Awane, Shiro
Ayabe, Yukio

Azuma, James H.
Azuma, Mike Masahiro
Baba, George Shiro
Baba, Kay Katsumi
Baba, Kenjiro
Baba, Mitsuru
Baba, Sadao
Baba, Soshiro Paul
Baba, Takashi Thomas
Ban, Robert Y.
Ban, Takeo
Bannai, Paul Takeo
Bessho, Asa Masao
Betsui, Richard Kiyoge
Budo, Yoshiro
Buto, Junichi
Butow, Robert J. C.
Butsuda, Yoshinori Clinton
Chena, Teiho Walter
Chihara, Joseph
Chihara, Toshio
Chikamura, Kaiji
Chinen, Hideo
Chisaki, Shunichi
Dairiki, Sadao
Daty, Henry Isamu
Deguchi, Masato
Deguchi, Seiichi
Dobana, Masaru
Doi, Asao
Doi, Carl Kaoru
Doi, Isao James
Doi, Mamoru
Doi, Terry Takeshi
Doi, Thomas Yoshi
Doike, Charles H.
Doizaki, William Masashi
Doue, Masao Stephen
Ebato, Larry Koichi
Ebesugawa, Yukio

Ebisuzaki, Taichi M.
Egami, George T.
Ego, Kisou
Eguchi, Eugene Minoru
Eijima, Warren
Endo, Herbert Yoshitada
Endo, Kunio
Endo, Roy R.
Endo, Tamotsu
Endow, Issac K.
Endow, Minoru
Endow, Noboru
Eno, Takao
Enomoto, Gulstan
Eto, Hiroshi
Eto, Joseph
Figundio, Elia M.
Fuchiwaki, Hiroaki Hilo
Fudenna, Harold Tarno
Fugami, Roy S.
Fujihara, George T.
Fujihara, Masaaki Paul
Fujii, Fred Yukio
Fujii, Keiji
Fujii, Masuto
Fujii, Paul Shinobu
Fujii, Tatsuo Ray
Fujii, Tsuyoshi Jim
Fujii, William Sueto
Fujikado, Kei
Fujikado, Yutaka Murphy
Fujikawa, Albert Hideo
Fujikawa, Masashi George
Fujikawa, Misuo John
Fujikawa, Nobuo
Fujikawa, Nobuyuki
Fujikawa, Toraki
Fujimori, Edward Matao
Fujimori, George Yoshio
Fujimori, Tokio

Fujimoto, Eddie N.
Fujimoto, Edwin Norio
Fujimoto, Fred T.
Fujimoto, George Jr.
Fujimoto, Harley T.
Fujimoto, Henry
Fujimoto, Isao
Fujimoto, John Nanahiko
Fujimoto, Kameso
Fujimoto, Masami
Fujimoto, Masao B.
Fujimoto, Ray
Fujimoto, Sachio R
Fujimoto, Thomas A.
Fujimoto, Tom Yukitake
Fujimoto, Yoshito
Fujimura, Henry A.
Fujimura, James Takao
Fujimura, Kiyoshi
Fujimura, Kunio
Fujimura, Susumu
Fujimura, Takuji
Fujinami, Masayo
Fujinami, Mitsuru
Fujino, Joe Yuzuru
Fujino, Russell Takeo
Fujio, Raymond Takamichi
Fujioka, Haruyuki
Fujioka, Hideo
Fujioka, Mamoru
Fujisaka, Takeshi
Fujise, George
Fujishima, Shoji
Fujita, David U.
Fujita, Joe
Fujita, Kazuma
Fujita, Kiyoshi
Fujita, Riyoichi
Fujita, Samuel I. J.
Fujita, Teruo

Fujita, William Kaoru
Fujita, Yasuhiro
Fujitani, George Yoshikazu
Fujitani, Tom Isamu
Fujitani, Yoshiaki
Fujiyama, Utaka
Fujiye, Kaneo
Fukada, Edward Masaichi
Fukada, Joseph
Fukai, Ace Yasuo
Fukano, Taneo Fred
Fukawa, Koji F.
Fukayama, Harry
Fukiage, Harry Shigeichi
Fukuba, Shuji
Fukuda, Kozo
Fukuda, Robert Kiyoshi
Fukuhara, Francis
Fukuhara, Frank Masakatsu
Fukuhara, George Yoshinori
Fukuhara, Harry Katsuhara
Fukuhara, Jimmy Kow
Fukuhara, Terasu
Fukui, Edwin Yukio
Fukui, Ralph Hisaichi
Fukui, Soichi
Fukui, Yoneichi
Fukuma, Mamoru Harold
Fukumitsu, Gilbert Takeo
Fukumoto, Masashi
Fukunaga, Jack Yujiro
Fukunaga, Masao
Fukunaga, Toshio Ken
Fukunaga, Yoshio
Fukushima, Fred M.
Fukushima, Jun

Fukushima, Masuo
Fukushima, Paul S.
Fukushima, Samuel J.
Fukushima, T.
Fukutaki, William Kaoru
Fukuyama, Hiroo
Fukuyama, Shigeo
Funabiki, Mason
Funabiki, Walter
Funada, George Shohei
Funamura, Isamu S.
Furuhashi, Shizuye Betsey (WAC)*
Furuiye, Nobuo
Furukawa, James Tsugio
Furukawa, Richard Isao
Furuki, Minoru
Furumoto, Howard Hoosaku
Furuno, George T.
Furuno, Kosaku
Furushima, Harry Haruo
Furusho, Don Yasusuke
Furusho, Toshio Marvin
Furuta, William H.
Furutani, Yaye (WAC)
Fusco, Edward T.
Futamase, Keiji
Gima, Shinyei
Gima, Warren S.
Goda, George Hagemu
Goi, George K.
Goi, Shoji K.
Goka, Kenneth Kenichi
Gorai, Arthur Seichiro
Goshikoma, Ralph Masoe
Gosho, Henry Hiroharu
Gotanda, Yukio

* The Women's Army Corps (WAC) was the women's branch of the U.S. Army in World War II. By the time the war ended, nearly five hundred Japanese American women had served as WACs or Army Nurses.

Goto, Hiroshi Norman
Goto, Susumu Paul
Goto, Takashi
Goto, Thomas Shinjiro
Goto, William Y.
Goya, K.
Goya, Yeijin
Gozawa, Jimmy Sadakazu
Gushiken, Koko
Hachiya, Frank Tadakazu
Hada, Howard Masao
Hada, Marjorie Yukue (WAC)
Hadomoto, Tom
Haga, Thomas Haruo
Hagihara, Grayson Hihuo
Hagino, Masao
Hagiya, Moses
Hagiya, Stanley Nato
Hakoda, Mamoru
Hamada, Dick Shigemi
Hamada, Kazuo
Hamada, Minoru
Hamada, Nobuo
Hamada, Thomas Tamotsu
Hamaguchi, Herbert Hiroshi
Hamai, Isamu
Hamaishi, Clarence J.
Hamakawa, Edward Shigeo
Hamamoto, Hakumasa
Hamamoto, Takumi
Hamamoto, Tatsuo
Hamamoto, Tsugio Robert
Hamanaka, Joseph Ushio
Hamanaka, Kozo G.
Hamane, Tadashi
Hamanishi, Willie Joe
Hamano, Shunji George
Hamasaka, Bunji
Hamasaki, Charles Hideyoshi
Hamasaki, James Yukio

Hamashige, Kintaro
Hamashita, Joe
Hanada, Katsumi
Hanafusa, George Yoshiki
Hanami, Yutaka Doug
Hanamoto, Asa
Hanamura, George Ritsuo
Hanano, Tsutomu
Hanaumi, Harold Hiroshi
Handa, Katsunori
Hanzawa, Fred Gisuke
Hara, Akira W.
Hara, Ben Kayji
Hara, Don M.
Hara, Frank S.
Hara, George F.
Hara, James S.
Hara, Minoru
Hara, Philip Toshio
Hara, Shigeru George
Harada, Clyde Takeo
Harada, George K.
Harada, George S.
Harada, Hisayoshi
Harada, Joe Leo
Harada, John H.
Harada, Kazumi
Harada, Michael F. M.
Harada, Masaru
Harada, Tomio
Harada, Tsuneo P.
Haramoto, Frank Hiroshi
Harano, Samuel Takashi
Haruki, James Tatsuo
Harunaga, Toshio Esq.
Haruta, Naoya Buster
Hasama, Isao
Hasegawa, Hideshiro
Hasegawa, Saburo
Hasegawa, Susumu

Hasegawa, Toru Tom
Hasegawa, Yutaka
Hashiguchi, Iwao
Hashimoto, Albert K.
Hashimoto, Herbert Kiyokazu
Hashimoto, Joichi
Hashimoto, Katsuki
Hashimoto, Masayuki
Hashimoto, Tadashi
Hashimoto, Ted Sakio
Hashimoto, Toshio
Hashimoto, Utaka
Hashisaka, Yukio Norman
Hashisaki, Joseph
Hashiwase, Ernest
Hashizume, Shiuchi
Hashizume, Shoichi
Hata, George Y.
Hata, Michael Mitsuru
Hata, Richard Yoshihiro
Hata, Seiji William
Hata, Yoshimi George
Hatada, Haruo Harry
Hatakeda, Itsuyoshi George
Hatakeda, Kazuo Charles
Hatakeyama, Coontz
Hatakeyama, Tsukasa
Hatashita, Kimio
Hattori, Eugene Hiroshi
Hattori, Harold M.
Hattori, Roy Nobuyoshi
Hattori, Yutaka
Hayakawa, George
Hayakawa, Tatsuo George
Hayakawa, Toshio H.
Hayami, Paul M.
Hayase, Robert Tsutomu
Hayashi, Akio
Hayashi, Albert M.
Hayashi, George

Hayashi, Gilbert Shigeo
Hayashi, Hajime
Hayashi, Harold Oliver
Hayashi, Harold Toshito
Hayashi, Hideo W.
Hayashi, Joe L.
Hayashi, Kazuma
Hayashi, Kazuo G.
Hayashi, Paul Yoshio
Hayashi, Richard Akira
Hayashi, Richard Kaoru
Hayashi, Sakaye
Hayashi, Shigeo
Hayashi, Utaka
Hayashi, William Masaru
Hayashi, Yoshimi
Hayashi, Yukio
Hayashida, George T.
Hayashida, Tetsuo
Hayashida, Yoshihiko
Hayataka, Masato
Hazama, John Yoneharu
Hazard, Benjamin H. Jr.
Hedani, Aeji
Hidaka, Susumi
Hieshima, Asaichi Shimidzu
Higa, Genchu Ralph
Higa, Kase
Higa, Leslie Hideyasu
Higa, Takejiro
Higa, Ted Mankichi
Higa, Thomas Shoshin
Higa, Warren Takemitsu
Higashi, George
Higashi, Harry Haruyoshi
Higashi, Kiyoshi
Higashi, Riyosaku
Higashi, Roy Masami
Higashi, Seiyu
Higashi, Shigeru

Higashi, Yoshikazu
Higashi, Yumiji Jim
Higashimura, Clifford Yoshio
Higashino, Edwin Takashi
Higashiyama, Tom
Higuchi, Eddie Sumio
Higuchi, Joe
Higurashi, Isamu S.
Hikawa, Richard Kazuyuki
Hikida, Henry T.
Hikida, Kazuo
Hikida, Tatsuo
Hikido, George Kensi
Hino, Hisashi
Hino, Kenji
Hino, Kenneth Shunma
Hinoki, Koe
Hirabayashi, Grant Jiro
Hirabayashi, Hirome H.
Hirabayashi, Takeo
Hirabayashi, Yoshiki
Hiraga, Keiji John
Hiraga, Tom Tanio
Hirahara, Tom Takeo
Hirai, Edwall S.
Hirai, George E.
Hirai, Hijiri Jerry
Hirai, Toshiyuki
Hirai, Wallace Satoru
Hiraide, Shori
Hirakawa, Frank T.
Hirakawa, Harriet Hisako (WAC)
Hirakawa, Henry Yoshio
Hiramatsu, Roy Y.
Hiranaga, Takao
Hiranaka, Robert A.
Hirano, Ben Mitsugi
Hirano, Frederick M.
Hirano, Henry Kiyoto
Hirano, Hiroshi Ben

Hirano, Hiroshi H.
Hirano, Kenneth
Hirano, Kiyoshi
Hirano, Kiyoshi Mike
Hirano, Phillip Teruichi
Hirano, Takeshi Angel
Hirano, Yutaka
Hiraoka, Masumi
Hiraoka, William Tsugio
Hirashima, Frank Fujio
Hirashima, William T.
Hirata, Clinton L.
Hirata, Hiroki
Hirata, Kentaro
Hirata, Masao
Hirata, Richard Yoshito
Hirata, Takegi Roy
Hirata, Teichiro
Hirata, Yuichi
Hiratani, Isao
Hiratsuka, Jordan F.
Hirayama, Taiji
Hiroki, Howard Katsuji
Hiromoto, Edward Shigeo
Hiromoto, Harry Yasuo
Hiromura, Yuji
Hironaka, Kisao H.
Hironaka, David T.
Hirooka, George Juichiro
Hirose, Jack Masatsugu
Hirose, Teruo
Hirose, Wataru
Hirose, William Eishi
Hirose, Yukio
Hiroshige, Naotaka Roy
Hiroshima, Arthur Toyoki
Hirota, Clinton L.
Hirota, Shinichi James
Hirota, Tadashi T.
Hirotsu, Roy Yutaka

Hisaka, Masakatsu
Hisaoka, Kiyoto George
Hisatake, Arthur Koji
Hiuga, Hiroyuki Harold
Hiura, Thomas M.
Hojo, Shizuo Kelly
Hokada, Garret Susumu
Hokama, Seian
Hokoda, Masato
Honda, Ben Tomaru
Honda, George Minoru
Honda, Hideo
Honda, Hiroshi George
Honda, Masami
Honda, Patrick Kunio
Honda, Robert Tatsuo
Honda, Robert Yoshiharu
Honda, Roy Matetsu
Honda, Sadao
Honda, Toshio
Honda, Tsutomu
Hongo, Shigeru
Honjiyo, John S.
Honke, Robert Katsuto
Honma, Richard Satoshi
Hori, Akira
Hori, Fukashi
Hori, Tsurumatsu
Horiba, Tsutomu
Horie, George
Horikiri, Takayuki
Horita, Hisashi
Horita, Tadashi
Horita, Tomio
Horiuchi, Masaru
Horiuchi, Nozomi Russell
Horiuchi, Seiji
Hoshide, Hideo
Hoshide, Yoshio
Hoshii, Henry N.

Hoshijo, Yasukichi Francis
Hoshimiya, David N.
Hoshiyama, John S.
Hosoda, Leo H.
Hosokawa, Hiroaki
Hosokawa, Kiyoshi
Hosokawa, Takayuki
Hotta, Yoshio
Hozaki, James Mitsuo
Iba, Shigeru
Ibara, Kazuo
Ichikawa, Benjamin K.
Ichikawa, George Torao
Ichikawa, Grant Hayao
Ichikawa, Joe Iwao
Ichikawa, Karl K.
Ichikawa, Roy
Ichikawa, Seiichi
Ichikawa, Tomio
Ichikawa, Toshio Stanley
Ichimura, Richard Takaichi
Ichimura, Toichi Thomas
Ichinokuchi, Tadao
Ichinose, Minoru George
Ichiriu, Edwin T.
Ichiriu, Kazuo George
Ichisaka, Mitsuo
Ichiyasu, Ben M.
Ichiyasu, Haruo V.
Ida, James Nubuo
Ida, Roy Masaaki
Idouchi, Kenneth Iwamatsu
Ieiri, Tetsuo
Igarashi, Goro
Igarashi, Lawrence Masao
Igata, Tadashi
Ige, Thomas H.
Iguchi, John
Iguchi, Tatsuo
Ihara, Hideo

Ihara, Toshiro A.
Iida, Andrew Y.
Iida, Harry Shinichi
Iijima, Iwao
Iinuma, Kaoru James
Iinuma, Satoru
Ikebe, Alata
Ikeda, Atsushi
Ikeda, Bennett Morio
Ikeda, Chiyoki
Ikeda, Frank Y.
Ikeda, George Tsuyoshi
Ikeda, Richard S.
Ikeda, Seito
Ikeda, Torao
Ikeda, Toshio
Ikeda, William Takaomi
Ikegami, Edward Katsuzo
Ikeguchi, Joseph
Ikehara, Yurikichi
Ikemoto, Haruyuki
Ikemoto, Masayuki
Ikemoto, Richard Kanji
Ikemoto, Ted Tsuyoshi
Ikemura, Tsutomu Harold
Ikeuchi, Kiyomi
Ikezawa, Michael Akira
Iko, Keiji K.
Ikuta, Joe Hisao
Imada, Shigemitsu
Imada, Tadashi William
Imada, Thomas Tsutomu
Imai, Akira B.
Imai, Charles Takeo
Imai, Hideo
Imai, Keiichiro
Imai, Richard K.
Imamura, Niso
Imamura, Shigeo
Imano, Susumu

Imaoka, Hichiro Raymond
Imazumi, Kanae K.
Imazumi, Shigetoshi R.
Imon, Frank Masao
Imori, Thomas T.
Imoto, William Shunichi
Imura, Takuo
Inaba, Futoshi
Inaba, Masaharu G.
Inaba, Mitsugi
Inada, Masao T.
Inafuku, Joseph
Inagaki, George Joji
Inamasu, Shigeru
Inashima, Minoru
Inashima, Osamu James
Inazaki, Tsugio
Inoshita, Masaji
Inouye, Charles S.
Inouye, Chikateru
Inouye, Harry Sakae
Inouye, Harry Takeshi
Inouye, Hiroshi Roy
Inouye, I.
Inouye Jack S.
Inouye, Kazuo
Inouye, Kazuyoshi
Inouye, Kiyoharu Reo
Inouye, Koichi David
Inouye, Masato
Inouye, Midori Milton
Inouye, Rikuo
Inouye, Saburo
Inouye, Satoru
Inouye, Tadao Eugene
Inouye, Theodore Tokuo
Inouye, Thomas Masaichi
Inouye, Toshio
Inouye, Tsutomu H.
Inouye, Wataru Walter

Inouye, Yoshiharu
Inouye, Yoshito Stanley
Inui, Hiroshi Roy
Irikura, James K.
Irinaga, Fred Mitsuharu
Iritani, Frances F.
Iritani, Frank Misao
Isa, Tooru Warren
Ishibashi, Kiyoshi
Ishida, Frank Kazuo
Ishida, Henry
Ishida, Hisao
Ishida, Masaru
Ishida, Nobushi Tom
Ishida, Theodore Joseph
Ishida, Toshio
Ishida, William Tsuyoshi
Ishida, Yoshio
Ishigami, Isao
Ishihara, Henry N.
Ishihara, James H.
Ishihara, Sakae
Ishii, Chris Kishio
Ishii, George T.
Ishii, Jack D.
Ishii, Mamoru
Ishii, Masayuki
Ishii, Shoji
Ishii, Sueo
Ishii, Togo Jack
Ishii, Tom Tomokichi
Ishikawa, Alvin Kiyohide
Ishikawa, Etsuzo
Ishikawa, George Y.
Ishikawa, Hidekazu Michael
Ishikawa, Masao Barrett
Ishikawa, Mitsuo Moffet
Ishikawa, Thomas M.
Ishima, Yasuto
Ishimaru, Tokuo Jim

Ishimoto, Arthur U.
Ishimoto, John
Ishimoto, Richard Tsutomu
Ishimoto, Shoichi
Ishio, Sunao Phil
Ishioka, Yutaka Ben
Ishisaka, Ted Minoru
Ishiyama, Sasuke
Ishizaki, Tadayuki
Iso, Yutaka James
Isokane, Setsuo Sam
Isomoto, Seiji
Isono, Masami
Itami, David Akira
Itan, Hajime
Itaya, Samuel Sumiharu
Ito, Arthur Tadashi
Ito, Donald Kanichi
Ito, Fred Yoshiaki
Ito, George Takashi
Ito, Harold K.
Ito, Harry Jiro
Ito, Hiroshi James
Ito, Ichiro
Ito, Isamu
Ito, Jack J.
Ito, James Osamu
Ito, Joji
Ito, Kiyoshi
Ito, Setsuo Stanley
Ito, Shigeo
Ito, Shigeto
Ito, Sueo
Ito, Tadao
Ito, Toshihiko
Ito, Yoichi Stanley
Itow, Hiroshi
Iwafuchi, Kingo K.
Iwafuchi, Kiyoshi R.
Iwahashi, Kazuo

Iwahashi, Paul Kazumi
Iwahashi, Shigenuki
Iwahashi, Tom Kiyoshi
Iwai, Donald Koso
Iwai, Gero
Iwai, Yoshiro J.
Iwakiri, Ben Tsutomu
Iwakiri, George K.
Iwamoto, Masato
Iwamoto, Nobuo
Iwamoto, Yoshito
Iwamura, James K.
Iwamura, Jimmy T.
Iwamuro, Arata Wallace
Iwana, Henry Nobukazu
Iwanaga, James Y.
Iwanaga, Kazuto
Iwanaga, Roy T.
Iwanaga, Sam S.
Iwasaki, Noriyuki
Iwasaki, Shogo
Iwashita, Kaoru C.
Iwata, Kay
Iwataki, Hideo Joseph
Iwatsubo, James Masutaro
Izu, Daniel Tadashi
Izumi, James Kiyoto
Izumi, Yutaka
Izumo, Hideo
Izumoto, Charles Kiyoharu
Jeniye, Esone Richard
Jinbo, James Masaru
Jinbo, Nobuto
Jio, Masateru
Joichi, Max S.
Kadani, Gary Tsuneo
Kadomoto, Thomas Soichi
Kadonaga, Satoshi Roland
Kadoyama, George Nobuharu
Kadoyama, Joe Yazuru

Kagawa, Kiyoshi D.
Kagawa, Masayuki Charles
Kai, James Tsutomu
Kaihatsu, Arthur Shigeki
Kaito, Frank M.
Kaizawa, Stanley Yoshinori
Kajihara, Hiroshi Roy
Kajihara, Takashi
Kajikami, Kenzo J.
Kajikawa, Masao R.
Kajikawa, Richard Tsutomu
Kajioka, Hiroshi Fred
Kakehashi, George Hiroto
Kakehashi, Hideo
Kakemoto, Satoru
Kako, George
Kakuuchi, Yuji August
Kameda, Robert K.
Kamei, Eiji
Kamei, Toshio
Kami, Frank Keijiro
Kami, Nagatoshi
Kamidoi, T.
Kamikawa, Yoichi
Kaminishi, James Hiroshi
Kamishita, Tsuyoshi
Kamitsuka, Joseph H.
Kamiya, Rodney Isamu
Kamiya, Smile
Kamoto, Harold Kazuo
Kan, Sidney T.
Kan, Wong Y.
Kanagaki, Hiroshi
Kanagaki, Kay
Kanazawa, James Einobe
Kanazawa, Kanemi
Kanazawa, Ryoji Jack
Kanda, Akira
Kanda, Hideko (WAC)
Kanda, Kazuo

Kanda, Robert T.
Kanega, Yoshio George
Kaneko, Edwin K.
Kaneko, Roy S.
Kanemitsu, Hitoshi
Kanemori, Michitada
Kanemoto, Edward Y.
Kanemoto, George Masato
Kanemoto, Kaoru Benjamin
Kanemoto, Kenzo
Kanemoto, Wayne Masao
Kaneshima, Edward Morimitsu
Kaneshiro, Henry Masao
Kaneshiro, Jay Jushin
Kaneshiro, Keith Kiyoshi
Kaneshiro, Patrick Kenshin
Kaneshiro, Toshiko (WAC)
Kanzaki, Albert Koichi
Kanzaki, Hitoshi
Kanzaki, Satoru
Kariya, Juette Ikuho
Kariya, Masazo
Kasai, Seiko Mitsugi
Kasai, Taro
Kasamoto, Hiroshi
Kashima, Takaaki Peter
Kashiwabara, Richard S.
Kashiwabara, Yoshimi
Kashiwada, James Tamotsu
Kashiwagi, Kazuo
Kashiwagi, Masayoshi
Kashiwase, Ernest J.
Kasubuchi, James Zenji
Katako, Jim Kazuo
Kataoka, Grant Ichiro
Kataoka, Yoshitaka
Katayama, Jerry J.
Katayama, Raymond Y.
Kato, Akio George
Kato, Akira

Kato, Benny Toshiyuki
Kato, David M.
Kato, Fred Yasuya
Kato, George Y.
Kato, Henry K.
Kato, John
Kato, Kenji K.
Kato, Raymond
Kato, Shigeo
Kato, William Naotsugu
Katsumata, Hiroshi C.
Katsura, Alan Y.
Katsuyama, Frank T.
Kawabata, Hideo
Kawabe, Yoshito Ray
Kawachi, Michiji
Kawada, Noboru Frank
Kawada, Teiichi
Kawaguchi, George Kametaro
Kawaguchi, Kazuo
Kawaguchi, Kojiro Francis
Kawaguchi, Masao Mike
Kawahara, Benjamin Aiso
Kawahara, Isami
Kawahara, Nero Niro
Kawahara, Richard H.
Kawahara, Rudy Haruo
Kawai, William Takeshi
Kawakami, Clarke H.
Kawakami, Iwao Jake
Kawakami, Norito
Kawakami, Shigeto
Kawakami, Toshio
Kawamoto, Casey Atsumu
Kawamoto, Dick S.
Kawamoto, Edward Kiyoshi
Kawamoto, Edward T.
Kawamoto, George J.
Kawamoto, Herbert Hiromu
Kawamoto, Hiroshi

Kawamoto, Jerry M.
Kawamoto, Keichi
Kawamoto, Nobuo
Kawamoto, Tatsumi
Kawamoto, Theodore T.
Kawamoto, Yukio
Kawamura, Masami James
Kawamura, Toshiko (WAC)
Kawamura, William Masami
Kawana, Haruo
Kawano, Tomio W.
Kawasaki, Hidemi Scott
Kawasaki, Kazuo Richard
Kawasaki, Tameo
Kawasaki, Toshio
Kawashima, Herbert
Kawashima, Raymond Masao
Kawashiri, Roy Iwao
Kawata, George S.
Kawata, Nobuo
Kawata, Robert M.
Kawata, Tedd Kishio
Kawaye, Harumi Harry
Kay, Morton M.
Kaya, Haruyoshi
Kaya, Setsuo
Kayano, George Kenichi
Kazahaya, Larry Takeshi
Kazahaya, Susumu Edward
Kebo, Frank Keijiro
Kenjo, John Yoshito
Kidani, Ralph Tokutaro
Kido, Fumio
Kido, George Hiroshi
Kido, Kiyoshi
Kido, Matsuko Harada
Kido, Matsuko K.
Kihara, Hayato
Kihara, Kenneth Yasushi
Kihara, Roy R.

Kihara, Samuel Mitsuo
Kihara, Ted T.
Kijima, Masaru Steve
Kikawa, Robert Shinobu
Kikudome, Michinori
Kikumoto, Paul Itsuo
Kikumoto, Teruo Sam Jr.
Kikuta, Hideo
Kikuta, Norman Noboru
Kikuta, Takashi
Kimoto, Francis M.
Kimoto, Herbert Masao
Kimoto, Mamoru
Kimoto, Robert Yoshio
Kimoto, Tatsumi Ralph
Kimoto, Toshio
Kimoto, Yoshio
Kimura, Charles H.
Kimura, Clarence Nagao
Kimura, Ernest Hideo
Kimura, George I.
Kimura, George Yoshito
Kimura, Henry Tsukao
Kimura, James
Kimura, Jim Yoshimi
Kimura, Makoto Max
Kimura, Robert Nobuichi
Kimura, Robert Torao Rusty
Kimura, Robert Yutaka
Kimura, Shigeru
Kimura, Takao
Kimura, Takeo
Kimura, Tatsushi T.
Kimura, Woodley H.
Kimura, Yoshikiyo
Kinjo, Isamu
Kino, Frank Shotaro
Kinoshita, Carl H.
Kinoshita, Clarence K.
Kinoshita, Hisato Jim

Kinoshita, Kiyoshi K.
Kinoshita, Masao
Kinoshita, Saburo Robert
Kinoshita, Yasuharu
Kinoshita, YukioKishi, Fred
Kishi, Hajime James
Kishi, Sharkey Kikumi
Kishimoto, Sadao
Kishimoto, Susumu
Kishinami, Wilbert Hiroshi
Kishiue, Dick Nobuo
Kishiyama, Yoshio R.
Kita, Hachiro
Kitagawa, Iwao
Kitagawa, Jack Susumu
Kitagawa, Kay I.
Kitagawa, Kenneth Naoto
Kitahara, Kei
Kitajima, Fred Sunao
Kitajima, George
Kitajima, Jimmy Miyoshi
Kitajima, Robert H.
Kitamura, Masuo
Kitamura, Toshio
Kitsuta, Masao
Kitsuwa, Naomitsu
Kiyabu, Lawrence Sadao
Kiyan, Joe
Kiyohara, Takeshi J.
Kiyokawa, Mamoru W.
Kiyonaga, Toshio
Kleeman, Richard P.
Kobara, Shoichi
Kobashi, Satoru Richard
Kobashigawa, Hiroshi
Kobata, Albert Eiji
Kobata, Calvin Takeshi
Kobata, Eugene Isamu
Kobata, George Zenichi
Kobayashi, Akira Larry

Kobayashi, Fred Isao
Kobayashi, Fritz F.
Kobayashi, George
Kobayashi, George Tsunekichi
Kobayashi, Gerald Jiro
Kobayashi, Hisao
Kobayashi, Howard Seishi
Kobayashi, Isamu
Kobayashi, James K.
Kobayashi, Joji George
Kobayashi, Key K.
Kobayashi, Thomas Takao
Kobori, Yutaka
Kodama, Edith K.
Kodama, Edith Y.
Kodama, Edward Toyoso
Kodama, Richard Yukio Dr.
Kodani, Naoto
Kodani, Teruo
Koga, James S.
Koga, Rikio Rickie
Koga, Tetsuo
Koike, Hajime James
Koike, Kenzo R.
Koike, Richard Yasuharu
Koito, Noboru
Kojima, Harry Tadashige
Kojima, Isao
Kojima, Susumu R.
Kojima, Toshio
Kojima, Unoyo (WAC)
Kojimoto, Chiaki
Kojiro, Masao
Kokubo, Koichi
Komae, Ryo
Komaki, George
Komatsu, Kimbow Benson
Komeiji, Toshio
Komori, Arthur S.
Komori, Hisashi

Komoto, Kazuo
Komoto, Tetsuo T.
Kondo, Seishin Andrew
Kondo, Shizuo
Konno, Clifford T.
Kono, Henry K.
Kono, Hideto
Kono, John Y.
Kono, Kern
Kono, Kiyoshi
Kono, Russell Katsuhiro
Kono, Tetsuko Alice (WAC)
Kora, Masa M.
Kora, Takashi T.
Koroki, Wallace Takeo
Koroki, Yoshio
Koshiba, Samuel Shigeru
Kosobayashi, Tom T.
Kotsubo, Mamoru
Koyama, Spady Ayato
Koyamatsu, Takeo J.
Koyanagi, Tamotsu
Koyanagi, Yasuo
Kozaki Kazuo, Harry
Kozono, Ardavan Kiyoshi
Kozu, Shinji
Kozuchi, George J.
Kuba, Seishun
Kubo, Harry Toshio
Kubo, Henry Tomio
Kubo, Hoichi Bob
Kubo, James
Kubo, Richard Hisao
Kubo, Takaji Richard
Kubo, Takashi
Kubochi, James Susumu
Kuboshima, Fumio
Kubota, Francis Masaki
Kubota, George M.
Kubota, Hiroshi

Kubota, Hisashi
Kubota, Kenichi
Kubota, Roy Toyoaki
Kubota, Saburo
Kubota, Takashi
Kubota, Tommy
Kubota, Yoshio Michael
Kubotsu, Kiyoshi
Kudaishi, Satoru
Kudo, Ben Benzo
Kuga, Fred T.
Kuge, Arthur
Kumabe, Iwao
Kumada, Arthur Tsukasa
Kumagai, Hakobu
Kumagai, Joe Y.
Kumagai, Patrick Hiroshi
Kumagai, Rikio
Kumamoto, Arthur Toshio
Kumamoto, Frank Masakatsu
Kumamoto, Katsumi
Kumamoto, Masuo
Kumasaka, Roy
Kumataka, Bryd Hajime
Kumataka, Wilson Takeshi
Kumura, John S.
Kunihiro, Harry Toshitsugu
Kunihiro, Shizuo
Kunihisa, Masuo
Kunimoto, Takeo
Kunimune, Makoto
Kunioki, Jitsumi
Kunitomi, Yoshisuke
Kunitsugu, Yoshimi
Kuniyuki, Arata
Kurahara, Janus Yoneo
Kurahashi, Shoichi
Kuramoto, Frank Kenji
Kuramoto, Sakae
Kuranishi, Tadaji Loyal

Kuratani, Kazuo
Kurihara, Dick Noboru
Kurimoto, Kiyoshi
Kurisu, David Sueichi
Kuroda, Haruo
Kuroda, Ichiro K.
Kuroda, T.
Kuroda, William Masatoshi
Kuroiwa, Mickey M.
Kurokawa, Ben Satoshi
Kurokawa, Tomoyoshi
Kuroki, Masao
Kuroko, Kenneth K.
Kurosaka, Tokuo
Kurose, Junelow
Kurotori, Harry Toji
Kurushima, Masato
Kusaba, George
Kusakai, Hiroshi
Kushihashi, Albert S.
Kusuda, Isao
Kusuda, Masashi
Kusuda, Masayoshi
Kusuda, Shigetoshi
Kusumi, George Takeo
Kusumoto, James Hajime
Kusumoto, Richard I.
Kusunose, Tadao
Kutara, Harumi Harry
Kuwabara, Henry Hideo
Kuwabara, Kenichi G.
Kuwabe, Shizuo
Kuwada, Joseph Takeo
Kuwahara, Kazuo G.
Kuwahara, M.
Kuwahara, Takashi
Kuwaki, Masao
Kuwasaki, Masaaki
Kuwata, Hiroshi
Kuwata, Noble N.

Kuwaye, Donald Y.
Kuwaye, Satoru
Kuyama, Paul Y.
Kyono, Noboru James
Laffin, William
Lee, Kyusul
Madokoro, Shigeshi
Maeda, George
Maeda, Ichiro
Maedo, Shigeo
Maehara, Edward Goro
Maeno, John T.
Maesato, Richard Takenobu
Maeshima, Seichi
Magata, George J.
Makino, Hideo
Makino, Roy C.
Makino, Takuro
Makino, William T.
Makishima, George
Makishima, Henry S.
Makishima, Tokuo J.
Makita, Harry
Makiya, Larry S.
Mamiya, Albert K.
Mamiya, George Y.
Mamura, Norio
Manabe, Mitsugi Benjamin
Mansho, Mitsuo
Marugame, Toraichi James
Marumoto, George Yoshiro
Maruya, David Takuzo
Maruyama, Eichi Wilson
Maruyama, Fukuo Henry
Maruyama, Joseph
Maruyama, Kazuo
Maruyama, Tom T.
Maruyama, Yoneo
Masaki, Mamoru
Masaki, Toshio

Masamitsu, Kaino Bob

Masuda, George Matsuo

Masuda, Henry Hiroshi

Masuda, Hisashi John

Masuda, Noriyuki

Masuda, Yutaka

Masuhara, Masato

Masui, Thomas T.

Masukane, Minoru

Masukawa, Leo S.

Masumoto, Edward T.

Masumoto, James M.

Masumotoya, Clarence

Masunaga, Herbert Hachiro

Masunaka, Yasuo F.

Masuoka, David Takashi

Masuoka, Frank Yoshio

Masuyama, Hisao Leroy

Matayoshi, Masaharu

Matayoshi, Milton Yoshio

Mato, George Kiyoshi

Matoba, Misao

Matoba, Michiyasu

Matsubara, Benjamin Y.

Matsubara, Shiyoichi

Matsuda, Hiroshi

Matsuda, Hiroshi I.

Matsuda, Hisaki

Matsuda, Sam Isamu

Matsuda, Tatsuo

Matsudaira, Michael Yoshihisa

Matsuhara, Howard S.

Matsuhara, Yoshiro William

Matsui, George Shigeo

Matsui, Jiro

Matsui, Matsuki

Matsui, Shichiro

Matsukawa, Kihachi Jack

Matsuki, Paul Shinji

Matsumoto, Charles K.

Matsumoto, Edwin Kusuo

Matsumoto, Hisao

Matsumoto, Masanori

Matsumoto, Masao

Matsumoto, Richard K.

Matsumoto, Hiroshi Roy

Matsumoto, Saburo

Matsumoto, Sam Yoshihara

Matsumoto, Tom Tamio

Matsumoto, Toshimitsu

Matsumoto, Yoshio

Matsumura, George M.

Matsumura, Tom Tokio

Matsunaga, George Mitsuru

Matsunaga, Hideo Arthur

Matsunaga, Ronald Shigeto

Matsunaga, Shigeru

Matsunaka, Charles Y.

Matsunaka, Sasao

Matsuno, Yoshio Ralph

Matsuo, Hisashi

Matsuo, James I.

Matsuo, Kenneth Kiyoshi

Matsuo, Toshio David

Matsuoka, Katsuji

Matsuoka, Kikuo

Matsushima, David Wataru

Matsushima, Theodore Tatsuya

Matsushino, John Koyo

Matsushita, Akira

Matsushita, Hiroshi

Matsushita, Kiyoshi

Matsushita, Matt Mitsuo

Matsushita, Shigeru Sam

Matsushita, Yutaka

Matsuura, Frank Tokio

Matsuura, George Kazuyoshi

Matsuura, George Yoshiro

Matsuura, Kazuo

Matsuura, Tom S.

Matsuura, Tommy Kiyoshi

Matsuura, Yoshimi

Matsuyoshi, Fugio

Mayeda, Albert Yoneo

Mayeda, Charles Shigeru

Mayeda, Fred Masaru

Mayeda, George Keishin

Mayeda, Ichiro George

Mayeda, Jack Noboru

Mayeda, Katsuto Jon

Mayeda, Kazuo

Mayeda, Masami M.

Mayeda, Tamiki

Mayekawa, Tommy

Mayeno, James Minoru

Mayewaki, Ben Benichi

Mayewaki, Hachiro

Mazawa, Shigeto Ken

Menda, Masao

Mento, Tetso

Michigami, Rose Sayoko (WAC)

Migaki, Yoshio

Migimoto, Tadao Mason

Migita, Torao

Mihara, Lawrence L

Mikuni, Hisao

Mikuriya, Kei

Mikuriya, Yasushi

Mimaki, Claude A.

Minaai, Walter Noboru

Minami, Kazuo

Minamoto, Harry Ichiro

Minamoto Masanori

Minata Marie Mickey (WAC)

Minato Howard M.

Minato Paul Fusao

Mine, William M.

Minemoto, Hajime

Mineta, Albert Kazuye

Mirikitani, Robert Akira

Misaka, Wataru Warren

Misaki, Takashi Richard

Misawa, Yaeko Barbara (WAC)

Mishima, Tom Erio

Misono, Calvin S.

Mita, Jim Masaomi

Mita, Toshiyuki

Mitani, Harry

Mitani, John Jitsuo

Mitani, Mike Michio

Mitsukado, Andrew N.

Mitsukado, Edward Hideo

Mitsunaga, Gary Y.

Mitsunaga, Sueki Bert

Mitsushima, Takeshi Robert

Mitsuyoshi, Keiji

Miura, Hiroshi

Miura, Hisahiro

Miura, Jack Eso

Miura, Kazuo

Miura, Ladd Tadashi

Miura, Roy Ryoichi

Miura, Stephen Hiroshi

Miwa, Ichiro T.

Miwa, Paul Maruo

Miwa, Ralph Makoto

Miyada, George T.

Miyagawa, Jitsuo Jay

Miyagi, Clarence Iwao

Miyagi, Edward Shigeo

Miyagi, Thomas Tetsuzo

Miyagishima, Harry H.

Miyagishima, Masanori M.

Miyagishima, Toshio

Miyahara, Hajime

Miyahara, John T.

Miyahara, Masao

Miyaji, Nobuo

Miyajima, Jitsuo

Miyakado, Gary Kazumi

Miyake, Hiroshi
Miyake, Isamu Charles
Miyake, Masayuki
Miyake, Morley K.
Miyake, Walter Susumu
Miyamoto, Fred
Miyamoto, Haruo Lou
Miyamoto, Hisao
Miyamoto, Hitoshi Alton
Miyamoto, Isami Richard
Miyamoto, Isamu Ike
Miyamoto, Tadami Tad
Miyamoto, Theodore Tatsuo
Miyamoto, Tsugio
Miyamoto, Walter T.
Miyamoto, Warren Y.
Miyao, Fumio Jesse
Miyao, Yutaka Roy
Miyasaki, Herbert Yoshiki
Miyasaki, Hisatomi
Miyasaki, Joseph M.
Miyasaki, Naotsuzuku Jim
Miyasaki, Seichi Mike
Miyasaki, Tateshi
Miyasato, Kokichi
Miyasato, Richard Jitbuo
Miyasato, Shigetoshi R.
Miyashiro, Harry Hiroshi
Miyashiro, Koei Michael
Miyashiro, Matsuo Larry
Miyashiro, Minoru
Miyashiro, Sadao
Miyashiro, Shigeo
Miyashiro, Susumu
Miyashita, Toshio
Miyata, Douglas Kikaku
Miyata, Fred Toshimasa
Miyata, Michio
Miyata, Roy Minoru
Miyata, Roy Tatsushi

Miyata, Tatsushi Roy
Miyatake, Masaichi
Miyatake, Michael Masami
Miyazaki, Kiyoshi
Miyazono, Barney Sadayuki
Miyoshi, George
Miyoshi, John Tomio
Mize, James S.
Mizobe, Yoshikazu
Mizokami, Takeo
Mizokawa, Hitoshi
Mizota, Masaharu
Mizue, Paul
Mizuire, Hiroshi
Mizuki, Takashi
Mizumoto, Larry Tamotsu
Mizumoto, Genso
Mizuno, Yasuki Frank
Mizusawa, Frank Shojiro
Mizushima, John S.
Mizutani, Joe Kojiu
Mizutani, Masayoshi Roy
Mizutari, Terry Yukitaka
Mochizuki, Tom T.
Momii, Tom Togo
Mori, Atau M.
Mori, Atsuko
Mori, Frank Sadao
Mori, Harry Y.
Mori, Isamu S.
Mori, Mikio
Mori, Mitoshi Sam
Mori, Ralph M.
Mori, Shigeru
Mori, Tadashi Tom
Moriguchi, Albert Masao
Moriguchi, Tom Namio
Morihiro, Mike Yoshito
Moriji, Kenneth Shigeo
Morikawa, Bill M.

Morikawa, Kenji
Morikawa, Shizuo Larry
Morimatsu, Calvin Goichi
Morimitsu, Arthur Takashi
Morimitsu, George Wataru
Morimoto, Isamu
Morimoto, Jimmy M.
Morimoto, Munaki
Morimoto, Rikio
Morimoto, Sunao
Morimoto, Theodore H.
Morimura, Joe Y.
Morinaga, Sueo
Morinaga, Yoshinori
Morinaka, Kenji
Morisako, Henry Hidemori
Morisato, Shigeo
Morishige, Sadao Alan
Morishige, Shun Cal
Morishige, Tadamasa
Morishita, Frank Shigemari
Morita, Masanori
Morita, Takashi
Morita, Yoshio
Morito, James Hatashi
Moritsugu, Richard Yutaka
Moriuchi, Gunji
Moriwaki, Ben M.
Moriwaki, Tadashi
Moriyama, Charles H.
Moriyasu, Masayuki Henry
Morozumi, John Itsuro
Mory, Tom Tamio
Motogawa, Lawrence N.
Motokane, Wilfred Masao
Motonagu, Susumu
Motoyama, Robert Kazuo
Motoyoshi, Yoshiyuki
Mouri, Sadayuki
Mugishima, Harold Haruo

Mukai, Frank
Mukai, Hajime
Mukai, Hiroto
Mukai, Takumi Don
Mukai, Thomas D.
Mukai, Wallace Sada
Mukasa, George Mitsugi
Mukaye, Bud Hiroshi
Munechika, Yukimitsu
Munekawa, Tomio
Munemasa, William Masato
Murai, Shigeki
Murakami, Benjamin Tomoichi
Murakami, Fred Kazuo
Murakami, George Shoji
Murakami, James M.
Murakami, Kenneth Kiyoshi
Murakami, Larry Toshio
Murakami, Mark Yutaka
Murakami, Masami
Murakami, Noboru James
Murakami, Paul K.
Murakami, S.
Murakami, Sam Kiyotaka
Murakami, Tadawo
Murakami, Thomas M.
Murakami, Tokiwo
Murakami, Tsuguo
Murakami, Tsuruo
Murakami, Yoshikazu Joe
Muraki, George
Muraki, Tom Tatsuo
Murakoshi, Henry S.
Muramatsu, George M.
Muramatsu, Joichi
Muramoto, Kay K.
Muramoto, Masaru
Muranaka, Hugh Tadao
Muranaka, Reynold Tadayoshi
Muranaka, Sadamu

Murao, Shigeyoshi
Muraoka, Harry Naoto
Muraoka, Katsuyuki
Muraoka, Masao Frank
Murasaki, Toshio
Murashige, Masaru
Murashima, Harry G.
Murashima, Itaru James
Murata, Harry S.
Murata, Herbert Hisao
Murata, Jimmy Mitsuyuki
Murata, Jiro
Murata, Sadaji R.
Murayama, Herbert Takashi
Murayama, Hironichi
Murayama, Hiroshi
Murayama, Leonard T.
Murayama, Milton A.
Murotani, Harry K.
Muto, George Senji
Nagahiro, Masao
Nagai, Masaaki
Nagai, Yoshinori
Nagaki, Tadashi
Nagamori, Takeo
Nagamoto, Kenny
Nagamoto, Sadao
Nagano, Charles Haruo
Nagano, George Chihiro
Nagano, George Kimiyoshi
Nagano, Jack Kiyoshi
Nagao, James A.
Nagao, Norito
Nagao, Tamotsu Tom
Nagao, Wallace Takeshi
Nagao, Yoshioki
Nagare, Fred Kunio
Nagasako, Kengo
Nagase, Masazumi
Nagata, Gilbert Yoshio

Nagata, Iwao
Nagata, Mac Nobuo
Nagata, Masao
Nagata, Nobuo
Nagata, Raymond Shogo
Nagata, Robert Isamu
Nagata, Robert Kusuo
Nagata, Tom Katsumi
Nagatani, George Yoshimasa
Nagayama, Katsuto
Nagayama, Takashi
Naito, Keita
Naito, Robert S.
Naito, Takeshi
Naito, William Sumio
Naito, Yoshinobu
Nakabayashi, Kazuo Ray
Nakada, Kenichi Roy
Nakada, Kenneth Yoshiro
Nakada, Minoru Paul
Nakada, Yoshio
Nakagama, Sam Isamu
Nakagama, Tetsuo Bill
Nakagawa, Charles Niro
Nakagawa, Edward K.
Nakagawa, Hiroshi
Nakagawa, Hisashi
Nakagawa, John Yasuyuki
Nakagawa, Kiyoshi George
Nakagawa, Kiyoto
Nakagawa, Kunso
Nakagawa, Mamoru
Nakagawa, Sam Masao
Nakagawa, Shunichi
Nakagawa, Toshio William
Nakagawa, Winslow Shoji
Nakagiri, Wakamatsu Fred
Nakahara, George K.
Nakahara, John Shuichi
Nakahara, Kenji

Nakahara, Masao
Nakahara, Peter Minoru
Nakahara, Shoichi Stanley
Nakahara, Yoshihiko Stanley
Nakahara, Yoshiaki
Nakahata, Yutaka
Nakaki, Hidetaka
Nakakihara, Henry
Nakama, Christian S.
Nakama, N.
Nakama, Seichi
Nakama, Yoshio
Nakamaejo, Koei
Nakamaru, Mitsuru
Nakamori, Kazuo
Nakamoto, Ben Ichiro
Nakamoto, Calvin M.
Nakamoto, Henry Hitoshi
Nakamoto, Larry Bunji
Nakamoto, Michitaka Sakata
Nakamoto, Richard M.
Nakamoto, Tom Tamotsu
Nakamura, Akimasa Amos
Nakamura, Akira
Nakamura, Charles K.
Nakamura, Edward Katsumi
Nakamura, Edward Nobu
Nakamura, Edward Y.
Nakamura, George Ichiro
Nakamura, George Itsuo
Nakamura, George S.
Nakamura, George Toshio
Nakamura, George Yonekuni
Nakamura, Harold Hisao
Nakamura, Harry Ichiro
Nakamura, Henry Kazumi
Nakamura, Hideki
Nakamura, Hiroshi
Nakamura, Howard Shigeyuki
Nakamura, Iwao

Nakamura, Junichi
Nakamura, Kazuo
Nakamura, Kazuto
Nakamura, Mary Hanako (WAC)
Nakamura, Masaki H.
Nakamura, Noboru
Nakamura, Richard Ichiro
Nakamura, Robert Masaki
Nakamura, Saburo
Nakamura, Sanao
Nakamura, Satoru Hank
Nakamura, Seichi
Nakamura, Seiji
Nakamura, Shoichi
Nakamura, Shuichi Roy
Nakamura, Susumu J.
Nakamura, Tadao
Nakamura, Tsugio
Nakamura, William Susumu
Nakamura, Yutaka
Nakanishi, Joe Masao
Nakanishi, Kameichi
Nakanishi, Keijiro P.
Nakanishi, Koichi
Nakanishi, Minoru
Nakanishi, Shigeji S.
Nakanishi, Stanley Jitsuo
Nakanishi, Terry Toyome (WAC)
Nakanishi, Toshio
Nakano, George Masatoshi
Nakano, Harvey Shizuo
Nakano, Hichiro
Nakano, J.
Nakano, Masanobu
Nakano, Masao Kenneth
Nakano, Roy S.
Nakano, Roy Yukiwo
Nakano, Shigeji
Nakano, Shiro
Nakano, Shizuo

Nakano, Yeichi Fred
Nakao, Errol Masayuki
Nakao, Pete Kunihiro
Nakashima, Fusao A.
Nakashima, Henry Hachiro
Nakashima, Ichiro
Nakashima, Joe
Nakashima, Roy Yoshihiro
Nakashima, Shigemitsu
Nakashima, Shigeru
Nakashima, Yoshito
Nakasone, Seiei
Nakata, Albert T.
Nakata, Charles Tadao
Nakata, Colbert K.
Nakata, G.
Nakata, Joe Hideo
Nakata, Masao Mac
Nakata, Sage Seige
Nakata, Takeo
Nakata, Yoneto James
Nakatani, Frank T.
Nakatogawa, Joe J.
Nakatsu, Daniel Toyoharu
Nakatsu, Masaharu Lorry
Nakatsuru, Toshito
Nakauchi, Tadashi
Nakauchi, Tsutomu
Nakayama, John S.
Nakayama, Yukio
Nakazaki, Tony Tsutomu
Nakazawa, Albert O.
Nakazawa, Yoshio
Nakazono, Eiichi
Nakazono, Hiroshi
Namatame, Teijiro
Namba, Isao Ken
Namba, Kitami
Namba, Mark M.
Namba, Minoru

Namba, Yoshio R.
Nanbu, George Tamotsu
Nao, Makoto
Narita, Masao
Naruto, Herbert Y.
Nash, Hugh Oriel
Natsuhara, George
Nawa, James Hidenao
Neishi, Hideso
Neishi, Torao Pat
Nekoba, Mamoru Nick
Nekota, Kazuo
Nihei, Joe Teruo
Nii, Fujio
Nii, Yoshito
Niizawa, Masamichi Henry
Niki, Joe Fujio
Nimura, Raymond Kaname
Nimura, Richard Takeshi
Nishi, Sumio
Nishi, Yosohachi J.
Nishibayashi, Masaru.
Nishida, George
Nishida, Kaoru
Nishida, Malcolm M.
Nishie, Masayoshi Norman
Nishiguchi, Benjamin M.
Nishihara, Herbert Kazu
Nishihara, Joe Atsushi
Nishiie, Masayoshi
Nishijima, Hiroshi
Nishijima, Satoshi Hisatoshi
Nishijima, Yoshio Victor
Nishikawa, Hiroshi Harry
Nishikawa, William S.
Nishimine, Kenro
Nishimori, Nobuo
Nishimoto, Hugh Makoto
Nishimoto, Kanoye K.
Nishimoto, Kenji

Nishimoto, Kiyoto T.
Nishimoto, Richard T.
Nishimoto, William Kazuyuki
Nishimura, Arthur Meguma
Nishimura, Dan Tamotsu
Nishimura, George Fumio
Nishimura, George Kazuo
Nishimura, George S.
Nishimura, Hank Minimasa
Nishimura, Harold Hiroyuki
Nishimura, Harold Sadami
Nishimura, Henry Yoshimitani
Nishimura, Herbert T.
Nishimura, Hiroshi
Nishimura, Katsuyoshi
Nishimura, William Y.
Nishinaga, Shoso
Nishioka, George Hiroshi
Nishioku, Masaru
Nishita, Hideo
Nishitomi, Tetsu
Nishitsuji, Fred Hiroshi
Nishiyama, Ted Tadashi
Nishizaka, Shunya Thomas
Nishizawa, Richard Yoshito
Nitta, Isamu
Nitta, Toshio Larry
Nitta, Warren Susumu
Niya, Hiroto George
Nobuhara, Saburo
Noda, Takashi N.
Noguchi, Harold M.
Noguchi, Isamu Ted
Noguchi, John Tamotsu
Noguchi, Kisa (WAC)
Noji, Mamoru
Nojima, Hiromu
Nojima, George Shoichi
Noma, Toshio
Nomura, Kenji

Nomura, Masashi
Nomura, Ruth Isuyo
Nomura, Shoichi
Nomura, Shoso
Nomura, Tadashi
Nomura, Tadashi Tad
Nonaka, Takeo Fred
Nonoguchi, Hajime
Norimoto, Frank Genji
Norisada, Tom Kay
Noritake, Yoshio Y.
Noro, Hidetoshi Don
Nosaka, Fred Kiyoshi
Nosaka, William Masuo
Nose, James C.
Nouchi, George
Nuno, William Y.
Obata, Benjamin Takeshi
Obata, James Kazuo
Obata, John K.
Obayashi, Kay Keiji
Obikane, Louis Ichiro
Ochi, Masao
Ochi, Satoru
Ochi, Seichi
Ochi, Shigeru
Ochi, Shunsuke
Ochi, Tetsuo
Oda, Akira
Oda, Dick Rikiho
Oda, Haruko Elaine (WAC)
Oda, Jack Wataru
Oda, Mamoru John
Oda, Robert Masaya
Oda, Ted Tsuruho
Odanaka, Fred Hideo
Odanaka, Woodrow
Odano, Henry Haruo
Odano, Wesley Toshio
Odo, Sadao

Odow, Terno
Ogasawara, Minoru
Ogata, Dye
Ogata, Robert S.
Ogata, Sue S. (WAC)
Ogata, Yoshio
Ogawa, Albert Isamu
Ogawa, Haruji
Ogawa, Hoagy Hogumo
Ogawa, Ichiro Howard
Ogawa, Kenneth Yasuo
Ogawa, Luther
Ogawa, Paul Kiyoto
Ogawa, Tadashi
Ogawa, Toshio
Ogi, Mitsuru
Ogino, George
Ogisaka, James H.
Ogita, Yoshiaki
Ogoso, Francis Takaaki
Ogura, Keiko (WAC)
Oguro, Richard Shigeo
Ohama, Katsumi
Ohama, Robert Kazuo
Ohara, Michael Yoshio
Ohira, Hiroshi Steve
Ohki, Kenneth
Ohno, Joe E.
Ohori, Akira
Ohta, Clarence Hitoshi
Ohta, Herbert I.
Ohta, Hiroshi
Ohta, John M.
Ohta, Tim Tokuyuki
Ohtaki, Paul T.
Ohye, Keisuke George
Oi, Junsuke Sammy
Oi, Susumu
Oie, Harold Toshio
Oie, Harold Wazo

Oikawa, Frank Eiichi
Oike, William S.
Oishi, Goro Roy
Oishi, Hayao Hal
Oishi, Mamoru
Oishi, Masaichi
Oishi, Masami
Oishi, Takanori
Oishi, Yoshiro
Oita, Itsumi J.
Oita, Katashi
Oji, Chester Susumu
Oji, Sukeo
Oka, Clarence Kazuyoshi
Oka, Don Chikara
Oka, Hide
Oka, Isao
Oka, James Ichiro
Oka, James N.
Oka, Kayji
Oka, Kazuo
Oka, Kiyoshi
Oka, Taka Steve
Okabayashi, Frank K.
Okada, Frank
Okada, George Patrick
Okada, Harry Hideo
Okada, Haruo
Okada, Hiroshi L.
Okada, Inoru L.
Okada, James M.
Okada, James Sadami
Okada, Minoru
Okada, Mitoshi Eldon
Okada, Peter Kazunori
Okada, Ryoichi
Okada, Seiichi Roy
Okada, Shigeo
Okada, Shigeru
Okahara, Akio

Okamoto, George
Okamoto, Hiroshi Steve
Okamoto, Kaname
Okamoto, Kazuto
Okamoto, Keiji
Okamoto, Masaji
Okamoto, Masato
Okamoto, Mitsugi
Okamoto, Noel Yuzuru
Okamoto, Samuel I.
Okamoto, Shore Frank
Okamoto, Susumu
Okamoto, Tito Uyeoka
Okamoto, William I.
Okamura, Saburo
Okamura, Shinji Jack
Okamura, Takao
Okamura, Toshio
Okanaka, W.
Okano, Keiji G.
Okano, Koichi George
Okano, Minoru
Okano, Teiji F.
Okasaki, Akeo
Okasaki, Amile
Okata, Hideo
Okawa, Stanley T.
Okayama, Steve Hisayuki
Okazaki, Elbridge Kazuso
Okazaki, George
Okazaki, Hachiro G.
Okazaki, Keisou K.
Okazaki, Seiichi Jerry
Okazaki, Seiji
Okazaki, Shoichi Jerry
Oki, Akira
Oki, Kiyoto Bob
Oki, Wataru
Okida, Terry Tokuo
Okido, Shoji

Okimoto, Chester S.
Okimoto, Minoru Henry
Okimoto, Yukio
Okimura, Hitoshi
Okimura, Shigenobu
Okinaga, Jiro
Okinaka, Masaharu S.
Okinishi, Imaichi
Okita, George Teraro
Okita, James Tatsumi
Oku, Muneo Larry
Oku, Shigeo
Okubara, Makoto Sam
Okubo, Andrew Kohei
Okubo, Donald Shigeru
Okubo, Harry Seichi
Okubo, Minoru William
Okubo, Shigeo
Okubo, Sumi
Okubo, Yasushi
Okubo, Yoshie John
Okuda, Sam Sadanobu
Okuda, Toshio
Okuhara, Masuwo T.
Okumura, George T.
Okumura, Makoto
Okumura, Susumu
Okumura, Suyeki
Okuno, Tetsuo Ted
Okura, Frank Masaru
Okura, Jimmie Mitsuru
Okura, Ross M.
Omachi, Henry Takashi
Omatsu, Frank Kay
Omatsu, Oliver George
Omiya, Hitoshi Robert
Omori, Kunitake Thomas
Omori, Richard Toshio
Omoto, Clarence Y.
Omoto, Sadayoshi

Omura, Kenneth Kenji
Omura, Minoru Jerry
Omura, Thomas Taro
Omura, Yasuo
Onaga, Mitsuru David
Oniki, Shozi Garry Rev.
Onishi, Harold Masao
Onishi, Hiroshi
Onishi, Katsumi
Onishi, Ray H.
Onishi, Tom T.
Onizuka, Keiji
Ono, Frank Fumio
Ono, Fred Y.
Ono, Gene I.
Ono, George Hiroshi
Ono, Jackson Matsuo
Ono, Jitsuo
Ono, Junji
Ono, Seichi Champ
Ono, Shigeshi
Ono, Takashi Nathaniel
Onoda, Johnny Seiichi
Onodera, Ken
Onuma, Shoichi
Oride, Rikio
Orikasa, Noboru
Orite, Ray
Osaka, Toshii
Osaki, Masuo
Osaki, George
Osako, Hiroshi Lloyd
Osasa, Thomas Takaomi
Osato, Isami Sam
Osato, Reginald Masaichi
Oshida, John S.
Oshikata, Mitsuo
Oshiki, Kazuo
Oshima, George Takashi
Oshima, Keiji K.

Oshima, T.
Oshiro, Eisei R.
Oshiro, Kamakichi O.
Oshiro, Kosei
Oshiro, Seiki
Oshiro, Toshiichi
Oshiro, Yoshinobu
Oshita, Albert Utaka
Oshita, Dennis
Oshita, Hosen
Oshita, William T.
Osuga, William Makoto
Osumi, David Takeshi
Ota, Daniel C.
Ota, George Masaichi
Ota, Harry Toshio
Ota, Haruo Paul
Ota, J.
Ota Kenichi
Ota, Ken Kenichi
Ota, M.
Ota, Satoru
Ota, Takeshi
Otaguro, Masaru
Otake, Harry T.
Otake, Jack M.
Otake, Raymond Kaname
Otani, Akira
Otani, John Seiichi
Otani, Takeo
Oto, Toshio
Otomo, John Hiroshi
Otsuka, Frank Masatoshi
Otsuka, Kenji Joe
Otsuki, Harry T.
Ouye, George Riyoji
Owashi, Harumi
Oya, John Jun
Oyakawa, Yoshio
Oyama, Hiromi H.

Oyama, Noboru
Ozaki, Junji
Ozaki, Mike Masayuki
Ozawa, Harry Hideo
Ozawa, Yoshio
Ozeki, Roger Kasabure
Ozima, Shigenobu
Rokutani, Samuel Shinobu
Ryono, Teruo
Ryuto, Masaru
Sado, Masami Mas
Sado, Tomokatsu Tom
Sagami, Toshio John
Sagara, Isamu Sam
Sagara, Masao
Sagawa, Masaichi
Saiki, Barry Minoru
Saiki, Sam Osamu
Saiki, Teddy Tetsuo
Saiki, Toshio
Saito, Billy Masaharu
Saito, Chester K.
Saito, Frank Manabu
Saito, Herbert S.
Saito, Isamu
Saito, James Hiroshi
Saito, Larry Yoshimi
Saito, Leo Takeshi
Saito, Mitsuo
Saito, Ralph Minoru
Saito, Richard Katsuyoshi
Saito, Saburo
Saito, Sakae Richard
Saito, Shozo
Saito, Takeo George
Saito, Tsukasa
Saito, Tsutomu Gregory
Sakaguchi, George Masatsugu
Sakaguchi, James T.
Sakaguchi, Paul Kuni

Sakaguchi, Sam Toshiyuki
Sakaguchi, Sanpei Sam
Sakai, George
Sakai, George Takashi
Sakai, Hisaji
Sakai, James Y.
Sakai, John J.
Sakai, John S. Jr.
Sakai, John Takashi
Sakai, Kadushi
Sakai, Kenichi
Sakai, M.
Sakai, Robert Kenjiro
Sakai, Roy T.
Sakai, Sakuji
Sakai, Shoichi
Sakai, Toshio Paul
Sakai, Yoshiyuki Ronald
Sakaki, Shiro Paul
Sakakida, Richard Motoso
Sakakura, Joe
Sakamoto, Calvin Kiyoki
Sakamoto, Edward Mitsuru
Sakamoto, Elton H.
Sakamoto, Gengo
Sakamoto, George S.
Sakamoto, John
Sakamoto, John Minoru
Sakamoto, K.
Sakamoto, Kiyoshi Kei
Sakamoto, Makoto (Max)
Sakamoto, Michael Michio
Sakamoto, R.
Sakamoto, Shigeo
Sakamoto, Shugetsu
Sakamoto, Thomas Tokio
Sakamoto, Tomochika Tom
Sakamoto, Toshiaki
Sakanari, George Ryoichi
Sakanashi, Noriyuki Frank

Sakashita, George J.
Sakata, Blanche M. (WAC)
Sakata, Frank S.
Sakata, Hiroshi Kato
Sakata, Raymond Tetsuo
Sakato, Kaoru Frank
Sakauye, Eiichi
Sakauye, Tatsuo Roy
Sakihara, Seikichi
Sako, Tokuma
Sakoki, Larry Mikio
Sakuma, Atsusa
Sakuma, Charles Takeo
Sakuma, Milton Tsukasa
Sakuma, Robert K.
Sakuma, Takashi
Sakuma, Warren S.
Sakurai, Tomio
Sakurai, Zeke Haruichi
Sameshima, Hitoshi George
Sanbongi, Fred Shigeru
Sanehira, Jitsuo
Sankey, George Kiyoshi
Sano, George K.
Sano, Tetsuro Patrick
Sanwo, Frank Tetsugo
Sasahara, Harry Koichi
Sasaki, Chris Kazuo
Sasaki, Eddie T.
Sasaki, Edwin K.
Sasaki, Everett Shigeo
Sasaki, Francis Toru
Sasaki, George T.
Sasaki, Harold Atsushi
Sasaki, Harry T.
Sasaki, Hitoshi Gary
Sasaki, Jiro
Sasaki, Joseph Jyo
Sasaki, Joseph Yuzuru
Sasaki, Katsumi

Sasaki, Kiyoshi
Sasaki, Nobuyuki
Sasaki, Roy Hiromi
Sasaki, Sam K.
Sasaki, Sam Satoru
Sasaki, Takashi T.
Sasaki, Thomas M.
Sasaki, Thomas Toru
Sasaki, Thomas Toshio
Sasaki, Toshio
Sasano, James Kumataro
Sasano, Lawrence Tsuneji
Sasano, Samuel K.
Sasao, Eiichi J.
Sase, Nobuyoshi
Sasuga, Nelly A. (WAC)
Satake, Sadashi
Sato, Eiichi Larry
Sato, Hajime
Sato, Hayami Russell
Sato, Herbert Shotaro
Sato, Hideo
Sato, Hideo James
Sato, Hiroyuki
Sato, Jiro Andrew
Sato, Kenichi
Sato, Kiyoji Richard
Sato, Richard Kichisaku
Sato, Rikio
Sato, Shigeru Lloyd
Sato, Sho Andrew
Sato, Tadao T.
Sato, Tadashi
Sato, Takeo
Sato, Takeo George
Sato, Toichi
Sato, Vernon K.
Satow, Jack Kenzo
Satow, Roy Toshio
Satow, Tomio

Sawada, Yukio Kenneth
Sawai, Ryoichi
Sawai, Shuichi Byron
Sawasaki, Harry M.
Sayama, Kenji
Sei, Hideo
Seikaku, Yoshio
Seike, Shu Ben
Seki, Liance Martin
Sekiguchi, Kenichiiro K.
Sekijima, Haruto John
Sekiya, Harry Noboru
Sekiya, Takeo Tom
Sen, Joseph W.
Senda, Kane Kazuo
Sera, Shiro
Seriguchi, George Toyotsugu
Seto, Hugh Y.
Seto, Kazuto
Seto, Masaharu Richard
Seto, Mathew M.
Seu, Yung Lum
Shiba, Frank
Shibao, Tatsumi
Shibata, Charles S.
Shibata, George Mitsuru
Shibata, Mitsuru
Shibata, Yoshimi
Shibata, Yoshito Jerry
Shibayama, Goro
Shibuya, Yoshimaro
Shigekawa, Frank Koji
Shigematsu, Joe
Shigemoto, Iwao
Shigemoto, Richard Sakaye
Shigemura, Yoshihiko
Shigeta, Sachio
Shigeta, Tsutomu
Shigeta, Yutaka James
Shigezawa, Jeffery Toshikazu

Shigihara, Kenichi
Shigihara, Takeshi
Shigihara, Teruo Harold
Shigio, Matao Matt
Shiigi, Lawrence E.
Shiigi, Shinichi
Shiine, Hideo
Shiinoki, Tom S.
Shikata, George M.
Shikina, Sachiko (WAC)
Shikuma, Richard H.
Shima, James I.
Shimabukuro, Joe Tsuneo
Shimabukuro, Sam Koyei
Shimabukuro, Stanley Seiko
Shimada, Bell Masayuki
Shimada, Kiyoshi
Shimada, Mitsuyoshi
Shimada, Susumu
Shimamoto, Edgar Akikazu
Shimamoto, Iwao
Shimamoto, Tetsuo
Shimamoto, Yoshio
Shimanuki, Goichi
Shimasaki, Kiyoshi
Shimaura, Mutsuo
Shimazaki, Tamotsu Thomas
Shimazu, Hiroyoshi
Shimbo, Kenneth Kenso
Shimizu, Allen Yoshimi
Shimizu, George
Shimizu, George Tadashi
Shimizu, George Yoshio
Shimizu, Harry
Shimizu, Iwao
Shimizu, Kenneth Kiyomi
Shimizu, Manabu
Shimizu, Masaru
Shimizu, Noboru B.
Shimizu, Satoru

Shimizu, Yoshiaki
Shimo, Cedrick Masaki
Shimoda, Fushiwo F.
Shimoda, Tadao
Shimojima, Henry
Shimokawa, Clyde M.
Shimokawa, James W.
Shimomura, Kenichi Andrew
Shimomura, Michio
Shimomura, Taro
Shimotakahara, Yukio F.
Shimotori, George H.
Shimoyama, Isao
Shimoyama, Midori (WAC)
Shimoyama, Mitori
Shimozono, Norio
Shimozono, Willis Y.
Shinagawa, Shizuko Sue (WAC)
Shinbo, Arthur
Shindo, Motomi
Shindo, Takeshi
Shingai, Isamu Sam
Shingu, Ken K.
Shinjo, Robert S.
Shinkawa, Terry H.
Shinmoto, Kiyoto
Shinmoto, Minoru
Shinoda, Michio Mickey
Shinohara, Harold S.
Shinsato, K.
Shinsato, Lloyd Kenzo
Shintaku, Harry
Shintaku, Harry Minoru
Shintaku, James
Shintaku, Kiyoshi Mac
Shintaku, Kiyoto John
Shintaku, Toshiaki
Shintaku, Wataru
Shintani, Toshiyuki Jim
Shinto, Harry Higashi

Shiode, Jimmy Hajime
Shiomi, Hardy Atsumichi
Shiotani, Tamiji
Shiozaki, Toshio H.
Shiozawa, Shiro
Shiraga, Toshiyuki
Shirai, Isamu
Shirai, Sanji
Shiraishi, George Jr.
Shiraishi, Joe Mitsuru
Shiraishi, Joe S.
Shiraishi, John K.
Shiraishi, Shigeo
Shiraishi, Yoshitsugu
Shiraiwa, Seichi
Shirakawa, Masaji Jack
Shirakawa, Raymond Hiroshi
Shiraki, Giichiro
Shiraki, Hideo
Shiroishi, Shiogeomi
Shiroma, David M.
Shiroma, George
Shiroma, Howard H.
Shiroma, Masao John
Shiroma, Yoshiharu Charles
Shiromoto, Nobuo
Shiroyama, Benji
Shishido, Minoru
Shishido, Saburo
Shishido, T.
Shitabata, Yoshio Walter
Shoji, Joseph T.
Sodetani, Roy Ritsuji
Sogi, Masaru Harold
Soken, Yeishun Allen
Sono, George Fumiyuki
Sono, Tom Fumio
Sonoda, George
Soyeshima, Ted Kiyoshi
Suda, George Sanaye

Sue, Edward Hideo
Suehiro, Richard Yoshio
Suehiro, Robert K.
Suematsu, Toshiaki
Suenaka, Kingo Richard
Suga, Etsuji Roy
Suga, Yasuo
Sugai, Susumu
Sugai, Takeshi
Sugai, Tetsuo
Sugano, Raymond Katsuyoshi
Sugano, Stephen S.
Sugeno, Frank E.
Sugeta, Ben Shigeyoshi
Sugi, Haruko (WAC)
Sugihara, Henry Y.
Sugihara, Masato
Sugihara, Paul Tall
Sugimoto, George
Sugimoto, Masaji
Sugimoto, Robert S.
Sugimoto, Robert Takashi
Sugimoto, Sam S.
Sugimoto, Shigeo Fred
Sugimoto, Shizuo
Sugimoto, Takanori
Sugimoto, Toshiro
Sugimoto, Yoshinori
Sugimura, James
Sugino, Arthur Tetsu
Sugino, Seichi Shoichi
Sugiyama, Isamu Sam
Sugiyama, Tadayoshi
Sugiyama,Taneo
Sumada, Tsuguo
Sumi, Takashi
Sumi, Tsutomu
Sumida, Edward Masaaki
Sumida, John Yutaka
Sumida, Makoto Maxie

Sumida, Marshall Masaru
Sumida, Nobuyuki
Sumida, Paul Hoomi
Sunamoto, Satoru Tony
Sunouchi, Sidney Seiji
Suski, Joe Clement
Sutow, Lawrence H.
Suyama, Mineo
Suyehira, Henry Genichi
Suyeishi, Charles M.
Suyemoto, Masaru Barry
Suyenaga, Taro
Suyeoka, Robert F.
Suzawa, Hiromu
Suzui, Richard S.
Suzukawa, Francis F.
Suzukawa, Fred Fukashi
Suzukawa, Harry
Suzukawa, Henry Hiroshi
Suzukawa, Kiyoshi
Suzukawa, Masao
Suzuki, Donald H.
Suzuki, Donald Isao
Suzuki, Frank H.
Suzuki, Frank K.
Suzuki, George Edwin
Suzuki, Gilbert T.
Suzuki, Henry Eichi
Suzuki, Jack Susumu
Suzuki, John Yoshitsugu
Suzuki, Masaharu George
Suzuki, Tatsuro
Suzuki, Toshio Thomas
Suzuki, Yoshikazu Robert
Suzuki, Yukio
Suzumoto, Sueo
Suzumoto, Tetsuo
Tabata, Jack Masuo
Tabata, Katsutoshi
Tachibana, Hideo

Tachibana, Ray K.
Tachino, Yoshio
Tada, Takeshi T.
Tadakuma, Katsutoshi
Taenaka, Toshikuni
Taga, James Yasunori
Tagami, Chiharu
Tagami, Kakumi Kay
Tagami, Kan
Tagami, Matazo Kenneth
Tagawa, Kay K.
Taguchi, Takeshi
Tahara, Charles Satoru
Tahira, Masami
Taira, Lincoln Toko
Taira, Marshall Hiroshi
Taira, Robert Rokuro
Taira, Sam S.
Taira, Walter Takeo
Taji, Thomas
Tajima, Ted Tsuneo
Takabayashi, Edward H.
Takabayashi, George Hideo
Takagaki, Takeo
Takagi, George H.
Takagi, Harry Osamu
Takahara, Sam Osamu
Takahashi, Harry H.
Takahashi, Hiroki
Takahashi, Hiroshi J.
Takahashi, Sadao
Takahashi, Terry Yoshio
Takahashi, Tom N.
Takahashi, Tony N.
Takahashi, William Hideo
Takahashi, Yukio
Takahata, Yoshinori
Takai, Kunio
Takai, Roy Tetsuo
Takai, Shizuo

Takaki, Fujio
Takaki, Kenichi J.
Takaki, Matsuo Henry
Takaki, Morinaka
Takakura, Tadashi
Takamiya, Kenneth Jitsuei
Takamori, Hideyuki
Takamura, Sojiro
Takamura, Yosaburo Samuel
Takane, Robert Fujio
Takanishi, Dick S.
Takanishi, Hajime
Takanishi, Mamoru
Takano, Tadashi
Takano, Theodore Kozuyuki
Takao, Frank T.
Takasaki, Richard Sadaji
Takasaki, Yasuo
Takashima, Kazue
Takasumi, Yoshio T.
Takata, Masao
Takata, Tateo
Takata, Tom Masaharu
Takatsuka, Bobby T.
Takaue, Yuji
Takayama, Hideo
Takayanagi, Tetsuo
Takebayashi, Tatsushi
Takechi, Clyde Shunji
Takeguchi, Hidenobu
Takehana, James Tamio
Takehara, Edward T.
Takehara, Eiji Daniel
Takehara, Sumio
Takehara, Yoshio
Takekawa, John A.
Takekawa, Yutaka D.
Takemoto, Ben
Takemoto, Satoru
Takemoto, Setsuo Richard

Takemoto, Shido
Takemoto, Waichi
Takemura, George S.
Takenaka, Michio Stanley
Takesako, Kow T.
Takeshima, Masaru
Takesue, Thomas Akira
Taketa, George Shioichiro
Taketa, Harry Haruo
Taketa, James Shosaburo
Taketa, Kazuto
Taketa, Morris Masao
Taketa, Shojiro Tom
Taketa, Thomas
Takeuchi, Masaji
Takeuchi, Yukio
Takeyasu, Motoi
Takishita, Yoshito
Takiue, Hakuto Henry
Takiue, Yuji
Takizawa, Etsumi
Takusagawa, Norman Takateru
Tamada, Kay
Tamaki, Carl Minoru
Tamaki, Paul Isamu
Tamanaha, Larry Shigeru
Tamane, Hideo
Tamao, Jiro
Tamashiro, James S.
Tamashiro, Samuel Y.
Tamashiro, Tamayo Uetake (WAC)
Tamashiro, Tsuneo
Tambara, George Kazuna
Tamura, Albert Kazuo
Tamura, Albert Yoshikagi
Tamura, Asaka Robert
Tamura, Kazunobu
Tamura, Ken
Tamura, Kunima
Tamura, Masaru

Tamura, Yukio
Tanabe, Edward S.
Tanabe, Frank Shinichiro
Tanabe, Harry Harushi
Tanabe, Henry Teruo
Tanabe, Hideo
Tanabe, Hiroshi Harold
Tanabe, Nobuo Dave
Tanabe, Robert Hiromichi
Tanabe, Tadashi
Tanabe, Takao
Tanabe, Yoshinobu
Tanada, Emiko Ichida
Tanada, Rose Sayoko
Tanada, Takuma
Tanagi, Shigeo Frank
Tanaka, Akira J.
Tanaka, Charles Kunio
Tanaka, George
Tanaka, Haruo
Tanaka, Hiroshi G.
Tanaka, Jack M.
Tanaka, James H.
Tanaka, James Zenzo
Tanaka, Jiro
Tanaka, Katherine S. (WAC)
Tanaka, Katsuki
Tanaka, Ken
Tanaka, Kenji Robert
Tanaka, Linda (WAC)
Tanaka, Masami
Tanaka, Masao Albert
Tanaka, Paul Hajime
Tanaka, Ritsuo Alan
Tanaka, Samuel H.
Tanaka, Shigeo
Tanaka, Stanley K.
Tanaka, Takeshi Eugene
Tanaka, Tatsuo
Tanaka, Teddy

Tanaka, Thomas T.

Tanaka, Tomio

Tanaka, Victor S.

Tanaka, Walter

Tanaka, William Thomas

Tanaka, Yoshito

Tanakatsubo, Satsuki Fred

Tanamachi, Masao

Tando, George Hiroshi

Tani, Bushichi

Tani, Frederick S.

Tani, George Tadashi

Tani, Jack I.

Tani, Paul Shunji

Tani, Tom Tamotsu

Tanigaki, Irene Sumiko (WAC)

Tanigawa, Hitoshi

Tanigawa, Mitsuru J.

Taniguchi, Eisei

Taniguchi, George Takeshi

Taniguchi, Harry Hiroshi

Taniguchi, James Kenji

Taniguchi, Kenneth K.

Taniguchi, Kiyoto

Taniguchi, Masao

Taniguchi, Sachio

Taniguchi, Seiso

Taniguchi, Tatsuo

Taniguchi, Tom Yoshiteru

Taniguchi, Toshio

Taniguchi, Wilfred T.

Taniguchi, Yukio

Tanimoto, Jack Shigeo

Tanimoto, Nobuyuki Frank

Tanimura, Ishizo

Tanita, Kaoru

Tanita, Satoshi Jimmy

Tanizawa, Milton Toshio

Tanizawa, Tom Tomu

Tanji, Goro

Tanji, Gilbert Toru

Tanji, James I.

Tanouye, Hiroshi Russ

Tanouye, Roy M.

Tanouye, Sumio Albert

Tanouye, T.

Taoka, George Mazumi

Tasaka, Hajime Hiram

Tasaki, Toma

Tateishi, Satoshi Stanley

Tateishi, Toyoaki Ted

Tateyama, Harold

Tatsuda, Charles

Taura, Joe

Tazuma, Noboru

Terada, George Ryoichi

Terada, Takuya Roy

Teragawa, Edward M.

Teragawa, Richard M.

Teragawa, Robert N.

Terai, Masao

Teraji, Yozo

Terakami, Fujio

Teramae, Takashi Derek

Teramoto, Toshiaki

Terao, Nobuyoshi Norman

Terao, Norio

Terao, Sadao Roy

Teraoka, Tatsuo

Teraura, Tadashi

Terazawa, Tokio George

Teshima, Harry Toshio

Teshima, James

Teshima, Robert Sadaki

Tetsutani, Nobuo S.

Toba, Tsutomu Ben

Toda, Harry Haruyoshi

Toda, James K.

Toda, James Yukio Rev.

Toda, Katashi Kay

Toda, Wilbert Yasuho
Todo, Jiro
Toguchi, Seishu
Toguchi, Takemitsu
Toi, Kiyomi
Toimoto, Arthur Asa
Toji, Tsugio
Tokirio, Frank Masaru
Tokubo, Frank Teruo
Tokuda, Roy Masaichi
Tokuda, Shizuo Billy
Tokunaga, George
Tokunaga, Isao
Tokuno, Shiro
Tokushige, William Tokuo
Toma, Jiro
Toma, Masao
Toma, Rodney Shiei
Toma, Takeyuki Dick
Tomihiro, Thomas Takashi
Tominaga, Hideo
Tominaga, Masayuki M.
Tomita, Frank Tetsuro
Tomita, Isao
Tomita, Kendall H.
Tomita, Masao
Tomita, Satoshi Robert
Tomita, Shigeru
Tomita, Tadao
Tonokawa, Etsuo
Torakawa, Takashi
Torigoe, Toichi
Toriumi, William Yoichi
Tottori, Calvin Atsushi
Towata, Robert S.
Toya, George Yoshinobu
Toyama, Roy
Toyama, Sadao
Toyama, Tom K.
Toyofuku, Suetsuki

Toyoshima, Shigeto A.
Toyota, Kiyoshi John
Toyota, Ralph Hiroshi
Tsubota, Bert Toshio
Tsubota, Kiyoshi Tom
Tsubota, Sadamu
Tsubota, Shigeru M.
Tsuchida, Jack Yoshio
Tsuchida, Kiwamu
Tsuchida, Satoshi
Tsuchikawa, Osao Ossie
Tsuchimochi, Minoru
Tsuchimoto, Isamu
Tsuchiya, Harry Taketo
Tsuchiya, Junso Carl
Tsuchiyama, Henry Tomio
Tsuchiyama, Tamie (WAC)
Tsuchiyama, Yoshio
Tsuda, Albert Takeshi
Tsuda, Isamu
Tsuji, Keiji
Tsuji, Kiyoshi
Tsuji, Shigeo Larry
Tsuji, Takeo
Tsujimoto, Fred H.
Tsujimoto, Richard K.
Tsujimoto, Ted M.
Tsukada, Masao
Tsukahara, Taro
Tsukahira, Keiji Peter
Tsukamoto, Bill Tadashi
Tsukazaki, Masayuki
Tsukazaki, Norman Takayuki
Tsukichi, George Sadaji
Tsukiyama, Ted Tatsuya
Tsumura, George Kenichi
Tsumura, James Masanori
Tsunashima, Akira
Tsuneishi, Hughes Takuma
Tsuneishi, Noel Keiichi

Tsuneishi, Warren Michio

Tsunezumi, Takeshi

Tsuno, Isao J.

Tsunoda, Tsutomu Tom

Tsuruda, Tomochi Tom

Tsuruoka, Teruo George

Tsurutani, James Shigeo

Tsusaki, Willie

Tsushima, Harry Tsunezo

Tsutsui, Harry Toshio

Tsutsui, Isao Jerry

Tsutsui, Katsumi Fred

Tsutsumi, Barney Shigeru

Tsutsumi, Frank A.

Tsutsumi, Harry M.

Tsutsumi, Hiromi

Tsuyuki, Hideo

Tsuyuki, Kiyoshi Jerry

Uchida, George

Uchida, Jack Mitsutoshi

Uchida, Megumi Barney

Uchida, Yoshio

Uchigaki, Tadashi

Uchimura, Minoru

Uchino, Fumio

Uchiyama, Fusao

Uda, Ben

Uda, Gilbert Kiyoshi

Ueda, George Hiroshi

Ueda, Robert Yoneo

Uehara, James Minobu

Uehara, Kunichi

Uehara, Wallace Tsugimi

Uejima, Tomonobu

Ueki, Calvin K.

Ueki, Harold Haruo

Ueki, Hisayoshi

Ueki, Leonard Tadae

Ueki, Nils K.

Uematsu, Joe S.

Uemoto, Tony Tokio

Uemura, Mitsuo

Ueno, James Morio

Ueno, Norman Shiro

Ueoka, Meyer Masato

Uesato, Toshio

Uetake, Harry Manabu

Uetake, Shinobu

Uetake, Tamayo Mildred (WAC)

Ugaki, Yoshihisa Yosh

Ujifusa, Robert Lee

Ujiie, Shigeru Sam

Ujimori, Eddie M.

Ujimori, Herbert H.

Ukishima, John Satoru

Umade, Samuel Yasuko

Umeda, Ben Tsutomu

Umeda, Harry Tsutomu

Umemoto, Charles Naoki

Umemoto, Joe Fumio

Umemoto, Kazuo

Umetani, Sam Yasuo

Umezu, Bill Shiro

Umezu, Yasuo Jack

Uni, Kenneth Mack

Uno, Hirobumi

Uno, Howard Yasumaru

Uno, Roy Hiroshi

Uno, Stanley Toshimaru

Uno, Toshiichi Jack

Ura, Aiko (WAC)

Uramoto, Yukio

Uranaka, Francis Y.

Urasaki, Harry Masaichi

Urata, Edward Yoshio

Urata, James Hajime

Urata, Wallace Takeshi

Uratsu, Gene Masaji

Uratsu, Marvin Tetsushi

Uriu, Masashi Royden

Uriu, Tadashi
Ushijima, George W.
Ushijima, Shigeyasu
Ushiro, Arthur Katsuyoshi
Ushiro, Masaru
Ushiroda, George T.
Usui, Masaru
Usui, Mitsuo
Uto, Hideo
Uyechi, Edward Kotaro
Uyeda, Akio
Uyeda, Harrison Etsuji
Uyeda, Kenichi
Uyeda, Kiyoshi James
Uyeda, Masao Bud
Uyeda, Robert Sadayuki
Uyeda, Takeshi
Uyeda, Tom Tomio
Uyeda, Tomoyoshi Tom
Uyehara, Harry Kaoru
Uyehara, Henry Toshiharu
Uyehara, Hideo Fred
Uyehara, Isamu
Uyehara, Kazuyo
Uyehara, Masanori
Uyehara, Matsunobu
Uyehata, Roy Toshitsura
Uyemura, Harry
Uyemura, Katsumi
Uyeno, Joe Yuzuru
Uyeno, Kenichi Thomas
Uyeno, Toyome Terry
Uyeoka, Charles Tadashi
Uyesugi, Kenji Kenneth
Uyesugi, Masao Mark
Wada, Benji
Wada, Douglas T.
Wada, George Hiromu
Wada, Hiromu William
Wada, Kenzaburo Kennnie

Wada, Larry M.
Wada, Masayoshi Edward
Wada, Yoritada
Wakai, Harry Hajime
Wakai, Theodore Y.
Wakai, Warren T.
Wakakuwa, Franklin Chuichi
Wakamatsu, Joe S.
Wakamiya, James M.
Wakamiya, Katsushi
Wakano, Victor Ichiro
Wakasa, Ben Shigeru
Wakasa, Robert Tatsumi
Wakayama, George
Wakayama, Ginzo
Wakayama, Jack Tsunae
Wakayama, Kinya
Wakayama, Mitsuo
Wakayama, William Susumu
Wakida, Momoichi
Wakimoto, Tsutomu Mac
Wakimura, Masao
Wakumoto, Noboru
Walsh, George W. Jr.
Watada, Takeshi Alfred
Watanabe, Chikara Stanley
Watanabe, Ernest Tsuneo
Watanabe, Harvey Hideo
Watanabe, Iris A. (WAC)
Watanabe, Jiro
Watanabe, Kamekichi
Watanabe, Katsuo
Watanabe, Kazuo
Watanabe, Kazuo Larry
Watanabe, Masami
Watanabe, Masao
Watanabe, Minoru
Watanabe, Mitsuo
Watanabe, Mitsuru
Watanabe, Saburo

Watanabe, Sadao
Watanabe, Satoru
Watanabe, Shizuo
Watanabe, Takashi Richard
Watanabe, Tamotsu
Watanabe, Tom
Watanabe, Tomoichiro
Watanabe, Toru
Watanabe, Tsugio
Watanuki, Masashi Max
Wataru, Shigeo
Watasaki, Kiyoshi
Watasaki, Masao
Watasaki, Sadao
Watson, Richard L.
Yaatame, Robert Masao
Yada, Edward Kotaro
Yada, Joe Jusaku
Yafuso, Hiroshi
Yagawa, Salem Seiran
Yagi, Fumio Dr.
Yagi, Steve Kaoru
Yagihara, Teruaki
Yagihara, Teruo
Yagyu, Paul Kiyoshi
Yajima, Tadashi T.
Yakura, Hiroshi David
Yama, Toshiharu
Yamada, Edward
Yamada, Hatsumi
Yamada, James Shinji
Yamada, Kazuhiko
Yamada, Kazuto
Yamada, Masahide
Yamada, Masamitsu
Yamada, N.
Yamada, Noboru
Yamada, Raymond Sunao
Yamada, Sachio
Yamada, Tatao

Yamada, Tetsuji
Yamada, Tom Tsutomu
Yamada, Tomio
Yamada, Tomoyuki .
Yamada, Toshimi
Yamada, Towru
Yamada, W.
Yamada, Yasuo
Yamada, Yoshikazu
Yamagami, Jiro
Yamagami, Yoneichi Tom
Yamagata, Clarence S.
Yamagata, George Yoshio
Yamagata, Jack
Yamagata, John Yukio
Yamagata, Mineo
Yamagata, Taisuke
Yamaguchi, Edward Tokio
Yamaguchi, Gary M.
Yamaguchi, George
Yamaguchi, George S.
Yamaguchi, George Soichi
Yamaguchi, George T.
Yamaguchi, Harold Shigeo
Yamaguchi, Iwao
Yamaguchi, James
Yamaguchi, Jimmie Noboru
Yamaguchi, Ken
Yamaguchi, Kaoru
Yamaguchi, Kazuo
Yamaguchi, Masao
Yamaguchi, R.
Yamaguchi, Shigeru
Yamaguchi, Shogo
Yamaguchi, Tokio
Yamaki, Bill Shuichi
Yamaki, Shigenobu
Yamamizu, Torao
Yamamoto, Ben Izumi
Yamamoto, Clarence Masaru

Yamamoto, Edward Soichi
Yamamoto, Ernest Torakazu
Yamamoto, Floyd Masayuki
Yamamoto, Francis Ryozo
Yamamoto, Genji J.
Yamamoto, George Haruyoshi
Yamamoto, George Katsuichi
Yamamoto, Harry K.
Yamamoto, Hiroshi
Yamamoto, Hirotoshi
Yamamoto, Ikuo
Yamamoto, Kiyodo
Yamamoto, Kiyoshi Kio
Yamamoto, Kiyoshi Kiyo
Yamamoto, Kunio
Yamamoto, Masatsuki
Yamamoto, N.
Yamamoto, Noboru Jack
Yamamoto, Osame Sammy
Yamamoto, Osamu
Yamamoto, Paul Hiroshi
Yamamoto, Robert Hajime
Yamamoto, Shinobu
Yamamoto, Shoichi Eddie
Yamamoto, Stanley Asao
Yamamoto, Stanley Yoshito
Yamamoto, Steve Shizuma
Yamamoto, Tatsuo
Yamamoto, Tetsuo
Yamamoto, Tom T.
Yamamoto, Yoshiharu William
Yamamoto, Yoshiyuki
Yamamura, George Terumi
Yamanaka, Daizo Roy
Yamanaka, Hideki
Yamanaka, James Yukio
Yamanaka, Narihiko
Yamanaka, Takashi
Yamanaka, William Masami
Yamane, Charles Saburo

Yamane, Kazuo Ernest
Yamane, Kosei
Yamane, Takeo
Yamane, Tatsuo Richard
Yamaoka, Garo
Yamaoka, Masakazu
Yamaoka, Ted Y.
Yamasaki, George M.
Yamasaki, George T.
Yamasaki, Masao Virgil
Yamasaki, Royoichi Roy
Yamasaki, William A.
Yamase, Charles Saburo
Yamashige, Fred H.
Yamashiro, George
Yamashiro, Hiroshi
Yamashiro, Hugh I.
Yamashiro, James Jiro
Yamashiro, Paul Touru
Yamashita, George J.
Yamashita, Harry Kaichi
Yamashita, Henry Y.
Yamashita, Hisako (WAC)
Yamashita, Isamu
Yamashita, Kanshi Stanley
Yamashita, Koichi
Yamashita, Nobuo
Yamashita, Shigeru
Yamashita, Takashi
Yamashita, Takeshi
Yamashita, Tom T.
Yamashita, Yasuo George
Yamate, Sohei
Yamauchi, Jackson M.
Yamauchi, Louis Kazuo
Yamauchi, Yoshito Roy
Yamazaki, Tadami
Yamazaki, Tomomasa
Yanagihara, Kyoichi Qupie
Yanaginuma, Kiyoshi

Yanamura, Herbert Kiyoto
Yano, Albert Hisayuki
Yano, Edward H.
Yano, Kataru
Yano, Tsutomu Thomas
Yasuda, Isao
Yasuda, Jiro
Yasuda, Tsukasa James
Yasui, Kenji Kenny
Yasui, Tatsumi
Yasukawa, Leo Isamu
Yasunaga, George
Yasunobu, Kerry Tsuyoshi
Yasutake, George M.
Yasutake, Hiroki
Yasutake, Shigeo Michael
Yasutake, Yasushi
Yatabe, Akira
Yatogo, Shigeru Frank
Yego, Tadashi
Yeki, Ben T.
Yempuku, Ralph T.
Yenari, Susumu William
Yenari, Theodore Touru
Yoda, Tetsuya
Yodogawa, Masao
Yokobe, Fumio
Yokogawa, Nobuyuki
Yokogawa, Tadashi
Yokoi, Harris Shoshi
Yokomizo, Shichiro
Yokota, Masaru
Yokota, Richard Shigeru
Yokota, Shigeo
Yokoyama, F.
Yokoyama, G.
Yokoyama, Henry Naoki
Yokoyama, Herbert N.
Yokoyama, Jimmie Noboru
Yokoyama, Mamoru Steve

Yomogida, Sam Isamu
Yoneda, Karl Goso
Yonehara, Tamotsu Tom
Yonehiro, Horace H.
Yoneji, George H.
Yoneji, Mitsuso
Yoneji, Takeo
Yonekawa, Tokio
Yonemori, Daniel M.
Yonemura, Joe
Yonemura, Masatatsu
Yonemura, Minoru
Yonemura, Yonezo
Yoneshige, Itsuo
Yoneshige, Shoji
Yoneyama, Isamu
Yorichi, Alex Nobuo
Yorioka, Joshi Joe
Yoshida, Charles A.
Yoshida, George S.
Yoshida, George Yoshio
Yoshida, Hideo
Yoshida, Hiroshi
Yoshida, Hiroshi P.
Yoshida, James Shunichi
Yoshida, John Takao
Yoshida, Katsumi Archie
Yoshida, Kazuo
Yoshida, Magoichi
Yoshida, Minoru
Yoshida, Mitsuo Ronald
Yoshida, Shoichi
Yoshihara, Hideo
Yoshihashi, Taro
Yoshihata, Kazu
Yoshika, Takashi Lefty
Yoshikawa, Thomas Hisayuki
Yoshimoto, Katsuyuki
Yoshimoto, Kazuo
Yoshimoto, Noboru

Yoshimoto, Tadao
Yoshimoto, Terasu Terry
Yoshimura, Akigi
Yoshimura, Francis K.
Yoshimura, Frank Toshio
Yoshimura, Kiyoshi
Yoshimura, Kiyoto
Yoshimura, Masao K.
Yoshimura, Noboru
Yoshimura, Takashi
Yoshimura, Teruo
Yoshinaga, George
Yoshinaga, James Yoshio
Yoshinaga, Tsugio John
Yoshinaka, Tokuo
Yoshino, Elmer
Yoshino, Hiroo Stanley
Yoshino, Ikuro Ike
Yoshino, John Yoshitaka
Yoshino, Masaaki Jack
Yoshino, Paul
Yoshino, Yowge B.
Yoshinobu, James S.

Yoshioka, Gunichi
Yoshioka, Charles Takeo
Yoshioka, Giichi
Yoshioka, James Shizuma
Yoshioka, Masaru Robert
Yoshioka, Nobuo
Yoshioka, Robert Kazuso
Yoshioka, Robert M.
Yoshioka, Robert Tsukio
Yoshioka, Takeo
Yoshioka, Toshio Richard
Yoshioka, Yoshito Roy
Yoshisato, George
Yoshitake, Shigeyuki
Yoshiwara, Grove Shinji
Yoshiwara, Joe Josaku
Yoshizawa, Izumi
Yota, Tom Tsutomu
Yotsuya, Keiji
Yuki, Harvard Katsumi
Yukimura, Jiro
Yumibe, Kiyoshi
Yuzawa, George Katsumi

JAPANESE AMERICAN SOLDIERS WHO LOST THEIR LIVES IN THE PACIFIC THEATER IN WORLD WAR II

Fujino, Russell Takeo
Fukui, Edwin Yukio
Goshikoma, Ralph Masoe
Hachiya, Frank Tadakazu
Hara, Ben Kayji
Hirano, Frederick M.
Ikeda, George Tsuyoshi
Ikemoto, Haruyuki
Imano, Susumu Imano
Imoto, William Shunichi
Inouye, Kazuyoshi
Ishii, Masayuki
Kadoyama, Joe Yazuru
Kashiwagi, Kazuo
Kataoka, Yoshitaka
Kato, John
Kumura, John S.
Kurokawa, Ben Satoshi
Kuwada, Joseph Takeo
Laffin, William
Matoba, Michiyasu
Migita, Torao
Miura, Jack Eso
Mizumoto, Larry Tamotsu
Mizutari, Terry Yukitaka
Mori, Shigeru
Motokane, Wilfred Masao
Motonaga, Susumu

Murakami, Tokiwo
Muramoto, Masaru
Nakahara, Shoichi Stanley
Nakamura, George Ichiro
Nakamura, Iwao
Nakamura, Masaki H.
Nii, Yoshito
Okido, Shoji
Oku, Muneo Larry
Omura, Kenneth Kenji
Osato, Reginald Masaichi
Ota, Daniel C.
Saito, Tsukasa
Shibata, George Mitsuru
Shiigi, Shinichi
Shikata, George M.
Shirakawa, Raymond Hiroshi
Shiroishi, Shiogeomi
Sogi, Masaru Harold
Soken, Yeishun Allen
Tani, Bushichi
Teramoto, Toshiaki
Yamaguchi, George T.
Yamamizu, Torao
Yamazaki, Tomomasa
Yano, Albert Hisayuki
Yonemura, Yonezo

BIBLIOGRAPHY

Anthony, J. Garner. *Hawaii Under Army Rule*. Stanford, CA: Stanford University Press, 1955.

Applegate, Rex. *Kill or Get Killed: A Manual of Hand-to-Hand Fighting*. Boulder, CO: Paladin Press, 2007.

Appleman, Roy E., James M. Burns, Russell A. Gugeler, and John Stevens. *Okinawa: The Last Battle*. Washington, DC: Center of Military History, 1948.

Astor, Gerald. *The Jungle War: Mavericks, Marauders, and Madmen in the China-Burma-India Theater of WWII*. New York: John Wiley and Sons, 2004.

Astroth, Alexander. *Mass Suicides on Saipan and Tinian, 1944: An Examination of the Civilian Deaths in Historical Context*. Jefferson, NC: McFarland and Co., 2019.

Bartley, Whitman S. *Iwo Jima: Amphibious Epic*. Washington, DC: Historical Branch, G-3 Division, Headquarters, U.S. Marine Corps, 1954.

Benedict, Ruth. *The Chrysanthemum and the Sword: Patterns of Japanese Culture*. New York: Houghton Mifflin Harcourt, 1946.

Bergamini, David. *Japan's Imperial Conspiracy*. New York: William Morrow, 1971.

Blume, Lesley M. M. *Fallout: The Hiroshima Cover-up and the Reporter Who Revealed It to the World*. New York: Simon and Schuster, 2020.

Boomhower, Ray E. *Dispatches from the Pacific: The World War II Reporting of Robert L. Sherrod*. Bloomington, IN: Indiana University Press, 2017.

Burton, Jeffery F., Mary M. Farrell, Florence B. Lord, and Richard W. Lord. *Confinement and Ethnicity: An Overview of World War II Japanese American Relocation Sites*. Tucson, AZ: Western Archeological and Conservation Center, 1999.

Byas, Hugh. *Government by Assassination*. New York: Alfred A. Knopf, 1942.

Cary, Otis, ed. *War-Wasted Asia: Letters, 1945–46*. Tokyo, Kodansha International, 1975.

Chan, Won-loy. *Burma: The Untold Story*. Novato, CA: Presidio Press, 1986.

Chapin, John C. "The Fifth Marine Division in World War II." Washington, DC: Historical Division, U.S. Marine Corps (August 1945).

Chase, William C. *Front Line General: The Commands of William C. Chase*. Houston: Pacesetter Press, 1975.

Cloe, John Haile. *Attu: The Forgotten Battle*. Washington, DC: National Park Service, 2018.

Coffman, Tom. *How Hawaii Changed America: The Movement for Racial Equality 1939–1942*. Honolulu: EpiCenter, 2015.

Commission on Wartime Relocation and Internment of Civilians. *Personal Justice Denied: Reports of the Commission on Wartime Relocation and Internment of Civilians*. Seattle: University of Washington Press, 1997.

Conner, Howard M. *The Spearhead: The World War II History of the 5th Marine Division*. Washington, DC: Infantry Journal Press, 1950.

Conrat, Maisie and Richard. *Executive Order 9066: The Internment of 110,000 Japanese Americans*. Los Angeles: UCLA Asian American Studies Center Press, 1992.

Corbin, Alexander D. *The History of Camp Tracy: Japanese WWII POWs and the Future of Strategic Interrogation*. Fort Belvoir, VA: Ziedon Press, 2009.

Corner, George Washington. *Two Centuries of Medicine: A History of the School of Medicine, University of Pennsylvania*. New York: Lippincott, 1965.

Cray, Ed. *Chief Justice: A Biography of Earl Warren*. New York: Simon and Schuster, 1997.

Crost, Lyn. *Honor by Fire: Japanese Americans at War in Europe and the Pacific*. Novato, CA: Presidio Press, 1994.

Daniels, Roger. *Asian America: Chinese and Japanese in the United States since 1850*. Seattle: University of Washington Press, 1988.

———. *Concentration Camps USA: Japanese Americans and World War II*. New York: Holt, Rinehart and Winston, 1971.

———. *Prisoners Without Trial: Japanese Americans in World War II*. New York: Hill and Wang, 1993.

David, Saul. *Crucible of Hell: The Heroism and Tragedy of Okinawa, 1945*. New York: Hachette Books, 2020.

Davidson, Orlando R., J. Carl Willems, and Joseph A. Kohl. *The Deadeyes: The Story of the 96th Infantry Division*. Washington, DC: Infantry Journal Press, 1947.

Davie, Maurice R. *Refugees in America: Report of the Committee for the Study of Recent Immigration from Europe*. New York: Harper and Brothers, 1947.

Day, Ronnie. *New Georgia: The Second Battle for the Solomons*. Bloomington, IN: Indiana University Press, 2016.

Department of the Army. *The Army Almanac*. Harrisburg, PA: Stackpole Co., 1959.

Dower, John W. *Embracing Defeat: Japan in the Wake of World War II*. New York: W. W. Norton, 1999.

———. *War Without Mercy: Race & Power in the Pacific War*. New York: Pantheon Books, 1986.

Drea, Edward J. *Japan's Imperial Army: Its Rise and Fall, 1853–1945*. Lawrence, KS: University Press of Kansas, 2009.

Dulles, Allen W. *The Craft of Intelligence*. Guilford, CT: Lyons Press, 2006.

Dunlap, Richard. *Behind Japanese Lines: With the OSS in Burma*. New York: Rand McNally and Co., 1979.

Dyer, George C. *On the Treadmill to Pearl Harbor: The Memoirs of Admiral James O. Richardson USN*. Washington, DC: Naval History Division, Department of the Navy, 1973.

Eldridge, Fred. *Wrath in Burma: The Uncensored Story of General Stilwell*. Garden City, NY: Doubleday, 1946.

Ellis, John. *Brute Force: Allied Strategy and Tactics in the Second World War*. New York: Viking, 1990.

Emmerson, John K. *The Japanese Thread: A Life in the U.S. Foreign Service*. New York: Holt, Rinehart and Winston, 1978.

Falk, Stanley L., and Warren M. Tsuneishi, eds. *American Patriots: MIS in the War Against Japan*. Washington, DC: Japanese American Veterans Association, 1995.

Finnegan, John Patrick. *Military Intelligence*. Washington, DC: Center of Military History, 1998.

Fiset, Louis, and Gail M. Nomura, eds. *Nikkei in the Pacific Northwest: Japanese Americans and Japanese Canadians in the Twentieth Century*. Seattle: University of Washington Press, 2005.

Flewelling, Stan. *Shirakawa: Stories from a Pacific Northwest Japanese American Community*. Seattle: University of Washington Press, 2002.

Flynn, George Q. *The Draft: 1940–1973*. Lawrence, KS: University Press of Kansas, 1993.

Frank, Richard B. *Downfall: The End of the Imperial Japanese Empire*. New York: Random House, 1999.

Frierson, William C. "The Admiralties: Operations of the 1st Cavalry Division, 29 February–18 May 1944." Historical Division, War Department, 1946.

Fuller, Richard. *Shokan Hirohito's Samurai: Leaders of the Japanese Armed Forces, 1926–1945*. London: Arms and Armour Press, 1992.

Furuiye, Nobuo, and Clarke M. Brandt. *I Am MIS: Experiences of a Member of the Military Intelligence Service in the Pacific Theater of Operations During WWII*. Aurora, CO: Privately published, 1999.

Gabbett, Michael. *The Bastards of Burma: Merrill's Marauders and the MARS Task Force Revisited*. Albuquerque, NM: Desert Dreams Publishers, 1989.

Gailey, Harry A. *"Howlin' Mad" vs. the Army: Conflict in Command: Saipan 1944*. Novato, CA: Presidio Press, 1986.

Gaither, John B. "Galahad Redux: An Assessment of the Disintegration of Merrill's Marauders." Fort Leavenworth, KS: Army Command and General Staff College, 1975.

Garfield, Brian. *The Thousand-Mile War: World War II in Alaska and the Aleutians*. Fairbanks, AK: University of Alaska Press (1969).

Girdner, Audrie, and Anne Loftis. *The Great Betrayal: The Evacuation of the Japanese-Americans During World War II*. New York: Macmillan Co., 1969.

Glacken, Clarence. *The Great Loochoo: A Study of Okinawan Village Life*. Berkeley: University of California Press, 1955.

Gruber, Ruth. *Inside of Time: My Journey from Alaska to Israel*. New York: Carroll and Graf Publishers, 2003.

Haller, Stephen A. *The Last Word in Airfields*. San Francisco: Golden Gate National Parks Association, 2001.

Halsey, William F., and J. Bryan III. *Admiral Halsey's Story*. New York: McGraw-Hill, 1947.

Hamm, Diane L., ed. *Military Intelligence: Its Heroes and Legends*. Honolulu: University Press of the Pacific, 2001.

Harries, Meirion and Susie. *Soldiers of the Sun: The Rise and Fall of the Imperial Japanese Army*. New York: Random House, 1991.

Harrington, Joseph D. *Yankee Samurai: The Secret Role of Nisei in America's Pacific Victory*. Detroit: Pettigrew Enterprises, 1979.

Hawaii Nikkei History Editorial Board. *Japanese Eyes, American Heart*. Honolulu: Tendai Educational Foundation, 1998.

Haynes, Fred, and James A. Warren. *The Lions of Iwo Jima: The Story of Combat Team 28 and the Bloodiest Battle in Marine Corps History*. New York: Henry Holt and Co., 2008.

Hays, Otis Jr. *Alaska's Hidden Wars: Secret Campaigns on the North Pacific Rim*. Fairbanks, AK: University of Alaska Press, 2004.

Henderson, Bruce. *Rescue at Los Baños: The Most Daring Prison Camp Raid of World War II*. New York: William Morrow, 2015.

Hersey, John. *Hiroshima*. New York: Alfred A. Knopf, 1985.

Higgins, John J. *A History of the First Connecticut Regiment, 1671–1963*.

Hill, Max. *Exchange Ship*. New York: Farrah and Rinehart, 1942.

Hirabayashi, Gordon K. *A Principled Stand: The Story of* Hirabayashi v. United States. Seattle: University of Washington Press, 2013.

Hirrel, Leo P. *U.S. Army Campaigns of World War II: Bismarck Archipelago*. Washington, DC: U.S. Army Center of Military History, 1994.

Historical Division, War Department. *The Admiralties: Operations of the 1st Cavalry Division, 29 February–18 May 1944*. Washington, DC: U.S. Army, Center of Military History, 1990.

Hollinger, David A. *Protestants Aboard: How Missionaries Tried to Change the World but Changed America*. Princeton: Princeton University Press, 2017.

Holmes, W. J. *Double-Edged Secrets: U.S. Naval Intelligence Operations in the Pacific During World War II*. Annapolis, MD: Naval Institute Press, 1979.

Hopkins, James E. T. *Spearhead: A Complete History of Merrill's Marauder Rangers*. Baltimore: Galahad Press, 1999.

Hoppes, Jonna Doolittle. *Just Doing My Job: Stories of Service from World War II*. Santa Monica, CA: Santa Monica Press, 2009.

Horie, Seiji. *Aru Okinawa Hawai Imin no Shinjuwan* [*One Okinawan Immigrant's Pearl Harbor*]. Tokyo: PHP Kenkyusho Press, 1991. Translated by Sonya Johnson, 2020.

Hosokawa, Bill. *Nisei: The Quiet Americans: The Story of a People*. New York: William Morrow, 1969.

———. *The Two Worlds of Jim Yoshida: A New and True Story of a Man Without a Country*. New York: William Morrow, 1972.

Hotta, Eri. *Japan 1941: Countdown to Infamy*. New York: Vintage Books, 2013.

Houston, Jeanne Wakatsuki, and James D. Houston. *Farewell to Manzanar*. Boston: Houghton Mifflin Co., 1973.

Howard, John. *Concentration Camps on the Home Front: Japanese Americans in the House of Jim Crow*. Chicago: University of Chicago Press, 2009.

Hunter, Col. Charles Newton. *Galahad*. San Antonio, TX: Naylor Company, 1963.

Ichinokuchi, Tad. *John Aiso and the M.I.S.: Japanese-American Soldiers in the Military Intelligence Service, World War II*. Los Angeles: Military Intelligence Service, 1988.

Ige, Tom. *Boy from Kahaluu*. Honolulu: Kin Cho Jin Kai, 1989.

Inouye, Daniel K., with Lawrence Elliott. *Journey to Washington*. New York: Prentice-Hall, 1967.

Irons, Peter. *Justice at War: The Story of the Japanese American Internment Cases.* New York: Oxford University Press, 1983.

———. *Justice Delayed: The Record of the Japanese American Internment Cases.* Middletown, CT: Wesleyan University Press, 1989.

Jacoby, Harold Stanley. *Tule Lake: From Relocation to Segregation.* Grass Valley, CA: Comstock Bonanza Press, 1996.

Jones, John M. *The War Diary of the 5307 Composite Unit (Provisional).* Merrill's Marauders Association, 2012.

Kase, Toshikazu. *Journey to the Missouri.* New Haven, CT: Yale University Press, 1950.

Katcher, Leo. *Earl Warren: A Political Biography.* New York: McGraw-Hill Book Co., 1967.

Keene, Donald. *On Familiar Terms: A Journey Across Cultures.* New York: Kodansha America, 1994.

Kenney, Dave. *Minnesota Goes to War: The Home Front During World War II.* St. Paul, MN: Minnesota Historical Society, 2005.

King, Dan. *A Tomb Called Iwo Jima: Firsthand Accounts from Japanese Survivors.* North Charleston, SC: CreateSpace, 2020.

Kinnison, Henry L. IV. *The Deeds of Valiant Men: A Study in Leadership: The Marauders in North Burma, 1944.* Carlisle Barracks, PA: U.S. Army War College, 1993.

Kitagawa, Daisuke. *Issei and Nisei: The Internment Years.* New York: Seabury Press, 1967.

Kiyota, Minoru. *Beyond Loyalty: The Story of a Kibei.* Honolulu: University of Hawaii Press, 1997.

Kotani, Roland. *The Japanese in Hawaii: A Century of Struggle.* Honolulu: Hawaii Hochi, 1985.

Lash, Joseph P. *Eleanor and Franklin.* New York: W. W. Norton, 1971.

Lehman, Anthony L. *Birthright of Barbed Wire: The Santa Anita Assembly Center for the Japanese.* Los Angeles: Westernlore Press, 1970.

Love, Edmund G. *The 27th Infantry Division in World War II.* Nashville, TN: Battery Press, 1949.

Lyons, Fred O. As told to Paul Wilder in 1945. "Merrill's Marauders in Burma: Here's What Really Happened." *Ex-CBI Roundup*, April 1969.

MacArthur, Douglas. *Reminiscences.* New York: McGraw-Hill, 1964.

MacArthur's General Staff. *Reports of MacArthur: The Campaigns of MacArthur in the Pacific.* Washington, DC: U.S. Government Printing Office, 1966.

MacGarrigle, George L. *Central Burma.* Washington, DC: U.S. Army Center of Military History, 1996.

MacKenzie, S. P. "The Treatment of Prisoners of War in World War II." *Journal of Modern History* 66, no. 3 (September 1994): 487–520.

Magoon, Christopher. "The 20th General Hospital." *The Pharos,* Alpha Omega Alpha Honor Medical Society (Autumn 2016).

Mandel, Lee. *Unlikely Warrior: A Pacifist Rabbi's Journey from Pulpit to Iwo Jima.* Gretna, LA: Pelican Publishing, 2015.

Marrin, Albert. *Uprooted: The Japanese American Experiences During World War II.* New York: Alfred A. Knopf, 2016.

Marshall, S. L. A. *Bringing Up the Rear: A Memoir.* San Rafael, CA: Presidio Press, 1979.

Masaaki, Aniya. "Compulsory Mass Suicides, the Battle of Okinawa, and Japan's Textbook Controversy." *Japan Focus: The Asia-Pacific Journal* (2008).

Masaharu, Ano. "Loyal Linguists—Nisei of World War II Learned Japanese in Minnesota," *Minnesota History,* vol. 45 (Fall 1977).

Mashbir, Sidney Forrester. *I Was An American Spy.* New York: Vantage Press, 1953.

Matsumoto, Valerie J. *Farming the Home Place: A Japanese American Community in California, 1919–1982.* Ithaca, NY: Cornell University Press, 1993.

McDonald, Andrew T., and Verlain Stoner McDonald. *Paul Rusch in Postwar Japan: Evangelism, Rural Development, and the Battle Against Communism.* Lexington, KY: University Press of Kentucky, 2018.

McNaughton, James C. *Nisei Linguists: Japanese Americans in the Military Intelligence Service During World War II.* Washington, DC: Department of the Army, 2006.

McWilliams, Carey. *Prejudice: Japanese-Americans: Symbol of Racial Intolerance.* Boston: Little, Brown and Co., 1944.

Merrill's Marauders, February–May 1944. Historical Division, War Department, for American Forces in Action series. Washington, DC: U.S. Government Printing Office, 1945.

Miller, Donald L. *D-Days in the Pacific.* New York: Simon and Schuster, 2005.

Miller, Edward G. "Action in the Admiralties." *WWII Quarterly, Journal of the Second World War* (Fall 2017).

Miller, John Jr. *United States Army in World War II. The War in the Pacific. Cartwheel: The Reduction of Rabaul.* Washington, DC: Department of the Army, 1959.

Morison, Samuel Eliot. *Aleutians, Gilberts and Marshalls,* vol. 7 of *History of United States Naval Operations in World War II.* Edison, NJ: Castle Books, 2001.

————. *Breaking the Bismarcks Barrier*, vol. 6 of *History of United States Naval Operations in World War II*. Edison, NJ: Castle Books, 2001.

————. *Leyte, June 1944–January 1945*, vol. 22 of *History of United States Naval Operations in World War II*. Edison, NJ: Castle Books, 2001.

————. *The Struggle for Guadalcanal*, vol. 5 of *History of United States Naval Operations in World War II*. Edison, NJ: Castle Books, 2001.

————. *Victory in the Pacific 1945*, vol. 14 of *History of the United States Naval Operations in World War II*. Edision, NJ: Castle Books, 2001.

Mortimer, Gavin. *Merrill's Marauders: The Untold Story of Unit Galahad and the Toughest Special Forces Mission of World War II*. Minneapolis, MN: Zenith Press, 2013.

Moyar, Mark. *Oppose Any Foe: The Rise of America's Special Operations Forces*. New York: Basic Books, 2017.

Muranaka, Reynold T. *Practicality of the Japanese Language in the United States Army*. Lakewood, WA: Muranaka Press, 2010.

Nakasone, Edwin M. *The Nisei Soldiers: Historical Essays on World War II and the Korean War*. White Bear Lake, MN: J-Press, 1999.

Nelson, Craig. *The First Heroes: The Extraordinary Story of the Doolittle Raid—America's First World War II Victory*. New York: Viking Penguin, 2002.

Newcomb, Richard F. *Iwo Jima*. Garden City, NJ: Nelson Doubleday, 1983.

Niiya, Brian. *Encyclopedia of Japanese American History: An A-to-Z Reference from 1868 to the Present*. New York: Facts on File, 2001.

Ninomiya, Calvin. *Patriots/2: About World War II and Two Americans Who Made Our Country a Better Place for All of Us*. Unpublished, 2012.

Nishimura, Hiro. *Trials and Triumphs of the Nikkei*. Mercer Island, WA: Fukuda Publishers, 1993.

Obmascik, Mark. *The Story of Our Shores: One Island, Two Soldiers, and the Forgotten Battle of World War II*. New York: Atria Books, 2019.

O'Brien, Francis A. *Battling for Saipan: The True Story of an American Hero*. New York: Ballantine Books, 2003.

Odo, Franklin. *No Sword to Bury: Japanese Americans in Hawaii During World War II*. Philadelphia: Temple University Press, 2004.

O'Donnell, Patrick K. *Into the Rising Sun: In Their Own Words, World War II's Pacific Veterans Reveal the Heart of Combat*. New York: Free Press, 2002.

Ogburn, Charlton Jr. *The Marauders*. New York: Harper and Brothers, 1956.

Oguro, Richard S. *Senpai Gumi*. Colusa, CA: Self-published, 1982.

Okada, John. *No-No Boy*. Tokyo, Japan: Charles E. Tuttle, 1957.

Okihiro, Gary Y. *Cane Fires: The Anti-Japanese Movement in Hawaii 1865–1945*. Philadelphia: Temple University Press, 1991.

O'Neill, Robert, ed. *The Road to Victory: From Pearl Harbor to Okinawa*. Oxford: Osprey Publishing, 2011.

Perras, Galen Roger. *Stepping Stones to Nowhere: The Aleutian Islands, Alaska, and American Military Strategy, 1867–1945*. Annapolis, MD: Naval Institute Press, 2003.

Pike, Francis. *Hirohito's War: The Pacific War 1941–1945*. New York: Bloomsbury Publishing, 2015.

Prange, Gordon W. *At Dawn We Slept: The Untold Story of Pearl Harbor*. New York: McGraw-Hill, 1981.

Prefer, Nathan N. *Vinegar Joe's War: Stilwell's Campaigns for Burma*. Novato, CA: Presidio Press, 2000.

Reeves, Richard. *Infamy: The Shocking Story of the Japanese American Internment in World War II*. New York: Henry Holt and Company, 2015.

Richardson, Donald M. "Random Recollections." Unpublished article, 1991.

Romanus, Charles F., and Riley Sunderland. *Stilwell's Mission to China*. Washington, DC: U.S. Army Center of Military History, 1987.

———. *Time Runs Out in CBI*. Washington, DC: U.S. Army Center of Military History, 1968.

Ross, Bill D. *Iwo Jima: Legacy of Valor*. New York: Vanguard Press, 1985.

Rottman, Gordon L. *World War II Pacific Island Guide*. Westport, CT: Greenwood Press, 2002.

Saiki, Patsy Sumie. *Ganbare!: An Example of Japanese Spirit*. Honolulu: Kisaku, Inc., 1982.

Sakakida, Richard. As told to Wayne Kiyosaki. *A Spy in Their Midst: The World War II Struggle of a Japanese-American Hero*. New York: Madison Books, 1995.

Sakamaki, Kazuo. *I Attacked Pearl Harbor: The True Story Told by the Midget Submarine Officer Who Became United States POW #1*. Honolulu: Rollston Press, 2017.

Sakamoto, Pamela Rotner. *Midnight in Broad Daylight: A Japanese American Family Caught Between Two Worlds*. New York: Harper, 2016.

Sakihara, Mitsugu. *Okinawan-English Wordbook: A Short Lexicon of the Okinawan Language with English Definitions and Japanese Cognates*. Honolulu: University of Hawaii Press, 2006.

Schrager, Adam. *The Principled Politician: The Ralph Carr Story*. Golden, CO: Fulcrum Publishing, 2008.

Scott, James M. *Target Tokyo: Jimmy Doolittle and the Raid That Avenged Pearl Harbor*. New York: W. W. Norton, 2015.

Shively, John C. *The Last Lieutenant: A Foxhole View of the Epic Battle for Iwo Jima*. Bloomington, IN: Indiana University Press, 2006.

Slesnick, Irwin L., and Carole E. *Kanji & Codes: Learning Japanese for World War II*. Bellingham, WA: I. L. and C. E. Slesnick, 2006.

Shigemitsu, Mamoru. *Japan and Her Destiny: My Struggle for Peace*. New York: E. P. Dutton and Co., 1958.

Sodei, Rinjiro. *Were We the Enemy?: American Survivors of Hiroshima*. Boulder, CO: Westview Press, 1998.

Soviak, Eugene, ed. *A Diary of Darkness: The Wartime Diary of Kiyosawa Kiyoshi*. Princeton: Princeton University Press, 1980.

Spector, Ronald H. *Eagle Against the Sun: The American War with Japan*. New York: Free Press, 1985.

Stannard, David E. *Honor Killing: How the Infamous "Massie Affair" Transformed Hawaii*. New York: Viking Penguin, 2005.

Sterner, C. Douglas. *Go for Broke: The Nisei Warriors of World War II Who Conquered Germany, Japan, and America Bigotry*. Clearfield, UT: American Legacy Historical Press, 2015.

Stilwell, Joseph W. *The Stilwell Papers*. New York: William Sloane Associates, 1948.

Stone, James A. "Interrogation of Japanese POWs in World War II: U.S. Response to a Formidable Challenge." *Interrogation: World War II, Vietnam and Iraq*. Washington, DC: National Defense Intelligence College, 2008.

Stone, James H. *Crisis Fleeting: Original Reports on Military Medicine in India and Burma in the Second World War*. Washington, DC: Office of the Surgeon General, 1969.

Straus, Ulrich. *The Anguish of Surrender: Japanese POWs of World War II*. Seattle: University of Washington Press, 2003.

Swift, David W. Jr. *First Class: Nisei Linguists in World War II*. San Francisco: National Japanese Historical Society, 2006.

Taaffe, Stephen. *MacArthur's Jungle War: The 1944 New Guinea Campaign*. Lawrence, KS: University Press of Kansas, 1998.

Takei, George. *To the Stars: The Autobiography of George Takei*. New York: Pocket Books, 1994.

Tamura, Linda. *Nisei Soldiers Break Their Silence: Coming Home to Hood River*. Seattle: University of Washington Press, 2012.

Tanaka, Yuki. *Hidden Horrors: Japanese War Crimes in World War II*. Lanham, MD: Rowman and Littlefield, 2018.

Toland, John. *The Rising Sun: The Decline and Fall of the Japanese Empire*. Vols. 1 and 2. New York: Random House, 1970.

Toll, Ian W. *Pacific Crucible: War at Sea in the Pacific, 1941–1942*. New York: W. W. Norton, 2012.

————. *Twilight of the Gods: War in the Western Pacific, 1944–1945*. New York: W. W. Norton, 2020.

Toyn, Gary W. *The Quiet Hero: The Untold Medal of Honor Story of George E. Wahlen at the Battle for Iwo Jima*. Clearfield, UT: American Legacy Media, 2006.

Tsukamoto, Mary, and Elizabeth Pinkerton. *We the People: A Story of Internment in America*. Elk Grove, CA: Laguna Publishers, 1988.

Tsukano, John. *Bridge of Love*. Honolulu: Hawaii Hosts, Inc, 1985.

Tsukiyama, Ted T. "The Battle of Okinawa Revisited." Unpublished manuscript.

————. *My Life's Journey: A Memoir*. Honolulu: Watermark Publisher, 2017.

Tsukiyama, Ted T., ed. *Secret Valor: M.I.S. Personnel, World War II, Pacific Theater*. Honolulu: Military Intelligence Service Veterans Club of Hawaii, 1993.

Tuchman, Barbara. *Stilwell and the American Experience in China 1911–1945*. New York: Macmillan, 1970.

U.S. Army. *The MISLS Album, 1946*. Nashville, TN: Battery Press, 1990.

U.S. War Department, General Staff. *Merrill's Marauders*. Washington, DC: Government Printing Office, 1945.

Uyeda, Clifford, and Barry Saiki, eds. *The Pacific War and Peace: Americans of Japanese Ancestry in Military Intelligence Service 1941 to 1952*. San Francisco: Military Intelligence Service Association of Northern California, 1991.

Vea, Sandra. *Masao: A Nisei Soldier's Secret and Heroic Role in World War II*. DMA Books, 2016.

Wallace, Chris, with Mitch Weiss. *Countdown 1945: The Extraordinary Story of the Atomic Bomb and the 116 Days That Changed the World*. New York: Avid Reader Press, 2020.

Webster, Donovan. *The Burma Road: The Epic Story of the China-Burma-India Theater in World War II*. New York: Farrar, Straus and Giroux, 2003.

Weckerling, John. *Japanese Americans Play Vital Role in United States Intelligence Service in World War Two*. 1946. San Francisco: Diversified Business Forms, 1974.

Weglyn, Michi Nishiura. *Years of Infamy: The Untold Story of America's Concentration Camps*. Seattle: University of Washington Press, 1976.

Wei, William. *Asians in Colorado: A History of Persecution and Perseverance in the Centennial State*. Seattle: University of Washington Press, 2016.

Weston, Logan E. *"The Fightin' Preacher."* Cheyenne, WY: Vision Press, 1992.

Willoughby, Charles A. *MacArthur: 1941–1951*. New York: McGraw-Hill, 1954.

Winik, Jay. *1944: FDR and the Year That Changed History*. New York: Simon and Schuster, 2015.

Wright, Bertram C., ed. *The 1st Cavalry Division in World War II*. Tokyo: Toppan Printing Co., 1947.

Yahara, Hiromichi. *The Battle for Okinawa: A Japanese Officer's Eyewitness Account of the Last Great Campaign of World War II*. New York: John Wiley and Sons, 1995.

yamada, gayle k. *Uncommon Courage: Patriotism and Civil Liberties*. A film produced, directed, and written by gayle yamada. Bridge Media, 2011.

Yenne, Bill. *Rising Sons: The Japanese American GIs Who Fought for the United States in World War II*. New York: Thomas Dunne Books, 2007.

Young, Edward. *Merrill's Marauders*. New York: Osprey Publishing, 2009.

Youngs, J. William T. *Eleanor Roosevelt: A Personal and Public Life*. New York: Little, Brown and Co., 1985.

Zimmer, Joseph E. *The History of the 43rd Infantry Division 1941–1945*. Bennington, VT: Merriam Books, 2012.

INDEX

Page numbers in *italics* refer to illustrations.

ILLUSTRATION CREDITS

A NOTE ON THE TYPE

This book was set in Adobe Garamond. Designed for the Adobe Corporation by Robert Slimbach, the fonts are based on types first cut by Claude Garamond (ca. 1480–1561). Garamond was a pupil of Geoffroy Tory and is believed to have followed the Venetian models, although he introduced a number of important differences, and it is to him that we owe the letters we now know as "old style." He gave to his letters a certain elegance and feeling of movement that won their creator an immediate reputation and the patronage of Francis I of France.

Composed by North Market Street Graphics,
Lancaster, Pennsylvania

Printed and bound by Berryville Graphics,
Berryville, Virginia

Designed by Betty Lew